EXPLORER'S GUIDE

SARASOTA, SANIBEL ISLAND, & NAPLES

SEVENTH EDITION

CHELLE KOSTER WALTON
with photographs by the author

THE COUNTRYMAN PRESS
A division of W. W. Norton & Company
Independent Publishers Since 1923

To my husband, Rob, with whom I first discovered
Southwest Florida's treasures and pleasures.

EXPLORE WITH US!

Here's how this book works: The area bounded on the north by the Manatee River and on the south by Ten Thousand Islands is often lumped under the heading Southwest Florida. Sometimes the Bradenton–Sarasota area is omitted from the region this heading defines and otherwise grouped with Tampa as Central West Florida. For the purpose of this guide, the Bradenton–Sarasota area is included in the coverage. It explores in depth the cities, towns, and communities from Bradenton–Palmetto in the north to Naples–Marco Island and the Everglades in the south.

I have sliced this delectable pie into five regional chapters, north to south: Bradenton & Mid-Coast, Sarasota Bay Coast, Charlotte Harbor Coast, Island Coast, and South Coast. Within these chapters I scan under separate headings each region's culture, recreation, lodging, dining, shopping, and annual events.

HIGH FIVES In the "Information" chapter, I have rated listings within a number of fun—and sometimes quirky—categories, from Splurge Accommodations and Martini Meccas to Kid Cool and Paddle Happy. They begin under the Chelle's High Fives heading on page 308.

Within the chapters, listings that have earned a High Five get a ✪ next to their name.

WHAT'S WHERE In the beginning of the book is an alphabetical listing of special highlights and important information that you may want to reference quickly. There you'll find everything from good places to spot alligators to the location of the best beaches.

LODGING I've selected lodging locations for mention in this book based on their merit alone; we do not charge innkeepers and hoteliers to be listed. I check every property personally and have stayed at most of them.

KEY TO SYMBOLS

- ✪ **High Five**. See Chelle's High Fives, page 308. These are marked with a star.
- ⚭ **Weddings**. The wedding-ring symbol appears next to lodging venues and other venues that specialize in weddings.
- 🎗 **Special value**. The blue-ribbon symbol appears next to selected lodging venues and restaurants that combine quality and moderate prices.
- 🐾 **Pets**. The dog-paw symbol appears next to venues that accept pets.
- ✎ **Child-friendly**. The crayon symbol appears next to lodging, restaurants, activities, and shops of special interest or appeal to youngsters.
- ♿ **Handicapped access**. The wheelchair symbol appears next to lodging, restaurants, and attractions that are partially or completely handicapped-accessible.
- ((ᵗ)) **Wireless Internet**. The wireless symbol appears next to lodging, restaurants, and attractions that offer wireless Internet access.

PRICES Rather than give specific prices, this guide rates dining and lodging options within a range.

Lodging prices are normally based on per-person/double occupancy for hotel rooms and per unit for efficiencies, apartments, cottages, suites, and villas. Price ranges reflect the difference in the off-season and high season (usually Christmas through Easter).

Generally, the colder the weather up north, the higher the cost of accommodations here. Rates can double during the course of a year. Many resorts offer off-season packages at special rates. Pricing does not include the 6 percent Florida sales tax. Furthermore, many large resorts add gratuities or housekeeping charges, and most counties also impose a bed or tourist tax, proceeds from which are applied to beach and environmental maintenance.

If rates seem high for rooms on the Gulf Coast, it's partially because many resorts cater to families by providing kitchen facilities. Take into consideration what this could save you on dining bills.

Dining cost categories are based on the range of dinner entrée prices or, if dinner is not served, of lunch entrées. Restaurants at some large resorts add gratuities to the tab. This is also customary for large parties at most restaurants, so check your bill carefully before leaving a tip. Satisfied diners are expected to tip 15 percent or more.

Heavy state taxes on liquor served in-house can boost a drinking tab quickly. Paying as you drink is a wise way to prevent sticker shock.

PRICE GUIDE

Code	Lodging	Dining
Inexpensive	Up to $100	Up to $15
Moderate	$100 to $200	$15 to $25
Expensive	$200 to $300	$25 to $35
Very Expensive	$300 and up	$35 or more

(An asterisk after the pricing designation indicates that the rate includes at least a continental breakfast in the cost of lodging and possibly more extensive meal service as noted in the listing.)

We would appreciate any comments or corrections. Please write to:

Explorer's Guide Editor
The Countryman Press
A division of W. W. Norton & Company
500 Fifth Avenue
New York, NY 10110

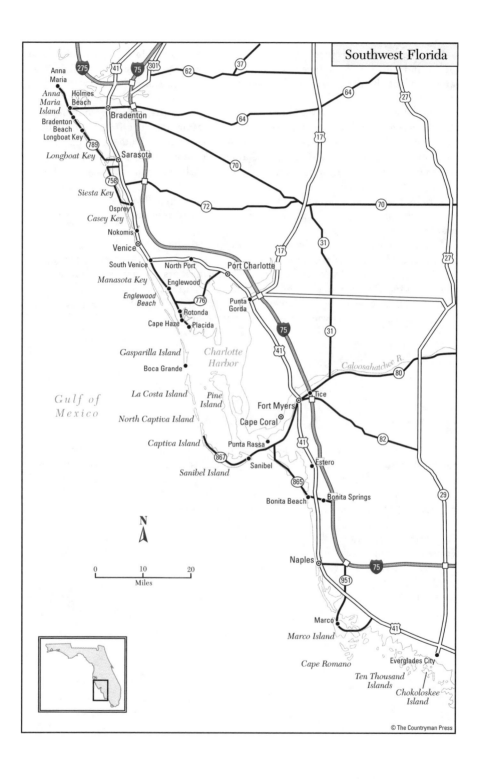

Southwest Florida

Anna Maria
Anna Maria Island
Holmes Beach
Bradenton
Bradenton Beach
Longboat Key
Longboat Key
Sarasota
Siesta Key
Osprey
Casey Key
Nokomis
Venice
South Venice
North Port
Manasota Key
Englewood
Englewood Beach
Rotonda
Cape Haze
Placida
Port Charlotte
Punta Gorda
Charlotte Harbor
Gasparilla Island
Boca Grande
La Costa Island
Pine Island
North Captiva Island
Captiva Island
Punta Rassa
Sanibel
Sanibel Island
Bonita Beach
Bonita Springs
Gulf of Mexico
Caloosahatchee R.
Tice
Fort Myers
Cape Coral
Estero
Naples
Marco
Marco Island
Cape Romano
Everglades City
Ten Thousand Islands
Chokoloskee Island

N

0   10   20
Miles

© The Countryman Press

CONTENTS

MAPS

INTRODUCTION

Morning dawns like a boater's dream. The sky is clear except for a trace of last night's moon: wispy, like a wadded-up cloud. The water stretches cellophane-taut between Sanibel and Pine Islands. It is a morning to wonder why anyone does anything else on days off except return to the sea. On cue, a family of three dolphins pierces the surface with their fins and their smiles. The show has begun.

In the course of our leisurely, two-hour cruise between Sanibel Island and Boca Grande, we are entertained by leaping stingrays, a school of mackerel, and the usual dive-bombing squadron of brown pelicans.

At lights-out call—after lunch in a marina-side fish house, beach time on an unbridged island, and a duck-the-afternoon-rains cocktail at a historic island inn—nature's revue reaches its spectacular finale. In the moonless dark, the wake behind our boat sparkles like a watery fireworks display. The Gulf has thrown an electric breaker switch. Liquid lightning strikes all around us as our twenty-one-foot Mako powerboat parts the seas. Whitecaps puff like nuclear popcorn.

Scientists call the phenomenon dinoflagellates or bioluminescence. Lay folks call the glowing organisms phosphorescents. Jamaicans call them sea-blinkies. The Ancient Mariner called them death-fires. I call their unpredictable visits to our summer waters magic, imparting a topsy-turvy, ethereal feeling that someone—without warning—has transformed the sea into a starry sky.

Such a perfect day isn't required to fully appreciate this inimitable slice of Florida's Gulf Coast, but such days do help to remind me why I moved here from long-johns land thirty-some years ago. Like so many who constitute our hodgepodge population, I escaped, I loved, I dug in. I stayed for the exotic, warm quality of tropical nature. I remain because of the miracles I discover—and watched my young son discover—every day.

I can't list all the people on whose patience and understanding I counted to see me through this project. First dibs on my gratitude must go to my husband, Rob, for not divorcing me, and my son, Aaron, who helped particularly with my beach and "kids' stuff" research through the years.

Jennifer Huber with Charlotte Harbor & the Gulf Island Visitor's Bureau, Jonell Modys representing Collier County, Erin Duggan and Lynn Hobeck Bates at the Sarasota Convention & Visitors Bureau, and Kelly Clark with Manatee County tourism have been particularly helpful.

—Chelle Koster Walton, Sanibel Island, Florida

WHAT'S WHERE IN SARASOTA, SANIBEL ISLAND & NAPLES

General Information

AREA CODE The 941 area code applies to the Sarasota Bay Coast and Charlotte Harbor Coast; the Island Coast and South Coast regions use 239. Numbers prefixed with 800, 888, 855, 866, and 877 are toll-free.

GETTING HERE BY CAR Southwest Florida is plugged into Florida's more highly charged areas by both major conduits and small feeders. Tampa/St. Petersburg lies at Bradenton's back door, via US 41, I-75, and I-275. The Tamiami Trail ends here, but US 41 continues on. The interstate proceeds north and connects to Orlando and the east coast via I-4. US 19 takes up the coastal route in St. Petersburg, heading toward Georgia. FL 70 cuts across the state above Lake Okeechobee to connect the east coast to Bradenton, and at Sarasota and Punta Gorda via FL 72 and US 17 respectively. These roads meander into Native American reservation territory, the town of Arcadia's cowboy country, and the expansive Myakka River State Park. The route runs jaggedly among the Island Coast, the big lake, and West Palm Beach, following a series of lazy two- and four-lane roads, including FL 80, US 27, US 441, and US 98. Alligator Alley (I-75) crosses the Everglades with a certain mystique. Once a two-lane toll road on which encounters with crossing gators and panthers were common (tragically, cars inevitably fared better in such encounters), today I-75 has been widened to four lanes, with underpasses for wildlife. At certain times of the year, it continues to earn its name, and a sharp eye can spot hundreds of gators sunning on water banks. But it's still a toll road and less than user-friendly. Gas up before you approach: fuel station/restaurant exit breaks are few and far between on the two-hour drive before it reaches the east coast at Fort Lauderdale. US 41 takes you into Miami and branches off into US 1 to the Florida Keys.

GETTING HERE BY AIR Two major airports service the lower Gulf Coast: Sarasota–Bradenton International Airport (SRQ) and Southwest Florida International (RSW) in Fort Myers. The Sarasota–Bradenton facility gives a proper introduction to the region, with shark tanks and tropical orchids from local attractions, a two-story waterfall, and works from its prolific artist community. RSW boasts one of the newer major airports in the nation. Smaller airports and fields service shuttle, charter, and private planes. The Punta Gorda Airport caters mainly to private craft but does service small charter airlines. North Captiva Island and Everglades City have their own landing strips for private planes, and seaplane service is available to some islands. See individual chapters for information on airlines and other airport specifics.

CAR RENTALS Rental agencies with airport offices or shuttle service include:
   Alamo: 800-732-3232; www.alamo .com
   Avis: 800-331-2112; www.avis.com

Budget: 800-527-0700; www.budget .com

Dollar: 800-800-3665; www.dollar.com

Hertz: 800-654-3131; www.hertz.com

National: 800-227-7368; www.nationalcar.com

Thrifty: 800-847-4389; www.thrifty .com

AIRPORT TAXIS/SHUTTLES Some hotels and resorts arrange pickup service to and from the airport. Taxi and limousine companies operate in most areas. See each chapter for details.
Boca Grande Limousine (239-964-0455 or 800-771-7433; www .bocagrandelimo.com) provides twenty-four-hour connections to all Florida airports. For a more dramatic arrival or departure, call **Boca Grande Seaplane** (941-964-0234). **Airport Limo & Car Service** (941-505-9400 or 800-954-9404; www.airportlimoandcarservice.com) has a fleet that includes Lincolns and SUVs.

From Southwest Florida International Airport in Fort Myers, **Aaron Airport Transportation** (239-768-1898 or 800-998-1898; www.aarontaxi.com) makes pickups and deliveries throughout the region. For lifts to and from the islands, call **Sanibel Taxi** (239-472-4160 or 888-527-7806; www.sanibeltaxi.com). **Pine Island Taxi** (239-283-7777 or 888-777-9653; www.pineislandtaxi.com) provides 24-hour service anywhere with advance notice.

In the south coast area, call **Taxi Time** (239-200-0000; taxinaples.com. On Marco Island, call **Classic Transportation** (239-394-1888 or 800-553-8294; www.classicluxurytransportation.com).

BANKS Several old and established banks have branches located throughout Florida's Gulf Coast. Some are listed here with their toll-free information numbers.

Bank	Number
Bank of America	800-299-2265
Fifth Third	866-671-5353
SunTrust	800-786-8787

HANDICAPPED ACCESS Within this book, all lodging, restaurants, and attractions are handicapped accessible unless noted in the description.

MEDIA Even with the digital information revolution, print media continue to flood the Gulf Coast like high tide. Many publications are directed toward tourists, and some are only as permanent as the shoreline during a tidal surge. Magazines come and go, and radio stations often shift formats.

Four daily newspapers stand out for their endurance and dependability against today's odds: the *Bradenton Herald*, the *Sarasota Herald-Tribune*, the Fort Myers *News-Press*, and the *Naples Daily News*. Weeklies are also firmly established in their respective communities, primarily because many are owned collectively by one corporation. Specialty tabloids address seniors, shoppers, fishermen, women, and other groups.

Magazines show the most fluctuation. Traditionally they were created to appeal to the region's upscale, mature population, which is concentrated in Sarasota and Naples. *Sarasota Magazine*, *SRQ Magazine*, *Naples Illustrated*, and *Gulfshore Life* have been the stalwarts of regional lifestyle glossies, but even they shift focus to address changing populations and economic trends.

Fort Myers carries the majority of the region's broadcast media, which reach to the Charlotte Harbor and the South Coasts. Much of the Sarasota Bay coast's TV comes from Tampa.

BRADENTON & MID-COAST

Newspapers: Bradenton Herald (941-748-0411; www.bradenton.com), 111 Third Ave. W., Bradenton 34205. Daily.

Longboat Observer (941-383-5509; www.yourobserver.com), 5570 Gulf of Mexico Dr., Longboat Key 34228. Weekly.

CLIMATE, SEASONS & WHAT TO WEAR

The tropics brush the Mangrove Coast but do not overwhelm it.
—Karl Bickel, *The Mangrove Coast*, 1942

Florida's nickname, the Sunshine State, was once as fresh as it was apt. Although overuse has tended to cloud the once-perfect image, Florida still remains the ultimate state of sunshine through the sheer power of statistics. The sun beams down on the Gulf Coast for nearly 75 percent of all daylight hours and constitutes the one asset that locals can bank on.

To residents, the sun's smile can seem more like a sneer as they await fall's begrudging permission to turn off air conditioners and open windows. They suffer their own brand of cabin fever during the summer months, which often seems to linger as long as a Canadian winter. Although visitors revel in the warmth and sunlight, they often wonder how residents endure the monotony of seasonal sameness.

The seasons *do* change along the southern Gulf Coast, although more subtly than "up north." Weather patterns vary within the region. The Sarasota Bay and Charlotte Harbor areas often get more rain. However, weather can be very localized—it may rain on the southern end of twelve-mile-long Sanibel Island while the north end remains dry. Islands generally stay cooler than the mainland in summer and warmer in winter, thanks to the insulating jacket of gulf water. This is especially true where Charlotte Harbor runs wide and deep, creating a small pocket of tropical climate.

Winter is everyone's favorite time of year, weather-wise. Temperatures along the coast generally reach into the seventies during the day and drop into the low fifties and upper forties at night. Visitors find green, balmy relief from snow blindness and frostbite. Floridians enjoy the relative coolness that brings a reprieve from sweltering days, steamy nights, and bloodthirsty insects. The fragrance of oranges, grapefruits, and Key limes fills the air. When it's time for activity, one can safely schedule a tee time past noon. Resort areas fill up, and migratory houseguests from the north arrive.

Spring comes on tiptoe to the coast. No thaw-and-puddle barometer alerts us; the sense of spring giddiness affects only longtime residents. Gardenias, Hong Kong orchids, and jasmine bloom, and everything that already looks green and alive bursts forth with an extra reserve of color. It's a time to celebrate the end of another tourist season and to greedily enjoy the domain that's been shared with visitors during the winter months.

Summers used to be reserved for die-hard Floridians. All but the most devoted residents boarded up their homes and businesses and headed somewhere—*anywhere*—cooler. Now

CHARLOTTE HARBOR COAST

Newspapers: Boca Beacon (941-964-2995 or 800-749-2995; www.bocabeacon.com), P.O. Box 313, Boca Grande 33921. Weekly.

Charlotte County Florida Weekly (941-621-3422; charlotte.floridaweekly.com), 1205 Elizabeth St. #G, Punta Gorda 33950. Local and national news and features.

Charlotte Sun-Herald (941-206-1000 or 877-818-6204; www.yoursun.com), 23170 Harborview Rd., Charlotte Harbor 33980. Daily.

Englewood Sun (941-681-3000 or 877-818-6204; www.yoursun.com), 120 W. Dearborn St., Englewood 34223. Daily.

Gasparilla Gazette (941-964-2728; www.breezenewspapers.com/news/gasparillagazette.asp), 5800 Gasparilla Rd., Boca Grande 33921. Weekly.

Magazines: Gasparilla Magazine (941-964-2995 or 800-749-2995) 431 Park Ave., P.O. Box 313, Boca Grande 33921. Bimonthly glossy.

Harbor Style (941-206-1284; www.harborstyle.com), 308 Sullivan St., Punta Gorda 33950. Covers lifestyle in the Charlotte Harbor area.

there's a summer trade, composed of Floridians, Europeans, and northern families—enough to keep the resort communities alive through temperatures that inch up to one hundred degrees. Although technically classified as subtropical, the region, starting in June, feels the bristles of a tropical brush. The pace of life slows, and late-afternoon rains break the sun's constancy. Mangoes and guavas blush with sweet temptation. Moonlit nights bring magic to the cereus vine and its white starburst blooms the size of Frisbees.

Fall appears in October as a sharpening of vision after a blur of humidity. Residents don't exactly go out and buy wool plaids, but they do break out sweatshirts. Many build fires in hearths that have held dried floral arrangements for eight months. The leathery leaves of the sea grape tree turn as red as the northern oak, and fallen leaves gather around decidu-ous gumbo-limbo trees. The best part about a Gulf Coast fall, for those residents who once endured northern winters, is that it doesn't forebode snow boots and long underwear.

Winter temperatures dip, albeit rarely, into the freezing range, so be prepared for just about any weather between December and February. Fortunately, swimsuits take up little room, so pack more than one. (Florida's high humidity often prevents anything from ever really drying out.) Loose-fitting togs and cotton work best in any season. Long sleeves are welcome in the evenings during winter. Summer showers require rain gear, especially if you plan on boating or playing outdoors.

Don't worry about dress codes in most restaurants. Ties and pantyhose are strictly for the office and (possibly) the theater. Worry more about comfort, particularly if your skin burns easily. Pack hats and lots of sunscreen. Bring insect repellent, too, especially if you plan on venturing into the jungle—or simply watching an island sunset, for that matter. Counties do spray for mosquitoes, but spraying has little effect on the tiny but prolific no-see-um (sand-fly). The best protection against both pests is sitting under a ceiling fan—practically standard equipment in homes and hotels.

On the cloudier side, Florida weather includes a high incidence of lightning, summer squalls, tornadoes, waterspouts, and the dreaded "H-word." Hurricane season begins in June, but activity increases toward season's end, August through October. Watches and warn-ings alert you in plenty of time to head inland or north; to be safest, make sure not to linger after the first warning, especially if you are staying on an island.

Florida's celebrated sunshine is at its best on the Gulf Coast. Ol' Sol visits practically every day, and it's also where he slips into bed. Gulf Coast Florida boasts the most spectacular sun-sets in the continental United States. (Okay, so I'm a little biased.)

ISLAND COAST

Newspapers: Cape Coral Breeze (239-574-1110; www.breezenewspapers.com), 2510 Del Prado Blvd., Cape Coral 33904. Daily.

Fort Myers Beach Bulletin (239-463-4421; www.breezenewspapers.com), 19260 San Carlos Blvd., Fort Myers Beach 33931. Weekly.

Fort Myers Florida Weekly (239-333-2135; fortmyers.floridaweekly.com), 4300 Ford St. Ext., #105, Fort Myers 33916. Local and national news and features, weekly.

Islander (239-472-1587; www.breezenewspapers.com), 2340 Periwin-kle Way, Sanibel Island 33957. Weekly.

News-Press (239-335-0200 or 800-468-0233; www.news-press.com), 2442 Dr. Martin Luther King Jr. Blvd., Fort Myers 33901. The tenth-largest daily in the state in terms of circulation, it pub-lishes editions for Charlotte County and Bonita Springs.

Pine Island Eagle (239-283-2022; www.breezenewspapers.com), 10700 Stringfellow Rd., Suite 60, Bokeelia 33922. Weekly.

Television: **WBBH-TV**, Fort Myers, NBC
WFTX-TV, Cape Coral, FOX
WINK-TV, Fort Myers, CBS
WZVN-TV, Fort Myers, ABC

SARASOTA BAY COAST

Newspapers: Siesta Key Observer (941-366-3468; www.yourobserver.com), 1970 Main St., Sarasota 34236. Weekly, covering Siesta Key and Sarasota.
Sarasota Herald-Tribune (941-953-7755; www.heraldtribune.com), 1741 Main St., Sarasota 34236. Florida's eighth-largest daily in terms of circulation. *Venice Gondolier Sun* (941-207-1000; www.venicegondoliersun.com), 200 E. Venice Ave., Venice 34285. Biweekly.
Magazines: Sarasota Magazine (941-487-1100 or 800-881-2394; www.sarasotamagazine.com), 330 S. Pineapple Ave., Suite 205, Sarasota 34236. Lifestyle for upscale Sarasotans.
Sarasota Scene (941-487-8276 www.scenesarasota.com), 5939 Approach Rd., Sarasota 34238. Weekly covering the Sarasota-Bradenton area.
SRQ (941-365-7702; www.srqmagazine.com), 331 S. Pineapple Ave., Sarasota 34236. SRQ is Sarasota-Bradenton International Airport's code; this slick magazine covers the dining, political, and shopping scene.
West Coast Woman (941-954-3300; www.westcoastwoman.com), P.O. Box 819, Sarasota 34230. Monthly free publication.
Television: **BLAB-TV**, Sarasota
SNN-TV, Sarasota News Now
WWSB-TV, Sarasota, ABC

SOUTH COAST

Newspapers: The Banner (239-263-4839; www.naplesnews.com/community/banner), 26381 S. Tamiami Trail #116, Bonita Springs 34134. Weekly Wednesday tabloid-size paper serving Bonita Springs, Estero, and vicinity.

Marco Eagle (239-213-6000 or 877-263-6047; www.naplesnews.com/community/marco-eagle/), 1100 Immokalee Rd., Naples 34110. Weekly tabloid-size newspaper operated by *Naples Daily News.*
Marco Island Sun Times (239-394-4050; www.marcoislandflorida.com), 606 Bald Eagle Dr., Marco Island 34145. Free distribution paper. Weekly.
Naples Daily News (239-262-3161; www.naplesnews.com), 1100 Immokalee Rd., Naples 34110. Daily; publisher of the three newspapers listed above.
Naples Florida Weekly (239-325-1960; naples.floridaweekly.com), 9051 Tamiami Tr. N., Naples 34109. Local and national news and features.
Magazines: Gulfshore Business (239-449-4111 or 800-220-4853; www.gulfshorebusiness.com), 1421 Pine Ridge Rd., Naples 34109. Monthly covering Southwest Florida's business news.
Gulfshore Life (239-449-4111 or 800-220-4853; www.gulfshorelife.com), 1421 Pine Ridge Rd., Naples 34109. Longtime slick lifestyle and news guide to the southwest coast.
Naples Illustrated (239-434-6966; www.naplesillustrated.com), 3066 Tamiami Trail N., Suite 102, Naples 34103. Haute lifestyles glossy.
Television: **WTVK-TV**, Bonita Springs, CW

REAL ESTATE Real estate prices run the gamut from reasonable to ultra-expensive. In parts of Bradenton, Sarasota, and Fort Myers, planned communities cater to young families. Exclusive areas such as Longboat Key, Casey Key, Manasota Key, Sanibel Island, Captiva Island, and Naples are known for their pricey waterfront homes and golfing developments. The most reasonable real estate, naturally, lies inland, away from the water. Florida's $25,000 homestead exemption gives residents a tax break on primary home purchases.
Real estate publications can be found on the newsstands, or check local

newspapers. Otherwise, contact the following agencies.

Florida Association of Realtors (407-438-1400; www.floridarealtors.org), 7025 Augusta National Dr., Orlando 32822.

Naples Area Board of Realtors (239-597-1666; www.naplesarea.com), 1455 Pine Ridge Rd., Naples 34109.

Punta Gorda, Port Charlotte, North Board of Realtors (239-629-8261; www.pgpcnprealtors.com), 3320 Loveland Blvd., Port Charlotte 33980.

Royal Palm Coast Realtor Association (239-936-3537; www.swflrealtors.com), 2840 Winkler Ave., Fort Myers 33916.

Sanibel & Captiva Islands Association of Realtors (239-472-9353; www.sanibelrealtors.com), 2353 Periwinkle Way #201, Sanibel Island 33957.

Realtor Association of Sarasota and Manatee (941-952-3400; sarasotamanateerealtors.com), 32320 Cattleman Rd., Sarasota 34232.

REGIONAL READING Books about the region are available in bookstores and through online outlets.

Biography & Reminiscence: Brown, Loren G. *Totch: A Life in the Everglades.* Gainesville, FL: University Press of Florida, 1993. A folksy, firsthand adventure tour of Ten Thousand Islands through the words of a former native.

Lindbergh, Anne Morrow. *Gift from the Sea.* New York: Pantheon/Village Books, 1955. A small book packed with sea-inspired wisdom from Charles Lindbergh's wife, who died in 2001. Strong evidence points to Captiva as the book's inspiration.

Newton, James. *Uncommon Friends.* New York: Harcourt, Brace, Jovanovich, 1987. Local man's memories of his friendships with Fort Myers's illustrious winterers: Thomas Edison, Henry Ford, Harvey Firestone, and Charles Lindbergh.

Orlean, Susan. *The Orchid Thief: A True Story of Beauty and Obsession.* New York: Random House, 1998. Set in Fakahatchee Strand Preserve State Park, Naples, and other local venues, Orlean tells a bizarre nonfiction tale about the elusive ghost orchid and the people who sought it.

St. Claire, Dana. *Cracker: The Cracker Culture in Florida History.* Daytona Beach, FL: The Museum of Arts and Sciences, 1998.

Weeks, David C. *Ringling: The Florida Years, 1911–1936.* Gainesville, FL: University Press of Florida, 1993.

Cookbooks: White, Randy Wayne. *Randy Wayne White's Gulf Coast Cookbook: With Memories and Photos of Sanibel Island.* Guilford, CT: The Lyons Press, 2006. Southwest Florida's most popular murder-mystery novelist combines local history with cuisine.

Fiction: Hiaasen, Carl. *Nature Girl.* New York: Alfred A. Knopf, 2006. Florida's favorite mystery man sets his thirteenth novel in Everglades City.

Hiaasen, Carl. *Hoot.* New York: Alfred A. Knopf, 2002. Award-winning book for young readers based on the burrowing owls of Cape Coral. Scenes from its spinoff movie adaptation were filmed locally.

Hudler, Ad. *All This Belongs to Me.* New York: Ballantine Publishing, 2006. Set in Fort Myers, its plot revolves around the Edison Estates.

King, Stephen. *Duma Key.* New York: Simon & Schuster, 2009. A horror novel set on a fictitious island near Casey Key, where King owns a home.

MacDonald, John D. Many of his Travis McGee mysteries, as well as others, take place in a Sarasota Bay coast setting, where he had a home.

Matthiessen, Peter. *Bone by Bone.* New York: Random House, 1999. The parents of this award-winning author lived on Sanibel Island. This is the final book in a historical trilogy about the posse killing of a murderer who hid out in the frontier of Ten Thousand Islands.

———. *Killing Mr. Watson.* New York: Random House, 1990. First book in the trilogy.

———. *Lost Man's River*. New York: Random House, 1997. Second book in the trilogy.

Smith, Patrick D. *A Land Remembered*. Sarasota, FL: Pineapple Press, 1984. This definitive historical novel about Florida's Cracker and cow-hunting eras features many scenes set in the Fort Myers and Everglades areas.

White, Randy Wayne. *Sanibel Flats*. New York: St. Martin's Press, 1990. Mystery by a local fishing guide/journalist in a local setting. Several books in his Doc Ford series take place mostly along the Gulf Coast.

History: Anholt, Betty. *Sanibel's Story: Voices & Images from Calusa to Incorporation*. Virginia Beach, VA: Donning, 1998. Written by a longtime island resident and historian.

Boca Grande Historical Society. *Boca Grande: Lives of an Island*. 2006. A human history with black-and-white photographs.

Buck, Pat Ringling et al. *A History of Visual Art in Sarasota*. University Press of Florida, 2003. Written by a Ringling heir, with illustrations.

Hill, Yvonne and Marguerite Jordan. *Sanibel Island*. Charleston, SC: Arcadia Publishing, 2008. Part of the Images of America series, it concentrates on the island's African-American heritage through historic photographs.

Smoot, Tom. *The Edisons of Fort Myers: Discoveries of the Heart*. Sarasota, FL: Pineapple Press, 2011. Chronicling the lives of Thomas and Mina Edison during their Fort Myers years.

Natural History: Douglas, Marjory Stoneman. *The Everglades: River of Grass*. St. Simons, GA: Mockingbird Books, 1947. The book that focused the nation's attention on the developing plight of the pristine Everglades.

Toops, Connie. *The Florida Everglades*. Stillwater, MN: Voyageur Press, 1998. Written by a former national park ranger.

Pictorial: Butcher, Clyde. *Clyde Butcher: Portfolio I*. Fort Myers, FL: Shade Tree Press, 1994. The master of natural landscape photography collects his haunting, black-and-white, large-format images in a coffee table edition.

Travel: MacPerry, I. *Indian Mounds You Can Visit*. St. Petersburg, FL: Great Outdoors Publishing, 1993. Covers the entire west coast of Florida, arranged by county.

Check It Out: Out-of-print books you can find in local libraries when you're visiting.

Bickel, Karl A. *The Mangrove Coast: The Story of the West Coast of Florida*. 4th ed. New York: Coward-McCann, 1989. Vintage regional history of the area from Tampa Bay to Ten Thousand Islands, from the time of Ponce de León to 1885, spiced with romantic embellishments.

Beater, Jack. *Pirates & Buried Treasure*. St. Petersburg, FL: Great Outdoors Publishing, 1959. Somewhat factual, ever-colorful account of José Gaspar and his cohorts, by the area's foremost legendaire.

Board, Prudy Taylor, and Esther B. Colcord. *Historic Fort Myers*. Virginia Beach, VA: Donning, 1992. Largely photographic treatment, written by two of the area's leading historians.

———. *Pages from the Past*. Virginia Beach, VA: Donning, 1990. Largely photographic treatment of Fort Myers's history.

Briggs, Mildred. *Pioneers of Bonita Springs (Facts and Folklore)*. Bonita Springs, 1976. Pirates, Indian healers, outlaws, and more.

Campbell, George R. *The Nature of Things on Sanibel*. Fort Myers, FL: Press Printing, 1978. Factual yet entertaining background on native fauna and flora.

Dormer, Elinore M. *The Sea Shell Islands: A History of Sanibel and Captiva*. Tallahassee, FL: Rose Printing, 1987. The definitive work on island and regional history.

Fritz, Florence. *Unknown Florida*. Coral Gables, FL: University of Miami Press, 1963. Focuses on the southernmost Gulf Coast.

Gonzales, Thomas A. *The Caloosahatchee: History of the Caloosahatchee River and the City of Fort Myers, Florida*. Fort Myers Beach, FL: Island Press, 1982. Memories of a native son, descendant of the city's first settler.

Grismer, Karl H. *The Story of Fort Myers*. Fort Myers Beach, FL: Island Press, 1982.

———. *The Story of Sarasota*. Tampa, FL: The Florida G Press, 1946.

Hann, John H., ed. *Missions to the Calusa*. Gainesville, FL: University of Florida Press, 1991.

Jordan, Elaine Blohm. *Pine Island, The Forgotten Island*. Pine Island, FL: n.p., 1982.

———. *Tales of Pine Island*. Ellijay, GA: Jordan Ink Publishing, 1985.

Marth, Del. *Yesterday's Sarasota*. Miami, FL: E. A. Seemann Publishing, 1977. Primarily pictorial history.

Matthews, Janet Snyder. *Edge of Wilderness: A Settlement History of Manatee River and Sarasota Bay*. Sarasota, FL: Coastal Press, 1983.

———. *Journey to Centennial Sarasota*. Sarasota, FL: Pine Level Press, 1989.

———. *Venice: Journey to Horse and Chaise*. Sarasota, FL: Pine Level Press, 1989.

Matthews, Kenneth, and Robert McDevitt. *The Unlikely Legacy*. Sarasota, FL: Aaron Publishers, 1980. The story of John Ringling, the circus, and Sarasota.

Peeples, Vernon. *Punta Gorda and the Charlotte Harbor Area*. Virginia Beach, VA: Donning, 1986. Pictorial history authored by a local politician.

Ripple, Jeff. *Southwest Florida's Wetland Wilderness: Big Cypress Swamp and the Ten Thousand Islands*. Gainesville, FL: University Press of Florida, 1992. This book celebrates the natural history of one of the most diverse, endangered, and beautiful ecosystems in the world. Stunning black-and-white photography by Clyde Butcher.

Romans, Bernard. *A Concise Natural History of East and West Florida*. Gainesville, FL: University of Florida Press,

1962. A facsimile reproduction of the 1775 edition.

Schell, Rolfe F. *De Soto Didn't Land at Tampa*. Fort Myers Beach, FL: Island Press, 1966.

———. *History of Fort Myers Beach*. Fort Myers Beach, FL: Island Press, 1980.

Tebeau, Charlton W. *Florida's Last Frontier: The History of Collier County*. Coral Gables, FL: University of Miami Press, 1966.

Widmer, Randolph J. *The Evolution of the Calusa*. Tuscaloosa, AL: University of Alabama Press, 1988. Very technical discussion of the "nonagricultural chiefdom on the Southwest Florida Coast."

Zeiss, Betsy. *The Other Side of the River: Historical Cape Coral*. Cape Coral FL: n.p., 1986.

ROAD SERVICE Information on the **AAA Auto Club** can be found at www.aaa.com. Each of the following offices provides 24-hour emergency road service.

941-798-2211; 6210 Manatee Ave. W., Bradenton

941-929-2299; 3844 Bee Ridge Rd., Sarasota

941-627-1544; 21229-A Olean Blvd., Port Charlotte

239-939-6500; 2516 Colonial Blvd., Fort Myers

239-594-5006; 5410 Airport Pulling Rd. N., Naples

SERVICES FOR THE PHYSICALLY IMPAIRED Regulations concerning disabled access vary, depending on locale. In general, most restaurants, parks, attractions, and resorts provide physically impaired visitors with special ramps, bathroom stalls, and hotel rooms. Some beaches provide wheeled beach chairs for the physically challenged.

KIDS' STUFF Southwest Florida prides itself on being a family destination that is the quieter flip side of the Orlando scene. You will find children's museums in Fort Myers and Naples, but what lies outdoors is what kids love most. No nature-deficit disorders here—between the beaches, the seas, and the nature parks, there's no end to what families can explore. Many of the parks, preserves, and nature centers offer special programs just for families. Some nature tours are geared toward teaching kids about the environment, using seining nets, touch tanks, games, and other tools. Throughout this book, attractions, restaurants, and resorts that are of special interest to children are indicated by the crayon symbol ✐.

LATE-NIGHT FOOD & FUEL Certain categories of Florida liquor licensing require bars to serve food, which provides a good source for late-night eating. Many chain restaurants located along major thoroughfares—such as Denny's and Perkins—stay open late or all night. Chain convenience stores, gas stations, and fuel/food marts also are open around the clock. These include 7-Eleven, Wawa, and Circle K.

TOWN GOVERNMENT All incorporated cities within the region are self-governing and have councilpersons, commissioners, mayors, and city managers in various roles. The unincorporated towns and communities are county ruled.

The incorporated cities of the Bradenton Mid-Coast include Bradenton, Anna Maria, Holmes Beach, and Bradenton Beach. Bradenton is the county seat for Manatee County. In the Sarasota Bay area, Sarasota, Longboat Key, North Port, and Venice are incorporated; Sarasota is the county seat for Sarasota County. On the Charlotte Harbor Coast, Punta Gorda (county seat) is incorporated. Bonita Springs, Cape Coral, Estero, Fort Myers (county seat), Fort Myers Beach, and Sanibel make up Lee County's incorporated cities. Naples is Collier County's seat; Naples, Marco Island, and Everglades City are incorporated.

VISITOR INFORMATION Local visitors bureaus, tourism development councils, and chambers of commerce are adept at the dissemination of materials and information about their area. These are listed in Chapter 5, "Information." For information on the entire region and other parts of Florida, contact Visit Florida (888-735-2872; www.visitflorida.com), 2540 Executive Center #200, Tallahassee, FL 32301.

WEDDINGS Within the book, properties that specialize in weddings are noted with the ring symbol ⚭.

Arts

PERFORMANCE Sarasota claims a lively theater scene downtown and at **The Ringling** (941-355-5101; www.ringling.org) complex. Performance art ranges from the **Sarasota Ballet** (941-351-8000 or 800-361-8388; www.sarasotaballet.org) and the **Sarasota Opera House** (941-366-8450; www.sarasotaopera.org) to Broadway shows at **Van Wezel Performing Arts Hall** (941-953-3368 or 800-826-9303; www.vanwezel.org) and the circus, an art form deeply embedded in Sarasota's genes. Fort Myers and Naples have their performing arts halls and professional and community acting troupes, too. In Fort Myers, **Florida Rep** (239-332-4488 or 877-787-8053; www.floridarep.org) professionals stage dramas and comedies in a historic theater downtown. For musical dinner theater, try **Broadway Palm** (239-278-4422; www.broadwaypalm.com) in **Fort Myers** and **BIG ARTS Strauss Theater** (239-472-6862; www.bigarts.org) on Sanibel Island. **Sugden Community Theatre's** (239-263-7990) **Naples Players** (www.naplesplayers.org) and **Gulfshore Playhouse** (866-811-4111; www.gulfshoreplayhouse.org) perform in downtown Naples.

VISUAL Sarasota has always been the region's headquarters for the arts, a

THE SCULPTURE *APPLAUSE* GREETS VISITORS TO THE VAN WEZEL PERFORMING ARTS CENTER

reputation established early on by circus master and avid art collector John Ringling. That still holds true with **The Ringling Museum of Art** (941-359-5700; www.ringling.org) complex, the Ringling School of Art, and the town's multitude of galleries. Naples, however, is catching up with its lively gallery scene and highly respectable **The Baker Museum** (239-597-1900 or 800-597-1900; artisnaples.org). Sarasota, Punta Gorda, Fort Myers, and Naples all offer art walks on a monthly basis.

Food & Drink

CRAFTY SPIRITS New Florida legislation and a growing trend have caused an explosion in the craft beer and spirits industry in Southwest Florida. Every town has at least one craft brewery: **Motorworks Brewing** (941-567-6218; motorworksbrewing.com) in Bradenton, **JDubs Brewing Company** (941-955-2739; www.jdubsbrewing.com) in Sarasota, **Fat Point Brewing** (800-380-7405; www.fatpoint.com) in Punta Gorda, **Cape Coral Brewing Company** (239-257-1033; capecoralbrewing.com), **Bury Me Brewing** ((239-332-2337; www.burymebrewing.com) and **Point Ybel**

Brewing Company (239-603-6536; ♿ www.pointybelbrew.com) in the Fort Myers area, **Momentum Brewhouse** (239-949-9945; www.momentumbrewhouse.com) in Bonita Springs, and **Naples Beach Brewing** (239-304-8795; www.naplesbeachbrewery.com) and **Riptide Brewing Company** (239-228-6533; riptidebrewingcompany.com) in Naples. A new Florida law, which a few years back allowed small-batch distilleries to sell a limited amount of product onsite, has seen the industry grow from **Siesta Key Rum** (941-358-1900; www.drumcircledistilling.com) in Sarasota and **Wicked Dolphin Rum** (239-242-5244; www.wickeddolphin.com) in Cape Coral to the new **Alligator Bay Distillers** (941-347-8419; www.alligatorbaydistillers.com) in Punta Gorda. Stop in for a sampler while you're around. More information about breweries, distilleries, and wineries is listed in each chapter.

FRUIT Citrus and tropical fruit thrives in the sunny climes of Southwest Florida. Besides grapefruit, oranges, Key limes, and tangerines, local residents and commercial farmers grow mangoes, guavas, sapodillas, papayas, coconuts, jackfruits, mameys, lychees, and avocados (which differ from California avocados in terms of size, sweetness, and oil content as

THE MOTORWORKS BREWERY

TROPICAL FRUITS ADD AN EXOTIC FLAVOR TO THE
SARASOTA FARMERS' MARKET

Florida's is lower). **Pine Island** on the
Island Coast is particularly known for its
fruit farms and **MangoMania** festival
every July.

GROUPER The grouper sandwich—crisp
fried fillet of a local white, meaty fish—is
the most signature dish of the coast. The
mild flavor of the large fish lends itself to
multiple preparations, however, and
most menus list more than one. Its popularity, unfortunately, has led to overfishing, and now grouper fishing season is
closed for a few months during the
winter.

KEY LIMES Yellow and the size of ping
pong balls, these cousins of the more
common green Persian lime are typically
juicier and more flavorful. They are the
only fruit that should go into a Key lime
pie. If you see a dark green Key lime pie,
it's either not the real thing or it's been
colored—a travesty to Key lime pie lovers. Hardly a coastal restaurant neglects
the ubiquitous dessert on its menu. The
best I've tasted in the region? Those renditions at **Gramma Dot's** (239-472-8138;
www.sanibelmarina.com/gramma.html)
on Sanibel Island and **Ophelia's on the
Bay** (941-349-2212; opheliasonthebay
.net) in Sarasota.

SEAFOOD Besides the grouper, shrimp,
and stone crab I cover individually here,

local fishermen and chefs bring to the
table a vast selection of fish and shellfish. Snapper comes in mangrove and red
varieties locally. Pompano, redfish, and
cobia sometimes show up on menus, but
any other fish is imported. Yellowtail
snapper, mahi mahi, hogfish, Florida lobster, and Apalachicola oysters come from
other parts of Florida. Shrimp fleets
bring pink shrimp into port at Fort Myers
Beach's working waterfront. (Make sure
to ask if they're wild shrimp; otherwise,
they're probably imported and possibly
treated with antibiotics and other
unknowns.) Blue crab is also caught
locally (again, ask if it's local). The best
place to relish it is **Peace River Seafood &
Crab Shack** (941-505-8440) in Punta
Gorda.

SHRIMP Gulf shrimp are graded by size
and assigned all sorts of vague measure-
ments: jumbo, large, medium-size, boat
grade, and so on. The surest way to know
what size shrimp you are ordering is to
ask for the count-per-pound designation.
This will be something like "21–25s,"
meaning there are twenty-one to twenty-five shrimp per pound. "Boat grade"
normally designates a mixture of sizes,
usually on the small side.

STONE CRAB CLAWS WERE "DISCOVERED" IN THE
EVERGLADES, AND YOU DON'T FIND 'EM ANY FRESHER
THAN AT LOCAL RESTAURANTS AND FISH MARKETS

STONE CRABS Possibly Florida's most exquisite dining pleasure, stone crabs are harvested from local waters between October 15 and May 15. Named for their tough-to-crack shells, they are cherished for their sweet, meaty flesh, usually eaten chilled and dipped in tangy mustard sauce. **Everglades City** and **Marco Island** are the major home ports for the sensational shellfish, but you'll find them fresh up and down the coast. Downtown Naples throws a Stone Fish Festival in October to celebrate the season's kick-off.

DON'T LET WINTER-SEASON TRAFFIC RUFFLE YOUR FEATHERS. HIT THE SCENIC BACK ROADS

Nature

ALLIGATORS Southwest Florida has a love-hate relationship with this prehistoric survivor. The reptiles prefer fresh or brackish water and so they congregate most heavily in the Everglades' River of Grass, largely removed from human habitation. Sometimes, however, they show up unannounced in someone's yard. They may steal a pet from time to time, and that's where the hate comes in. They prey on humans infrequently, usually under circumstances where the gator has been fed by them. Sanibel Island figures importantly in the complex relationship locals have with these beasts, because it is one of Florida's few islands with freshwater and one of the state's most conservation-minded cities. With its groundbreaking laws against feeding, it helped bring back alligators from endangerment. However, after two beloved citizens were taken down by gators a few years back, the city cracked down on nuisance gator removal, effecting a solid decrease in their population on the refuge island as gator trappers were allowed to take more than just the nuisance gator when they showed up. The best place to see alligators remains the Everglades, especially (and most safely) at the Oasis Visitor Center in **Big Cypress National Preserve** (239-695-1201; www.nps.gov/bicy).

BARRIER ISLANDS Islands line the shores of the Southwest Florida coastline, buffeting it from waves and weather, and providing it with its famed beachfront. The chain of islands starts in the north with **Anna Maria Island** and runs continuously to **Marco Island** and some of the **Ten Thousand Islands** in Everglades territory. The islands are constantly in flux, shaped by forces of nature and man—erosion, mangrove building on their leeward sides, and seawalls and other structures. The **Intracoastal Waterway** runs between the islands and the mainland on the islands' east side.

BEACHES Boasting some of the best beaches in the world, Southwest Florida can also claim great variety and superiority in its coastal makeup. **Siesta Key** in Sarasota, for instance, wins accolades for having some of the whitest sand in the world, made up of ground quartz that originated in the Appalachian Mountains. Dr. Beach voted it #1 in the nation in 2011. TripAdvisor echoed the ranking in 2015. **Venice Beach**, on the other hand, is known for its dark flecks and shark's teeth fossils, while **Sanibel Island** has a world-renowned reputation for seashell picking.

BIRDS Much of Southwest Florida lies along a major "flyway" for migrating birds. This means superb birding, particularly in late fall through the spring months. White pelicans and warblers are among the most spectacular migrating species. Brown pelicans, roseate spoonbills (in the southern latitudes), reddish egrets, great blue and green herons, great white and snowy egrets, bald eagles, white ibis, gulls, terns, sandpipers, oystercatchers, mangrove cuckoos, indigo buntings, and more than two hundred other species inhabit the region year-round. Dozens of parks and preserves along the coast are part of the **Great Florida Birding & Wildlife Trail** (www.floridabirdingtrail.com).

DOG BEACHES **South Brohard Park** (941-316-1172) in Venice and **Bonita Beach Dog Park** (239-707-1874; www.leegov.com/parks) on Lovers Key, south of Fort Myers Beach are the only area beaches where dogs can run leash-free. Dogs must have all the proper tags. **Sanibel Island** allows dogs on the beach when leashed. Most other beach parks do not allow dogs at all. Throughout this book, lodgings and other selected places that accept pets are indicated with the dog-paw symbol 🐾. It's a good idea to call ahead when traveling with your pet.

EVERGLADES "The Everglades" refers to the dominant type of environment in southern Florida. It actually begins in Central Florida with the downflow of the Kissimmee River. A large portion of the habitat is protected locally by Everglades National Park, Big Cypress National Preserve, Florida Panther and Ten Thousand Islands National Wildlife Refuges, and state parks. Its ecological composition ranges from slow-moving river and saltwater marshes to mangrove forest and barrier islands. Vital to the region's water supply and the survival of hundreds of species of animals, many threatened or endangered, the Everglades is undergoing a multibillion-dollar restoration.

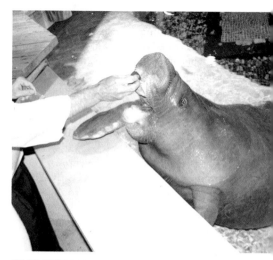

SNOOTY, SOUTH FLORIDA MUSEUM'S CELEBRITY MANATEE, TAKES THE STAGE

MANATEES One of Florida's most well-loved and docile creatures, this prehistoric marine mammal teeters on the brink of survival. Cold spells, red tide, and boat propellers threaten its existence in our waterways. Boat tours in Fort Myers and Naples take you into their habitat to see them. In winter, you can watch them at **Manatee Park** (239-533-7440 or 239-690-5030; www.leegov.com/parks), where they come to bask in the warm runoff waters from the local electric company. For a close-up educational experience, visit them in captivity at the **South Florida Museum** (941-746-4131; www.southfloridamuseum.org) in Bradenton or **Mote Marine Aquarium** (941-388-4441 or 800-691-MOTE; www.mote.org) in Sarasota.

Outdoors

FISHING Recreational fishing brings much of the region's tourism. **Boca Grande Pass** has a big reputation for tarpon fishing and holds annual tournaments in the late spring/early summer. Another tarpon tourney takes place from Fort Myers Beach. Other prized catches include snook, redfish, shark, snapper, ladyfish, mackerel, and sheepshead. Any

SURF FISHING COMBINES TWO OF THE COAST'S GREATEST OUTDOOR PLEASURES

number of fishing charters and head boats can take you to the fish, or you can cast from land or fishing piers throughout the area. You will need a fishing license if you're not covered by a boat's or pier's licensing.

GARDENS Everything grows like crazy in this part of the world, so it's only natural that public gardens play an important role in the landscape. Many gardens are part of a greater attraction, such as **Sarasota Jungle Gardens** (941-355-5305 or 877-861-6541; www.sarasotajungle gardens.com) and **The Ringling** (941-355-5101; www.ringling.org) in Sarasota, **Lakes Regional Park** (239-533-7575; www.leegov.com/parks) and **Edison & Ford Winter Estates** (239-334-7419; www.edisonfordwinterestates.org) in Fort Myers, and the **Naples Zoo** (239-262-5409; napleszoo.org) and **Palm Cottage** (239-261-8164; www.napleshistorical society.org) in Naples. The **Naples Botanical Garden** (239-643-7275 or 877-433-1874; www.naplesgarden.org) is the area's one such attraction devoted entirely to the appreciation of plants.

INSECTS Among the rich wildlife one finds in Southwest Florida is an abundance of bugs, spiders, and butterflies. Of course the last is the most appreciated, and you can find butterfly houses at several nature centers, such as **Calusa Nature Center** (239-275-3435; www .calusanature.org) in Fort Myers, which also devotes an entire room—the Insectarium—to bugs. Also in Fort Myers, the **Butterfly Estates** (239-690-2359 or 877-690-2359; http://thebutterflyestates .com) immerses curious visitors in a winged experience. In the great wide open and quite possibly even on your doorstep, you will see (or feel) a wide variety of less desirable insects, including palmetto bugs (our euphemism for flying cockroaches), biting mosquitoes and no-see-ums (sand flies), huge lubber

GIANT LILYPADS ADD DRAMA TO A WATER FEATURE AT NAPLES BOTANICAL GARDEN

grasshoppers, golden orb spiders, ants in assorted varieties (avoid the red, biting fire ant), and the occasional scorpion (whose bite is usually less than toxic to those who are not allergic).

PARKS & PRESERVES Southwest Florida's rare ecology deserves keeping, and a number of government entities—from city to county to federal—take up the cause. Federal parks and preserves include **De Soto National Memorial** (941-792-0458; www.nps.gov/deso) in Bradenton, **J. N. "Ding" Darling National Wildlife Refuge** (239-472-1100; www.fws .gov/refuge/jn_ding_darling/) on Sanibel Island, and in the Everglades area **Florida Panther National Wildlife Refuge** (239-657-8001; www.fws.gov/refuge/ florida_panther/)**, Ten Thousand Islands National Wildlife Refuge** (239-657-8001)**, Everglades National Park** (239-695-3311; www.nps.gov/ever), **Big Cypress National Preserve** (239-695-1201; www .nps.gov/bicy), and **Rookery Bay National Estuarine Research Reserve** (239-530-5940; www.rookerybay.org). You'll find state parks and wildlife management areas in every section of this

book. Private organizations—such as **Corkscrew Swamp Sanctuary** (239-348-9151; corkscrew.audubon.org) near Naples, the **Conservancy of Southwest Florida** (239-262-0304; www .conservancy.org) in Naples, and the **Sanibel-Captiva Conservation Foundation** (239-472-2329; www.sccf.org)—have stepped up to preserve vast tracts of fragile land and water.

A TYPICAL TIMUCUA INDIAN VILLAGE HAS BEEN RE-CREATED AT DE SOTO NATIONAL MEMORIAL PARK IN BRADENTON

SEAFOOD DOESN'T GET ANY FRESHER OR MORE AFFORDABLE THAN AT NEW PASS GRILL

SEASHELLS BY THE SEASHORE Sanibel Island is the recognized leading shell-collecting beach in the region, perhaps in the whole country. The offshore island of **Cayo Costa** also attracts rabid shellers. **Bonita Springs**, too, can boast its shellacious treasures. Shelling is a favorite pastime throughout the region, and the variety is infinite. Prize shells include the junonia, lion's paw, and wentletrap. Shell shops throughout the region sell perfect specimens that cost anywhere from twenty cents to four figures.

SHELL MOUNDS The ancient Calusa built midden mounds, sort of early compost heaps, where they disposed of their dinner bones, seashells, pottery shards, and other materials. They also built mounds for burial purposes and to provide elevation for their homes and temples. Two sites along the Gulf Coast let visitors peek into cutaways of actual mounds built by the Calusa. They reside at **Historic Spanish Point** (941-966-5214; www.historicspanishpoint.org) south of Sarasota and **Mound House** (239-765-0865; www.moundhouse.org) on Fort Myers Beach. You can walk or drive up lofty shell mound remains in Palmetto, Pineland (Pine Island), and Marco Island.

SURFING Most surfers equate Florida's east coast with the best wave action. Storms and fronts, however, do reward the west coast with breakers of surfable quality. Best spots are at the jetties on **Venice Beach** and at **Turner Beach** on Sanibel Island. Both, however, have dangerous undercurrents, so they are not for beginners or weak swimmers.

TIDES Unlike some coastal areas, the Gulf Coast usually only experiences one low and one high tide every day, meaning its tides are diurnal. Several websites give times for high and low tides, which are important mostly to fishermen, boaters, birders, and shellers. Bait shops and local newspapers can also provide this information.

HISTORY

T he essence of Gulf Coast Florida seems to be a balance of polar extremes: the ultimate in both natural wilderness and social civility. To understand the region and the
richness of its heritage, culture, and environment, one must understand its roots,
learn the names, and revel in the legends of its past—a past steeped in romance, adventure, and power.

The story begins with a single mangrove tree and evolves around humanity's need
to conquer that tree's primeval world. Enter the characters: Ambition, Wealth, and
Social Grace. How does the story end? Happily, we can hope, with the modern redis-
covery of the coast's unique natural and historical heritage.

Natural History

FROM GRAINS OF SAND

> Each wave helps build a ridge of accumulating sand and shell that
> runs roughly parallel to the beach. Over a period of hundreds or thou-
> sands of years, a ridge may become a barrier island.
> —Lynn Stone, Voyageurs Series, *Sanibel Island*, 1991

> On the floor is a straw mat. Under the mat is a layer of sand that has
> been tracked into the cottage and has sifted through the straw. I have
> thought some of taking the mat up and sweeping the sand into a pile
> and removing it, but have decided against it. This is the way keys form,
> apparently, and I have no particular reason to interfere.
> —E. B. White, "On a Florida Key," 1941

Billions of years ago, the Florida peninsula existed only as a scattering of volcanic
keys, akin to the Caribbean islands. The passing years, silt, and the sea's power eventually buried all evidence of these volcanic origins. What is now Florida remained submerged until some twenty million years ago, when matter buildup brought land to the
surface in the form of new islands.

Ice Age sea fluctuations molded Florida into solid land, and islands continued to
grow along its fringes. From a single grain of sand or a lone mangrove sprout they
stabilized into masses of sand and forests composed of leggy roots and finger shoots.
As shells and marine encrustations accumulated, islands fell into formation along the
Gulf Coast, protecting it from the battering of a storm-driven sea. In the gaps between
the islands, the gulf's waters scoured the shore to forge inlets, estuaries, bayous,
creeks, and rivers. The sea chiseled a mottled, labyrinthine shoreline that kept the
southern Gulf Coast a secret while the rest of the state was being tamed.

During its infancy, the region hosted a slow parade of ever-changing creatures. In
prehistoric graveyards modern archaeologists have found mummified remains of rhi-
noceroses, crocodiles, llamas, camels, pygmy horses, saber-toothed tigers, mastodons,
and great woolly mammoths—Florida's first winter visitors at the advent of the Ice Age.

Another era brought giant armadillos, tapirs, and other South American creatures. Fauna and flora from these ancient eras survive today: cabbage palms (the state tree), saw palmettos, garfish, seahorses, horseshoe crabs, alligators, manatees, armadillos, and loggerhead sea turtles.

AN EARLY PICTURE

> In the bay of Juan Ponce De León, in the west side of the land, we meet with innumerable small islands, and several fresh streams: the land in general is drowned mangrove swamp . . . From this place Cape Romano, latitude 25:43 to latitude 26:30 are many inconsiderable inlets, all carefully laid down in the chart, here is Carlos Bay, and the Coloosa Hatchee, or Coloosa river, with the island San Ybell, where we find the southern entrance of Charlotte harbour.
> —Bernard Romans, 1775

One of the earliest recorders of Florida native life and topography, Bernard Romans is credited with naming Charlotte Harbor after the queen of his adopted homeland, England, and Cape Romano in Ten Thousand Islands after himself. Native Americans and earlier Spanish explorers are responsible for other regional place names.

The harbor was already the center of west-coast life when the first explorers discovered it. Its deep waters and barrier-island protection created a pocket of unusually mild climate, attracting early aborigines and their descendants.

Romans and his contemporaries found the Gulf Coast alive with wild turkeys, black bears, white-tailed deer, golden panthers, bobcats, possums, raccoons, alligators, river otters, lizards, and snakes. Wild boars and scrub cattle roamed freely, descendants of stock brought by Spanish explorers and missionaries. Land birds and waterfowl of all varieties—some permanent, some migratory—filled the skies and back bays. Majestic ospreys and bald eagles swooped; kites soared effortlessly; sandhill cranes foraged the countryside; wood storks nested; pelicans came in brown and white; gulls, terns, and sandpipers patrolled seashores; cormorants, ducks, anhingas, ibises, egrets, roseate spoonbills, and herons fed among the mangroves.

Marine life flourished. Manatees cleared waterways, dolphins frolicked in the waves, and mullet burst from bay waters like cannon-shot. Tarpon, rays, snapper, snook, flounder, ladyfish, and mackerel churned the otherwise calm backwaters. Grouper, tripletail, tuna, and shark lurked in deep waters offshore.

On land, a wide variety of indigenous vegetation abounded. Sea grapes, sea oats, nickerbeans, and railroad vines anchored sandy coasts. Thick, impenetrable jungles clogged inland areas. Cabbage palms and gumbo-limbo trees stood tall. Papayas flourished along with flowering shrubs. In mixed-wood forests, pines climbed skyward and live oaks fluttered their eerie veils of Spanish moss. Cedars fringed islands along the Sarasota Bay coast. Ferns and grasses carpeted the marshes. Swamplands were home to great cypress trees with bony knees and branches full of parasitic mistletoe, resurrection fern, and epiphytic orchids and bromeliads.

Primeval and teeming, Florida held an exotic and mysterious aura. The swamp and the estuary nurtured all of life, from the Everglades upward along the lowlands of the Gulf Coast. It was a perfect ecosystem, designed by nature to withstand all forces—except humankind.

FACE-LIFTS & IMPLANTS With the arrival of the first settlers, the natural balance that existed along the Gulf Coast began to tilt. The Spanish brought citrus seedlings and livestock. Naturalists and growers introduced specimens from the north and south: mangoes, avocados, bougainvillea, hibiscus, frangipani, coconut palms, pineapples, sapodillas, tomatoes, and legumes. For the most part, these exotics proved harmless to the fragile environment.

Three nonnative plants brought to the area in the past century, however, have harmed the ecosystem and changed the profile of the land. The prolific melaleuca tree (or cajeput), casuarina (Australian pine), and Brazilian pepper choke out the native vegetation that wildlife feeds on and harm both man and property. Many communities are attempting to eradicate these noxious plants, particularly the pepper tree.

In the animal world, exotic species, such as the Burmese python and Nile monitor lizards, thrive to the detriment of native ones, and government agencies have set eradication programs in motion.

The complexion of the west coast was changed further by dredging and plowing. In times when swampland was equated with slimy monsters and slick real estate agents, developers and governments thought nothing of filling it in to create more buildable land. This, too, threw the ecosystem off balance. Fortunately, such mistakes were recognized before their effects became irreversible. Today the government strives to preserve, even restore, the delicate balance of the wetlands, most notably through the massive, multi-billion-dollar, thirty-year Everglades restoration project.

Social History

TIME LINE: GULF COAST FLORIDA The modern settlement of Florida's southwest coast can be traced like a timeline that begins on the shores of Sarasota Bay in 1841 and ends at Naples in 1887. At first glance, this time frame makes the region look young, without the gracious patina of age and the wrinkles of an interesting past. Common is the belief, in fact, that the Gulf Coast has no history because it lacks Williamsburg's colonial homes and Philadelphia's monuments.

True, the Gulf Coast's early pioneers left no standing architecture. Termites, flimsy building styles, erosion, and tropical storms saw to that. But earlier settlers did leave other proof of their existence—artifacts that date as far back as ten thousand years. If that isn't history, what is?

CALUSA KINGDOM Archaeologists of this century and the last have discovered remnants of early architecture and lifeways in the shell mounds of the Calusa and Timucua tribes, who settled the coastlines more than 2,500 years ago. The Timucua inhabited the Bradenton area and Sarasota Bay coast for many years and then migrated northward and to the east; the Calusa later moved into the Sarasota area and were centered around Charlotte Harbor.

Evidence of still earlier civilizations has been found, placing Florida's first immigrants, possibly from Asia, in the upper coast regions around 8200 BC. Little is known about these early arrivals except that they used pointed spears.

THE FOUNTAIN FROM THE OLD HOTEL CHARLOTTE HARBOR NOW GRACES THE GROUNDS OF PUNTA GORDA HISTORY PARK

Archaeological excavations and the writings of Spanish explorers give us a more complete picture of the Calusa and other tribes, who built shell mounds to bury their dead and debris. Learned consensus brings the Calusa and the Timucua to southern Florida from Caribbean islands—evidence of similar lifestyles and sustained contact suggests a connection to the peaceful Arawak Indians of the West Indies. Similarities have also been found between the Calusa and South American tribes, and, given indications of the Florida's tribes' great engineering skills, some historians consider them wayward relatives of the Maya or Aztec. (Others say they are connected to the Maya and Aztec by trade rather than origin.)

The name Calusa, or Caloosa, was used first by Spanish conquerors who understood the name of the tribe's chief to be Calos. They were said to be tall people with hip-length hair that men wore in a topknot. When clothed, men dressed in breeches of deerskin or woven palmetto fiber, and women fashioned garments out of Spanish moss. They fished for mullet and mackerel with harpoons and palmetto-fiber nets; hunted for turkey, deer, and bear with bow and arrow, deer-bone dirks, and Aztec-style weapons; and harvested wild sea grapes, fruit, yams, swamp cabbage (hearts of palm), and the coontie root, out of which they pounded flour for bread. Conch and whelk shells were crafted into tools for building, fishing, and cooking. The natives spent their leisure time wrestling, celebrating the corn harvest, and worshiping the sun god. Great seafarers, the Calusa built dugout canoes and traveled in them to Caribbean islands and the Yucatán. A different style of pirogue took them along rivers and bay waters to visit villages of their own tribe and those of other nations.

Much of our information about the Calusa comes from the son of a Spanish official stationed in Cartagena, in what is now Colombia. The youngster, Hernando de Escalante Fontaneda, was shipwrecked along Calusa shores en route to Spain. He lived among the tribe for seventeen years, learned its language, and, upon returning to Spain in 1574, recorded its customs. In 1895, Frank Hamilton Cushing explored Charlotte Harbor's Amerindian heritage. He surmised that the Calusa's religious structures and palmetto-piling homes had perched on shell mounds along riverbanks and coastlines. Terraces and steps bit into the towering mounds where gardens and courts had been built. Man-made canals up to thirty feet wide connected neighboring villages. Manasota Key, Pine Island, Mound Key, and Marco Island were important religious and governmental centers for the Calusa.

Excavations along the Gulf Coast continually provide new information about the region's native inhabitants and their symbiotic relationship with nature. The University of Florida in Gainesville funds a research center on Pine Island for the sole purpose of excavating mounds to discover more truth about the vanished civilization.

SPANISH IMPOSITION Greed and religious fervor eventually warped this idyllic picture, and the Calusa showed themselves to be vicious warriors when it came to preserving the life they knew. Juan Ponce de León first crashed the party in 1513. It's possible that early slavers from the Caribbean were responsible for the Calusa hostility he encountered, or perhaps the Amerindians' early hatred of the conquistadors was gained secondhand, from trading with island natives. Whatever the reason, Ponce was "blacklisted" by the Calusa shortly after he began his search, according to legend, for Bimini, a storied land of treasure and youth.

Ponce de León first landed on Florida's east coast at Eastertime without strife, and the conqueror named the land after the Spanish name for the holiday, "Pascua Florida." However, on his second landing, days later, he was met by shell-tipped spears and bows and arrows. His three wounded sailors were the first Europeans known to shed blood in Florida. Ponce de León's ship continued to the west coast, where it

IN PALMETTO, VISITORS CAN CLIMB TO THE TOP OF AN ANCIENT INDIAN MOUND AT EMERSON POINT PRESERVE

stopped in the vicinity of Marco Island. Here one native astounded him by speaking to him in Spanish—learned, perhaps, from West Indies contacts. Impressed, Ponce de León allowed his party to be tricked by a marauding native army in canoes, but escaped with the loss of only one man's life.

After several trips to Florida and the Gulf Coast, Ponce de León returned to Puerto Rico—still treasureless and now middle-aged—to plot a new scheme. In 1521, he set out to establish a Gulf Coast colony as a base for treasure explorations. This time, the party he crashed had been forewarned, possibly by smoke signals. Calusa arrows pierced the heavy armor of the Spaniards, killing and wounding many, including the great seeker of youth himself. After returning to Havana for medical attention, Ponce de León died there at the age of sixty.

Lust for gold overcame common sense as more explorers and invaders followed in Ponce de León's tragic footsteps. In 1539, Hernando de Soto sailed from Havana and headed up the Gulf Coast, seeking, it would seem, a way to confuse future historians. Three different crewmen described the expedition three different ways. The Smithsonian has published a report some locals still dispute, which claims that de Soto landed first on Longboat Key and then, looking for fresh water, headed toward Tampa Bay. According to the Smithsonian, de Soto set up his first mainland camp at an abandoned native village at the mouth of the Manatee River, near modern-day Bradenton. Others are convinced that his first landfall was at Fort Myers Beach. Regardless of where the landing took place, we know that de Soto scoured the coast for gold, all the while torturing and killing Native Americans who would not, could not, lead him to it.

Sarasota and its environs embrace the Smithsonian study's findings. Some say the name of the town itself, initially written as "Sara Sota," comes from the conqueror. Others prefer a more romantic legend regarding his fictional daughter, Sara. Sarasota's first hotel, in any case, took its name from de Soto. Near Bradenton, a small national park marks the alleged spot of his first landing.

In 1565, Pedro Menéndez de Avilés came to the Gulf Coast, searching for a son lost to shipwreck and a group of Spaniards being held captive by the Calusa. With the aid

THE MIRACLE OF THE MANGROVE

The mangrove forest is both a fertile incubator and a marine graveyard, the home of an island construction crew and a vegetative ballet troupe. It is a self-sustaining world marked by vivid contrasts. The Mangrove Coast (as one local historian termed it) is riddled with red, black, and white species of the tree. Red mangroves strut along mainland coastlines, canals, and the leeward sides of islands on graceful prop roots—or at least they look graceful until low tide reveals the oysters, barnacles, and tiny marine metropolises that weigh them down and keep them connected to the sea.

Farther inland, black and white mangroves create thick, impenetrable forests that buffer waves, filter pollutants, send out shoots, and always busily build. Encrustations of shellfish grab algae, silt, and sand, creating rich soil out of decaying material. Fish, crabs, and mollusks skitter among the roots, nibbling dinner, depositing eggs, and tending to their young. Birds rest and nest in the mangroves' scraggly branches, ready to dive for the fish on which they feed. Mother trees send their tubular offspring bobbing upon sea currents to find a foothold elsewhere and perhaps begin a new island.

The cycle is ancient and ongoing, threatened only by the chainsaws of developers. A few decades ago, these natural builders, the mangroves, were leveled in favor of cement seawalls. Today, strict regulations prohibit mangrove destruction. The crucial role of the mangrove in the survival of Florida's sea life finally has been realized—and cherished.

---

of one of Chief Calos's Spanish captives, Menéndez befriended Calos with flattery and gifts, then built a fort and a mission at a spot called San Anton, believed to have been on Pine Island. But Menéndez insulted the great chieftain by rejecting his sister as a wife and allying himself with enemy tribes. Sensing Calos's anger, Menéndez tricked the leader into captivity and had him beheaded. When Menéndez later executed Calos's son and heir to the throne, along with eleven of his subchiefs, tribesmen burned their own villages, forcing the settlers to bail out on the settlement in search of food.

The century that followed is considered the Golden Age of the Calusa. It was marked by freedom from European intrusion and great cultural advances, heightened by the contribution of Spanish captives who had refused to be saved by Menéndez's rescue party and by others who found Calusa ways preferable to "civilization."

Eventually, peaceful trading softened the hostility between Spanish settlers and the Calusa. Cuban immigrants began building a fishing industry around Charlotte Harbor. Although the Calusa had won the war against Spanish invaders, they were defenseless against the diseases the Europeans brought with them. By the turn of the nineteenth century, smallpox and other diseases had killed off most Calusa; the remainder were absorbed by intermarrying with the Cubans and newly arriving tribes. The most prominent of the latter were the Seminole—a name meaning "wanderer"—a mixture of Georgian Creek, African, and Spanish bloodlines.

THE VARMINT ERA "A haunt of the picaroons of all nations," explorer James Grant Forbes wrote in 1772, referring to Charlotte Harbor—layover, if not home, for every scoundrel who sailed its island-clotted waters. The southern Gulf Coast's maze of forbidding bayous and barely navigable waterways made it a favorite hideout for escaped criminals, bootleggers, government refugees, smugglers, and—that most popular of all local folk characters—buccaneers.

Pirate legends color the pages of regional history books in shades of blood red and doubloon gold. Besides willing to residents a certain cavalier spirit, these pirates have left—if one believes the tales—millions of dollars in buried treasure. "After researching the subject in 1950 . . . then state attorney general Ralph E. Odum estimated that some

$165 million is still buried beneath Florida's sands and waters," reported a 1978 issue of the *Miami Herald*'s *Florida Almanac*, "$30 million of it originally the property of Jose Gaspar."

Besides the mostly mythical Gaspar, other picaresque names resound along the Gulf Coast: Jean Lafitte, of New Orleans fame; Bru Baker, Gaspar's Pine Island cohort; and a dark soul named Black Caesar. Henry Castor supposedly buried treasure on Egmont Key in the mid-1700s. Local legend places the notorious Calico Jack Rackham and his pirate lover, Anne Bonny, on the shores of Fort Myers Beach for a playful honeymoon. Black Augustus lived and died a hermit on Mound Key, to the south. On Panther Key, John Gomez, Gaspar's self-proclaimed cabin boy, lived to be 122 and sold maps purportedly leading to Gasparillan gold to many a gullible treasure hunter.

According to more reliable historical records, island pirate havens were replaced by or coexisted with crude Spanish fishing ranchos, which cropped up as early as the 1600s. The camps—which provided Cuban traders with salted mullet and roe to eat—consisted of thatched shacks, some built on pilings in shallow waters. Here families lived, according to customs inspector Henry B. Crews, "in a state of Savage Barbarism with no associate but the Seminole and the lowest class of refugee Spaniards who from crime have most generally been compelled to abandon the haunts of civilized life."

Ice-making and railroads changed the direction of fish exportation from southern points to northern destinations. Punta Gorda, with the area's first railroad station, became the center for the transshipment of fresh fish. Major fish-shipping companies built stilt houses for the more than two hundred men who harvested their mullet crops. These structures straddled shallows from Charlotte Harbor to Ten Thousand Islands, providing homes for the fishermen and their families until the late 1930s, when modern roads and the burning of Punta Gorda's Long Dock brought the era to a close. Fewer than a dozen of the historic fish shacks have survived hurricanes, erosion, and the state's earlier determination to tear them down as a public nuisance. They strut along the shallows in greatest concentration offshore of North Captiva Island.

"It is highly important that no person should be permitted to settle on the Islands forming 'Charlotte Harbor' . . . which are of no value for the purpose of agriculture, being in general formed of sand and shells," advised Assistant Adjutant General Captain Lorenzo Thomas in 1844. Nonetheless, out of this era of varmints sprouted a tradition of farming. Plucky pioneers raised coconuts, citrus, tomatoes, and other crops, despite hardship and heartbreak, as they trickled in to coax their livelihood from a hostile environment.

YEARS OF DISCONTENT The bloody years of the Wars of Indian Removal began in 1821, when Andrew Jackson—then governor of the territory—decided to claim northern Florida from the Seminole tribes that were wreaking havoc on American settlers. By 1837, fighting had spread to the southern reaches of the peninsula, and two forts were built upriver from present-day Fort Myers. The following year the government reached an agreement with the Seminole, restricting them to mainland areas along the Charlotte Harbor coast, the Caloosahatchee River, and southward.

News of imminent peace prompted Josiah Gates to build a hotel on the banks of the Manatee River, near modern-day Bradenton, in anticipation of the influx of settlers from Fort Brooke (Tampa) that the treaty would bring. A modest community rose up around this precursor of southwest Florida resorts. Families of soldiers and wealthy Southern planters settled in the area. The latter brought their slaves and built sugarcane plantations on vast expanses of land that they bought for $1.25 an acre.

Sarasota got its first permanent settler in 1842 when William Whitaker, a fisherman, built his home on Yellow Bluff, overlooking Sarasota Bay. He and his new wife, daughter of one of the Manatee planters, had ten children and later went into cattle ranching and farming.

The year after the peace treaty was signed, a tribe of Seminole attacked a settlement across the river from their village, on the same site as present-day Fort Myers. The Harney Point Massacre rekindled the war. Fort Harvie was built near the site of the violent attack. Chief Billy Bowlegs led his people in evasive tactics through the wild and mysterious Everglades, but by 1842, the government had captured 230 of his people and shipped them west. Further pursuit was abandoned. Only Fort Harvie and one other fortification remained operational. A new agreement contained the Seminole along the Caloosahatchee and barred them from the islands to protect the fishermen and their families. The treaty made no mention of the swampland, probably because the government considered it useless; the Seminole assumed the territory was theirs.

By 1848, three years after Florida's admission to the Union as the twenty-seventh state, there was a surge of interest in the wetlands. The government, envisioning drainage projects to create more land, offered the Seminole $250 each to relocate in the West. When they refused, a systematic plan to conquer them went into effect. This plan included the repair of Fort Harvie, which was renamed Fort Myers after a US colonel who had served for many years in Florida and was engaged to the commanding general's daughter. Manpower was increased there, and the fort was reinforced and enlarged. Scouting parties stalked the Seminole but usually found only the remains of abandoned and burned villages when they arrived.

In December 1855, after soldiers destroyed Billy Bowlegs's prize banana patch, the Seminole chief and his people retaliated. Fort Myers became the center of war activity. The government placed a bounty on the head of any Seminole brought to the fort and

THE STORY OF THE CALUSA AND SEMINOLE PEOPLES, INCLUDING SEMINOLE CHIEF BILLY BOWLEGS, FINDS AN AUDIENCE ALONG VENICE'S MAIN THOROUGHFARE

offered $1,000 to each Seminole warrior ($100 to each woman and child) who agreed to leave the area. Finally, in 1858, after soldiers had captured his granddaughter and other women of the tribe, Billy Bowlegs capitulated, thus bringing an end to thirty-seven years of killing and deception by the government and the military. Fort Myers was abandoned, and the remaining Seminole dispersed deep into the Everglades. Farmers, planters, fishermen, and cattlemen continued peacefully in their trades, although government vigilance against alliances with the Seminole forced some of the island fishing *ranchos* to close during the war's final years. Today, the Seminole live on reservations, earning an income from tourism, fishing, and casinos.

In the late 1850s, Virginia planter Captain James Evans purchased Fort Myers on the auction block. He brought in his slaves to work the crops he envisioned—tropical fruits, coconut palms, coffee, and other exotic plants. But the Civil War interrupted his venture, sending him back home. Florida joined the Confederacy in 1861. West coast inhabitants generally remained uninvolved until a federal blockade at Key West cut off supplies, at which point they turned to the profitable business of blockade running.

CATTLE KINGS, CARPETBAGGERS & CRACKERS Jacob Summerlin epitomized the Florida cattle king. He dressed in a floppy hat, leather boots, and trail dust. Having established a steady trade between Florida and ports south before the Civil War, Summerlin was in a good position to provide the Confederate Army with contraband beef. Working with his blockade-running partner, James McKay Sr., he drove his cattle from inland Florida to Punta Rassa, where the causeway from Sanibel Island makes landfall today. There he sold his scrub cattle, descendants of livestock left by the early Spaniards. The US Navy eventually learned of these illegal dealings and stationed boats at Sanibel and Punta Rassa. Despite attempts to thwart their trade, however, Summerlin and McKay sold twenty-five thousand steers to the Confederates between 1861 and 1865.

Jake Summerlin lived by the seat of his pants, driving cattle to Punta Rassa and collecting big bags of Cuban gold—which he spent at the end of the line on drinking and gaming. In 1874, he built the Summerlin House at Punta Rassa, where he and his men could bunk and invest the profits of the business in frivolity.

The rough, free-and-easy lifestyle of the cow hunter attracted young post–Civil War drifters. In addition, Summerlin's success lured Civil War officers into the prosperous life of the cattle boss, including Captain F. A. Hendry, founder of an ongoing Fort Myers dynasty. Between 1870 and 1880, stockmen sold 165,000 head of cattle at Punta Rassa for more than $2 million. Into the 1900s, the cow hunters drove their herds through the streets of downtown Fort Myers, past the homes of investors, bankers, and other wealthy settlers, including Thomas Edison.

Reconstruction brought more settlers to Florida's west coast. One notable rebel refugee, Judah P. Benjamin—who had served as the Confederacy's secretary of state—ducked indictment as a war criminal by hiding out in Florida. His weeklong asylum at the old Gamble plantation near Bradenton ensured the landmark's preservation by the United Daughters of the Confederacy.

The first postwar visitors to Fort Myers were the vultures that picked the fort clean of coveted building materials. Then came men who remembered the old fort in its heyday and hoped to settle with their families in this land of plenty. The first settler, Captain Manuel A. Gonzalez, had run a provisions boat from Tampa during the Seminole War. He and his family moved from Key West with another family named Vivas. Other war officers and refugees settled in and around the ruins of the old fort, planting gardens, opening stores, and living a blissful existence unknown elsewhere in the devastated South.

Captain James Evans returned to Fort Myers from Virginia to find his land comfortably occupied. After struggling in the courts to keep the land out of government hands, he split it with the squatters in exchange for a share of his legal fees. In 1872, the first school in Fort Myers was built. County government was centered 270 miles away, in Key West.

Some historians credit the cow hunters with contributing the name "Cracker" to early Florida settlers, which they say derives from the cracking of the long whips the cowmen used to drive their herds. Others say it originated with the Georgia settlers who cracked corn for their hush puppies, corn pone, and fritters. Georgians did, in fact, drift down to southwest Florida, most notably the Knight clan, which founded a settlement

STOCK LEFT ON FLORIDA SHORES GAVE HOOF TO LUCRATIVE CATTLE-DRIVING ENTERPRISES IN THE MID- TO LATE 19TH CENTURY

at Horse and Chaise, named by seamen to describe a landmark clump of trees. (The name was changed to "Venice" in 1888 by developer Frank Higel, who was reminded of the Italian city by the area's many bayous and creeks.)

The Homestead Act, passed in 1862, entitled each settler in Florida to 160 acres of land, provided the individual built a home and tended the land for five years. As had been intended, the act brought a flood of intrepid settlers into the area from all over the eastern seaboard and Deep South. Traveling by foot or boat, they built rough palmetto huts, burned cow chips to ward off mosquitoes that carried yellow fever, ate raccoon purloo and turtle steaks, and stubbornly endured the heat, hurricanes, and freezes that stymied a number of enterprises: sugar refining, fish-oil production, and pineapple and citrus farming among them.

Florida's cow hunters eventually proved detrimental to the agriculturally based ventures associated with the Crackers of the Sarasota Bay region. They allied themselves with greedy land speculators who, by 1883, underhandedly nullified the beneficial effects of the Homestead Act. These speculators had discovered a loophole in Florida's land development legislation, namely the Swamp Land Act, which allowed them to purchase flooded land at rock-bottom prices while overriding homestead claims. They succeeded in declaring arable property swampland and ultimately bought up a good 90 percent of present-day Manatee County, much of which had been worked for years by hardy pioneers. Together the speculators and the cattlemen fought farmers' protests against "free ranging," the practice of letting herds roam and feed without restriction. A Sara Sota Vigilance Committee formed in opposition, and by the time the fighting ended, two men lay dead.

As thatch homes gave way to wooden farmhouses—the tin-roofed vernacular style today termed Cracker—Gulf Coast settlements entered a new era, an era that made "riffraff" out of Crackers, rich men out of schemers, and exclusive getaways out of crude frontier towns.

AT THE DROP OF A NAME When your first guests are Juan Ponce de León and Hernando de Soto, whom do you invite next? After such an impressive pair, it wouldn't do to host just anybody. So began west coast Florida's tradition of larger-than-life visitors with impressive names and pedigrees, all of whom, just as impressively, influenced the region's development. Thomas Edison, Henry Ford, Harvey Firestone, John and Charles Ringling, Charles Lindbergh, Teddy Roosevelt, Henry du Pont, Andrew Mellon, Rose Cleveland, and Shirley Temple were among the wide array of early southwest Florida winterers. Their fame and following quickly elevated the status of the lower Gulf Coast from crude and backward to avant-garde and exclusive, attracting the cutting-edge elite. They set national trends by declaring new hot spots—fresh, wild, unspoiled places about which no one else knew, especially the paparazzi. They balanced the very wild coast with a very civilized clientele. The area's natural endowments of fish, fowl, and game attracted adventurers, fishermen, and hunters with the means to make the long, slow journey.

The first and most influential name in any Gulf Coast retrospective is Thomas A. Edison. Disappointed by the cold winters of St. Augustine, the ailing inventor embarked on a scouting cruise along the Gulf Coast in 1885, the same year Fort Myers was incorporated. As Edison sailed along the Caloosahatchee River, he sighted a stand of bamboo trees. Then and there he decided to move to Fort Myers. And he wanted that property!

The bamboo worked well as filament in Edison's light bulb experiments, and the climate bolstered his failing health, helping to add another forty-six years to his life. On the banks of the Caloosahatchee, the inventor fashioned his ideal winter home, Seminole Lodge, complete with laboratory and tropical gardens. Holder of more than one thousand patents, the crafty genius experimented with rare plants in his quest to produce inexpensive rubber for his friend, tire mogul Harvey Firestone. So enamored with Fort Myers was Edison that he persuaded Firestone to spend his winters there. He also set up fellow visionary Henry Ford on an estate next to his. A self-styled botanist, Edison planted the frequently photographed row of royal palms lining the street that eventually ran past his home, McGregor Boulevard, thereby earning the town its nickname: City of Palms.

Meanwhile, the Florida Mortgage and Investment Company—connected with such notables as the archbishop of Canterbury and estate owner Sir John Gillespie—lured a colony of politically disgruntled Scotsmen to Sara Sota, a paradise of genteel estates, bountiful orange groves, and cheap land. Or so the brochures promised. But instead of the Garden of Eden and ready-made manor houses about which they had read, the newcomers found shortages of food and building materials. Only through the kindness of the Whitakers and other pioneers did they survive their first month. Then the Gulf Coast's unpredictable winter weather dealt another cold blow, causing most of the colonists to return to their homeland. Those who stayed, however, brought life to the struggling village and sparked it with a determined spirit.

Most influential among the Scottish ranks was John Hamilton Gillespie, son of Sir John. He built the city's first hotel, the De Soto, and introduced the game of golf to Florida. Gillespie initially transplanted the sport from his homeland by building a two-hole links down Main Street, near his hotel; he later built the area's first real course and clubhouse nearby. When the town of Sarasota was incorporated on October 14, 1902, Gillespie became its first mayor.

It was an American woman, however, who firmly and definitively upgraded Sarasota's image. At the turn of the twentieth century, the name Mrs. (Bertha Honoré) Potter Palmer stood for social elitism. In her hometown, Chicago, her famed Palmer House was at the top of the nation's "it list," and in London and Paris, she kept homes and hobnobbed with royalty. When the widowed socialite decided to visit Sarasota in 1910, hearts palpitated: She could make or break the new town. Enchanted by the area's beauty and the town's quaintness, Mrs. Palmer immediately bought thirteen acres that eventually grew to 140 thousand. She built her home, The Oaks, and a cattle ranch in a community south of Sarasota called Osprey and from there proceeded to spread the word.

Mrs. Palmer's much-publicized love affair with the Gulf Coast drew the attention of John and Charles Ringling, the youngest of the illustrious circus family's seven sons. The two brothers, in a contest of one-upmanship, began buying property around town. They became active in civic affairs, built bridges to Sarasota's islands, and stoked the economy by making the town the winter home for the Ringling Circus. John Ringling especially, and his wife, Mable, brought to Sarasota a new worldliness born of their extensive travels and love of European art.

The fate of the Charlotte Harbor coast lay mostly in the hands of one powerful man, Henry B. Plant. The west coast's counterpart to Henry Flagler—builder of the east coast's railroad and great hotels—Plant brought the railway to Tampa, where he built a fabulous resort of his own, always in competition with Flagler. At the same time, another railway company extended its tracks to an unknown, unsettled spot in the wilderness of Charlotte Harbor's shores and erected the Hotel Charlotte Harbor. It reigned briefly as the latest posh outpost for wealthy sportsmen and adventurers, counting Andrew Mellon and W. K. Vanderbilt among its patrons. But in 1897, after Plant had acquired the railway to Punta Gorda, he decided that the town's deepwater port and resort posed too much competition for his Tampa enterprises. So he choked the life out of a thriving commercial and resort town by severing the rails to Punta Gorda's Long Dock.

Deepwater ports, railroads, and fabulous hotels went hand in hand in those days: Developers had to provide transportation before they could attract visitors. And at the end of the line, the visitors needed a place to stay. In Boca Grande, where a railroad had been built in 1906, the deep waters of Boca Grande Pass attracted Rockefellers, du Ponts, J. P. Morgan, and other industrialists who used the port for shipping phosphate from central Florida. To accommodate them, the graciously refined Gasparilla Inn opened in 1913.

Another man who was to influence the discovery and development of the Gulf Coast came to town in 1911. John M. Roach, Chicago streetcar magnate and owner of Useppa Island, introduced Barron Collier to the area. Collier eventually bought Useppa from his friend and there established the Useppa Inn and the Izaak Walton Club. Both attracted, according to local lore, such tarpon-fishing enthusiasts as Shirley Temple, Gloria Swanson, Mae West, Herbert Hoover, Zane Grey, and Mary Roberts Rinehart; the latter author then bought nearby Cabbage Key for her son and his bride.

Collier went on to infuse life into the southwest coast by underwriting the completion of the Tamiami Trail, stalled on its route from Tampa to Miami. He acquired land throughout the county that today bears his name after earlier attempts by Louisville publisher Walter Haldeman had failed to put Naples on the map.

Along the lower Gulf Coast of Florida, Collier bought more than a million acres, much of it under the infamous Swamp Act. Although he dreamed of development on the scale of Flagler and Plant, anti-corporation outcry, hurricanes, the Depression, and war staunched his success. His sons inherited his kingdom, which they ruled with a heart for the unique environment their father so loved. Collier's influence increased awareness of the Gulf Coast as a refuge for crowd-weary stars and illuminati. Its islands are still popular with the rich and famous who seek anonymity.

But what about the ordinary people—Native Americans, fishermen, cattlemen, Crackers, pioneers, and common folk—who loved this land long before it became fashionable to do so? For the most part they lived side by side with this new brand of resident, called the winterer or snowbird. (In Boca Grande they were termed "beachfronters" for their unusual-at-the-time idiosyncrasy of building dangerously close to the shore.) The locals became their fishing guides, cooks, and innkeepers. In some cases, their heads were turned by brushes with great wealth. In other instances, heightened standards put an end to cruder lifestyles and trades. For example, the cow hunter's boisterousness and preference for free-running stock hastened his extinction.

Sometimes the common folk protested big-bucks development and were classified as riffraff. The "Cracker" label today, despite the culture's enriching influence on architecture and cuisine, is considered an insult by some native Floridians. However, the epithet is gaining popularity as a source of pride in the past.

BOOMS, BURSTS & OTHER EXPLOSIONS The Gulf Coast's resort reputation came of age at the turn of the twentieth century. Sarasota's De Soto, the Hotel Charlotte Harbor, Boca Grande's Gasparilla Inn, the Useppa Inn, Fort Myers's Royal Palm Hotel, the Naples Hotel, and the Marco Inn pioneered in the hotel field, hosting visitors in styles ranging from bare bones to bend-over-backward. They sparked an era touched with Gatsby-type glamour, giddiness, and graciousness.

The Gulf Coast's halcyon days peaked in the early 1920s as the state entered a decade known as the Great Florida Land Boom. Growth came quickly to the young communities of Bradenton, Sarasota, Punta Gorda, Fort Myers, and Naples. The good people of the Gulf Coast grew dizzy with the whirl of growth and success.

According to the 1910 census, Sarasota's population was 840; before the 1920s drew to a close, almost 8,400 people called it home. In the meantime, the city shaped itself with sidewalks, streets, schools, a newspaper, a pier, an airfield, and the establishment of its own county, having split from Bradenton's Manatee County. A bridge to Siesta Key added a whole new element to the town's personality by plugging it into the gulf and attracting a seaside resort trade.

World War I briefly interfered. Prohibition brought to the coast yet another roguish character: the rumrunner. Homes and hotels popped up like toadstools after a summer rain shower. Increased lodging options opened the Gulf Coast to a wider range of vacationers. The average traveler could now afford Florida's Gulf Coast, no longer just a socialites' haven. A new class of winterer arrived in force, known as tin-can tourists for the trailers and campers they pulled behind their vehicles. Tourist camps sprang up overnight, and southwest Florida became an Everyman's paradise. Real estate profits added to the lure of tourism, and many visitors decided to remain permanently.

The 1920s created Charlotte County along the Charlotte Harbor coast. A bridge was built across the Peace River, connecting the pioneer towns of Charlotte Harbor and Punta Gorda, spurring growth, and spawning subdivisions by the score.

Fort Myers became the seat of a new county named for Confederate General Robert E. Lee. Between 1920 and 1930, the population grew from 3,600 to 9,000, boosted by the completion of the Tamiami Trail in 1928. Fort Myers evolved from a raucous cattle town into a modern city with electricity (thanks to Edison), telephone lines, and a railroad. The Royal Palm Hotel treated guests to a regal departure from the cow trails that ran adjacent to the property. A country club put Fort Myers on the golfing map, and a bridge to Estero Island's beautiful beaches (today Fort Myers Beach) further boosted tourism. Real adventurers took the ferry to Sanibel Island, to be accommodated at Casa Ybel or the Palm Hotel.

South of Fort Myers, the farming community of Survey was renamed Bonita Springs. In 1923, Naples—previously a well-kept secret among buyers from such faraway places as Kentucky and Ohio and distinguished vacationers from the upper echelons—became a city just in time to feel the effects of the tourism boom. The same year, Collier County seceded from Lee County. Everglades City became the first county seat;

EARLY GUESTS TO SANIBEL'S HISTORIC ISLAND INN ARRIVED BY WAGON, AS PORTRAYED IN THIS CIRCA-1910 PHOTO

later, growing, thriving Naples took the honors. In 1927, the Naples Pier, which had served as a landing point for visitors and cargo since 1887, was replaced in importance by a railroad depot.

Gulf Coast skies had never been sunnier: Visitors spent lots of money. Residents prospered. Real estate prices soared. It seemed too good to be true. And indeed it was.

A 1926 hurricane hit Fort Myers, worsening a condition of already deepening debt. In Sarasota, John Ringling suffered severe financial losses from which he never recovered. On the southernmost coast, however, the national economy had little impact on the surge of interest sparked by the opening of the Tamiami Trail.

The Depression blunted the momentum with which the Gulf Coast had developed during the 1920s, but in many ways it affected the region less drastically than it did other parts of the country. Since it most tragically affected the middle class, wealthy Gulf Coast residents were largely spared. Works Progress Administration (WPA) recovery projects built Fort Myers its waterfront park, its yacht basin, and the city's first hospital. The WPA also funded the building of Bayfront Park, a municipal auditorium, and the Lido Beach Casino in the Bradenton–Sarasota area. Despite serious financial problems, Ringling kept his promises to build bridges and an art museum.

By the beginning of World War II, southwest Florida had firmly joined the twentieth century, with modern conveniences that made it popular among retirees. New golf courses accommodated active seniors, who often participated in the civic affairs of their adopted communities more vigorously than they had in those of their hometowns. Professional golf tournaments were introduced, first in Naples and then along the coast, making the area golf's winter home. Later, spring baseball camps brought another spectator sport to this land of year-round recreation.

Warmth-seekers turned their attention to the Gulf Coast's islands and beachfronts. Golfing communities and waterfront resorts swallowed up local farming and fishing industries. High-rise condominiums replaced Cracker houses, posh resorts toppled tourist fishing camps, and the Gulf Coast continued to grow—albeit not quite as loudly or erratically as in pre-Depression times.

Some areas learned to control their growth. Sanibel Island served as a model, taking grip of its fate after a causeway connected it to the mainland in 1963. It incorporated and introduced measures to protect wilderness areas and limit takeover by developers. The southward expansion of Interstate 75 during the 1970s and 1980s changed the Gulf Coast from a series of towns connected by two-lane roads to communities keeping pace with the world. Communication and transportation systems improved. Commercial development spread to the freeway corridor, leaving downtown areas to fade in bygone glory. Light industry and winter-weary entrepreneurs relocated. Post-secondary schools worked to prepare local youth for the changing marketplace, while the construction and tourism industries continued to prosper.

The Gulf Coast remained seemingly untouched by the fluctuations of the American economy. Urban blight was a distant reality. Northerners fled to the Gulf Coast to escape overcrowding, smog, and crime. In previous decades, this had caused unnatural development in some of the metropolitan areas. The delicate balance of infrastructure, human services, nature, heritage preservation, and the arts spun out of kilter. The coast lived very much in the present, deaf to the demands of residents, both human and otherwise.

Finally, though, the new trends of eco-tourism and social responsibility amplified the voices of the few who had screamed over the decades for preservation of the environment against tourism and cultural sterility. While Sarasota and Naples served as cultural prototypes, Sanibel Island and Charlotte County provided environmental models. The 1990s brought an awareness of the frailty of the west coast's islands, wetlands, and shorelines. At the same time, interest in the area's history grew, and movements were launched to preserve architectural treasures that so far had been spared by the bulldozer. Eventually, the dipping economic trends of the early 1990s and mid-2000s affected the Gulf Coast. Construction slowed its racing pace, and unemployment figures jumped as Northerners continued to arrive, looking for jobs in this legendary land of treasure and youth.

All of these factors have contributed to the current perspective on the Gulf Coast. Economic fluctuations give city planners occasion to pause and rethink. Future growth is being mapped out with more care than ever before. Dying downtown neighborhoods and abandoned Cracker homes are being revitalized, now recognized as important parts of the area's heritage. Government is drawing into its blueprints the need for environmental preservation, cultural enrichment, and historic renovation. A new blight is having a profound effect on the pristine environment of Sanibel Island, which once served as an environmental model. Nutrient runoff from sugar farming around Lake Okeechobee, in the center of the state, reaches the region's estuaries via the Caloosahatchee River when heavy rainfall occurs, as it did in the wake of 2004's hurricanes and again in more recent years. The resultant algae kills sea grasses, thereby diminishing fish and bird populations in the sanctuary island and its environs. Grassroots movements struggle to remedy the situation and make plodding headway. They have inspired the state to seek methods to rechannel and filter the water before it's too late, hoping that the grain of sand and the mangrove pod from which this land was wrought will once again play a role in its future.

COASTAL CULTURE One of southwest Florida's great contradictions is that it lies more to the north than to the south on the cultural map. North of it or inland, you will find Deep South cookery, clog dancing, bluegrass music, and traditional Southern arts. In southwest Florida, however, Midwestern and Northeastern US influences sway

KINGDOM OF GASPARILLA

Of all the rum-chugging and throat-slashing visitors to have set foot upon Southwest Florida's tolerant shores, José Gaspar (known by the more properly pirate-sounding name "Gasparilla") is the one remembered most fondly. Gaspar set up headquarters, it is said, on Gasparilla Island, where Boca Grande now sits. In his time it was called High Town, according to legend. He built a palmetto palace there and furnished it with the finest booty. Low Town he placed on a separate island so as to distance himself from the crude lifestyles of his rowdy shipmates. Gasparilla's fort stood on Cayo Costa.

Legends also tell that Gasparilla got his start as a pirate after some nasty business with the wife of a crown prince. He gave up his cushy position as Admiral of the Spanish Navy for the hardships of life at sea and in the jungles of late eighteenth-century Florida.

His address might have changed, but his love of beautiful women did not. He kidnapped the fairest and wealthiest of them from captured ships and whisked them off to another Gulf Coast island named for its inhabitants—Captiva—until ransom money arrived. Gasparilla took the most beautiful of his captives to High Town to woo them with fine wines, jewels, and Spanish poetry. One object of his affection, a Mexican princess named Joséfa, would have nothing to do with such a barbarian. Finally, driven to madness by her insults, Gasparilla beheaded his beloved. He carried her body to another key in his island fiefdom, where he buried her with remorse and sand. He named the island "Joséfa," which, through the years and the twistings of rum-swollen tongues, has been perverted to "Useppa." And so the exclusive island is called today.

Nearby Sanibel Island, according to one legend, got its name from the abandoned lover of Gaspar's gunner. However, variations abound and improve with each telling. The legend began with the ramblings of old "Panther Key John" Gomez and was perpetuated by railroad press agents and optimistic treasure hunters.

Serious historians doubt the existence of a man named Gasparilla but concede that one of the many Gulf Coast pirates might have borrowed the island's name. Others hold tenaciously to the legend, plying coastal sands with shovels and dredges in search of his ill-gotten booty.

heavily. The only truly indigenous art forms have their origins in the Seminole traditions of weaving, dancing, basket-making, and festivals. Other cultures have arrived through the centuries to create one of the nation's richest melting pots. African Americans, East Indians, Latinos, Haitians, and Germans have most indelibly enriched the coastal makeup.

The arts have been heavily influenced through the years by the region's winter population. Many Northern-based artists have relocated here, lured by the sea and tropical muses. Others bring with them their appetite for culture, sparking the finest in visual, performing, and culinary arts.

SOUTHWEST FLORIDA ARCHITECTURE Years of simmering together Seminole, Cracker, "Yankee," and Caribbean traditions have yielded a unique southwest Florida style, particularly in architecture and cuisine. If one overall style could be said to represent local architecture, it would have to be Mediterranean—specifically, Italian and Spanish-mission forms.

Lumped together under the label "Mediterranean Revival," these southern European influences are found primarily in public and commercial buildings constructed during the boom years of the Roaring Twenties. They're revealed in stucco finish, mission arches, red barrel-tile roofing, bell towers, and rounded step facades. Re-revived Mediterranean Postmodern—updated Mediterranean Revival blended with elements of tropical styles adopted from the Cracker era—serves as a popular style for upscale housing developments and commercial enterprises.

Cracker vernacular runs a close architectural second. Pure Cracker style began as folk housing. From the single-pen home—a wood-frame, one-room house featuring a shady veranda, a high tin roof, an elevated floor, and wood siding—grew more sophisticated interpretations of the style. With Gothic touches, Victorian embellishments, Palladian accents, and New England influences, the humble Cracker house evolved into a trendy, modern-day version termed Old Florida. Boxy and built on stilts, its most distinctive characteristics include a tin roof and wide wraparound porch.

The latest influence on the Cracker house comes from the Caribbean and the Bahamas via the Keys. Since indigenous West Indian styles are greatly similar to Cracker, especially in their suitability to tropical weather, the convergence was inevitable. The result: sherbet colors and hand-carved fretwork—used as much for ventilation as for decoration—that add charm and whimsy to the basic unit.

Like the Cracker home, the Seminole chikee, or chickee (pronounced chi-KEY), hut conformed to the tropical climate with its high-peaked roof, wide overhangs, and open sides. Today, the thatched roofing that is the chikee's most distinctive feature has become an art form. Still a popular style of housing for the Seminole and Miccosukee of the Everglades, the chikee has evolved as a trademark of the Gulf Coast watering-hole tradition known as chikee, or tiki, bars.

With the mid-1920s influx of tin-can tourists, the mobile home replaced the Cracker house on the low end of the architectural totem pole. Mobile homes—that would "look a lot better as beer cans," according to an old Jimmy Buffett tune—still provide low-cost housing, mostly to part-time winter residents. The brutal winds of Hurricane Charley

A NEW MUSEUM GIVES NEW LIFE TO THE OLD NAPLES DEPOT, WHERE CELEBRITIES DISEMBARKED DURING THE ROARING TWENTIES

THE FLORIDA MARITIME MUSEUM IS FREE TO THE PUBLIC

in 2004 went a long way toward eliminating many of the structures. But despite their unsuitability, many mobile homes still remain.

The concrete-block ranch, a popular residential style of the 1970s, was built to withstand hurricanes. The flood regulations of the 1980s raised these up on pilings; lattice and fretwork added interest. Art deco returned later in the decade, as Miami Beach's Art Deco District attracted attention.

Today's Gulf Coast towns are seasoned with period styles and spiced with contemporary looks that strive for compatibility with nature. Screened porches (often called lanais), windowed "Florida rooms," and lots of sliding glass doors let the outside in, enabling residents to take full advantage of the unique, enviable climate and environment.

COASTAL CUISINE As for culinary *richesse*, southwest Florida has wowed hungry visitors since the first Europeans came ashore and discovered nature's abundantly stocked pantry. The seas were teeming with Neptune's bounty, and wild animals filled the forests.

Today, naturalized tropical fruits introduced into the environment add exotic flavor: mangoes, bananas, coconuts, pineapples, avocados, sapodillas, carambolas (star fruit), and lychees. Citrus fruit, particularly the orange, is of course the region's most visible and profitable crop. Key lime trees grow mostly in backyards. Practically year-round producers, they are a standard part of any good Florida cook's landscaping scheme. Here on the Gulf Coast, as in the Florida Keys, where the tree got its name and fame, Key lime pie is a culinary paradigm, and each restaurant claims to make the best. In the finest restaurants with the most extravagant dessert menus, Key lime pie inevitably outsells the rest. The classic recipe, created by Florida cooks before refrigeration, uses canned sweetened and condensed milk and is elegant in its simplicity. The most important factor is the freshness of the limes—sometimes a problem for restaurants because the fruit does not lend itself to commercial farming. One sure sign of an inauthentic version is the color green. Key limes turn yellow-green when ripe and, unless the cook adds food coloring, should impart a light, almost buttery hue to the pie.

Historically, crop farming has provided coastal residents with economic sustenance. Weather conditions bless farmers with two growing seasons for most ground crops. As land becomes too valuable to farm, agriculture has been pushed inland. Pine Island, known for its tropical fruits, is the region's final bastion of the agricultural tradition.

Seafood is most commonly associated with Gulf Coast cuisine, including some delicacies unique to Florida. Our prize catch, stone crabs (Florida author Marjorie Kinnan Rawlings once described the taste as being "almost as rare as nightingales' tongues"), were discovered as a food source in the Everglades. They are in season from October 15 through May 15, and restaurants serve them hot with drawn butter or more commonly cold with tangy mustard sauce. Their aptly named shells are usually pre-cracked to facilitate diners' enjoyment.

The highly sustainable gulf shrimp is an emblem of local cuisine. Look for labels telling you it's "wild shrimp," otherwise you might be buying Asian imports treated with antibiotics and other unregulated additives. Its poorer cousin, the rock shrimp, gets less publicity because of its hard-to-peel shell. More economical and with a flavor and texture akin to lobster, the rock shrimp is certainly worth tasting. Restaurants change their menus—or at least their daily specials—according to what's in season. Grouper, the most versatile food fish in the area, traditionally has been available year-round, but overfishing is limiting its availability. A large and meaty fish, its taste is so mild that you hardly know it's fish. Winter months bring red and yellowtail snapper—my favorite—to diners' plates. Warmer weather means pompano, cobia, shark, and dolphinfish (also known as mahi mahi). Tuna and flounder are caught year-round, but sporadically. Some restaurants serve less well-known species, such as triggerfish and catfish, to offset spiraling costs caused by dwindling supplies of the more popular varieties. Fish farming also addresses these shortages. Catfish and a Brazilian fish called tilapia (which tastes similar to snapper) are cultivated most commonly. Fresh fish from around the world supplement local bounty.

A SEMINOLE TRADEMARK, CHIKEE HUTS HAVE DOTTED THE EVERGLADES LANDSCAPE SINCE THE SEMINOLE WARS FORCED THE NATIVE AMERICANS INTO THE HOSTILE SWAMPLAND

The best Gulf Coast restaurants buy their seafood directly from the docks of local commercial fishermen to ensure the utmost freshness. The traditional style of cooking seafood in Florida is deep-frying. Although constituting a mortal sin in this age of gourmet standards and health awareness, it is a true art when properly executed. There's a vast difference between what you find in the frozen

OLD FISH HOUSES, LIKE THIS ONE IN CORTEZ, SURVIVE FROM THE 1930S, WHEN FISHERMEN'S FAMILIES LIVED IN AND WORKED OUT OF THE STILTED STRUCTURES

food department at the supermarket and what comes hand-breaded, crunchy, and flavor-sealed on your plate at the local fish house.

New Florida style, at the other extreme, has evolved from California, new American, New World, global, and eclectic styles of cuisine. This type also depends on freshness— of all its ingredients. For this reason it uses local produce prepared in global culinary styles. Regional cookery—sometimes termed Floribbean cuisine—prefers tropical foods and ingredients, inspired by the cuisines of New Orleans, Mexico, Cuba, Puerto Rico, Haiti, the Bahamas, Jamaica, and South America. Pacific Rim influences also are prominent. Southern traditions have experienced a recent resurgence in popularity in these parts. The outcome of all this blending, at its tamest, merely twists the familiar; at its most adventurous, it can treat your taste buds to a virtual bungee jump.

Between the two extremes of old and new Florida styles, Continental cuisine survives in both classic and reinvented forms. Along with restaurants that serve the finest in French and Italian haute cuisine, you will find others that represent the Gulf Coast's melting pot, with authentic renditions or interpretations of a wide variety of cuisines: Native American, Thai, East Indian, Iranian, German, Irish, Greek, Cuban, Jamaican, Amish, Jewish, Mexican, Puerto Rican, and Peruvian.

In its cuisine and cultural makeup as well as its history, the map of Gulf Coast Florida resembles a patchwork quilt. It blankets its people in warmth, checkers its past with colorful and contrasting patterns, and layers its character with intriguing, international textures.

TRANSPORTATION

The Gulf of Mexico and its mighty rivers and Intracoastal Waterway compose the region's oldest and lowest-maintenance transportation system. From the days when the Calusa paddled the streams and estuaries in dugout canoes, through the romantic steamboat era, and until 1927, when the railroad to Naples was completed, boat travel was the most popular means of getting around. Early homes lined the waterways, and historic houses face the water rather than the roads that accommodate modern-day traffic. Even today, the Caloosahatchee River, which empties into the sea along the Island Coast and connects to the east coast via canals and Lake Okeechobee, constitutes part of a major intercoastal water route.

The railroad first came to Charlotte County's deepwater port in 1886 and created the town of Punta Gorda—much to the chagrin of Fort Myers's leaders, who had tried for years to persuade company officials to extend their Florida Southern Railroad to the Caloosahatchee River. Instead, an unpopulated location was selected and a fabulous hotel built there, according to the custom of Florida's great railroad builders of the day. Besides transporting wealthy winterers to the nation's southernmost railroad stop, the trains hauled fresh fish, cattle, and produce.

ONCE AN INDIAN TRADING POST, SMALLWOOD STORE TODAY SERVES AS A MUSEUM IN THE SECLUDED EVERGLADES OUTPOST OF CHOKOLOSKEE ISLAND

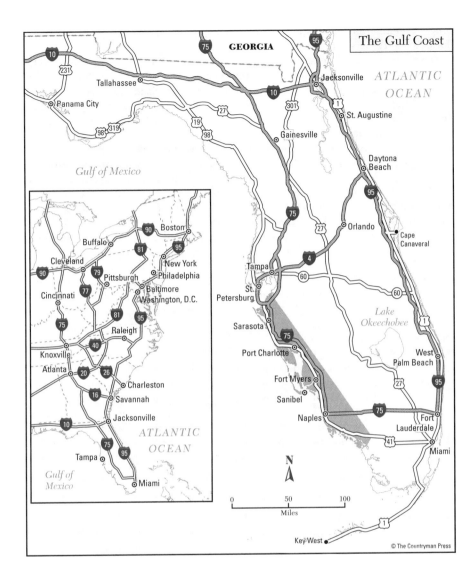

A train nicknamed "Slow and Wobbly" ran between Bradenton and Sarasota from 1892 to 1894. The Seaboard Railroad built a more reliable version to Bradenton in 1902. In 1911 it was extended beyond Venice under the influence of Chicago socialite and major landholder Bertha Palmer. When Palmer named the railway terminus Venice, infuriated residents of the original Venice changed their town's name to "Nokomis." Then the Charlotte Harbor and Northern Railway laid track in 1906 to ship phosphate from inland mines to the deep waters of Boca Grande Pass, off Gasparilla Island. Another refined resort came with it.

Fort Myers finally got its first railroad station in 1904. In 1922, the trestles reached Bonita Springs and were later extended to Naples via the Orange Blossom Special in 1927. Famous passengers such as movie stars Hedy Lamarr, Greta Garbo, and Gary

Cooper rode the rails to vacation at the posh Naples Beach Hotel & Golf Club, one of Florida's first resorts to boast golf greens on the property.

The concept of the Tamiami Trail made headway when, in 1923, a group called the Trail Blazers traveled the proposed route that would connect Tampa and Miami. Mules, oxen, and tractors were used to complete that first motorized crossing of the Everglades. Builders lived at the work site, and a whole body of legend grew up around the monumental task. Progress was slowed by dense jungles, forbidding swampland, devastating heat, and mosquitoes so thick that they covered exposed skin like a buzzing body glove. The project was further hampered by war and depletion of funds.

A special new dredge had to be invented to build the section across the Everglades, and before the trail was paved, it had a sand surface. Summer rains caused such heavy flooding that old-timers recall getting out of their cars to catch fish in the road while their parents worked to get vehicles unstuck. Even after the rains subsided, jarring, muck-crusted ruts made the trip less than comfortable.

As the trail's west coast leg inched toward its destination, it changed the communities it penetrated. Thirteen years in the building, the Tamiami Trail was met with euphoria when it was completed in 1928, opening communities to land travel, trade, and tourism. Today, the Trail—also known as US 41—strings together the region's oldest towns and cities, and newer communities have grown up around it.

With the extension of parallel I-75, the Tamiami Trail has lost its role as the sole intercoastal lifeline. Nonetheless, it remains the backbone of the lower west coast. Probing both metropolitan interiors and rural vistas, it provides glimpses of a cross-section of life—as it was and as it is—in southwest Florida.

US 41 runs through the middle of the area covered in this book. At the Gulf Coast's northern and southern extremes, the highway edges close to the shoreline. In midsections, it reaches inland to communities built along harbors and rivers.

I-75 draws the eastern boundary for most of this guide's coverage. The freeway glimpses, at top speed, Gulf Coast life as it zips through the twenty-first century. Although convenient and free of traffic lights, it misses the character that the more leisurely pace of the Tamiami Trail reveals. It does, however, extend the boundaries of US 41's family of communities to create new ones.

BRADENTON &
MID-COAST

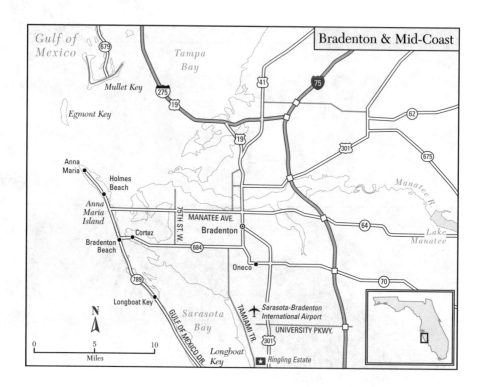

BRADENTON & MID-COAST

River City, Island Beaches

Bradenton draws much of its historical identity from the reputed landing of Hernando de Soto on local shores. Old Hernando—scoundrel and sadist though he turned out to be—gives the town a reason to celebrate its heritage. Each year, the town reenacts the momentous arrival of the Indian-slaying conquistador at a national park.

Later in the history of Bradenton and the surrounding mainland communities, two pioneering influences dictated a low-key attitude and light development. The first, the wealthy plantation owners of the 1840s, ranked Manatee County as the largest area in the state for sugar and molasses production. Sugar's aristocratic families set the social standards of the town until the Civil War turned the sweetly lucrative industry sour. The second, nineteenth-century land speculators, exploited Florida's Swamp Act, which had a counterproductive, stunting effect on the area's development. By having homestead properties fraudulently declared wetlands, they prevented agricultural expansion and delayed its by-product, the building of railroads.

Most of **Bradenton's** modern growth has occurred since 1970, when tourism and shipping into deepwater Port Manatee became major income sources. Today, downtown waterfront restoration projects and an artists' colony have helped return Bradenton to its earlier status as a vital city textured with an interesting past.

Across the Manatee River, preservation of the Gamble Plantation and original village structures—along with the development of sleepy, agriculturally driven **Palmetto**—extends Bradenton-area visitors' options to include more historic attractions and riverfront activity.

The village of **Cortez** lies southwest of Bradenton and several eras in the past. Fishing made this peninsular community, and fishing remains its livelihood. Along its southern waterfront, a working fishing operation and its toilers reside in a time-stilled setting.

Fishing, resorts, and heterogeneous neighborhoods mark the three incorporated towns of **Anna Maria Island: Anna Maria, Holmes Beach,** and **Bradenton Beach.** The first Anna Maria Island settlers of record, George Emerson Bean and his family, arrived around 1890. Bean developed the island in the early 1900s for tourists, who came by boat to the Anna Maria city pier. In 1921, the first bridge to the island was built from Cortez.

Longboat Key, to the south of Anna Maria Island, was mentioned often on the maps and journals of early Spanish explorers. It supposedly got its name from the longboats that Hernando de Soto's scouting party used to come ashore. Aside from one tucked-away village with a salty, local flavor, Longboat Key is known for its prim-and-properness. A series of historic markers relate Longboat Key's history as a sixteenth-century destination for Timucua canoes and Spanish galleons, a World War II bombing target, and a major shipping port destroyed by the hurricane of 1921.

GETTING HERE Arrivals fly into **Sarasota–Bradenton International Airport (SRQ)** (941-359-2770; www.srq-airport.com; 6000 Airport Circle, Sarasota 34243). Airlines include Air Canada, Alitalia, Delta, JetBlue, United, and WestJet. If traveling by bus,

OLD FISHING TRADITIONS ENDURE IN THE VILLAGE OF CORTEZ

the Greyhound Lines (941-342-1720; www.greyhound.com), the closest depot is located at 5951 Porter Way in Sarasota, By car, take Interstate 75 or US 41 from the north and FL 70 from Florida's East Coast. See pages 12–13 for rental car phone numbers and web sites. Alamo, Avis, Budget, Dollar, National, and Thrifty have rental facilities at SRQ.

GETTING AROUND Taxi companies that provide transportation to and from the Bradenton-Sarasota airport include **Diplomat Taxi** (941-365-8294 or 877-859-8933; www .diplomattaxi.com) and **Longboat Limousine** (941-383-1235 or 800-525-4661; www .longboatlimousine.com).

US 41 and US 301 are major trunk roads. Principal through-streets for east–west traffic in this area are generally those with exits off I-75, north to south: US 301 to Palmetto, Manatee Avenue (FL 64) and 53rd Ave. (FL 70). Bradenton's 75th Street West (De Soto Memorial Highway) skims the town's western reaches close to the bay front. From Exit 220, FL 64 travels straight into downtown and out to Anna Maria Island at Holmes Beach. From the south, take exit 217 and follow FL 70 to US 41. Head north on US 41, then turn west on FL 684 (Cortez Road/44th Avenue), which takes you across the south bridge to Bradenton Beach. Both bridges lead to Gulf Drive (FL 789), the island's main road. Longboat Key lies to the south of Anna Maria Island, across a bridge, along Gulf of Mexico Drive.

In the Bradenton area and its islands, **Manatee County Transit (MCAT)** (941-749-7116; www.ridemcat.org) provides bus service and free trolley transportation on Anna Maria Island.

HOSPITALS&CLINICS **Blake Medical Center** (941-792-6611; www.blakemedicalcenter. com), 2020 59th St. W., Bradenton. Emergency room open twenty-four hours. Free Consult-a-Nurse hotline 888-685-1599.

Manatee Memorial Hospital (941-746-5111 or 941-745-7564 for emergencies; www .manateememorial.com), 206 Second St. E., Bradenton. Emergency room open twenty-four hours. Find-a-Doctor service 941-708-8100.

    Bradenton Area Convention & Visitors Bureau (941-729-9177; www.bradenton gulfislands.com), P.O. Box 1000, Bradenton 34206.

    Longboat Key Chamber of Commerce (941-387-9000; www.longboatkeychamber .com), 5390 Gulf of Mexico Dr. #102, Longboat Key 34228.

    Manatee Chamber of Commerce (941-748-3411; www.manateechamber.com), 222 Tenth St. W., Bradenton 34205.

✳ To See

ARCHITECTURE In the Bradenton area, the Greek Revival–style plantation house has left its mark. The best example of this style survives grandly at ✪ Gamble Plantation (see "Historic Sites"). Pioneer styles are preserved at the Manatee Historical Village, which includes a Cracker Gothic farmhouse, a one-room schoolhouse, and an early brick store. In downtown Bradenton you'll find a Mediterranean influence in commercial buildings, such as the South Florida Museum and the newly restored historic building now occupied by the Hampton Inn & Suites. Old Florida–Victorian style survives in the homes of neighborhoods around downtown. Along the riverfront in Palmetto, you will find some examples of fine historic homes, such as the Palmetto Riverside Bed & Breakfast.

    On **Longboat Key**, resorts and mansions are modern and ostentatious. In the village once known as Longbeach, one finds a return to comfortable, older styles and a bit of New England charm.

CINEMA **Regal Oakmont 8** (844-462-7342 ext. 178; www.regalcinemas.com), 4801 Cortez Rd. W., Bradenton.

GARDENS **Palma Sola Botanical Garden,** (941-721-2866; palmasolabp.com), 9800 17th Ave. NW, Bradenton. Small, but worth the stop if you're in the neighborhood of De Soto National Memorial (See "Historic Homes & Sites"). Its garden of fruiting trees is of special interest. Open daily dawn to dusk. Free admission.

HISTORIC HOMES & SITES **Braden Castle Ruins,** Braden Castle Dr. off 27th St. E. and FL 64, Bradenton. At the juncture of the Manatee and Braden Rivers, antebellum memories crumble gracefully in a setting recognized by the National Register of Historic Sites. Just short of spectacular, the plantation house ruins are surrounded by chain-link fences and posted with KEEP OUT, DANGER signs. They hide at the center of a historic retirement community in a riverside park that's not easy to find. A marker tells the story of Dr. Joseph Addison Braden from Virginia and his ill-fated, eponymous plantation. Open daily sunrise to sunset. Free admission.

A SCULPTURE AT BRADENTON PIER PAYS HOMAGE TO THE COUNTY'S NAMESAKE

🐟 **Cortez Village**, Cortez Rd. and 123rd St., Bradenton. Vital remnants of a fishing village from the 1880s include old tin-roofed seafood houses, boat works, and seafood processing plants. Exhibits and painted murals throughout the salty district describe local culture and environmental practices. A maritime museum complex and cultural museum (see "Museums") preserve the heritage of this community—once the largest fishing center on Florida's West Coast. A walking tour map of the village on the National Register of Historic Places points out ninety-two historic structures and sites.

✪ 🐟 ♪ **De Soto National Memorial** (941-792-0458 ext. 105; www.nps.gov/deso), 8300 De Soto Memorial Hwy., Bradenton. Somewhat off the beaten path, this is a place where you can imagine yourself back in the sixteenth century with conquistadors in heavy armor trying to survive among irate Native Americans, mosquitoes, and sweltering heat. Engraved plaques, a re-created Amerindian village and Spanish camp, and the Memorial Trail tell the story of Hernando de Soto's life and adventures here, where supposedly he first breached the shores of the Florida mainland to begin his heroic trek to the Mississippi River. A visitors' center holds artifacts and shells, a twenty-two-minute video presentation, and helmets and Amerindian tools kids can try out. In the winter, rangers and volunteers dress up and play the parts of sixteenth-century inhabitants, demonstrating weaponry and methods of food preparation. Right outside the park's gates, Riverview Pointe Trail takes hikers to historic sites along the De Soto Expedition Trail. Visitors' center open daily 9–5; park open daily sunrise to sunset. Free admission.

Downtown Bradenton, Main St. and Manatee Ave. (FL 64), 12th St. W (a.k.a. Old Main Street), and the city yacht basin form the historic downtown district's nucleus. Because the area is compact, it's easy to walk and experience the old architecture, a fine museum, park benches, sidewalk eateries, pubs, and brick-paved crosswalks. Locals are trying hard to pump new life into a river town that died with the advent of the automobile. The 1.5-mile Riverwalk, completed in October 2012, takes strollers along the Manatee River. Visit the shops on Main Street and have lunch, then stroll around nearby Point Pleasant for a taste of Bradenton's oak-canopied neighborhoods and heritage. Every Saturday, October through May, visit the farmers' market.

♂ **Gamble Plantation Historic State Park** (941-723-4536; www.floridastateparks .org/park/Gamble-Plantation), 3708 Patten Ave., US 301 near I-75, exit 224, Ellenton. Major Robert Gamble, originally from Scotland, learned about sugar planting in Virginia and Tallahassee before he moved to the Manatee River. He eventually cleared 1,500 acres of jungle, using slave labor, and built a Greek Revival–style home. He constructed the mansion's crowning touch—eighteen Greek columns—with a mortar known as tabby, made of crushed and burned seashells. The spacious (by the time's standards) palace served as the area's social hub until hurricane and frost damage and market losses forced the major to sell it in 1856. In 1925, the United Daughters of the Confederacy rescued the mansion from decades of neglect. The site was declared a Confederate shrine for its role in sheltering Judah P. Benjamin, Confederate Secretary of State, when he fled for his life after the Civil War. The United Daughters donated the monument to the state a couple of years later. Visitors can see the inside of the home only by guided tour, which takes less than an hour. The two floors contain period furnishings and housewares, which the park ranger explains in lively, interesting dialogue. You'll learn, for example, how such expressions as "hush puppy," "sleep tight," and "don't throw the baby out with the bath water" came to be, and about the lives of nineteenth-century plantation owners and slaves. Note that the home is not air conditioned, and can get quite warm in the summer. The museum in the visitors' center tells the plantation's story through the eras. A picnic shelter accommodates lunchers. Visitors' center open 9–5; tours depart at 9:30, 10:30, and on

THE STEPHENS HOUSE REPRESENTS PIONEER HOME LIFE AT MANATEE VILLAGE HISTORICAL PARK

the hour from 1 to 4; closed Tuesday and Wednesday. Admission: the mansion tour is $6 adults and $4 children ages six to twelve. Free admission to visitors' center museum.

🔍 ⚓ **Manatee Village Historical Park** (941-749-7165; www.manateevillage.org/historical/ManateeVillage.aspx), 1404 Manatee Ave. E., Bradenton. Several buildings with local historical significance have been restored and moved to a pleasant, oak-shaded park strongly representative of Bradenton's old wooded and winding neighborhoods. The County Courthouse, completed in 1860, is the oldest and also the oldest remaining building constructed as a county courthouse in Florida. Others include a circa-1889 church (the oldest congregation south of Tampa), a Cracker farmhouse, a one-room schoolhouse, a smokehouse, and a brick general store from the early nineteenth century. A museum of artifacts, photographs, and period-furnished rooms occupies the general store. The Cracker-Gothic Stephens House is stocked with preserves, period kitchen items, furniture, and farm implements. Bat Fogarty Boat Works reflects Bradenton's boatbuilding heritage. Kids can climb aboard "Old Cabbage Head," a historic timber-hauling locomotive, and blow off steam on the railroad-themed playground. The staff sometimes wears historically accurate dress. Across the street lies the Manatee Burying Ground, which dates from 1850. All in all, the park is a romantic site, grossly underrated and lightly visited (except when school groups arrive). Open 9–4 weekdays and 9–4 the second and fourth Saturday of each month. Admission: suggested donation $5 adults, $4 seniors, $3 students.

🔍 ⚓ **Palmetto Historical Park** (941-723-4991; www.manateeclerk.com/historical/PalmettoPark.aspx), 515 10th Ave. W., Palmetto. The park's circa-1914 Carnegie Library contains historic museum exhibits. It also includes a circa-1880 post office, a wedding chapel that is a composite of three Palmetto historic churches, a circa-1920 one-room schoolhouse, and the Cypress House Museum, which is devoted to military artifacts. The park conducts tours of the buildings' interiors for free at 10 a.m. on Fridays and at 2 p.m. Tuesday through Friday and the first and third Saturdays of each month. Within the park, the **Manatee County Agricultural Museum & Hall of Fame** (941-721-2034;

AN EXHIBIT AT THE MANATEE COUNTY AGRICULTURAL MUSEUM IN PALMETTO ILLUSTRATES THE IMPORTANCE OF COMMERCIAL FISHING TO THE REGION'S ECONOMIC DEVELOPMENT

www.manateeclerk.com/historical/AgMuseum.aspx) is a staffed facility housed in a barnlike structure; it holds hands-on and other kinds of displays demonstrating the importance of farming to Manatee County past and present. For families, there's also a park with a playground across the street. Open 10 to noon and 1–4 Tuesday through Friday, the first and third Saturday of the month, and Monday by appointment. Free admission.

KIDS' STUFF ✔ **Riverwalk** (941-621-6471; www.realizebradenton.com), from Business 41 to Second St. W., Bradenton. Along this 1.5-mile paved walk overlooking the Manatee River, families can find a Family Fun Zone with playground and interactive fountain, a skate park, a fishing pier, a kayak launch, volleyball courts, and event spaces.

✔ **South Florida Museum, Bishop Planetarium & Parker Manatee Aquarium** (941-746-4131; www.southfloridamuseum.org), 201 10th St. W., Bradenton. This downtown museum has a designated Discovery Place for kids' hands-on enjoyment. In the regular museum, youngsters especially love the prehistoric skeleton casts, live manatees, and the drawers of artifacts in the "visible storage" area. Special first Saturday Family Night programs most months keep the museum open until 8 p.m. with manatee presentations, crafts, special tours, and, at 8:15, a planetarium show. Open January through April, July, 10–5 Monday through Saturday, noon to 5 Sunday; closed Monday during all other months. Admission: $19 adults, $17 seniors, $14 children ages four to twelve, children under age four free with paying adult. Admission for Family Nights after 3 reduced to $9, $8, and $7.

MUSEUMS For art museums, see "Visual Arts Centers & Resources."
❂ **Anna Maria Island Historical Museum** (941-778-0492; www.amihs.org), 402 Pine Ave., Anna Maria. A homey little museum inside a 1920s icehouse, newly renovated in 2015, holds a heartwarming wealth of photos, maps, records, and books; a shell collection; a new Leisure on the Beach lifestyle display; and vintage movies on YouTube. Next door sits the old jail, its humorous graffiti worth a chuckle. The newest adjunct to the museum, circa-1920 Belle Haven Cottage, is filled with period pieces and shares space with a natural garden. It once sat on the Anna Maria pier and took a tumble into the sea in 1926. Open January to March, Monday to Friday 10–4; April to December Monday to Friday 10–1. Closed September. Donations accepted.
🖊 **Florida Maritime Museum of Cortez** (941-708-6120; floridamaritimemuseum .org), 4415 119th St. W., Cortez. Housed in the 1912 Cortez Rural Graded Schoolhouse, this museum explores the state's maritime heritage from Cedar Keys to the Florida Keys, with special emphasis on Cortez. Displays include artwork, vignettes of early fishing and Cuban fishing ranchos, models of boats that were once made in Cortez, a 1932 pole skiff, other artifacts, and photographs from prehistoric times to present. The circa-1890 Bratton Store, which was relocated next to the schoolhouse, undergoes regular renovation for use as a folklore research center and library. The Pillsbury Boatshop has also come to rest on-site for family and other programs to restore historic watercraft and build models from historic plans. The four-acre complex abuts a ninety-five-acre nature preserve where the Cortez Village Cultural Center displays photos and artifacts in a historic home. Museum open Tuesday to Saturday 9–4:30 (closes at 4 in summer). Cultural center open Thursday to Saturday 10–4.

MUSIC & NIGHTLIFE Check the *Bradenton Herald*'s "Weekend" to learn what's happening in area clubs.

MUST SEE

⚓ **South Florida Museum, Bishop Planetarium & Parker Manatee Aquarium** (941-746-4131; www.southfloridamuseum.org), 201 10th St. W., Bradenton. This two-story museum holds impressive displays and a stadium-style, all-digital planetarium. The first floor focuses on ancient history and features prehistoric skeleton casts, realistic life-size Native American dioramas, and appropriate sound effects. One of the museum's most prized exhibits, the Tallant Collection, displays Amerindian artifacts excavated mostly from Manatee County. Upstairs holds collections of historic artifacts. A seashell display showcases some twenty thousand different shells. Other exhibits simulate different local environments and virtually take you underwater in a river, mangrove forest, and the gulf. It segues into the re-created habitat of Snooty, the star of the museum and the oldest known manatee born in captivity (since 1948) in the United States. You can watch him and his current temporary playmate(s) underwater through aquarium windows or from above at the Parker Aquarium, where interactive exhibits explain the plight of the endangered manatee and educational presentations and feedings take place throughout the day. The museum's outdoor Spanish Plaza holds a replicated sixteenth-century chapel. Bishop Planetarium shows include IMAX-like movies and film special events. Open January to April, July, Monday to Saturday 10–5, Sunday noon–5; closed Monday during all other months. Admission: $19 adults, $17 seniors, $14 children ages four to twelve, children under age four free with paying adult. Admission for Family Nights after 3 reduced to $9, $8, and $7.

BRADENTON BEACH

Beach House (941-779-2222; beachhouse.groupersandwich.com), 200 Gulf Dr. N., Bradenton Beach. Live reggae and island music most evenings in a new, large indoor-outdoor beachside facility.

SPECIALTY LIBRARIES **Family Heritage House Museum** (941-752-5319; www.familyheritagehousemuseum.com), State College of Florida, Manatee/Sarasota, 5840 26th St. W., Bradenton. Part of Florida's Black Heritage Trail, it contains traveling exhibits, children's books and displays, adult books, art, photographs, and other materials relevant to the Underground Railroad and to black heritage, arts, and culture.

THEATER **Anna Maria Island Players** (941-778-5755; www.theislandplayers.org), 10009 Gulf Dr. at Pine Ave., Anna Maria Island. October through May, community theater has been presented in this Old Florida–style building for more than sixty years.

Manatee Performing Arts Center (941-748-5876; www.manateeperformingartscenter.com), 502 Third Ave. W., Bradenton. The new home of Manatee Players, it presents popular dramas and musicals, plus kids' theater.

VISUAL ARTS CENTERS & RESOURCES The following entries introduce you to opportunities for experiencing art as either an appreciator or a practicing artist. A listing of commercial galleries is included under "Shopping."

Art Center Manatee (941-746-2862; www.artcentermanatee.org), 209 Ninth St. W., Bradenton. Classes and demonstrations in all media for all ages; sales gallery.

Longboat Key Center for the Arts (941-383-2345; www.ringling.edu/lbkca), 6860 Longboat Dr. S., Longboat Key. Hidden from mainstream traffic, here is a find for the buyer and would-be artisan. Galleries sell works mostly by Florida artists. Changing and permanent exhibits feature local, emerging, and experimental artists. A crafts shop sells wares made at the center's surrounding workshops, where classes are taught

MUST SEE

✪ ☙ **Village of the Arts** (941-747-8056; www.villageofthearts. com), eighteen-block radius around 12th St. and 11th Ave. W., Bradenton. Officially welcomed in 2001, this artist colony revitalized a former drug neighborhood, turning it into a point of pride for the community. More than thirty artists and artisans from all disciplines—visual arts, healing arts, culinary arts—have moved into the neighborhood to work and sell their art and services. Most are concentrated around 10th Avenue and 12th Street and open December through July, Friday through Sunday; look for banners with bright appliqués in front of participating houses. Art walks take place the first Friday (6–9:30) and Saturday afternoon of each month. One of my favorites is **The Baobab Tree Gallery** (941-447-3795, baobabtree-gallery.wix.com/thebaobabtreegallery; 1113 12th St. W.).

BRADENTON'S VILLAGE OF THE ARTS BRIGHTENED A DRUG-INFESTED NEIGHBORHOOD WITH THE STUDIOS AND WORKSHOPS OF WORKING ARTISTS

in basketry, watercolor, jewelry making, metal craft, pottery, and more. In season, second Tuesdays bring jazz concerts to the center.

The Manatee Arts Council Gallery (941-746-2223; www.manateearts.org), 926 12th St. W., in Village of the Arts, Bradenton. Hosts monthly or bimonthly shows by local artists on a rotating basis.

❋ To Do

BEACHES ☙ ✐ **Anna Maria Bayfront Park** (941-742-5923; www.mymanatee.org), 316 North Bay Blvd., northeast end of Anna Maria Island. One of the region's more secluded beach parks, this one is narrower than the rest of the island's beaches. The

FAMILIES ENJOY BRADENTON BEACH

bay offers a magnificent view of St. Petersburg's Sunshine Skyway Bridge. A historical marker tells about the island's early settlers. Heed danger signs that mark where heavy tidal currents make swimming perilous. Facilities: picnic areas, restrooms, showers, playground, recreational facilities, fishing pier.

✪ ✇ ✿ **Coquina Beach** (941-742-5923; www.mymanatee.org), 2651 Gulf Dr., southern end of Gulf Dr., Bradenton Beach, Anna Maria Island. This large and popular park boasts plump, wide sands edged in Australian pines and small, sea-oat dunes. Waters at the south end provide good snorkeling. The park continues on the bay, where swimming should be avoided because of currents and boat traffic. Bayside trails take you to environmentally restored thirty-acre Leffis Key with a twenty-six-foot hill overlook. Facilities: picnic areas, restrooms, showers, lifeguard, café, volleyball, playground, concessions, boat ramps, and paddle craft launch (bayside).

Cortez Beach (941-742-5923; www.mymanatee.org), Gulf Dr., Bradenton Beach, Anna Maria Island. Here's a long stretch of revamped, undeveloped sand at the end of the Cortez Bridge and stretching north. To the south, it meets up with Coquina, its more popular cousin. Surfers like it here. It's convenient for the heavily laden beachgoer because you can park right along the sand's edge. Facilities: picnic tables.

Longboat Key (941-742-5923; www.mymanatee.org), public access at Broadway St. on the north end of island. Longboat Key has beautiful beaches, mostly enjoyed by resort guests and waterfront residents. Public accesses are marked subtly with signs. Parking, however, is limited, and there are no facilities or lifeguards. The beach stretches wide as well as long and has fluffy white sand and dramatic sunset views. Greer Island, at the north end, is endearingly known as Beer Can Island because of its party-people popularity.

✪ ✇ ✿ **Manatee Beach Park** (941-742-5923; www.mymanatee.org), 4000 State Road 64 and Gulf Dr, Holmes Beach. The hot spot of Anna Maria Island beachgoing, this park appeals to families because of its full complement of facilities. The beach is wide enough to accommodate rows and rows of beach towels. Australian pines shade picnic areas, and the café is popular for breakfast, ice cream, and live music. Facilities: picnic

THE ANNA MARIA CITY PIER PUNCTUATES THE ISLAND'S NORTHERN SHORELINE

area, restrooms, showers, lifeguard, playground, restaurant, ice cream shop, beach rentals, volleyball.

Palma Sola Causeway Beach (941-742-5923), 9000 Manatee Ave. W., Anna Maria Bridge, FL 64. Fairly narrow sands edge the causeway between the mainland and Anna Maria Island. Australian pines add character to the area, which is popular with windsurfers and jet skiers. Facilities: picnic area, restrooms, boat ramps.

BOATS & BOATING *Paddle Sports:* In addition to the following outlets, some resorts and parks rent canoes, kayaks, and stand-up paddleboards. Best trails include those that run along the Manatee River and in intracoastal waters.

Almost Heaven Kayak Adventures (941-504-6296; www.kayakfl.com), 7134 87th Ln. E., Palmetto. Offers tours in and around the islands, bays, and rivers of Sarasota and Bradenton; lessons included. Daily and weekly rentals and drop-off and pickup service.

ENTRANCE TO ROD & REEL PIER

Beach Bums (941-778-3316; www.beach bumsami.com), 427 Pine Ave., Anna Maria. Rents kayaks and leads eco-tours. Also bike and golf cart rentals.

Native Rentals (941-527-6355), 5418 Marina Dr., Holmes Beach. Quality kayak and paddleboard rentals and guided and self-guided tours through bay waters and bird islands.

Personal Watercraft Rental/Tours: Florida law now requires operators between ages eighteen and twenty-one to have a boater safety card. Many rental agents can qualify you for the card.

Powerboat Rentals: **Bradenton Beach Marina** (941-778-2288; www.bradenton

beachmarina.com), 402 Church Ave., Bradenton Beach. Jet Skis, runabouts, center-console fishing boats, and pontoons.

Cannons Marina (941-383-1311; www.cannons.com), 6040 Gulf of Mexico Dr., Long-boat Key. Rentals by the half- or full day and week; runabouts, deck boats, and water skis.

Public Boat Ramps: **Coquina Beach Bayside Park**, Gulf Blvd., Bradenton Beach. Two ramps, plus picnic and recreational facilities; restrooms nearby.

Kingfish Ramp, FL 64 on causeway to Anna Maria Island. Two ramps and picnic facilities.

Palma Sola Causeway, Palma Sola Bay and FL 64. There are three ramps along the causeway, plus restrooms and picnicking.

Palmetto, Riverside Park on Riverside Dr., just west of the Green Bridge. One ramp accommodates two boats on the Manatee River, picnicking.

Sailboat Charters: **Kathleen D Sailing Catamarans** 9941-896-6400; www .kathleend.net) Mainsail Marina, Holmes Beach. Excursions include 2- or 3-hour dolphin watch sails; sunset sail; and a day trip to Egmont Key, home to a national wildlife refuge, lighthouse, and fort ruins.

Sara-Bay Sailing (941-914-5132; www.sarabaysailing.com), 4134 Gulf of Mexico Dr., Longboat Key. Captained charters by the half or full day, sailboat rentals, and American Sailing Association (ASA) certification courses.

Spice Sailing Charters (941-704-0773; spicesailingcharters.com), 840 S. Bay Blvd., at the Galati Yacht Basin, Anna Maria. Half-day and sunset sails to Egmont Key aboard a thirty-foot yacht. Sailing lessons available.

Sailboat Rentals & Instruction: Some resorts have concessions that rent Hobie Cats and other small sailboats. Instruction is often available with the rental. For something more sophisticated, try:

Coastal Watersport Rentals (941-778-4969; coastalwatersportsami.com), 1301 Gulf Dr., Bradenton Beach. Free lessons with catamaran rentals; also rents WaveRunners and kayaks, as well as stand-up paddleboards.

KAYAKING AT ROBINSON PRESERVE

Sara-Bay Sailing (941-914-5132; www.sarabaysailing.com), 4134 Gulf of Mexico Dr., Longboat Key. ASA-certification courses.

Seaduced Watercraft Adventures (941-779-5228; www.seaducedagain.com) Twin Dolphin Marina, Bradenton. Its Discover Sailing Adventure offers 2.5 hours of introductory instruction. Longer classes and sailing excursions also available.

Sight-Seeing & Entertainment Cruises: Look under "Wildlife Tours & Charters" for nature excursions.

Riverside Tours (941-779-3606, riversidetoursinc.com), Regatta Pointe Marina, Palmetto. Two-hour day cruises aboard a pontoon along the Manatee River to see mansions and wildlife; also, two-hour sunset tours. Bring your own food and drink.

Water Taxi (941-586-3210), 801 N. Casey Key Rd. at Second Wind Marine, Casey Key. Good for pub-hopping to local watering holes in the Venice–Sarasota area aboard a twenty-five-foot pontoon boat.

BICYCLING By state law, bicyclists must conduct themselves as pedestrians when using sidewalks. Where they share the road with other vehicles, they must follow all the rules of the road. Children under age sixteen must wear helmets.

Best Biking: **Riverwalk** (941-621-6471; www.realizebradenton.com), from Business 41 to Second St. W., downtown Bradenton. This 1.5-mile paved path along the Manatee River not only offers great views but a score of fun features such as Family Fun Zone, a fishing pier, and sand volleyball.

In Palmetto, **Emerson Point Preserve** offers a pleasant bike ride on an almost 3-mile, partially paved path that runs along waterfront vistas and sometimes shares the road with vehicles.

✪ **Longboat Key's** twelve miles of bike paths and lanes parallel Gulf of Mexico Drive's vista of good taste and wealth on both sides of the road.

Rental Shops: **Fun and More Rentals** (941-462-2719 or 866-931-9840; www.funandmorerentals.com), 5347 Gulf Dr., Holmes Beach. Rents adult and children's bikes and child bike trailers. Free delivery. Also stand-up paddleboards.

Island Scooter Rentals (941-726-3163; www.islandscooters.com), 9908B Gulf Dr. N., Anna Maria. Rents bikes to the public by the hour, day, and week. Also scooters, kayaks, and paddleboards. Customer pickup and drop-off available.

FISHING Nonresidents sixteen and older must obtain a license unless they are fishing from a vessel or pier that's covered by its own license. You can buy inexpensive, temporary, nonresident licenses at county tax collectors' offices and most Kmarts, hardware stores, marinas, and bait shops.

The Bradenton area is known for its mammoth grouper (formerly known as jewfish). Other fine catches include mangrove snapper, sheepshead, and pompano in backwaters, and grouper, amberjack, and mackerel in deep seas. Check local regulations for season, size, and catch restrictions.

Fishing Charters/Outfitters: To find fishing guides, check with major marinas such as Cortez Village.

Stray Dog Charter Boat (941-794-5615; www.straydogcharters.com), 12507 Cortez Rd. W., Cortez. One of several guide charters docked along "Charter Row" alongside the Cortez Bridge, it takes fishermen offshore on a forty-three-foot custom boat with private head.

Fishing Piers: **Bradenton Beach City Pier** (941-778-1005; www.cityofbradentonbeach.com/home/city-pier), Bridge St., Bradenton Beach. Reaching into intracoastal waters, the pier was originally part of the first bridge from the island to the mainland. AMOB on the Pier restaurant (see "Restaurants") and bait concession.

Green Bridge Pier, Business 41 over the Manatee River, downtown Bradenton.

Historic Anna Maria City Pier, Pine Ave., Anna Maria Island. This pier juts 678 feet into Anna Maria Sound at the south end of Bayshore Park.

Rod & Reel Pier (941-778-1885; www.rodreelpier.com), 875 North Shore Dr., Anna Maria. A privately owned fishermen's complex extending 250 feet into Tampa Bay. Includes a café and bait shop.

GOLF Bradenton has its share of golf courses, many of them private or semiprivate. For a wider selection, head to Sarasota. In winter season, rates are highest and greens are the most crowded. Carts are often required. Make tee times well in advance.

Golf Centers: **IMG Golf Academy** (800-872-6425; www.imgacademy.com/sports/golf), IMG Academies, 5500 34th St. W., Bradenton. A highly respected full-time boarding school that also offers summer and weeklong lesson programs.

Public Golf Courses: ✿ **Manatee Golf Course** (941-792-6773; www.golfmanatee. com), 6415 53rd Ave. W., Bradenton. One of the county's most popular courses. Eighteen holes, par seventy-two with five different sets of tees. Clubhouse and restaurant. Reasonable rates; afternoon and twilight discounts apply.

HEALTH & FITNESS CLUBS **Anna Maria Island Health and Fitness Center** (941-778-5446; www.amihealthandfitness.com), 5364 Gulf Dr., Holmes Beach. Open twenty-four hours, it offers a complete selection of cardio and weights equipment, plus a juice and smoothie bar and therapeutic massage. Daily, weekly, and monthly memberships available.

HIKING **Emerson Point Preserve** (941-721-6885; www.mymanatee.org/), 5801 17th St. W., Palmetto. This lovely chin of land on Snead Island lays out trails up ancient Indian mounds, along the bay, through thick woods, and to an observation tower. Bring your binoculars for some worthwhile birding and a lunch for picnicking on Terra Ceia Bay.

Robinson Preserve (941-742-5923; www.mymanatee.org/parks), 1704 99th St. W., Bradenton. Within 487 acres of Bradenton's residential area near De Soto Memorial National Park, visitors will find more than five miles of trails for hiking through mangrove and marsh habitat to a forty-foot observation tower and fishing accesses.

HORSEBACK RIDING ⚘ **Beach Horses** (941-907-7272 or 800-807-7656; www .beachhorses.com). Ever heard of horse-surfing? Possibly invented by this operation, horse-surfing tours take you for an easy, more-or-less bareback stroll down the beach on Palma Sola Causeway. You and your mount then enter the water, where you eventually stand up on the horse's back, and then get a tail pull through the waters.

KIDS' STUFF ⚘ **The Fish Hole** (941-778-3388; www.thefishhole.com), 115 Bridge St., Bradenton Beach. A welcome addition to Bradenton Beach's family friendliness. Its eighteen holes of mini golf are fishing-themed and open daily.

⚘ **Holmes Beach Skateboard Park**, 5801 Marina Dr., Holmes Beach. Open to BMX bikers, skateboarders, and inline skaters. Also playground and shuffleboard.

⚘ **Smuggler's Cove Adventure Golf** (941-756-0043; www.smugglersgolf.com), 2000 Cortez Rd. W., Bradenton; and (941-351-6620). Eighteen holes of "adventure-style" miniature golf and live gators, with a pirate motif. Admission $12.49 adults, $11.49 ages twelve and younger; second game $1.99.

RACQUET SPORTS **Anna Maria Community Center**, Magnolia Ave., Anna Maria Island. Two lit tennis courts. Fee.

Bayfront Park (941-316-1980; www.longboatkey.org/departments/rec/rec.htm), Longboat Key. Two lit courts.

Glazier Gates Park, Manatee Ave. E., Bradenton. Two unlit, cement, public tennis courts.

Holmes Beach Courts, near City Hall, Holmes Beach. Three lit tennis courts.

Jessie P. Miller Elementary School, 601 43rd St. W., Bradenton. Four lit cement tennis courts and one handball court.

Nick Bollettieri Tennis at IMG Academies (800-872-6425; www.imgacademy.com/sports/bollettieri-tennis), 5500 34th St. W., Bradenton. Training camp for adults and juniors. Includes state-of-the-art tennis, seventy-two courts (six of them indoors), swimming pools, a sports-therapy care center, and high-tech sports center. Andre Agassi, Venus and Serena Williams, Maria Sharapova, and other pros have trained here.

Walton Racquet Center (941-742-5973; www.mymanatee.org), 5512 33rd Ave. Dr. W., at G. T. Bray Park, Bradenton. Eight each of cement, clay, and racquetball courts, plus a tennis practice wall and pro shop.

SPECTATOR SPORTS *Pro Baseball:* **McKechnie Field** (941-748-4610; http://pittsburgh.pirates.mlb.com), 161 Ninth St. W. at 17th Ave. W., Bradenton. Site of the Pittsburgh Pirates' exhibition games during March and into April and Bradenton Marauders in the summer season; a small but fun park.

🏖 **Pirate City** (941-747-3031; http://pittsburgh.pirates.mlb.com), 1701 27th St. E., Bradenton. Spring-practice field for the Pittsburgh Pirates' major and minor leagues. Catch the major leaguers during spring season working out from 10 a.m. to 1:30 p.m. The minor leaguers train here in March and early April.

COOL PLAYGROUNDS ATTRACT FAMILIES TO FAMILY KID ZONE ALONG THE RIVEWALK

WATER SPORTS *Parasailing & Waterskiing:* **Bradenton Beach Parasailing** (855-968-3592; www.bradentonbeachparasailing.com), 200 Bridge St., Bradenton Beach. Up to four ride behind a dedicated parasailing boat. "Free fall" option available.

YOLO Adventures (941-792-6000; www.floridafunboat.com), 4330 127th St. W., Cortez. Dry take-offs and landings; single, double, and triple rides.

Sailboarding & Surfing: Sailboarders (a.k.a. windsurfers) find fine conditions all along the coast. Kiteboarding, one of the newer water sports to hit Florida seas, requires extensive training and lots of cash. As far as Florida's west coast surfing reputation goes—which isn't very far—Bradenton Beach is one of the prime spots for hitting the waves, especially in winter when cold fronts approach or in summer before and after tropical storms.

WILDLIFE SPOTTING *Birds:* Birders can find feathered friends at parks and refuges such as the Passage Key National Wildlife Refuge north of Anna Maria Island (bring binoculars—landing ashore is forbidden). Look for peacocks roaming the streets of the north-end village on Longboat Key.

Dolphins: Dolphins often follow in the wake of tour boats, but they're unpredictable. You can't plan on them; you can only be thrilled and charmed when they do appear. If you learn their feeding schedules, you have a better chance of catching their act.

Manatees: Named after the lovable creatures, Bradenton's Manatee County has erected MANATEE WATCH signs at manatee-frequented areas: on the bridges and city pier of the Manatee River, on the Palma Sola Causeway, and on Anna Maria Island at Bayfront Park, Coquina Beach and Boat Ramp, and Kingfish Boat Ramp.

Nature Preserves & Eco-Attractions: 🌸 **Quick Point Nature Preserve** (941-316-1988; www.longboatkey.org), 100 Gulf of Mexico Dr., south end of Longboat Key. The town of Longboat Key worked to restore the natural environment of this thirty-four-acre plot, once covered over and nearly destroyed by sand dredged from New Pass. Park on the west side of the road and follow a boardwalk under the pass bridge to get to the trails through beach, uplands, mangrove, and lagoon habitats. It's a popular spot for ospreys, egrets, ibises, and shorebirds. Open daily. Free admission.

✳ Lodging

Most vacationers to Bradenton Bay gravitate toward Anna Maria Island and Longboat Key, where instead of the usual chains you are more likely to find mom-and-pops, B&Bs, inns, destination resorts, and privately owned places.

Privately owned second homes and condominiums provide another source of accommodation along the Sarasota Bay coast. Vacation brokers who match visitors with such properties are listed under "Home & Condo Rentals" at the end of this section.

I've listed here a well-rounded selection of Sarasota-area accommodations, including a few of the better chain hotels. Toll-free 800, 888, 877, 866, or 855 reservation numbers, where available, are listed after local numbers.

Prices are normally per-person/double occupancy for hotel rooms and per unit for efficiencies, apartments, cottages, suites, and villas. The range spans low- and high-season rates. Many resorts offer off-season packages at special rates and free lodging for children. Pricing does not include the 6 percent Florida sales tax or Sarasota County's 5 percent tourist tax, which

HOLY SEA COWS!

Today we know them as Florida manatees: 1,300-pound blimps, with skin like burlap and a face only a nature buff could love. They also go by the name sea cows, although they are more closely related to the elephant. In days of yore, many a sea-weary sailor mistook them for mermaids.

Well, Ariel they're not, but bewitching they can be. Gentle and herbivorous—consuming up to one hundred pounds of aquatic plants daily—they make no enemies and have only one stumbling block to survival: man. Being mammals, manatees must surface for air, like whales and dolphins. Their girth makes them a prime target for boaters speeding through their habitat. Warning signs designate popular manatee areas. Instead of zipping through these waters and further threatening the endangered manatee population, boaters can slow down to spot the reclusive creatures when they come up for air. It requires a sharp eye, patience, and experience. Watch channels during low tides, when the manatees take to deeper water. Concentric circles, known as manatee footprints, signal surfacing animals. They usually travel in a line and resemble as drifting coconuts or fronds.

is allotted to beach revitalization, arts funding, and tourism promotion. Some large resorts add service gratuities or housekeeping surcharges.

Rate Categories

Inexpensive	Up to $100
Moderate	$100 to $200
Expensive	$200 to $300
Very Expensive	$300 and up

An asterisk after the pricing designation indicates that the rate includes at least a continental breakfast in the cost of lodging and possibly more extensive meal service as noted in the listing. Note that under the Americans with Disabilities Act (ADA), accommodations built after January 26, 1993 and containing more than five rooms must be usable by people with disabilities. I have indicated those small places that do not make such allowances.

ANNA MARIA

Pine Avenue Guest House Rentals (941-778-2167, www.annamariarental .net), 315 Pine Ave. Above the shops and offices along Anna Maria Island's main commercial strip on Pine Avenue, near the beach, nine one- and two-bedroom guest accommodations make a lovely way to experience the cool little village. Spacious and decorated in designer Florida style, they include full, modern kitchens, washers and dryers, covered decks, barbecue grills, and a private swimming pool out back. All units are built and decorated to green standards. Rates are typically by the week, but shorter stays can be arranged when available. Moderate to Expensive.

BRADENTON

Courtyard Marriott Bradenton Sarasota Riverfront (941-747-3727; www.marriott.com/srqbd), 100 Riverfront Dr. W., 34205. Despite its chain branding, this hotel maintains singular character with its old Spanish-style architecture, fountained courtyards, and riverside views. Completely modernized, the lobby holds a media center with free use of video games, fashionable furnishings, a little market with microwave oven, and a sleek bistro that serves Starbucks coffee, breakfast, lunch, and dinner. The courtyard outside drips with hibiscus and oleander blossoms. Here you'll also find the pool and whirlpool. All 153 rooms (fifty-seven of them suites) in the five-story hotel have narrow private balconies that overlook the river or courtyard (rooms) or pool (suites) and come with flat-screen TVs, clean lines, and earthy tones. The hotel is the only place to lie along the Riverwalk and has a sand beach and volleyball court fronting it. The Courtyard also has a fitness center and free wireless Internet access. Moderate.

HAMPTON INN & SUITES BRINGS NEW LIFE TO HISTORIC DOWNTOWN BRANDENTON DIGS

(((•))) **Hampton Inn & Suites Bradenton Downtown Historic District** (941-746-9400, hamptoninn3.hilton.com), 309 10th St. W. Bravo for the Hampton Inn for rescuing this historic beauty dating back to the 1920s. It does its important part in bringing downtown back to life with this seven-story icon. Adjacent to the South Florida Museum complex, its location is ideal for access to downtown's attractions. Original woodwork, vaulted ceilings, and polished stone floor recall the glamor of yesteryear. Yet modern amenities such as microwaves, refrigerators, free WiFi, and iHome clock radios bring the convenience of modern times to guest rooms. Amenities include free hot breakfast, a fitness center, and an outdoor swimming pool. Moderate to Expensive.

🦐 (((•))) **The Londoner Bed & Breakfast** (941-741-4981; www.germaninnbradenton.com), 304 15th St. W., 34205. Surrounded by a picket fence, this 1926 home was perhaps destined to be a B&B. Three of the six rooms—all with London names like Victoria Suite and The Westminster—have their own bath across the hall and a communal refrigerator. The three suites have in-room bathrooms and fridges. Flat-screen TVs, robes, pillow-top mattresses, and WiFi add homey and convenient touches to all of the rooms, which are furnished in individual styles to reflect their names, such as the Victorian furnishings in the Victoria suite. Rates include full breakfast in the sunny breakfast room. Traditional English afternoon tea convenes in the delightful tearoom Monday through Saturday 11:30–3, but is not included in the room rate. and is open to the public. The B&B is an easy walk to downtown's shops, restaurants, and other attractions. Moderate.*

BRADENTON BEACH

🏄 (((•))) **Bridgewalk, a Landmark Resort** (941-779-2545 or 866-779-2545; www.silverresorts.com), 100 Bridge St., 34217. Key West–Caribbean in look, the colorful Bridgewalk houses twenty-eight studio suites, town houses, and mini apartments in three tin-roofed low rises along the town's historic district. Units are comfortably spacious with full or mini kitchens. Deluxe touches include granite countertops, Jacuzzi tubs in some units, screened private balconies, and gulf views from one of the buildings. The beach is a short walk across the street; beach chairs are provided in the rooms, and shade umbrella use is available. The heated pool in the parking area cools off guests apres-beach. Its two restaurants serve up sunset views with cocktails to match. Buffet continental breakfast is complimentary. Moderate to Expensive.

🏄 (((•))) **SeaSide Inn & Resort** (941-778-5254 or 800-447-7124; www.seasideresort

.com), 2200 Gulf Dr. N., 34217. Spotless and decorated with charm, the six gulf-front studios and three rooms have tiled bathrooms, private patios, and modern kitchen facilities: toasters, refrigerators, and microwaves, with stovetops in the studios. The penthouse (Very Expensive) has a separate bedroom, two queen sofa beds, and luxury appointments, and it can connect to two other rooms for large family gatherings. Each room and the pool look out on the gulf with a patio or deck balcony, and the inn has its own private sea-walled beach above the public beach. Weekly rates are available. Expensive.

HOLMES BEACH

🦐 **Cedar Cove Resort & Cottages** (941-778-1010 or 800-206-6293; www.cedarcoveresort.com), 2710 Gulf Dr. N., 34217. The Nut House out back looks like a Gilligan or Moondoggie kind of place to hang out. Hammocks, swinging benches, and a tub of beach toys keep guests on the beach. Every one of the 19 one- and two-bedroom suites comes with a kitchen or kitchenette, along with surprises such as the scope and the pinball machine in the two-bedroom villa. They lie both on the beach side of the property and across the street. Run by a Florida native, the resort has a feel that is right on and conducive to its two rules: "zero stress, 100 percent relaxation." No wonder celebrities find their way to the unlikely spot and that it regularly wins awards from *USA Today* to TripAdvisor. Moderate to Expensive.

✪ ((ᵖ)) **Harrington House B&B** (941-778-5444 or 888-828-5566; www.harringtonhouse.com), 5626 Gulf Dr., 34217. One of Florida's loveliest and best-maintained bed-and-breakfasts, Harrington adds to its homey, historic allure with a beachfront. Built in 1925 of local coquina rock and pecky cypress with Mediterranean flourishes, the Main House was refurbished with casual elegance and magical touches. Each of the six rooms—such as Renaissance, Birdsong, and Sunset—is labeled with a needlepoint door sign. Room sizes vary from spacious, with a king-size bed, to comfortably cozy. Each guest room has its own bathroom, refrigerator, and TV. Six other rooms plus an assortment of suites are distributed throughout the Carriage House and two beach houses. An eclectic collection of hand-picked antique furniture enhances guests' comfort. A dramatic cut-stone fireplace dominates the sitting room in the Main House, where classical music recordings are interrupted only by an occasional piano solo and homemade chocolate chip cookies in the afternoon. Guests enjoy gourmet home-cooked breakfasts at individual tables amid Victorian pieces and filmy white curtains. Outdoor areas include sundecks, a pool, a wide beach, and colorful landscaping around picket fences and arched alcoves. Bikes and kayaks are available for guests' use. No smoking or children younger than age thirteen allowed. Moderate to Very Expensive* (two-night minimum weekends and holidays).

LONGBOAT KEY

✪ ⚲ ✎ ((ᵖ)) **Longboat Key Club & Resort** (941-383-8821 or 800-237-8821; www.longboatkeyclub.com), 220 Sands Point Rd. At the south end of Longboat Key, things get higher and higher-end. Highest of all, the high-rise condos and luxurious trappings of Longboat Key Club make for a tidily manicured landscape and high-density manscape. There's plenty to love about this private, gated scene. Let me count the ways: 291 slips in the deepwater marina, 223 plush rooms and condo suites, forty-five holes of golf, twenty Har-Tru tennis courts, nine miles of biking and walking pathways, eight restaurants, one spa, and zero toxic pesticides or herbicides used on the golf course. The latter two are part of an overall wellness philosophy that extends from guests to the planet Earth. Besides having the expected Florida green hotel and marina designations, Longboat uses mostly organic product in its signature Sands Pointe restaurant and a farm-to-table concept at the Tavern & Whiskey Bar. Snacks and lunches provided for Kids Klub participants are designed to be healthy. Wellness services range from nutritional seminars to yoga paddleboarding. Expensive to Very Expensive.

✪ ❦ ⟨⟨•⟩⟩ **Rolling Waves Beach Cottages** (941-383-1323; www.rollingwaves .com), 6351 Gulf of Mexico Dr., 34228. What more could you ask of a beach vacation than a cute little 1940s cottage furnished homely in bright colors, containing a full kitchen and bath, and complete with patio tables, umbrellas, classic-style painted metal chairs, a grill, sea grapes, huge pink hibiscus blossoms, and a quiet beach outside the door? Rolling Waves' seven one-bedroom and one two-bedroom cottages are kept meticulous and decorated with touches of character: clay-tile kitchen floors here, rag rugs over wood floors there, full-size futons in the living room, and an exterior paint job that evokes the chattel houses of the Caribbean. Sure, there are signs of wear and tear, and maid service is not provided, but we're talking sunset a few steps away and all the ingredients for a beach escape. Located in Longboat Key's old, historic section, it escapes the glitz and the throngs with classic class. Pets are allowed in the cottages but not on the beach. Moderate to Very Expensive. No handicapped access.

❦ 🦎 **Sandpiper Inn** (941-383-2552; www.sandpiperinn.com), 5451 Gulf of Mexico Dr., 34228. Barefoot beach vacations are my favorite, and Sandpiper Inn manages to shut out the world—effectively blocking the low-rise next door from the one-story, eleven-room property's view with clever veg-

etation and a focus on the sea. A paver walkway leads past the efficiencies, each set up with a patio table, umbrella, and rock-paved pad for its chaise lounge. It passes a picnic area with gas grills, a shuffleboard court, and a rock fountain on its way to a tin-roofed gathering area and the beach, fringed with palms, sea oats, and other vegetation. Rattan and white wicker furnish the tiled rooms with their fully equipped kitchens and palm tree accents. The pool is tiny, and there are a few rough edges in the rooms. The beauty lies in the details— your name posted on a plaque as you arrive, cushions on the lounge chairs, beachy art in the rooms, and innkeepers who greet you like family, sit you down at a table for check-in, and pay individual attention to all. Neat, orderly, and quiet, Sandpiper is everything you want in a beach escape. Small pets are allowed. Daily housekeeping is extra. Moderate to Expensive.

PALMETTO

✪ ♂ ⟨⟨•⟩⟩ **Palmetto Riverside Bed & Breakfast** (941-981-5331; www .palmettoriverside.com), 1102 Riverside Dr., Palmetto 34221. In a lovely home dating from 1913 and overlooking the Manatee River, this historic property is all graciousness and elegance. Vaulted ceilings, paddle fans, French antique furnishings, and luxury give the six suites and rooms individual style. The suites have extra sitting room and a fireplace. All have private baths, four-poster beds, high-speed WiFi, and other modern amenities. One of the rooms is ADA-accessible. A full hot breakfast on the sunny porch is included with the stay. Original wood molding and other accents beautify the common areas. Kids ages eight and older are welcome, but accommodations on weekends may be difficult to find because of the inn's brisk wedding business. Belgian innkeepers Mieke and Wim extend the utmost hospitality.

THE PALMETTO RIVERSIDE BED AND BREAKFAST

The inn lies within walking distance to the restaurants downtown and at the nearby marina and to the town's historic attractions. Expensive to Very Expensive.

HOME & CONDO RENTALS **Anna Maria Rentals** (941-778-4178 or 800-737-9855; www.amgcrentals.com), 5702 Marina Dr., Holmes Beach 34217. Anna Maria Island is a hot market for home and condo rentals, from charming beach cottages to swank condos and multiroom homes.

Anna Maria Island Accommodations (941-779-0733 or 866-264-2226; www.annamariaparadise.com), 5604-B Marina Drive, Holmes Beach 34217. More than 200 homes to rent by the week or month.

A Paradise Rental Management (800-237-2252; www.aparadiserentals.com), 5201 Gulf Dr., Holmes Beach 34217. Rental condos and homes on Anna Maria Island for short and long term, starting under $1,000 for a week.

RV RESORTS (📶) **Horseshoe Cove** (941-758-5335 or 800-291-3446; www

.carefreecommunities.com/rv-parks/florida/horseshoe-cove), 5100 60th St. E., Bradenton 34203. This sixty-acre oak-grove riverfront site includes a twelve-acre island with a pavilion and nature and biking trails. The resort has a heated pool and spa, a postal facility, hookup to phone and cable, lighted fishing docks on the Braden River, shuffleboard courts, and other recreational facilities. Music jam sessions happen regularly.

Linger Lodge (941-755-2757; www.lingerlodgeresort.com), 7205 85th St. Ct. E., Bradenton 34202. By dint of its old-Florida-style character and slightly bizarre restaurant, this place has gained a reputation for funky. RV sites lie along or near the Braden River. Amenities include a boat ramp, fishing, and laundry. Cabins available.

Sarasota Bay Travel Trailer Park (941-794-1200 or 800-247-8361; www.sarabayrvpark.com), 10777 Cortez Rd. W., Bradenton 34210. Located on the bay and having full hookups, a boat ramp and dock, fishing, horseshoes, exercise room, recreation hall, and entertainment, this park for seniors caters mostly to permanent abodes, with some spots for transients. This is an exceptionally well-kept and scenic facility.

✳ Where to Eat

Bravo! The individually owned restaurants of Sarasota and Manatee counties have banded together to fight chain-restaurant homogeneity and build their promotional muscle. Look for restaurants that display the "Eat Like a Local" logo (www.dineoriginals.com).

The following listings span the diversity of Bradenton area cuisine in these price categories:

Inexpensive	Up to $15
Moderate	$15 to $25
Expensive	$25 to $35
Very Expensive	$35 or more

Cost categories are based on the range of dinner entrée prices or, if dinner is not served, of lunch entrées.

Note: Florida law forbids smoking inside all restaurants and bars serving food. Smoking is permitted only in restaurants with outdoor seating.

ANNA MARIA ISLAND

♂ **Sandbar Seafood & Spirits** (941-778-0444; www.sandbar.groupersandwich .com), 100 Spring Ave. At the Sandbar you can dine alfresco or within a porch-like, wood-paneled dining room. Either way, you enjoy a close-up view of the gulf and beach. The view makes it a popular spot. It's one of those places where you can sit outdoors 'neath an umbrella on patio furniture and order a good sandwich, salad, or entrée for lunch or dinner. Selections are extensive, including peel-and-eat shrimp, soft-shell crab BLT, salmon Caprese, grouper tacos, seafood platters, crab-crusted scallops, and steak. Early-bird and gluten-free menus are also available. Sunday brunch features live jazz and a complete menu of Sandbar favorites plus house-made scones, crab cake benedict, brunch tacos, and other breakfast items. I have always preferred the atmosphere and beach cuisine on the deck. It's a great place to

BEACHFRONT SEATING AT SANDBAR

people-watch, and I've had better service there. Moderate to Expensive. No reservations.

BRADENTON

🦪 ♿ **Fav's Italian Cucina** (941-708-3287; www.favsitaliancucina.com), 419 12th St. W. Restaurants come and go in struggling downtown Bradenton, but this one has endured, and it's not difficult to reckon why. Simple: good food, easy-to-swallow prices. Packed into the tiny storefront corner of an arcade, it spills onto the arcade and sidewalk out front. The place bustles with the activity of locals coming in to pick up their take-out, chat with the staff, or sit down at a table topped with butcher block paper. Lots of windows mean a bright atmosphere inside or out. The menu is crammed with Italian favorites, hot and cold subs, and wraps. Order anything topped with Fav's homemade red sauce because it's perfect. The subs come on homemade Italian flatbread baked daily on-site, and that adds a whole new twist to the taste and texture. I tried the meatball sub—garlicky, not-too-crazy-big meatballs smothered in mozzarella. It rates #1 in a lifetime of loving meatball subs. Hand-tossed pizzas include deep dish, meatball, and a lunch special where you can order two slices and a soft drink for $4.50. Dinner entrées, most of which are not available until after 5, made my mouth water, especially the gnocchi and the baked tortellini with tomato cream sauce, sausage, mushrooms, and mozzarella. Inexpensive. No reservations.

((ୁ)) **Pier 22** (941-748-8087, www.pier22dining.com), Memorial Pier, 1200 First Ave. W., Bradenton. The pier has held dining space as long as anyone can remember, but restaurants have fluctuated. This one shows promise, keeping the indoor space elegant and the riverside open-air component casual and fun. The dinner menu is quite extensive, with a long list of small plates such as honey walnut shrimp and lamb lollipops, pizzas, salads, and seafood and meat entrées. Choose from grilled seabass, wasabi-crusted tuna, or fresh seafood, grilled or blackened, in the fish category. Landside, you will find chicken chevre, rack of lamb, and Thai beef with peanuts. The lunch menu is quite streamlined in comparison. The Pressed Cuban is tasty, but unusual—made gluten-free with flatbread instead of Cuban bread. Other eclectic options: chicken and balsamic portobello sandwich, fried alligator sandwich, salmon BLT club, and jambalaya. The restaurant also serves Sunday brunch from 11 to 3. Its outdoor bar becomes a lively gathering place for locals.

BRADENTON BEACH

🦪 🎣 ♿ **AMOB on the Pier** (941-778-2662; www.oysterbar.net), 200 Bridge St., on the Historic Bridge Street Pier. A spinoff of a chain of Bradenton area restaurants known as Anna Maria Oyster Bar (and shortened to AMOB) has most recently occupied the pier's restaurant space, which has been in a state of flux during the past decade. Given the brand's popularity and the nicely spruced, salty location, with indoor and outdoor seating, we can hope this one endures. Serving breakfast, lunch, and dinner, AMOB specializes in oysters. The menu at its pier location is more abbreviated than the extensive one at its sister restaurants. But it covers most of the seafood house bases, with fish & chips, salmon grilled or blackened with hollandaise sauce, grouper sandwich, and gulf shrimp. For breakfast and meat-eaters: omelets, breakfast burrito, baby back ribs, and burgers. Inexpensive to Moderate. No reservations.

HOLMES BEACH

✪ **Beach Bistro** (941-778-6444; www.beachbistro.com), 6600 Gulf Dr. The

SHORT FOR ANNA MARIA OYSTER BAR, AMOB OCCUPIES BRANDENTON BEACH'S HISTORIC FISHING PIER

talk of connoisseurs for many years, this little bit of gourmet heaven has fewer than twenty tables in its main dining area, a two-room cottage. (Most of them cluster around picture windows in a room with one of the best local-dining views of the sunset.) On every occasion we've visited, servers attended us with skilled timing and pleasant surprises. In recent years, Beach Bistro has added small plate and cocktail menu options for those who can't afford its classic specialty items in the $33 to $95 range. Dinner begins with herbed bread and a marvelous dip of tomatoes and basil. The exacting menu showcases the chefs' quirky talents, which are difficult to define but easy to enjoy. The "lobstercargots" appetizer, for instance, replaces those "chewy little slugs" with succulent morsels of Florida lobster in bubbling garlic butter and spinach. We had a hard time letting them cool before we ate them—they were that tantalizing. Bouillabaisse with lobster, calamari, shrimp, and fish is a signature ($54 to $66, depending on portion size), as is the "Food Heaven" marvel—lamb crowned with lobster and foie gras on brioche bread pudding ($95). Each dish is executed to perfection. The vegetable accompaniments to our main courses were delicious enough to fight them for attention, and our wine by the glass was poured from the bottle, a touch I always appreciate. In short, if you hear critics and regular folks raving about Beach Bistro, it's all true. Serving dinner only. Moderate to Very Expensive. Handicapped access is limited; close quarters and no bathroom wheelchair access.

LONGBOAT KEY

✪ **Mar Vista Dockside Restaurant & Pub** (941-383-2391; marvista .groupersandwich.com), 760 Broadway St., in the Village. Locals still refer to this as The Pub, a hangover from years gone by. Casual at its best, it has that lovely, lived-in, borderline ramshackle look on the outside, crowned by an appropriately rusting tin roof. Inside, tables don't match, napkins are paper, historic photos and sailors' dollar bills adorn the wall, boaters hoist beers at the bar, and a view of the harbor dominates the decorator's scheme. There's also seating on plastic chairs waterside on the patio, which has heaters when it's cool and fans when it's hot. The seafood is fresh and prepared with signature twists: scallops rumaki with plum sauce, a fresh-catch Reuben sandwich, grouper quesadilla, yellowfin tuna bowl, and Caribbean grilled chicken. A steamer pot brims with shellfish and vegetables, plus other steamed seafood dinners satisfy the urge for simplicity. The Key lime pie is creamy, dreamy, and authentic. We've enjoyed the well-executed cuisine and laid-back atmosphere here many times. Moderate to Expensive. No reservations; preferred seating. Handicapped access in the restaurant but not the restrooms.

PALMETTO

✪ 🍴 ♿ **Alvarez Mexican Food** (941-729-2232), 1431 Eighth Ave. W., Palmetto. Across the river from Bradenton, Palmetto is the seat of Manatee County's huge agricultural industry. That means a heritage of fresh produce and Mexican cuisine. Alvarez has ruled the latter category since 1976. Farmworkers mingle with white-collar tomato brokers for the real thing. The dining room is small, kitsch, and worn, but the patio has more of a festive air and is the first choice when weather allows. The menu spans all the Tex-Mex favorites along with Alvarez specialties: *huevos rancheros* and *chilaquiles* for breakfast, *camarones al Diablo* (spicy shrimp), beef- and raisin-stuffed *chiles poblanos*, and rich mole with either pork or chicken. Daily lunch special combinations offer bargains until 4. Beware of the salsa: it appears simple but packs a wallop and tastes entirely of fresh tomatoes. Inexpensive. No reservations.

BAKERIES 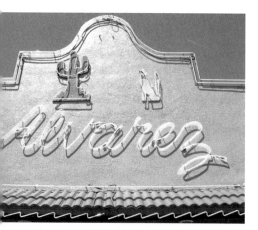 **Ginny's & Jane E's Café, Bakery & Store** (941-778-7370; www.annamariacafe.com), 9807 Gulf Dr., Anna Maria. Rustic breads, cakes, pies, muffins, pastries, and cookies baked fresh within a collectibles store. Also breakfast, sandwiches, coffee, and smoothies.

BREAKFAST 🍷 ✐ **Anna Maria Island Beach Café** (941-778-0784; www.amibeachcafe.com), 4000 Gulf Dr., at Manatee County Park, Holmes Beach. Locals know this window-service

ALVAREZ MEXICAN FOOD SERVES THE REAL THING AND HAS SINCE 1976

concession as one of the most affordable and scenic places to start the morning. Belgian waffles are a specialty, and the all-you-can-eat pancakes with sausage ($5.99) are a big draw. Also lunch and dinner.

Ginny's & Jane E's Café, Bakery & Store (941-778-7370; www.annamariacafe.com), 9807 Gulf Dr., Anna Maria. Vintage tables mingle among the merchandise of a delightful whatnot shop. It serves fresh bakery goods as well as eggs, pancakes, lunch items, coffee, and smoothies.

Peaches (941-721-7838; www.peachs.net), 2207 60th Ave. E., Ellenton. This makes a good breakfast stop before Ellenton Premium Outlets or Gamble Plantation History State Park. One of eleven in the area, this one keeps busy with its extensive menu of pancakes, omelets, and other breakfast specialties. I recommend the Cobb benedict with avocadoes and turkey.

Rod & Reel Pier Restaurant (941-778-1885; www.rodreelpier.com), 875 N. Shore Dr., Anna Maria. Wake up with a sweeping view of the sea all the way to Tampa Bay and its famed Sunshine Skyway Bridge. Typical selection of eggs, pancakes, biscuits and gravy, and coconut French toast.

Sage Biscuit Café (941-792-3970; www.sagebiscuitbradenton.com), 6656 Cortez Rd. W., Bradenton. Breakfast until 3 p.m. includes biscuits and gravy, Raging Breakfast Burrito, apple-cinnamon brioche French toast, plus omelets, skillets and healthy options like Southwestern Quinoa Scramble. Also serves lunch items.

BREWERIES, WINERIES, DISTILLERIES **Motorworks Brewing** (941-567-6218; motorworksbrewing.com), 1014 Ninth St. W., Bradenton. Close to downtown and Village of the Arts, Bradenton's first craft brewery resides in a 1923 car dealership, thus the name and overall theme. The spacious tasting room and beer gardens with a three-hole putting green host live music and special events. It's a friendly place to taste brews such as V Twin Vienna Lager, Indy IPA, and Lazarus Kumquat Wheat (seasonal).

CANDY & ICE CREAM **Corwin's Ice Cream and Smoothies** (941-748-3433; www.corwinsicecream.com), 1000 First Ave. W., Bradenton. Downtown at the riverside Twin Dolphin's Marina, this nautical spot sells almond milk-yogurt smoothies in five fruit flavors, plus various flavors of ice cream cones and toppings and sundaes.

✿ **Joe's Eats & Sweets** (941-778-0007; www.joeseatsandsweets.com), 219 Gulf Dr. S., Bradenton Beach. Forty gourmet flavors of ice cream (cotton candy and Nerds, Key lime cheesecake, almond turtle fudge, and pineapple coconut among them) made on the premises, including sugar-free, lactose-free, and fat-free varieties, plus low-fat yogurt. Homemade fudge in dozens of unusual flavors, sodas, creative sundaes (raspberry truffle cheesecake, latte crème, apple pickers,

MOTORWORKS BREWING OCCUPIES A PREVIOUS-LIFE CAR DEALERSHIP

and wet walnut, for instance), shakes, espresso, and cappuccino.

Two Scoops (941-779-2422; www.twoscoopsami.com), 101 S. Bay Blvd. #A2, Anna Maria. Near the city pier, this has become the talk of local sweet-tooth types. Offers scrumptious sundaes; thirty-two ice-cream flavors, such as birthday cake butter, gator tracks, and muddy sneakers; an espresso bar; plus bagels,

JOE'S EATS & SWEETS, A BRADENTON BEACH LANDMARK

breakfast sandwiches, chili dogs, and luncheon wrap sandwiches.

COFFEE & TEA ((ᵠ)) **Back Alley Treasures** (941-778-1800; backalleytreasures .com), 108 Bridge St., Bradenton Beach. Coffee, frappés, smoothies, wine, bakery goods, and WiFi inside a fun little gift shop.

((ᵠ)) **The B'Towne Coffee Co.** (941-745-3100; btownecoffee.com), 440 Old Main St., Bradenton. A variety of quality and flavored coffee and espresso, plus ice cream, bakery treats, sandwiches, and wireless Internet access.

((ᵠ)) **The Londoner Bed & Breakfast Tea Rooms** (941-748-5658; www .thelondonerinn.com), 304 15th St. W., Bradenton. The Londoner serves authentic English afternoon tea, cakes, and coffee Monday to Saturday 11:30–3 in a prim little B&B parlor. All of the scones and other goodies are made from scratch daily. Reservations recommended.

FRUIT & VEGETABLE STANDS **Bradenton Farmers Market** (941-621-6471; www .realizebradenton.com), Old Main St., downtown Bradenton. Every Saturday from 9 to 2 October through May, this market spreads a selection of fresh produce and local art with chef demonstrations and live music.

🐟 **Hunsader Farms** (941-322-2168; www.hunsaderfarms.com), 5500 Co. Rd. 675, ten miles east of I-75, Bradenton. A bit of a drive from Bradenton's tourist attractions, but worth it if you're in the market for fresh produce. You-pick and we-pick crops from September to June. Also a petting zoo and playground.

🐦 🐟 **Mixon Fruit Farms** (941-748-5829 or 800-608-2525; www.mixon.com), 2525 27th St. E., Bradenton. A large, old, family-owned business specializing in citrus. Tram tours of the grove and processing plant, a wildlife preserve, a café, a kid's maze, free samples, shipping, and a gift shop selling fruit, fudge, orange

FARM MARKET AND ANTIQUES DEALER AT HUNSADER FARMS

swirl ice cream, wine, and jellies. Closed Sundays and the first two weeks in September.

PIZZA & TAKE-OUT **Ciao! Italia** (941-383-0010), 5370 Gulf of Mexico Dr., Longboat Key, in the Centre Shops. Brick oven pizzas include margherita, white, and creative offerings such as the shrimp and crab with fresh tomatoes. Also pasta, fish, veal, and chicken Italian specialties for take-out.

Vertoris Pizza House (941-751-0333; www.vertorispizza.com), 6830 14th St. W., Bradenton. Specializes in brick-oven-baked thin-crust pizzas and gluten-free and vegan pies. Delivery available.

SEAFOOD **Island Fresh Market** (941-567-6130; www.thefishmarketami.com), 5604 Marina Dr., Holmes Beach. Local seafood, organic produce, take-out salads and chowders, desserts, beer, and wine.

✪ **Star Fish Company** (941-794-1243; www.starfishcompany.com), 12306 46th Ave. W., Cortez. To get any closer to the source, you'd have to get wet. This long-standing tradition is the anchor of Cortez village's working waterfront, where crusted old fishing and shrimp boats pull up, and murals and plaques deliver lessons on history and heritage. Buy fresh fish in the market to take home, or order it off the menu.

✳ Selective Shopping

The best shopping in the Bradenton area is scattered around Anna Maria Island.

SHOPPING CENTERS & MALLS **Bridge Street, Bradenton Beach**. An easy-to-walk selection of small shops carrying wares from beachy and affordable to handcrafted jewelry.

De Soto Square (941-747-5868; www .facebook.com/DeSotoSquare), 303 Hwy.

A SAMPLING OF COLORFUL WARES AT BRADENTON'S VILLAGE OF THE ARTS

301, Bradenton. Some seven hundred thousand feet of shop-till-you-drop opportunities in nearly one hundred stores, including Sears, Macy's, and J. C. Penney.

Longboat Key. You'll find a smattering of interesting shops and galleries at The Centre Shops (5370 Gulf of Mexico Dr.) and Avenue of Flowers (off Gulf of Mexico Dr.).

ANTIQUES & COLLECTIBLES **The Sea Hagg** (941-795-5756; www.seahagg.com), 12304 Cortez Rd. W., Cortez. With its stock of antique periscopes, sextants, rods and reels, and other nautical and fishing memorabilia, this is a place to buy a piece of Cortez maritime heritage. Browse its two shops and yards for everything from old crab traps to sea glass by the scoop and metal bird and fish sculptures.

CONSIGNMENT/THRIFT **Unique Boutique** (941-747-6797; www.wrcmanatee .org/unique-boutique), 1926 Manatee Ave. W., Bradenton. Sells women's clothing and accessories to benefit the Women's Resource Center.

CORTEZ'S SEA HAGG TAKES SHOPPING INTO A TREASURE-HUNTING DIMENSION

FACTORY OUTLET CENTERS Ellenton Premium Outlets (941-729-8615; www .primeoutlets.com), 5461 Factory Shops Blvd., at I-75 exit 224, Ellenton. More than 130 shops, a nice food court, and a children's playground in a Caribbean setting. Besides the typical kitchen and clothing stores, it boasts some top names, such as Brooks Brothers, Tommy Hilfiger, Saks Fifth Avenue, and a good, varied selection of others.

FLEA MARKETS & BAZAARS Red Barn Flea Market (941-747-3794 or 800-274-3532; www.redbarnfleamarket .com), 1707 First St. E., Bradenton. More than six hundred stores and booths selling everything from baseball cards to car parts in an air-conditioned facility. Fully open Friday, Saturday, and Sunday 8–4 (also Wednesday, November through April); mall-area stores (about forty) are open Tuesday to Sunday 10–4.

GALLERIES Island Gallery West (941-778-6648; www.islandgallerywest.com), 5368 Gulf Dr., Holmes Beach. This twenty-plus-year-old co-op represents more than twenty-five local artists of sculpture, ceramics, jewelry, stained glass, paintings, basketry, and more.

Restless Natives (941-779-2624; www .restlessnativesgifts.com), 5416 Marina Dr., Holmes Beach. Displays the art of more than eighty Anna Maria Island artists in all forms of artistic media.

GIFTS Back Alley Treasures (941-778-1800; backalleytreasures.com), 108 Bridge St., Bradenton Beach. Fun place to browse for beach art, jewelry, and T-shirts, and enjoy a coffee or glass of wine while you're at it.

Exit Art Gallery (941-387-7395 or 800-833-0894; www.exit-art.com), 201 Gulf of Mexico Dr., Longboat Key. Artistically designed home and office tools, pop art, colorful tableware, jewelry, and clothes.

The Island Cabana (941-896-4946; www.islandcabana.com), 403C Pine Ave., Anna Maria. "Main Street" Anna Maria, a short stretch of Pine Avenue, holds some delightful shops that carry a mix of beach-appeal inventory. This one, for instance, sells fun jewelry and clothing (including Lilly Pulitzer) as well as home décor items and gifts.

JEWELRY **Bridge Street Jewelers** (941-896-7800; www.amibracelet.com), 129 Bridge St., Bradenton Beach. Pretty custom and other beach-inspired jewelry—rings, bracelets, necklaces, and gemstones. Specializing in AMI (Anna Maria Island) destination jewelry.

Tide & Moon Jewelry Island Designs (941-778-4050), 200 Bridge St., at the Pier, Bradenton Beach. In a tiny shop at the foot of the fishing pier, silversmith Laura Shely creates original designs for pendants, rings, earrings, and other wearable art.

SHELL SHOPS **Raders Reef** (941-778-3211; radersreef.com), 5508 Marina Dr., Holmes Beach. Specimen and craft shells, handmade Christmas ornaments and other shell crafts, sponges, jewelry.

✳ Special Events

January: **Manatee County Fair** (941-722-1639; www.manateecountyfair.com), 1303 17th St. W., Palmetto. Ten days midmonth.

February: **Cortez Commercial Fishing Festival** (941-795-6620; www.cortez-fish .org/fishing-festival.html), village of Cortez. Food vendors, music, net-mending demonstrations, arts and crafts, boat tours, and educational exhibits describing the community of Cortez's one-hundred-year-old fishing industry. Third weekend of the month.

March: **Anna Maria Island Springfest** (941-778-2099; www.islandartleague .org), Holmes Beach City Hall Park. A celebration of island arts featuring artist and craft booths, local entertainment, and food concessions. Two days early in the month. **Manatee Heritage Days** (941-741-4070). The entire month is devoted to the celebration of local history and traditions throughout Bradenton and Manatee County. Special tours are arranged by local attractions, and demonstrators weave, quilt, and make baskets and doilies. **Palmetto Heritage Day** (941-723-4991;), Palmetto Historical Park, 515 10th Ave. W., Palmetto. Live entertainment, a chicken-and-yellow-rice luncheon, and one-day postage cancellations at the historic post office highlight this open house on the second Saturday as part of Manatee Heritage Days.

April: **De Soto Heritage Festival** (941-747-1998; www.desotohq.com), Bradenton. The month-long schedule of events (starting at the end of March) includes an illuminated night parade, seafood festival, children's parade, Easter egg hunt, and plastic-bottle boat regatta.

July: **De Soto Fishing Tournament** (941-747-1998; www.desotohq.com/ events), Bradenton Yacht Club, Palmetto. Inshore and offshore divisions. Entry fee and cash prizes. Takes place one weekend midmonth.

December: **Winterfest** (941-778-2099; www.islandartleague.com), Holmes Beach City Hall Park. Two days of arts and crafts shows, live entertainment, and food.

SARASOTA BAY COAST

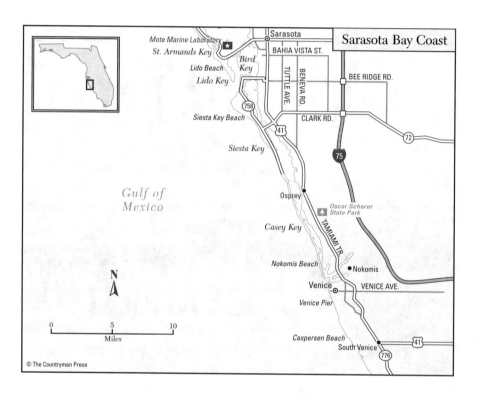

Sarasota Bay Coast

Mote Marine Laboratory
St. Armands Key
Lido Beach
Lido Key
Bird Key
BAHIA VISTA ST.
Sarasota
BEE RIDGE RD.
TUTTLE AVE.
BENEVA RD.
758
Siesta Key Beach
CLARK RD.
41
72
Siesta Key
75
Gulf of Mexico
Osprey
Oscar Scherer State Park
Casey Key
TAMIAMI TR.
Nokomis Beach
Nokomis
Venice
VENICE AVE.
Venice Pier
N
0   5   10
Miles
Caspersen Beach
South Venice
41
776
© The Countryman Press

SARASOTA BAY COAST
Seashore Sophisticate

The city of Sarasota dominates the Sarasota Bay coast, an expanse of metropolitan sprawl that melds with Bradenton, barricaded behind sybaritic, beach-centric islands. History and a heritage of high culture add dimension to this world of sand and city streets.

Wealthy social godparents guided Sarasota's early development. Mrs. (Bertha Honoré) Potter Palmer, known as "queen of Chicago society," settled south of town in 1910, which eventually drew John Ringling and his circus to Sarasota. Although lesser known today, Mrs. Palmer exerted an influence equal to Ringling's in attracting attention to the area around Sarasota Bay. Sarasota continues to grow as a wealth-conscious town—not too big, not too small, just right. In recent years, growth has been upward, as the downtown bayside skyline fills in with luxury condo and resort towers, the Ritz-Carlton and Hyatt Regency among them.

Just across Sarasota Bay from downtown, shopping mecca **St. Armands Circle** and beachy **Lido Key** begin the procession of dot-dash islands that connect to **City Island**, home of Mote Marine Aquarium to the north, then Longboat Key and Anna Maria Island. The chapter on Bradenton & Mid-Coast (page 51) covers the latter two islands.

South of downtown Sarasota, remote **Siesta Key** resisted settlement until the turn of the twentieth century, when a hotel launched the island's reputation as a restful place. A bridge built in 1917 finally brought permanent residents to the island. Siesta Key has historically attracted creative types. One of its best-known citizens was prolific writer John D. MacDonald, most famous for his Travis McGee detective novels. It is believed that while living on Siesta Key he wrote more than seventy novels. Witty essayist E. B. White was a regular visitor around the 1940s. Surrealist Jimmy Ernst, son of Dada master Max Ernst, spent much time on Casey Key during his life; today, horror novelist Stephen King keeps a home there, inspiration for his mystical book *Duma Key*.

The Webb family first arrived in the Sarasota area in 1867 to plant the seed for a town they named **Osprey** seventeen years later. Here is where Bertha Honoré Palmer headquartered when she arrived in 1910.

The original village of **Venice** sat where Nokomis does today. Venice moved south and seaward to its current location after the railroad bypassed it in 1922. Actually an island separated from the mainland by narrow waterways, the original Venice reflects the influence of John Ringling and visionary urban planner John Nolen, who was hired by the Brotherhood of Locomotive Engineers after it purchased much of the town in the 1920s.

Casey Key was built on the principle that island real estate should be reserved for the well-to-do. This has kept it exclusive and lightly developed, particularly at its north end, where a narrow road snakes through a forest of mansions à la Palm Beach. Nokomis Beach, at the southern end, is a more casual, beachy, fishing-oriented resort area.

The Sarasota area has conveniently organized its environmental and historical attractions on a *Gulf Coast Heritage Trail* map, available at visitor information centers around town or at sarasotabay.org.

GETTING HERE Arrivals fly into **Sarasota-Bradenton International Airport (SRQ)** (941-359-2770; www.srq-airport.com; 6000 Airport Circle, Sarasota 34243). Airlines include Air Canada, Alitalia, Delta, JetBlue, United, and WestJet. If traveling by bus, the **Greyhound Lines** (941-342-1720; www.greyhound.com) depot is located at 5951 Porter Way in Sarasota. By car, take Interstate 75 or US 41 from the north or south, and FL 72 from Florida's East Coast.

GETTING AROUND Taxi companies that provide transportation to and from the Bradenton–Sarasota airport include **Diplomat Taxi** (941-365-8294 or 877-859-8933; www.diplomattaxi.com) and **Blue Sky Limo** (941-366-3500 [Sarasota], 941-484-9796 [Venice]); www.blueskylimo.net). See pages 12–13 for rental car phone numbers and web sites. Alamo, Avis, Budget, Dollar, National, and Thrifty have rental facilities at SRQ.

In Sarasota, US 41 runs along bay shores and converges with US 301, another major trunk road. Principal through-streets for east–west traffic in this area are generally those with exits off I-75, north to south: University Parkway (closest to the Sarasota's Ringling museums), Fruitville Road (closest to Sarasota's downtown and the islands), Bee Ridge Road (closest to Siesta Key), Clark Road (FL 72), and Venice Avenue.

Streets hiccup through downtown Sarasota, starting and stopping without warning. Main Street and Ringling Boulevard run east–west, crossed by Orange Avenue, one of the neighborhood's longest streets. Bayfront Drive arcs around the water and skirts a lot of the town's water-based recreation action. Bahia Vista intersects Orange at its southern extreme and constitutes a major route. To cross town from north to south between US 41 and I-75, take Tuttle Avenue, Beneva Road, McIntosh Road, or Cattlemen Road.

To get to St. Armands Circle and Lido Key from downtown Sarasota, follow the signs on Tamiami Trail to cross the Ringling Causeway. To reach Siesta Key from I-75, take exit 205 (Clark Road) or 207 (Bee Ridge Road). From Bee Ridge Road, turn north on US 41 and west on Siesta Drive, which leads to the north bridge. Clark Road (FL 72) becomes Stickney Point Road and crosses the south bridge. On Siesta's north end, Higel Avenue and Ocean Boulevard are the main routes into the shopping district. Beach Road runs gulfside and merges with Midnight Pass Road, which travels to the island's south end, intersecting Stickney Point Road.

To get to Venice, take Jacaranda Boulevard off I-75 to Venice Avenue and the town's beaches and old Mediterranean-influenced neighborhoods. US 41's business route splits from the Tamiami Trail at Venice and takes you to the older part of town. Harbor Drive travels north–south along the beaches. The Esplanade and Tarpon Center Road reach into waterfront communities and South Jetty Park.

The Sarasota Bay coast boasts dependable public transportation, with discounts for schoolchildren and seniors. Buses run every day 6 a.m. to 6 p.m. A downtown trolley runs around Sarasota and St. Armands Circle. For route information, call **Sarasota County Area Transit (SCAT)** (941-861-5000; www.scgov.net/SCAT).

HOSPITALS & CLINICS **Doctors Hospital of Sarasota** (941-342-1100; doctorsofsarasota .com), 5731 Bee Ridge Rd., Sarasota. Emergency room open twenty-four hours. Free Consult-a-Nurse hotline 888-685-1599.

Sarasota Memorial Hospital (941-917-9000; www.smh.com), 1700 S. Tamiami Trail, Sarasota. Emergency room open 24 hours.

Venice Regional Bayfront Health (941-485-7711; www.veniceregional.net), 540 The Rialto, Venice. Emergency room open twenty-four hours.

EXCURSIONS: Scenic Island Routes

Follow the snaking road through a string of barrier islands, from downtown Sarasota through **St. Armands Circle** for shopping, **Lido Key** for beaching and kayaking, **City Island** (home of **Mote Marine Aquarium**), **Longboat Key**, and **Anna Maria Island**. FL 789 adopts a different name on each island: John Ringling Parkway, Gulf of Mexico Drive, and so on. Beach-famous **Siesta Key** is unconnected to the chain and south of downtown Sarasota. To avoid US 41 traffic between downtown and Siesta Key, turn west onto Orange Avenue, follow it through scenic neighborhoods along McClellan and Osprey Avenues to Siesta Drive, and then turn west again. FL 758, along Siesta Key, makes a short, beachy bypass between Siesta Drive and Stickney Point Road. The drive through lovely **Casey Key** begins between Sarasota and Venice at Blackburn Point Road, off US 41, then proceeds south through **Nokomis Beach** and back to the mainland.

VISITOR INFORMATION **Downtown Sarasota Alliance** (941-366-7040; www.dsasarasota.com), P.O. Box 11011, Sarasota 34278.

Visit Sarasota County (941-955-0991 or 800-800-3906; www.visitsarasota.org), 1777 Main St., #302, Sarasota 34236. This is a temporary home for Visit Sarasota.

Siesta Key Chamber of Commerce (941-349-3800 or 866-831-7778; www.siestakeychamber.com), 5118 Ocean Blvd., Siesta Key 34242.

Venice Area Chamber of Commerce (941-488-2236; www.venicechamber.com), 597 S. Tamiami Trail, Venice 34285.

✳ To See

Culture arrived on the Sarasota Bay coast with the early settlers of wealth and means. Eager at first to escape metropolitan ways for the simplicity of life on the beach, they eventually craved access to theater and fine arts, and so ensured the existence of both.

Sarasota benefited most from the generous cultural endowment of the Ringling brothers. Not only did the Ringlings bring circus magic to a quiet frontier town, they also exposed the pioneers to the wonders of Gilded Age European art and architecture. In their wake they left a spirit that is still palpable and unique to Southwest Florida. Art schools and theater groups in Sarasota breed a freshness, vitality, daring, and avant-garde attitude that is unusual for a town of this size. Siesta Key, especially, has an atmosphere that has attracted writers, artists, actors, cartoonists, and architects since folks began settling there.

Sarasota's cultural heritage began with an influx of Scottish settlers at the turn of the century. Now widely varied, its population includes a colony of Amish/Mennonite residents in a district known as Pinecraft, around Bahia Vista Street and Beneva Road. Here you'll see long-bearded men driving tractors or riding bikes down the streets, women in bonnets, a Mennonite church, simple homes, a neighborhood park, and Amish restaurants and markets. The historic African American neighborhood known as Rosemary District lies between US 41 and US 301 and between 10th and Myrtle Streets.

ARCHITECTURE **Sarasota's** downtown and bay areas hold a smorgasbord of old European styles, from the lavish, Italian-inspired ✪ **Cà d'Zan** at The Ringling Estate to the recently renovated and expanded ✪ **Sarasota Opera House**. Fine examples of old residential architecture are found on the fringes of the downtown area. In contrast, the Frank Lloyd Wright Foundation's ✪ **Van Wezel Performing Arts Hall** makes a bold statement with purple shells on the bay shoreline.

SARASOTA'S PLAIN PEOPLE

The Amish-Mennonite community of Pinecraft lies about fifteen minutes from flashy downtown Sarasota, known for its upscale snowbird population. The snowbirds of Pinecraft, however, are a different species. The tight community, eight blocks wide, has been winter home for Amish and Mennonite snowbirds since the 1940s. Contrary to their lives up north, they enjoy electricity, air conditioning, and other conveniences in their Sarasota homes. Other strictures relax here: flip flops instead of black stockings, bathing suits at the beach. Dividing lines between the Old Order and New, Amish and Mennonite blur. The local sect calls itself Beachy Amish-Mennonites.

Instead of growing and cooking all their own food, they line up with tourists to devour meatloaf, fried chicken, rhubarb pie, and other comfort food you want to eat and eat until you are quite, well, *un*comfortable. The food, in fact, brings most "outsiders" inside Pinecraft for a day visit that takes an extreme cultural departure from Sarasota's beach-and-eat scene. Pinecraft's culinary appeal can be summed up in one word: pie. The community celebrates pie every January with its Pie Baking Contest, when locals dole out free chili and pie to all takers. Year-round, order your pie at Yoder's for breakfast, lunch, or dinner, or at the take-out window—by-the-slice or whole. Besides thirty-two varieties of baked and cream pie—from coconut cream to shoofly—it packs the house with home-cooked marvels (see "Restaurants.") Part of Yoder's Amish Village, the restaurant anchors a gift shop, produce market, deli, and courtyard portraying with mural and statues the way of life up north. Nearby at Der Dutchman, the specialty is roasted chicken breaded and crispy. It also has a gift shop and retail area selling pies, cakes, breads, jams, and other Amish specialties. After lunch, stroll around the village to walk off the meal. Check out the quilt and furniture shops and explore neighborhood streets to gain a sense of culture and lifestyles

Season: Thanksgiving to the week before Easter brings the most activity. You'll see women in long dresses and white headwear hanging clothes to dry. Men wearing black suits and chin beards converse in High German or Pennsylvania Dutch. School kids board three-wheel bikes to head to church schools. Crowds gather midday at Pinecraft Park, bordered by Phillippi Creek, for shuffleboard and socializing. After dinner, Big Olaf Creamery constitutes the local nightlife as everyone gathers for home-churned Amish ice cream. Even in the off-season, you will see Pinecraft's "Plain People" in full dress around Florida's only Amish community, which becomes one of its most unusual resorts in winter.

In the 1950s, Sarasota revolutionized local architecture by developing a contemporary style suitable to the environment. Examples of the Sarasota School of Architecture are spread throughout the area. For a driving tour of Sarasota's architectural treasures, pick up a copy of its keepsake *Tour Sarasota Architecture* book at visitors' centers. A new separate tour covers Venice.

Often overlooked, **Venice** houses many architectural treasures created in the 1920s, when the Brotherhood of Locomotive Engineers selected it as a retirement center and subsequently built a model city in northern Italian style. Two shining examples of this style are the **Summit at Venice assisted living facility**—originally the Hotel Venice—at Tampa Avenue and Nassau Street, and the nearby **Venice Centre Mall**, once the San Marco Hotel, later the Kentucky Military Institute. The length of **West Venice Avenue** reveals stunning shops and homes in the prevailing Mediterranean Revival style, as does the **Venezia Park** neighborhood along nearby Nassau Street. You'll find architectural treasures throughout the city, which strives to preserve its historic gems. Walking tour maps are available at the Venice Museum & Archives [see "Museums."]

CINEMA **AMC 12 Theatres at Westfield Sarasota Square** (941-922-9609; www .amctheatres.com), 8201 S. Tamiami Trail, at Beneva Rd., Sarasota.

Burns Court Cinemas (941-955-3456; www.filmsociety.org), 506 Burns Ln., Sarasota. A bright pink movie theater showing art, foreign, and other mainstream and out-of-the-mainstream films on three screens.

Regal Hollywood Stadium 20 (844-462-7342 ext. 208; www.regalcinemas.com), 1993 Main St. at Hwy. 301, Sarasota. State-of-the-art theaters with stadium seating and surround-sound stereo.

In addition to run-of-the-mill movie theaters, Sarasota is also a hotbed for film, with its celebrated film festivals, alternative cinema, and ideal locations for filming.

Sarasota Film Society (941-364-8662, box office: 941-955-3456; www.filmsociety.org), Burns Court Cinemas, 506 Burns Ln., Sarasota; P.O. Box 3378, Sarasota 34230. This group is devoted to screening quality international films, both first-run and classic, year-round. It sponsors the Cine-World Film Festival (see "Special Events" at the end of this chapter).

DANCE **American International Dance Centre** (941-955-8363), 556 S. Pineapple Ave., Sarasota. Ballroom dancing instruction and competition for adults and children.

Gotta Dance Studio (941-486-0326; www.gottadancestudio.net), 303 Tamiami Trail S., Nokomis. Classes in tango, samba, and more for beginners and experienced dancers.

Sarasota Ballet (941-359-0099), 5555 N. Tamiami Trail, Sarasota. Classic and interpretative dance performances are staged by professionals at the FSU Center for the Performing Arts, Sarasota Opera House, and Van Wezel Performing Arts Center, from October to April.

Sarasota Dance Club (941-726-0569; http://ballroomdancefl.com), 3801 Bee Ridge Rd., Sarasota. Dancing and classes from ballroom to salsa.

GARDENS **Historic Spanish Point** (941-966-5214; www.historicspanishpoint.org), 337 N. Tamiami Trail, P. O. Box 846, Osprey. This multi-era historic attraction (see "Historic Homes & Sites") features the ornamental and native gardens built by Sarasota matriarch Bertha Honoré Palmer in the 1910s. The Duchene Lawn, the most dramatic, is lined with towering palms and holds a Greek-column portal that once framed a view of the sea. To create her lovely gardens, Mrs. Palmer built a miniature aqueduct system. A sunken garden and pergola, lychee field, and butterfly garden also provide oases of lush respite along the path at this thirty-acre site. Open Monday to Saturday 9–5, Sunday noon–5. Admission: $12 adults, $10 seniors, $5 children ages five to twelve. Docent tram tours $3 extra each; reservations are required.

The Ringling Bayfront Gardens (941-359-5700; www.ringling.org), 5401 Bay Shore Rd., Sarasota. Mammoth banyan trees (gifts from Thomas Edison, who had an estate in Fort Myers), a showy poinciana, statuesque royal palms, and a 1,200-bush rose garden planted in 1913 are the centerpieces of the lovely sixty-six-acre bayfront Ringling Estate. Near Cà d'Zan, family graves are situated in the Secret Garden, rediscovered about thirty years ago and recently rededicated. The Dwarf Garden—lined with stone little-people statues from Italy (perhaps the earliest yard gnomes?)—lies between the art museum and the visitors center. Open daily 10–5, Thursday until 8. Admission: free with admission to the Ringling complex. Bayfront Gardens Tours take place on select Fridays and Saturdays for $20 each.

✒ **Sarasota Jungle Gardens** (941-355-1112 or 877-681-6541; www.sarasota junglegardens.com), 3701 Bay Shore Rd., Sarasota. Although this is largely a kiddie attraction, plant lovers will enjoy the botanical gardens and cool, tropical jungle. Winding paved paths lead easily through the grounds' more than ten acres, one hundred varieties of palms, and countless species of indigenous and exotic flora, all identified. Private nooks,

MUST SEE

⚥ **Marie Selby Botanical Gardens** (941-366-5731; www.selby.org), 900 S. Palm Ave., Sarasota. This 1920s residence on Sarasota Bay occupies fourteen acres of gardens that wow plant-lovers with bayfront plots of palm, bamboo, hibiscus, tropical fruit plants, and herbs; a koi pond; and a canopy boardwalk with a rope bridge in the Children's Rainforest Garden. Selby is world renowned for its collection of more than 6,000 orchids and 3,600 bromeliads in a lush rainforest conservatory setting with waters trickling over rocks. Artsy interpretative signage tells the different plants' stories with poetry and science. Delightful shops and a barbecue café add to the natural pleasures. Open daily 10–5. Admission: $19 adults, $6 children six to twelve, free for children ages five and younger.

MARIE SELBY BOTANICAL GARDENS SHOWS OFF MORE THAN 6,000 ORCHIDS IN ITS LUSH SETTING

arbor benches, and bubbling brooks make this a lovely spot for quiet reflection, especially in the early morning before the throngs arrive. Exotic birds and other attractions are gravy for the connoisseur of nature. (See "Kids' Stuff.") Snack bar and gift shop. Open daily 10–5. Admission: $18 adults, $17 seniors, $13 children ages four to sixteen.

HISTORIC HOMES & SITES **Cà d'Zan Mansion** (941-359-5700; www.ringling.org), 5401 Bay Shore Rd., at The Ringling, Sarasota. A visitors center with gift shop, restored eighteenth-century European theater, and restaurant welcome you to the Ringling complex, which also contains the centerpiece art museum; a circus museum; miniature circus exhibit building, gardens; and John Ringling's fabulous palazzo, Cà d'Zan. The 32-room showpiece is a gem of Gilded Age glory. Visitors can take a self-guided tour of the first floor or pay extra ($10) for guided tours of the first and second floors. For $20, you can get the private tour of the tower and "secret" places. Using the Doges Palace in Venice as a model, circus king John Ringling spared no expense building this monument to success and overindulgence in the 1920s. He imported styles, materials, and pieces from Italy, France, and elsewhere around the world to embellish his eponymous (in an Italian dialect) "House of John." Baroque, Gothic, Moorish, and Renaissance elements; marble; colored tiles; and jesterlike, multicolor-tinted leaded windows contribute to a breathtaking, ornate Roaring Twenties opulence in the $1.5 million (nearly $19 million in today's currency) mansion on the bay at The Ringling (see "Visual Arts Centers & Resources"). Open daily 10–5. Admission to the Ringling complex: $25 adults, $23 seniors, $10 students with ID and children ages six to seventeen, and free for children under age six; covers admission to all Ringling attractions.

PRETTY PALMS AND HISTORIC ARCHITECTURE MAKE SHOPPING IN DOWNTOWN VENICE PAINLESS

☼ 🐾 🚲 〰 **Historic Spanish Point** (941-966-5214; www.historicspanishpoint.org), 337 N. Tamiami Trail, Osprey. This historic site spans multiple eras of the region's past—from 2150 BC through 1918. Its importance lies not only in its historical aspects, but in its environmental and archaeological significance. Assembled on the thirty-acre Little Sarasota Bay estate, once owned by Chicago socialite Bertha Palmer, are prehistoric Indian burial grounds, a cutaway of a shell midden mound, the relocated homestead and family chapel of the pioneering Webb dynasty, Mrs. Palmer's restored gardens (see "Gardens"), and a late Victorian pioneer home. Local actors give living-history performances on Saturdays and Sundays in the winter. Guided tours and docent-narrated tram rides are available; reserve ahead for both. Another tip: Bring mosquito repellent in warm weather. Open 9–5 Monday to Saturday, noon–5 Sunday. Admission: $12 adults, $10 seniors, $5 children ages five to twelve. Docent tram tours $3 extra each.

Sarasota Circus Heritage Trail (www.sarasotaarts.org), throughout Sarasota County. This website and its trail map take visitors through the county's Big Top past via ten sites, including "the church the circus built" (St. Martha's Catholic Church at 200 N. Orange Ave. in Sarasota), the Circus Ring of Fame at St. Armands Circle, The Ringling complex, the home of Charles and Edith Ringling at New College of Florida (5800 Bayshore Rd. in Sarasota), the Sailor Circus Big Top, Venice's Circus Bridge, and a statue of famed animal trainer Gunther Gebel-Williams at the historic Train Depot in Venice (see below).

🚂 **Venice Train Depot** (941-412-0151; www.venicehistory.com), 303 E. Venice Ave. at Seaboard Ave. Set in Railroad Park under the Business 41 bridge, this circa-1927 depot, the last remaining passenger station in the county, conducts tours of the Mediterranean Revival building. The depot has local significance because the Brotherhood of Locomotive Engineers owned much of Venice in the 1920s; and because in the 1960s, when Ringling headquarters moved here, the Seaboard Railroad transported the circus. In the park, you can also visit the statue of circus trainer Gunther Gebel-Williams and a Seaboard caboose. Visit by guided or self-guided tour 10–3 Monday, Wednesday and Friday, November through April; and 10–1 Saturday year-round. Free admission; donations accepted.

KIDS' STUFF 〰 🚂 **Bayfront Park**, downtown Sarasota. Toddlers especially love the playground and shallow pool, with its squirting fountains and climbable sculptures of frogs, manatees, turtles, gators, and fish. It's a good, tobacco-free place for strolling, people-watching from a park bench, jogging, and shopping for boat charters. A small, inexpensive restaurant and water-sports concession can be found within. Street sculpture exhibitions are year-round and feature artists from around the world. Free.

〰 **The Children's Garden** (941-330-1711; www.sarasotachildrensgarden.com), 1670 10th Way, Sarasota. This magical fantasy, an especially popular place for parties, uses

MUST SEE

✪ ✎ The Ringling Circus Museum & Tibbals Learning Center
(941-359-5700; www.ringling.org), 5401 Bay Shore Rd., at The Ringling, Sarasota. The circus museum was Florida's way of saying "thank you" to John Ringling back in 1948. Its re-creation of Big Top magic paid tribute to the man who bequeathed to the city a legacy of exotica, sophistication, and art appreciation. The museum reflects Ringling's seemingly contradictory interests—fine art and glitzy showmanship. Tasteful cloth mannequins model plumed and sequined costumes. Vignettes peek behind the scenes and framed art reflects the world of freak shows. The original museum plays up Sarasota's role as winter headquarters for the circus and its part in the filming of the movie *The Greatest Show on Earth*. Visitors can walk a gangway to look into its newest addition—the Ringlings' seventy-nine-foot, circa-1905 luxury railroad car, the *Wisconsin*. The newer Tibbals Learning Center, next to the museum, is a more modern tribute to the art and magic of the circus in a larger sense than Ringling and Sarasota. The experience begins with a short film of historic footage that deals with the logistics of the moving city known as a circus. The complexity of visiting 150 towns in one season with one hundred railcars inspired Howard Tibbals to create a 3,800-square-foot miniature model of the circus—the largest in the world—that covers every aspect of the circus from its arrival in town by train to what goes on behind the scenes and the Big Top main event. This multisensory experience re-creates the sounds of the circus while the lighting turns the scene from day to night. Upstairs, you can look down upon the massive display. Other exhibits include another miniature circus, memorabilia, and a timeline chronicling the circus from its ancient origins, through its Golden Age, and up to its modern incarnations. A new wing in the Tibbals appropriated some of the costumes and props originally exhibited in the circus museum for an interactive component, where kids can listen to calliopes and play at riding bareback and walking the tightrope. The museum and learning center are located on the grounds of The Ringling Museum of Art (see "Visual Arts Centers & Resources"). Open daily 10–5. Admission: $25 adults, $23 seniors, $5 children and students up to age eighteen with ID, free for children under age six; cost covers admission to all Ringling attractions.

THE TIBBALS LEARNING CENTER AT RINGLING ESTATES RE-CREATES THE MAGIC OF THE BIG TOP

recycled products and old-fashioned concepts to entertain children. Kids can dress up in their choice from a roomful of costumes; take the yellow brick road to play gardens where pirate ships, dragons, and an octopus lurk; find their way through the maze; visit the butterfly garden; and run, climb, jump, and make believe. Open 10–5 daily. Admission: $10 adults, $9 seniors, $5 children ages three to twelve.

THE VENICE MUSEUM RESIDES IN A PRETTY, OLD VENICE NEIGHBORHOOD

🐦 **Sarasota Jungle Gardens** (941-355-5305 or 877-681-6541; www.sarasotajunglegardens.com), 3701 Bay Shore Rd., Sarasota. A birds-of-prey exhibit and show, reptile and rainforest-bird shows, a Meet the Keeper program, free-strolling flamingos you can hand-feed, a playground with a jungle theme, a bird posing area, a playground, monkeys, swans, wallabies, and other live animals and feathered friends make this one of the area's favorite children's attractions. Its peaceful, junglelike gardens appeal to others. (See "Gardens.") Open daily 10–5. Admission: $18 adults, $17 seniors, $13 children ages four to sixteen.

✪ **Sarasota Classic Car Museum** (941-355-6228; www.sarasotacarmuseum.org), 5500 N. Tamiami Trail, Sarasota. More than one hundred antique, classic, muscle, and celebrity cars park under one roof here. See a 1981 DeLorean like the one from *Back to the Future*; John Lennon's '65 Mercedes Benz Roadster; John Ringling's Rolls-Royces and Pierce Arrow; Paul McCartney's Mini Cooper, and vintage motorized vehicles dating from 1905. The kids will get a kick out of the vintage games. Open daily 9–6. Admission: $9.85 adults, $8.50 seniors, $6.50 children ages six to twelve.

🖼 **Venice Museum & Archives** (941-486-2487; www.venicemuseum.org), 351 S. Nassau St., Venice. The most interesting relic here is the building that houses the facility. A 1927 Italianate structure with a triangular base and a Renaissance tower, it once was called the Triangle Inn. Stop for a peek at whatever exhibit is showing, a room full of local fossils, and another exhibit honoring city father Dr. Fred Albee, whose invention, the orthopedic and fracture table, you'll find among the other memorabilia. A botanical park lies across the street. Open May through September, Monday, Tuesday, and Wednesday 10–4; January through April also open first and third Saturdays 11–3. Admission is free or by donation ($3 per person or $5 per couple suggested).

MUSIC & NIGHTLIFE Thanks to its population of college students, Sarasota dances with action throughout the week and especially on weekends. Local bands and up-and-coming stars appear in theaters, cabarets, and nightclubs. Cores of activity include downtown, Siesta Key, and posh St. Armands Circle. Every Friday, check the *Sarasota Herald-Tribune*'s "Ticket" section to learn what's happening in area clubs.

NOKOMIS

Pelican Alley (941-485-1893; www.pelicanalley.com), 1009 W. Albee Rd., Nokomis. Check the Facebook page for live music happenings.

SARASOTA

🍸 **Five O'Clock Club** (941-366-5555; www.5oclockclub.net), 1930 Hillview St., Sarasota. The hottest thing going away from downtown, it hosts live bands and DJs nightly in an old (circa 1955), plain neighborhood bar setting—everything from reggae to pop. Happy hour here lasts from noon to 8 p.m.!

✪ **The Gator Club** (941-366-5969; www.thegatorclub.com), 1490 Main St., Sarasota. One of the hottest places downtown, in historic digs with a pressed-tin ceiling and straw paddle fans. Live music most nights.

McCurdy's Comedy Theatre (941-925-3869; www.mccurdyscomedy.com), 1923 Ringling Blvd., Sarasota. This downtown house of guffaws and giggles hosts major national acts such as Sinbad and Louie Anderson. It also hosts open mic nights and a Humor Institute.

Jazz Club of Sarasota (941-366-1552; www.jazzclubsarasota.org), 330 S. Pineapple Ave., Suite 111, Sarasota. This organization, founded by the former publicist for Benny Goodman in 1980, dedicates itself to the perpetuation and encouragement of jazz performance by presenting various monthly and annual events, jazz sessions, special presentations, and youth programs. It also has a musical instrument lending library and sponsors the weeklong Sarasota Jazz Festival in March (see "Special Events").

Ringling by the Bay (941-358-3180; www.ringling.org), The Ringling Museum of Art, 5401 Bay Shore Rd., Sarasota. On select Mondays from 5 to 8 p.m., live local musicians perform music from the '60s forward. Tickets are $10.

Sarasota Concert Band (941-364-2263; www.sarasotaconcertband.org), 6858 Sagebrush Circle, Sarasota. This ensemble's fifty-some members perform year-round at indoor and outdoor venues throughout the area. Regular concert season is November through May.

Sarasota Orchestra (941-953-3434 or 866-508-0611; www.sarasotaorchestra.org), 709 Tamiami Trail N., Sarasota. Besides holding classical symphony concerts in Bradenton and Sarasota counties from September to May, this group (formerly Florida West Coast Symphony) sponsors June's Sarasota Music Festival and the Youth Orchestra.

SIESTA KEY

✪ **Beach Club** (941-349-6311; www.beachclubsiestakey.com), 5151 Ocean Blvd., Siesta Key. This youthful pool hall–nightclub has been hosting local rock, jazz, and reggae groups nightly since 1947.

🍸 **Siesta Key Oyster Bar** (941-346-5443; www.skob.com), 5238 Ocean Blvd., Siesta Key. In the midst of Siesta Key Village hubbub, its open-air component and nightly live music make it a popular pub crawl stop.

VENICE

Venice Symphony (941-488-1010; www.thevenicesymphony.org), 230 Tamiami Trail S., Venice; mailing address: P.O. Box 1561, Venice. Classical and pops concerts December through April at Venice Performing Arts Center (1 Indian Ave.).

SPECIALTY LIBRARIES **The Ringling Art Library** (941-359-5700; www.ringling .org/art-library), 5401 Bay Shore Rd., Sarasota. One of the largest art libraries in the Southeast, it specializes in Italian and European Baroque art, Peter Paul Rubens, and decorative and theater art books, more than eight hundred of them from Ringling's own collection. Special programs include lectures, book discussions, and children's story time. Open to the public Monday through Friday 1–5, or by appointment (access through the Ringling Visitors Center).

✐ **Selby Public Library** (941-861-1100; www.scgov.net), 1331 First St., Sarasota. The city's central and most impressive-looking library, it schedules cultural events throughout the year. Arranged in a circular design, the library features an exciting youth wing that you enter through a glass aquarium arch.

THEATER ❂ ✐ **The Circus Arts Conservatory** (941-355-9805; circusarts.org), 2075 Bahia Vista St., Sarasota; This umbrella organization keeps alive Sarasota's deeply entrenched Big Top tradition with a holiday-time and February schedule of performances at the Big Top at 12th St. and Tuttle Rd. and also Circus Sarasota summer family performances at The Ringling. Conceived by Sarasota native Dolly Jacobs (daughter of the late, great circus clown Lou Jacobs), who continues to perform, it's a not-for-profit, educational organization hosting clown-arts seminars and Sailor Circus (see Events).

Florida Studio Theatre (941-366-9000; www.floridastudiotheatre.org), 1241 N. Palm Ave., downtown Sarasota. A major testing ground for budding playwrights (including elementary students) and new works, Florida Studio Theatre's professional troupe performs main stage, cabaret (with dining), and improv theater year-round. It also hosts summertime new playwright and improv festivals.

❂ **FSU Center for the Performing Arts** (941-351-8000 or 800-361-8388; www.asolo .org), 5555 N. Tamiami Trail, across from The Ringling, Sarasota. Formerly the Asolo Center, it incorporated into the interior of one of its venues a dismantled, historic European theater: a circa-1900 Scottish opera house. Carved box fronts, friezes, and ornate cornice work from the old theater decorate the new one, lending it an aura of Old World heritage. Opened in 1989 in partnership with the Florida State University acting department, the five-hundred-seat Harold E. and Esther M. Mertz Theatre hosts the

FLORIDA STATE UNIVERSITY'S CENTER FOR THE PERFORMING ARTS' DRAMA BRANCH IS AT HOME IN SARASOTA'S FORMER ASOLO CENTER, ON THE GROUNDS OF THE RINGLING ESTATES

excellent, fifty-year-old Asolo Rep troupe November through June. Free tours are available by advance reservation (941-351-9010 ext. 4714). A separate, more intimate, 161-seat theater, called the Jane B. Cook Theatre, is the home of FSU's conservatory program.

Glenridge Performing Arts Center (941-552-5300 or 888-999-4536; www.theglenridge.com), 7333 Scotland Way, Sarasota. In addition to live theater, this 267-seat state-of-the-art facility hosts films and concerts from chamber music to jazz.

Historic Asolo Theatre (941-359-5700; www.ringling.org/historic-asolo-theater), 5401 Bay Shore Rd., Sarasota. Recently restored and merged into The Ringling's visitors center, it hosts dance, music, theater, films, lectures, and a summer circus experience show. The theater is open on certain days for self-guided tours; check at the desk upon arrival.

The Players of Sarasota (941-365-2494; www.theplayers.org), 838 N. Tamiami Trail, Sarasota. Community theater group that stages Broadway musicals, plus live music and other programs year round.

✪ **Sarasota Opera House** (941-328-1300; www.sarasotaopera.org), 61 N. Pineapple Ave., downtown Sarasota. Don't even try to park or dine downtown on opera opening nights during the February–March season. (There's also a short October–November season.) Southwest Florida's oldest opera company's opening galas are popular events that require ticket purchase months in advance. In operation for more than fifty years, the Sarasota Opera Association stages all the classic and rare works in its beautifully restored, 1926 Mediterranean Revival–style structure, located in the Theater and Arts District. It also hosts concerts and other cultural events. You can tour the facility every Monday in fall and winter at 10:30 for $12. Check the website for dates.

Urbanite Theatre Sarasota (941-321-1397; www.urbanitetheatre.com), 1487 Second St., Sarasota. Alternative theater comes to the stage for winter and summer seasons.

✪ **Van Wezel Performing Arts Hall** (941-953-3368 or 800-826-9303; www.vanwezel.org), 777 N. Tamiami Trail, Sarasota. The Van Wezel, that purple eye-catcher radiating outward like a scallop shell from the shores of Sarasota Bay, was designed by the Frank Lloyd Wright Foundation and hosts name comedians, musicians, and dance groups; Broadway shows; major orchestras; ethnic music and dance groups; and chamber and choral music. In the off-season, May through October, the hall hosts Friday Fest on the Bay one Friday per month from 5–9 p.m., featuring live music from country to reggae.

Venice Theatre (941-488-1115; www.venicestage.com), 140 W. Tampa Ave., downtown Venice. In its Mediterranean Revival structure, the troupe performs six mainstage shows practically year-round. It conducts theater classes, workshops, and summer camp for adults and kids.

VISUAL ARTS CENTERS & RESOURCES The canvas of Sarasota Bay arts reveals a complex masterpiece, layered with the diverse patterns and local color of its many communities. With its backdrop of artistic types dating back to avid collector John Ringling, Sarasota leads the region to avant-garde heights. In fact, in 2012, *American-Style* magazine named Sarasota the #1 Small City for Art. A new museum, the Sarasota Museum of Art (239-309-7662; www.ringling.edu/SMOA), is expected to take up residence by 2017 in a historic high school currently under renovation.

The following entries introduce you to opportunities for experiencing art as either an appreciator or a practicing artist. A listing of commercial galleries is included under "Shopping."

Art Center Sarasota (941-365-2032; www.artsarasota.org), 707 N. Tamiami Trail, Sarasota. Exhibition and sales galleries feature the paintings, jewelry, sculpture, pottery, and enamelware of local and national artists. Art instruction and demonstrations are available. The gallery features an outdoor sculpture garden.

MUST SEE ✪ **The Ringling Museum of Art** (941-359-5700; www.ringling.org/museum-art), 5401 Bay Shore Rd., Sarasota. Sarasota's pride and joy, and designated the State Art Museum of Florida, this is not only an art museum but also the nucleus of tourism activity and the heart of the local art community. It shares its sixty-six-acre bayfront estate with Ringling's extravagant Cà d'Zan palace (see "Historic Homes"); a circus museum and learning center (see "Museums"); gardens (see "Gardens"); and a visitors center with an extensive gift shop (see "Shopping"), restaurant, and restored historic Italian theater (see "Theater"). The art collection, much of which was purchased by Ringling, covers five hundred years of European art and specializes in late-medieval and Renaissance Italian works. The Old Masters collection contains five original Rubens tapestries as well as Spanish Baroque, French, Dutch, and northern European works (largely portraits of a religious nature). The museum continually augments its collection of American and contemporary works in three wings, and the newer Ulla R. and Arthur F. Searing Wing, which houses traveling exhibits. The Center for Asian Art opened in 2016 to host rotating collections of The Ringling's Asian art possessions, The lushly landscaped courtyard features reproductions of classic statues and Italian decorative columns, which Ringling originally purchased for the hotel he hoped to build on Longboat Key. The museum is open daily 10–5 and until 8 p.m. on Thursdays; the grounds are open 9:30–6. Admission covers all Ringling property attractions and a tour of the art museum: $25 adults, $23 seniors, $5 students (with ID) and children ages six to seventeen, free for children under age six. On Thursdays from 5–8 p.m., admission is $10 adults. Admission is free to everyone all day Monday.

Artists' Guild of Anna Maria Island (941-778-6694; www.amiartistsguildgallery.com), 5414 Marina Dr., Holmes Beach. Local artists meet and display in the gallery.

The Fine Arts Society of Sarasota (941-330-0680; www.fineartssarasota.com), Van Wezel Performing Arts Hall, 777 N. Tamiami Trail, Sarasota. Van Wezel houses a permanent collection of prominent Florida artists' works dating from the 1930s on loan from the society, which conducts tours at 10 a.m. the first Tuesday of each month, October through May. Cost is $5 per person.

Ringling College Galleries (941-359-7563; www.ringling.edu/campus-galleries), 2700 N. Tamiami Trail, at the Ringling College of Art and Design, Sarasota. Five on-campus modern galleries exhibit the works of contemporary students, faculty, and local, national, and international artists and designers. Free admission.

✪ **Towles Court Artist Colony** (www.towlescourt.com), 1938 Adams Ln., Sarasota. A delightful, blossomy village of restored and brightly painted tin-roofed bungalows turned art colony. Showings, studios, and galleries. Third Friday gallery walks, 6-9 p.m.

Venice Art Center (941-485-7136; www.veniceartcenter.com), 390 S. Nokomis Ave., Venice. Local artists' exhibitions, gift shop, café, and art instruction.

To Do

Known both for its superlative white sand beaches and as the birthplace of Florida golfing, Sarasota and its environs draw lovers of the outdoors to their year-round playgrounds.

BEACHES The Sarasota area claims more than forty miles of sandy seashore. Island beaches are, for the most part, highly developed, with lots of facilities and

Brohard Park (941-486-2626; www.venicegov.com/parks. asp), 1600 S. Harbor Dr., Venice. This sea oats–edged, dark-flecked sand beach threads under the Venice Fishing Pier and around covered picnic tables. Folks come here to fish, hang out at the pier tiki bar, and hunt for shark's teeth. Facilities: handicap-accessible, picnic areas, restrooms, showers, fitness trail, fishing pier, bait shop, beach shop, restaurants, volleyball.

concessions. Recent years have seen a concession of another sort—to nature—as boardwalks and sea oat plantings restore the dunes. On the islands, erosion takes its toll and beaches must be periodically renourished. This stretch of the Gulf Coast boasts some of the whitest beaches this side of the Florida Panhandle—and some of the darkest. Like most Southwest Florida beaches, gulf waters here are typically calm and inviting. Parking is free at all area beaches. Pets (except where noted) and glass containers are prohibited. So is walking across dune vegetation any way but on the boardwalk crossovers. For current beach conditions, go to visitbeaches.org or call 941-BEACHES. The resources are especially useful in checking for the presence of red tide, an organism that appears in local waters from time to time and can cause respiratory problems.

Caspersen Beach (941-861-5000; www.scgov.net), 4100 Harbor Dr., Venice. At the end of the road lies natural Caspersen Beach, where a series of boardwalks cross high, scrub-vegetated dunes onto speckled sands. It's popular with shark's-tooth hunters and young beachgoers. From here you can walk to Manasota Key Beach to

SIESTA KEY'S SUNDAY DRUM CIRCLE DRAWS A COLORFUL CROWD

the south. On the bay side, the county has built a bike path, a fishing pier, and a kayak launch along the Venetian Waterway. Facilities: picnic areas, restrooms, showers, nature trail, fitness station/trail, covered playground, bike path, creekside fishing pier, kayak launch. Open daily 7–8.

🦞 ⚓ **Crescent Beach** (941-861-5000; www.scgov.net), south of Siesta Public Beach on Midnight Pass Rd., access near Stickney Point Rd. intersection, Siesta Key. Less populated than the main public beach, but with the same award-winning sand, this beach is a little tricky to find. It lacks the facilities and ease of parking of the main beach, but it does have a couple of access points. At its south end, Point of Rocks is popular with snorkelers and fishermen because of an accumulation of rocks that attracts marine life. The Point of Rocks Road access has no parking, however.

🦞 ⚓ ((ᵞ)) **Lido Beach** (941-861-5000; www.scgov.net), 400 Ben Franklin Dr., Lido Key. Heavily developed and popular, this is the main beach on Lido Key. Canvas cabanas and stylish, umbrella-shaded lounge chairs may be rented along the stretch of sand carpeted with small shells and shell hash. Signs warn about submerged rocks in the water. South of the pavilion at the Lido Beach Resort, you'll find water-sports equipment rentals. In 2001, residents rallied to save the circa-1926 community lap pool on the beach, a throwback to the glamour days of John Ringling and friends. Facilities: picnic areas, restaurant, ice-cream shop, restrooms, showers, lifeguards, historic swimming pool, volleyball, beach wheelchairs. Pool admission: $4 adults, $2 seniors and children ages four to eleven.

🦞 ⚓ **Maxine Barritt Park** (941-486-2626; www.venicegov.com/parks.asp), 1800 S. Harbor Dr., Venice. Venice's newest park is wedged between Brohard and South Brohard's Paw Park. It circles a fenced-off retention pond with a two-third-mile paved walkway. Dunes-top picnic shelters overlook the beach. Facilities: picnic area, restrooms, showers, swings, trails, handicap accessible.

✪ 🦞 ⚓ **Nokomis Beach** (941-861-5000; www.scgov.net), 100 Casey Key Rd. at Albee Rd., Casey Key. Remote and exclusive Casey Key gives way to beachy abandon toward its southern end. In the midst of the town's action, it is a popular destination, prettily landscaped and inviting. A series of parking lots provides public access, and a long boardwalk runs parallel between two of them. Join in the drum circle and bonfire every Saturday night. Facilities: picnic area and shelters, restrooms, showers, lifeguards, volleyball, playground, beach wheelchairs.

🦞 ⚓ **North Jetty Park** (941-861-5000; www.scgov.net), 1000 Casey Key Rd., Casey Key. The town of Nokomis Beach is a fisherman's haven, and its rock-shored North Jetty, at its southernmost point, lures anglers. (South Jetty lies across the pass on Venice Beach.) A bait shop keeps fishermen supplied and also sells sandwiches. A newer food concession has a larger selection. The beach's wide sands, festooned with Australian pines and sea grape trees, are well loved by serious local beachgoers. When the waves kick up, the surfing crowd heads here. Fast-moving pass waters can make swimming treacherous. Facilities: picnic area and shelters, playground, restrooms, showers, lifeguards, concessions, boat ramps, beach wheelchairs.

North Lido Beach (941-861-5000; www.scgov.net), 50 Ben Franklin Dr., Lido Key. This one extends from the main beach up to New Pass. A lack of facilities and limited parking keep the throngs away from the northernmost reaches of this naturally maintained park. It is wide, with fine, spic-and-span sand, plus trails for hiking and running. The main parking lot fills early in the day.

Service Club Park (941-486-2626; www.venicegov.com/parks.asp), 1190 S. Harbor Dr., Venice. An extensive system of boardwalks crosses scrub pinelands (watch for rare scrub jays and gopher tortoises) and provides picnic nooks off the beach.

MUST SEE

✪ 🦆 🏄 **Siesta Beach** (941-861-5000; www.scgov.net), 948 Beach Rd. at Midnight Pass Rd., Siesta Key. Siesta Key's sand was once judged "the finest, whitest beach in the world" by the Woods Hole Oceanographic Institute. (Anna Maria Island's beach placed third.) In 2011, Dr. Beach pronounced it the best beach in the United States, and in 2015, it ranked number one for the TripAdvisor Travelers' Choice best beach award. The blinding whiteness comes from its quartz (99 percent) origins; the sand's fineness comes from Mother Nature's efficient pulverizer, the sea. Unfortunately, these facts have not been kept secret. The park averages about twenty thousand visitors a day. Arrive early to find a parking space. Condos and motels line the wide beach. Swimming is wonderful because the beach has gradually sloping sands and typically clear waters. Public accesses along Beach Road to the north provide more seclusion, but parking is on the street and limited. On Sunday evenings, a drum circle starts an hour or two before sunset. Facilities: picnic areas and shelters, restrooms, showers, lifeguard, snack bar, playground, volleyball, tennis, ball fields, soccer field, fitness trail, beach wheelchairs.

This is quieter than neighboring Brohard Park and its fishing pier, but within walking distance of both. Facilities: picnic areas and shelters, restrooms, showers, volleyball.

South Brohard Park and Paw Park (941-486-2626; www.venicegov.com/parks.asp), S. Harbor Dr., Venice. Parking and boardwalks over mangrove wetlands provide access to a beach that is away from noise, fishhooks, and crowds. The undeveloped natural beach appeals to escapists, who are nonetheless within walking distance of facilities at Brohard. One acre of its twenty-two acres is a designated dogs-allowed beach and is outfitted with fenced areas for doggies and owners. Facilities: picnic table, restrooms, showers, drinking fountains for dogs and people.

South Jetty (941-486-2626; www.venicegov.com/parks.asp), 2000 Tarpon Center Dr., Venice. Also known as Humphris Park, the jetty at Casey's Pass—a favorite of fishing types—is shored with huge boulders. South of them stretches a span of condo-lined beach that's popular with surfers and sailboarders. Here, people while away time eating lunch and watching boat traffic through the pass. Across the pass lies Nokomis Beach's North Jetty. Facilities: restrooms, picnic tables, food concession.

🦆 🏄 **Ted Sperling Park at South Lido Beach** (941-861-5000; www.scgov.net), 2201 Ben Franklin Dr., Lido Key. A wide, natural beach wraps around the tip of Lido Key from the gulf to the bay, facing Siesta Key to the south. Picnic areas are overhung with Australian pines and carpeted by their needles. Within its one hundred acres several Florida ecosystems thrive on different waterfronts. Squirrels are the most evident wildlife throughout the park, which is smoke- and pesticide-free. Hiking trails lead you along the mangrove worlds of Little Grassy and Big Grassy lagoons. Brushy Bayou is a good place to kayak through mangrove canopies. Swift waters in the pass make swimming treacherous but fishing fine. Facilities: picnic areas, restrooms, showers, playground, volleyball, ball fields, horseshoes, soccer field, fitness trail, nature trail, canoe trail.

🦆 🏄 **Turtle Beach** (941-861-5000; www.scgov.net), south end of Blind Pass Rd., Siesta Key. The sands become coarser, darker, and more shell-studded at Siesta's lower extremes as the high-rise buildings become scarcer. Along here and Midnight Pass Road, the island's upper echelon resides behind iron gates. Less crowded than the other Siesta beaches, it's sports- and family-oriented but without lifeguards. If you walk southward, you'll come to ✪ **Palmer Point Beach** (otherwise only reachable by boat), where Midnight Pass between Siesta and Casey keys has filled in and shark's teeth are easy to find. Facilities: picnic areas, restrooms, showers, small playground, volleyball, boat ramps, horseshoes; restaurants and bars across the street.

○ ☃ ♂ **Venice Beach** (941-486-2626; www.venicegov.com/parks.asp), 101 The Esplanade, Venice. This beach feels cramped and more urban than Venice's spacious south-end beaches. Buildings border the sands, which spread wide here. Wooden benches provide places to gaze at the normally calm sea. This beach is especially popular with divers because a reef fronts the sands a quarter mile out. Its retro-look rock pavilion holds a food concession with beach necessities and even rents the "Florida snow shovels" that shark's teeth collectors use. Facilities: restrooms, showers, food concession, picnicking, volleyball, beach wheelchairs.

BICYCLING Sarasota's best bikeways lie on barrier islands, in parks, and in rural areas to the east. Most biking elsewhere is on the sides of roads or sidewalks.

By state law, bicyclists must conduct themselves as pedestrians when using sidewalks. Where they share the road with other vehicles, they must follow all the rules of the road. Children under age sixteen must wear helmets.

Best Biking: In Palmetto, **Emerson Point Preserve** offers a pleasant bike ride on an almost three-mile, partially paved path that runs along waterfront vistas and sometimes shares the road with vehicles.

Bike paths travel through parts of **Lido Key** and **Siesta Key**. The **Venetian Waterway Park** (941-861-5000; www.scgov.net) in Venice runs along both sides of the Intracoastal Waterway and stretches for 9.3 miles from the train depot on Venice Avenue,

THE SOUTH JETTY AND NORTH JETTY LINE CASEY'S PASS—AN ANGLER'S HAVEN

one of nine trailheads for **Legacy Trail** (941-861-5000; www.legacytrailfriends.org), which follows the old railroad route to Macintosh Road in Sarasota in the north. **Oscar Scherer State Park** provides a more natural backdrop for biking on nearly fifteen miles of trails. In Sarasota, county buses are equipped with bike racks for pedal-and-ride passengers.

Rental Shops: Resorts and parks often rent bikes or provide free use of them.

Beach Bikes & Trikes (941-412-3821; www.venicebikesandtrikes.com), Venice. Rentals, repairs, and sales. No storefront, but free local delivery and pickup twenty-four hours.

Siesta Sports Rentals (941-346-1797; www.siestasportsrentals.com), 6551 Midnight Pass Rd., Southbridge Mall, Siesta Key. Beach cruisers, speed bikes, kid bikes, tandems, surreys, jogger strollers, scooters, scooter cars, and beach stuff.

BOATS & BOATING *Paddlesports:* In addition to the following outlets, some resorts and parks rent canoes, kayaks, and stand-up paddleboards. Best trails include those that run along the Myakka River and in intracoastal waters.

Adventure Kayak Outfitters (941-779-7426; www.adventurekayakoutfitters.com), launch site at 190 Taft Dr., Sarasota. Free delivery and pickup for rentals. Also offers sunset fishing, birding, manatee sighting, and Lido Key mangrove tours.

CaliFlorida Surf & Skate Shop (941-346-0310; www.califloridarentals.com), 5253 Ocean Blvd., Siesta Key. Rent stand-up paddleboards, kayaks, surfboards, skimboards, Jet Skis, and skateboards.

Enticer Watersports (941-366-7245; www.sarasotawatersportsrentals.com), 5 Bayfront Dr., at Bayfront Park, Sarasota. Rents kayaks, paddleboats, paddleboards, small sailboats (two hour minimum) and row boats, and WaveRunners by the half-hour or hour.

✪ **Oscar Scherer State Park** (941-483-5956; www.floridastateparks.org/park/oscar-scherer), 1843 S. Tamiami Trail, Osprey. Canoe rentals and launch and tidal creek paddling along scrubby and pine flatwoods. River otters and alligators inhabit the waters; scrub jays, bobcats, and bald eagles inhabit the land. Ranger-led canoe programs are available every Wednesday, free with admission on a first-come basis.

Siesta Sports Rentals (941-346-1797; www.siestasportsrentals.com), 6551 Midnight Pass Rd., at Southbridge Mall, Siesta Key. Rents single and double kayaks, plus snorkels, boogie and skim boards, and other beach equipment.

Silent Sports (941-966-5477; www.silentsportsoutfitters.com), 2301 Tamiami Trail, Nokomis. Rents kayaks and stand-up paddleboards and leads three-hour tours (reservations required). Delivery available.

Personal Watercraft Rental/Tours: Florida law now requires operators between ages eighteen and twenty-one to have a boater safety card. Many rental agents can qualify you for the card.

Enticer Watersports (941-366-7245; www.sarasotawatersportsrentals.com), 5 Bayfront Dr., at Bayfront Park, Sarasota. Rents kayaks, paddleboats, paddleboards, sailboats, and WaveRunners by the half-hour, hour, day, or week.

Siesta Key Jet Ski (941-346-3000; www.siestakeyjetski.com), 1250 Stickney Point Rd., at CB's Saltwater Outfitters, Siesta Key. One- to four-hour rentals.

Powerboat Rentals: **Cannons Marina** (941-383-1311; www.cannons.com), 6040 Gulf of Mexico Dr., Longboat Key. Rentals by half-day, day, and week; runabouts, deck boats, and water skis.

CB's Saltwater Outfitters (941-349-4400; www.cbsoutfitters.com), 1249 Stickney Point Rd., Siesta Key. Runabouts, center console boats, pontoons, and deck boats; also rod and reel rentals, fishing licenses, tackle shop, and fishing guides.

Island Jet Ski (941-474-1168; www.islandjetski.com), 801 Blackburn Point Rd. at Casey Key Fish House, Osprey. Rents pontoon and deck boats and jet skis. Also has paddlecraft rentals and conducts guided dolphin tours.

Sarasota Boat Rental (941-951-0550; www.sarasotaboatrental.com), 2 Marina Plaza, at Marina Jack, Sarasota. Center console fishing boats, deck boats, and skiffs by the half- or full day.

Public Boat Ramps: **City Island**, Ken Thompson Pkwy. Three ramps.

Blackburn Point Park, Blackburn Point Rd. on the way to Casey Key. Two ramps, fishing pier, picnic tables.

Higel Park, Tarpon Center Dr., Venice Beach, Venice Inlet.

Marina Boat Ramp Park, 215 E. Venice Ave., Venice.

Nokomis Beach, Venice Inlet.

Turtle Beach, Blind Pass Rd., Siesta Key. Two ramps.

Sailboat Charters: **Key Sailing** (941-346-7245; siestakeysailing.com), 2 Marina Plaza E18, at Marina Jack, Sarasota. Small, customized private sails aboard a forty-one-foot Morgan with free sailing lessons.

Sight-Seeing & Entertainment Cruises: Look under "Wildlife Tours & Charters" for nature excursions.

⌀ **LeBarge Tropical Cruises** (941-366-6116; www.lebargetropicalcruises.com), 2 Marine Plaza, at Marina Jack in Bayfront Park, Sarasota. Island-style crooning, an aquarium bar, and on-board mermaid sculptures and live coconut palms put the tropical in this excursion. Sight-seeing and nature, dolphin and manatee, and sunset-party cruises depart daily. Light snacks and drinks available.

FISHING Nonresidents sixteen and older must obtain a license unless they are fishing from a vessel or pier that's covered by its own license. You can buy inexpensive, temporary, nonresident licenses at county tax collectors' offices and most Kmarts, hardware stores, marinas, and bait shops.

Snook are so plentiful in the Intracoastal Waterway between Sarasota and Venice, it's been dubbed "Snook Alley." Other fine catches include mangrove snapper, sheepshead, and pompano in backwaters and grouper, amberjack, and mackerel in deep seas. Check local regulations for season, size, and catch restrictions.

Deep-Sea Party Boats: **Flying Fish Fleet** (941-366-3373; www.flyingfishfleet.com), 627 Avenida del Norte, at Marina Jack in Bayfront Park, Sarasota. Half-day to twelve-hour deep-sea charters and party-boat excursions.

Fishing Charters/Outfitters: To find fishing guides, check with major marinas such as Marina Jack's in downtown Sarasota. Capacity is smaller and prices higher than for party-boat excursions.

Big Catch (941-366-3373; www.flyingfishfleet.com/charter-big-catch.asp), 627 Avenida del Norte, at Marina Jack's in Bayfront Park, Sarasota. Four- to twelve-hour private fishing charters.

CB's Saltwater Outfitters (941-349-4400; www.cbsoutfitters.com), 1249 Stickney Point Rd., Siesta Key. Light-tackle fly and spin sportfishing charters in Sarasota Bay, the gulf, Snook Alley, and Charlotte Harbor. Four to eight hours. Fly-casting instruction available. Orvis endorsed.

Charter Boat Shark (941-365-2161; www.charterboatshark.com), 2 Marina Plaza, at Marina Jack, Sarasota. Catch tuna, kingfish, mackerel, shark, and more offshore aboard an air-conditioned, forty-one-foot boat.

High Class Hooker Fishing Charters (941-806-8062; www.highclasshookercharters .com), Venice. Inshore, offshore, and kayak fishing excursions.

THE FLYING FISH FLEET MEETS EVERY ANGLER'S NEEDS

Sarasota Fishing Charters (941-587-9852; www.sarasotafishingcharters.com), 2576 Hillview St., Sarasota. Light-tackle sportfishing the flats, backcountry, and inshore for snook, trout, redfish, and tarpon. Half-day, six-hour, and full-day trips for one to three adult anglers or a family of four.

Fishing Piers: **Ken Thompson Pier** (941-316-1172), 1700 Ken Thompson Pkwy., City Island. Three small piers into New Pass.

✪ **Nokomis Beach's North Jetty** (941-316-1172), south end Casey Key Rd., Nokomis Beach. Man-made rock projection along the pass and into the gulf. Beach and picnic area.

Osprey Fishing Pier, west end of Main St., Osprey. A neighborhood pier in an off-the-beaten-path area; no parking.

Tony Saprito Fishing Pier, Hart's Landing, Ringling Causeway Park en route to St. Armands Key. The pier juts into the bay from the north side of the causeway; the bait store is on south side.

✪ **Venice Fishing Pier** (941-486-2626; www.venicegov.com/parks.asp), 1600 S. Harbor Dr., at Brohard Park, Venice. It's 740 feet long, complete with restrooms, showers, bait shop, rod and reel rentals, and restaurant. Admission to the pier is free.

Venice's South Jetty (941-486-2626; www.venicegov.com/parks.asp), Tarpon Center Dr., Venice. A stretch of boulder buffer with a paved walkway and food concession at Venice's north end.

GOLF In 1902 Sarasota's founder and first mayor, a Scotsman, built a two-hole golf course in the middle of town. Locals claim it was Florida's first golf course. Through the years, the sport has grown in Sarasota, and today there are more courses than you can swing a club at. The majority are private or semiprivate. Several large resorts have their own greens or arrange golf-around programs at local links. In winter season, rates are highest and greens are the most crowded. Carts are often required. Make tee times well in advance.

Golf Centers: **Evie's Family Golf Center** (941-377-0990; eviesonline.com), 4735 Bee Ridge Rd., Sarasota. Practice sand traps, chipping and putting greens, lessons with PGA pros, miniature golf, and wiffle ball; also food and a video arcade.

Public Golf Courses: **Bobby Jones Golf Course** (941-955-3529; www.bobbyjones golfclub.com), 1000 Circus Blvd., off Beneva Rd. or 17th St., Sarasota. Sarasota's only municipal course, it has thirty-six holes plus a nine-hole executive course, practice range, and chipping and putting greens. Restaurant and lounge. Named for one of the sport's late greats, who personally dedicated the course in 1927.

🐌 **Lake Venice Golf Club** (941-488-3948; www.lakevenicegolf.com), 1801 Harbor Dr. S., Venice. A par-seventy-two eighteen-hole course and par-thirty-six nine-hole course. Walk or ride the course; snack bar.

HEALTH & FITNESS CLUBS **Arlington Park & Aquatic Complex** (941-861-5000; www.scgov.net), 2650 Waldemere St., Sarasota. City-owned, county-operated facility with lap pool, fitness center, tennis, racquetball, and basketball. Admission.

🏄 **Babe Weiller Branch YMCA** (941-366-6778; www.sarasotaymca.org/babe), 1991 Main St., #200, Sarasota. Weight machines, sauna and steam room, classes. Daily, weekly, and monthly memberships available and transferable to other Sarasota Y's.

🏄 **Evalyn Sadlier Jones YMCA** (941-922-9622; www.sarasotaymca.org/esj), 8301 Potter Park, Sarasota. With an Olympic-size pool and children's water park, this Y goes beyond fitness to fun. For workouts, there are classes, a weight and cardio room, an indoor track, racquetball and basketball courts, an outdoor fifty-meter pool, diving boards, and a Jacuzzi area. At the water park, families will enjoy the activity pool, slides, water cannons, fountains, and other cool stuff, plus there's an adjacent climbing tower. A child-watch program supervises the little ones while parents work out. Daily, weekly, and monthly memberships available and transferable to other Sarasota Y's.

🏄 **South County Family YMCA** (941-492-9622; www.swflymca.org), 701 Center Rd., Venice. Wellness center with strength-building and extensive cardio equipment, plus two racquetball courts, massage therapy, a skate park, baby-sitting, and a food court.

HIKING **Jelks Preserve** (941-861-5000; www.scgov.net), 2300 N. River Rd., Venice. Not far off Interstate 75 exit 191, this preserve's more than eight miles of trail lead to the lovely Myakka River, a designated wild river and Florida Outstanding Water, through canopy hammock and pineland habitat.

⊙ **Oscar Scherer State Park** (941-483-5956; www.floridastateparks.org/park/oscar-scherer), 1843 S. Tamiami Trail, Osprey. A combined fifteen miles of six level-ground nature trails, including a half-mile barrier-free trail. An audio device introduces the scrub habitat of the marked, five-mile Yellow Trail.

Sarasota Bay Walk (sarasotabay .org), 1550 Ken Thompson Pkwy., next to Mote Marine Aquarium, City Island.

FEEL DELIGHTFULLY AWAY FROM IT ALL AT THE VENICE PIER

Self-guided nature boardwalk into a mangrove estuary and lagoon, part of a shoreline restoration project.

South Lido Nature Park (941-316-1172), 2201 Ben Franklin Dr. at Taft Dr., Lido Key. Adjacent to South Lido Beach Park, it has nature trails into the mangroves of Brushy Bayou.

HUNTING For information on hunting licenses, permits, and seasons, visit www .myfwc.com/hunting.

Knight Trail Park (941-488-3223; www.scgov.net/parks), 3445 Rustic Road, Nokomis, east of I-75 at exit 195. Public facility maintained by the Sarasota Parks and Recreation Department. Trap and skeet, pistol and rifle range, archery range, picnic areas.

KIDS' STUFF ✒ **Evalyn Sadlier Jones YMCA** (941-922-9622; www.sarasotaymca.org/ esj), 8301 Potter Park, Sarasota. Water park for families with activity pool, slides, water cannons, fountains, and climbing tower.

✒ (๏) **Leaping Lizards** (941-496-4386; www.leapinglizardsvenice.com), 4411 S. Tamiami Trail, Venice. This indoor inflatable playground includes a snack bar and TVs for parents to watch the game on weekends while the kids burn energy on nine large inflatables and a laser tag maze.

Sky Zone Trampoline Park (941-363-6FLY; www.skyzone.com/sarasota), 6180 Edgelake Dr., Sarasota, off Bee Ridge Rd. at I-75. A bowl of trampolines, a Foam Zone, and other fun features make this a workout the whole family will love. Special programs include Toddler Time, Skycamp, and Tuesday Family Four-Pack.

RACQUET SPORTS **Arlington Park & Aquatic Complex** (941-861-5000; www.scgov .net), 2650 Waldemere St., Sarasota. Lit tennis and racquetball courts. Fee.

Gillespie Park (941-316-1172), 710 N. Osprey Ave., Sarasota. Three unlit tennis courts.

Hecksher Park (941-486-2626; www.venicegov.com/parks.asp), 450 W. Venice Ave., Venice. Six tennis courts with lights and two racquetball courts. Also, shuffleboard.

Siesta Beach (941-861-5000), 948 Beach Way Dr., Siesta Key. Four tennis courts with lights.

South County Family YMCA (941-492-9622; www.swflymca.or), 701 Center Rd., Venice. Two racquetball courts, plus workout and fitness rooms and classes.

SHELLING Although not comparable to the coast's southern beaches for shelling, the islands of Sarasota do yield some unusual finds. Venice Beach, for instance, is known for its shark's teeth, which come in all sizes and various shades. The south end of Siesta Key also boasts toothy waters, but Venice's beaches have the best pickings.

Sharks continually shed teeth and grow new ones. Most of what you find is prehistoric. The white ones are recent sheddings. Teeth range in size from 1/8 inch to a rare three inches. Some resorts provide "Florida snow shovels"—screen baskets fastened to broomstick handles for sifting through the sand. You can also buy them in local stores. Digging for specimens is taboo.

SPAS **Mandala Medi Spa & Yoga Shala** (941-927-2278; http://mandalamedspa.com), 1715 Stickney Point Rd. Indonesian body treatments, massage, salon services, medical aesthetics, and yoga classes.

The Met (941-388-3991; www.themetsarasota.com), 35 S. Blvd. of Presidents, St. Armands Circle, Sarasota. Up a sweeping staircase from a posh clothing store in an elegant setting, The Met offers full spa and beauty facilities and treatments, including wraps, massages, and facials. The Marine Sea Salt Polish with Hydrating Cocoon is signature. Also offers a spa lunch.

Pixie Dust (941-366-6325, www.dustypixie.com), 1476 Main St., Sarasota. Besides psychic readings and "metaphysical" gifts, it does massage and other therapies such as hot Himalayan salt stone massage, energy crystal massage, and sound baths.

Sea-renity (941-779-6836; www.sea-renityspa.com), 112 Bridge St., Bradenton Beach. Massages for thirty, sixty, and ninety minutes in-house or at the beach, plus facials, manis, and pedis.

Sirena Island Day Spa (941-485-2922; www.sirenaislandspa.com), 211 Nassau St., Venice. In a cute cottage just off Venice Avenue, it offers a full complement of massages, scrubs, wraps, facials, waxing, tinting, and packages.

Warm Mineral Springs (941-426-1692; www.scgov.net/warmmineralsprings), 12200 San Servando Ave., south of Venice near North Port. Water of a rare quality attracts health seekers to a 1.4-acre lake fed by nine million gallons of mineral water each day. If you know your spas, you will appreciate the springs' chemical analysis of 19,870 parts per million of fixed solid minerals, the third highest in the world—good for the skin, joints, and sinuses. The lake, which maintains a year-round temperature of eighty-seven degrees, has soothing and, some believe, healing powers that attract people from around the world. Folks bathe at a roped-off beach and children's area, and they sun on a grassy lawn. Opened in 1940, the facilities are now under the auspices of the city of North Port. Archaeologists have discovered artifacts in the lake suggesting that Native Americans came here for a bit of mineral-washed R&R ten thousand years ago. Some claim this was the Fountain of Youth Ponce de León sought but never found because of his untimely death from an arrow inflicted nearby. Admission: $20 per person for all day, $8 for 5:30–8; $15 students for all day, $5 for evening hours, and $10 children ages two to twelve, $2 for evening hours. Open daily 9 a.m. to 8 p.m.

SPECTATOR SPORTS Southwest Florida is rich with spring training teams. The Baltimore Orioles currently practice and compete in the Sarasota Bay area. Word has it that the Atlanta Braves may be relocating to the south in North Port.

Greyhound Racing: **Sarasota Kennel Club** (941-355-7744; www.sarasotakennelclub. com), 5400 Bradenton Rd., Sarasota. Greyhound night and matinee racing from November to mid-April. Parimutuel betting, Texas Hold 'Em, and matinee and evening shows year-round. Thoroughbred horse racing is simulcast from Miami and other tracks year-round. Dining on-site. Closed Sunday. Admission. Must be eighteen or older to enter.

Polo: **Sarasota Polo Club** (941-907-0000; www.sarasotapolo.com), 8201 Polo Club Ln., Lakewood Ranch, 3.5 miles east of I-75 exit 213, Sarasota. Watch from the grandstands or bring a tailgate picnic. Game time is 1 p.m. every Sunday, mid-December to Easter.

Pro Baseball: **Ed Smith Stadium** (941-954-4101), 2700 12th St., Sarasota. It is the spring-training home (March and early April) of the Baltimore Orioles (888-848-BIRD; http://baltimore.orioles.mlb.com).

Waterskiing: 🦜 **Sarasota Ski-A-Rees Show** (941-388-1666; www.skiarees.com), 1602 Ken Thompson Pkwy. Adjacent to Mote Marine Aquarium, Sarasota. Free amateur waterskiing and wakeboarding performances in the bay at 2 p.m. Sundays, February to mid-May (except Easter). See website for off-season show schedule.

WATER SPORTS *Parasailing:* **Siesta Key Parasail & Jet Ski** (941-586-1972; siestakey parasailandjetski.com), 1536 Old Stickney Point Rd., Siesta Key. Single, double, and triple rides.

Sailboarding & Surfing: Sailboarders (a.k.a. windsurfers) find fine conditions all along the coast.

Kiteboarding, one of the newer water sports to hit Florida seas, requires extensive training and lots of cash.

As far as Florida's west coast surfing reputation goes—which isn't very far—Venice's and Nokomis' jetty parks are prime spots for hitting the waves, especially in winter when cold fronts approach or in summer before and after tropical storms.

Island Style Wind & Watersport (941-954-1009; www.islandstylesports.com), 2433 N. Tamiami Trail, Sarasota. Offers windsurfing and kiteboarding lessons plus paddleboarding.

Snorkeling & Scuba: Of all the southern Gulf Coast, this region generally boasts the best visibility for underwater exploration, especially in spring. Man-made reefs make up for the lack of natural reefs on Florida's west coast. At Venice Beach, a natural reef lies just a quarter-mile from the beach, making shore dives possible. South of Crescent Beach, at the island's central zone, rocks, underwater caves, and coral formations make good submerged sightseeing at Point of Rocks beach.

At Bradenton Beach, the sunken sugar barge *Regina* houses various forms of marine life. Both snorkelers and divers look for shark's teeth fossils.

Economy Tackle/Dolphin Dive & Kayak Center (941-922-9671; www.floridakayak .com), 6018 S. Tamiami Trail, Sarasota. Snorkel and spearfishing rentals.

SURF'S UP AT NOKOMIS BEACH!

MUST SEE

MOTE MARINE LABORATORY AQUARIUM BUILT ITS REPUTATION ON SHARK AND OTHER MARINE-CREATURE RESEARCH

✪ ✐ **Mote Marine Laboratory Aquarium** (941-388-4441 or 800-691-MOTE; www.mote.org), 1600 Ken Thompson Pkwy., on City Island, northeast of Lido Key, Sarasota. Mote Marine is known around the world for its research on sharks, marine mammals, and environmental pollutants. Its two visitors centers here educate the public on projects and marine life. A 135,000-gallon shark tank centerpieces the original facility and is kept stocked with sharks and fish typical of the area: grouper, snook, pompano, and snapper. Dozens of smaller aquariums and a touch tank hold more than two hundred varieties of common and unusual species. Colorful signs challenge kids to ponder and learn about aquarium denizens. The original visitors center expanded its shark focus in the new millennium with a Sharktracker interactive exhibit, shark encounters, and training sessions. A 1,500-gallon Ray Touch Pool sits outside in a chikee hut, and a mollusk exhibit features a preserved twenty-five-foot giant squid from two thousand feet down off the coast of New Zealand. In the Marine Mammal Visitors Center, the main attraction is a floor-to-ceiling glass tank that holds manatees Hugh and Buffett. The center also features a marine mammal rehabilitation tank and a sea turtle exhibit, both of which host some of the world's most fascinating sea creatures. Newest are an exhibit featuring playful river otters and Oh Baby!, which is a look at mating and juvenile species. Open daily 10–5. Admission: $19.75 adults, $18.85 seniors, $14.75 children ages four to twelve.

Scuba Quest (941-366-1530; www.scubaquestusa.com), 1129 S. Tamiami Trail, at Bahia Vista St., Sarasota. With several locations in Florida, this company offers NAUI certification classes, charters, and equipment sales.

WILDERNESS CAMPING ✪ **Oscar Scherer State Park** (941-483-5956; www.floridastateparks.org/park/oscar-scherer), 1843 S. Tamiami Trail, Osprey. This nearly 1,400-acre natural oasis provides ninety-four full-service campsites in a wooded, creek-side setting of palmettos, pines, and venerable moss-draped oaks. The threatened Florida scrub jay seeks refuge here, along with bald eagles, bobcats, river otters, gopher tortoises, and alligators. You can swim in a freshwater lake or enjoy a bird walk, nature and canoe trails, picnicking, and fishing. To reserve a campsite or cabin, call 800-326-3521 or go to the park's website or www.reserveamerica.com.

WILDLIFE SPOTTING **Birds:** The Sarasota coast is the least natural of the Gulf Coast's five regions. Determined bird spotters can find feathered friends at parks and refuges such as Rookery Islands north of Siesta Key (approachable by boat only); Venice Area Audubon Rookery at the end of Annex Road in South Venice, a half-mile south of the junction of US 41 and FL 776; and Oscar Scherer State Park in Osprey, home of the endangered Florida scrub jay.

Dolphins: Dolphins often follow in the wake of tour boats, but they're unpredictable. You can't plan on them; you can only be thrilled and charmed when they do appear. If you learn their feeding schedules, you have a better chance of catching their act.

Nature Preserves & Eco-Attractions:

✪ ✍ **Oscar Scherer State Park** (941-483-5956; www.floridastateparks.org/park/oscar-scherer), 1843 S. Tamiami Trail, Osprey. Home of the threatened Florida scrub jay plus bald eagles, bobcats, river otters, gopher tortoises, and alligators. Experience wildlife in a canoe along a saltwater tidal creek or by hiking an extensive system of nature trails. Take heed: If you swim in the freshwater lake, you may become more closely acquainted with an alligator than you would care to. Also, signs warn of amoeba threats in the warm summer months. The 1,384-acre park offers camping, swimming, canoeing (with rentals and a launch), fishing, and picnicking. Open sunrise to sunset. Admission: $5 per vehicle of two to eight people; $4 per single-occupant vehicle; $2 per pedestrian, cyclist, or extra passenger.

Save Our Seabirds (941-388-3010; www.saveourseabirds.org), 1708 Ken Thompson Pkwy., on City Island, east of Lido Key. This rehab attraction opened in January 2012 near Mote Marine and makes a good companion tour to its neighbor. Visitors can see select cases of the injured birds who cannot be returned to the wild. Open daily 10–5. Admission: $10 adults, $6 children ages four to twelve.

Wildlife Tours & Charters: ✍ **Sarasota Bay Explorers** (941-388-4200; www.sarasotabayexplorers.com), Mote Marine Laboratory Aquarium, 1600 Ken Thompson Pkwy., on City Island, Sarasota. A marine pontoon tour takes you into the Intracoastal waters between City Island and Siesta Key. Features include trawl-net tossing, binocular study of rookery islands, and a marine-biologist narration. Kids love the hands-on quality of this educational tour. The Nature Safari combines a boat ride, beach and nature trail walk, and slog onto a sandbar with waders to collect species with personal nets. It also offers kayak and custom boat tours.

✳ Lodging

Most vacationers on the Sarasota Bay coast gravitate toward the barrier islands. On Siesta Key you won't find many chain hotels; however, you will find accommodations large and small by the score. The other islands have their chains but more mom-and-pops, B&Bs, inns, destination resorts, and privately owned places. On the mainland, especially around the airport, business travelers find no-nonsense franchise and small motels plus a couple of luxury options: Ritz-Carlton and the Hyatt Regency, plus Hotel Indigo, the boutique branch of InterContinental Hotels Group. With downtown Sarasota's renewal, more and more vacationers are choosing mainland accommodations.

Privately owned second homes and condominiums provide another source of accommodations along the Sarasota Bay coast. Vacation brokers who match visitors with such properties are listed under "Home & Condo Rentals" at the end of this section.

I've listed here a well-rounded selection of Sarasota-area accommodations, including a few of the better chain hotels. Toll-free 800, 888, 877, 866, or 855, reservation numbers, where available, are listed after local numbers.

Prices are normally per-person/double occupancy for hotel rooms and per unit for efficiencies, apartments, cottages, suites, and villas. The range spans low- and high-season rates. Many resorts offer off-season packages at special rates and free lodging for children. Pricing does not include the 6 percent Florida sales tax or Sarasota County's 5 percent tourist tax, which is allotted to beach revitalization, arts funding, and tourism promotion. Some large resorts add service gratuities or maid surcharges.

Rate Categories

Inexpensive	Up to $100
Moderate	$100 to $200
Expensive	$200 to $300
Very Expensive	$300 and up

An asterisk after the pricing designation indicates that the rate includes at least a continental breakfast in the cost of lodging and possibly more extensive meal service as noted in the listing.

Note that under the Americans with Disabilities Act (ADA), accommodations built after January 26, 1993, and containing more than five rooms must be usable by people with disabilities. I have indicated only those small places that do not make such allowances.

ACCOMMODATIONS

LIDO KEY

❧ Historic Gulf Beach Resort Motel (941-388-2127 or 800-232-2489; www .gulfbeachsarasota.com), 930 Ben Franklin Dr., Sarasota 34236. Just a couple of doors down from the towering Lido Beach Resort, Gulf Beach takes you to a circa-1950 era of Florida vacationing. All forty-nine rooms of this "condo-tel" are privately owned and therefore decorated with individual personality. They range from tiny motel rooms with mini fridges, microwaves, and coffeemakers to roomy, two-bedroom, gulf-front apartments (Expensive) with all the comforts of home. Three one- and two-story cement-block buildings file between the main

beach drag and the wide sands of Lido. At ground level, there are individual screened porches; on the second floor, a shared balcony. There's a homey feel here. Owners have been coming for years, taking advantage of the welcoming pool, grilling area, shuffleboard, and sunset-perfect view. In 2003, Lido Key businesspeople saved this, Lido's first motel, from demise and high-rise takeover by getting it designated a historic landmark. Moderate.

✒ Lido Beach Resort (941-388-2161 or 866-306-5457 www.lidobeachresort .com), 700 Ben Franklin Dr., Sarasota 34236. Located next to Lido Key's public beach, the 223-unit, smoke-free resort provides attractive accommodations furnished in sand and sea tones, and a wide apron of sand with a beach bar and café in the thick of beach activity. Its tower holds fourteen floors, a city-view restaurant named Lido Beach Grille, and business facilities. Between it and the original four-story hotel squirms a cement creek crossed by wooden walkways with tin-roofed gazebos. Two pools and three whirlpools sit on the shell-scattered beach and have their own beach bar. Another café offers guests breakfast, lunch, and dinner in the lobby. Modern, nicely furnished rooms come with or without full kitchens. Some have a small refrigerator and microwave instead; all have coffeemakers. The resort provides a complimentary shuttle to shopping at St. Armands Circle. Moderate to Expensive.

NOKOMIS

⦿ A Beach Retreat (941-485-8771 or 866-232-2480; www.abeachretreat.com), 105 Casey Key Rd., 34275. A Beach Retreat owns efficiencies and apartments on both the beach and the bay. Fancied up with stucco and red tile roofs, it also has a swimming pool on the bay side, where boat docks and nine units accommodate guests and their vessels. (There's a boat launch next door.) The gulfside rooms, mostly ground level, are steps from a lovely, natural beach that borders the public beach. The twenty-five units—from efficiencies to three-bedroom suites—all have their own look and layout that is largely modern but with some imperfections that lend beach character. All but two have full kitchens, plus there are gas grills for guests' use. Moderate to Expensive.

SARASOTA

✪ (((•))) **Hotel Indigo** (941-487-3800 or 877-8-INDIGO; www.srqhotel.com), 1223 Boulevard of the Arts, 34236. Hotel Indigo provides a stimulating environment in a boutique setting. Trademarks of the boutique brand (a privileged Holiday Inn stepchild) include lobby and room murals that change with the season. An oversize wooden Adirondack-style beach chair and a waterfall under glass decorate the lobby, where you'll also find H2O Bistro, a bright little café serving breakfast, lunch, and dinner. The hotel's ninety-five rooms (twelve of which are suites) are inviting and decorated beach cottage style with hardwood floors, sleeper sofas, and glassed-in shower stalls (no bathtubs). Two large whirlpools—one hot, one cold—are the centerpieces of an outdoor lunching and sunning deck. A coffee-pastry counter and fitness room complete the description of this so-called lifestyle hotel. It is close to Van Wezel Center and downtown attractions. Moderate to Expensive.

♂ (((•))) **Hyatt Regency Sarasota** (941-953-1234 or 800-233-1234; sarasota.regency.hyatt.com), 1000 Blvd. of the Arts, 34236. Inspired by the Florida-style clothing design of Lilly Pulitzer, the décor is all a-splash in pinks, lime greens, oranges, and floral bursts. A soaring atrium makes way for a clubby lounge and refined restaurant Currents, with windows overlooking the water. At the front desk, the staff, in crisp uniforms, is efficient and helpful. Spaciousness and good taste characterize the twelve-story hotel's 282 rooms and twelve suites. They come equipped with flat-screen TVs and iPod docking stations. All have a view of Sarasota Bay or the hotel's marina, which has thirty-two boat slips, plus boat rentals and fishing charters. The full fitness center (which thoughtfully provides refrigerated towels), a zero-entry swimming pool with rock-arched waterfalls and its own grill bar, and close proximity to Van Wezel Performing Arts Hall and downtown attractions make this long-standing landmark a favorite with business and leisure travelers. Moderate to Very Expensive.

✪ ♂ ✎ 🌴 (((•))) **Ritz-Carlton Sarasota** (941-309-2000 or 800-241-3333; www.ritzcarlton.com), 1111 Ritz-Carlton Dr., 34236. One of the first in the Ritz-Carlton line to offer living quarters, this hotel has 266 rooms and suites that deliver all the luxury you expect from the name. Perched on the edge of downtown, it's more of a city hotel than Naples' Ritz-Carlton Florida properties, but it has its own off-site beach club. Some rooms have views of Sarasota Bay, others overlook a neighboring marina. White marble bathrooms, oversize rooms in butterscotch tones, wonderful beds, and wireless Internet make it equally accommodating for leisure and business travelers. Available on the main campus are a spa and fitness center, as well as a swimming pool and burger bar, and restaurants and bars. Small touches such as a free shoeshine service and over-the-top service define the inimitable Ritz experience. For the ultimate experience, book on the club floors and take advantage of the complimentary food and drink services. Nine floors of the seventeen-story high-rise are devoted to resort guests; the rest, plus two other buildings on the mainland and beach are residential units. An hourly shuttle transports guests to shopping on St. Armands Key and the Ritz's Beach Club on Lido Key, which includes a kids' club, pool, locker rooms, and a tropical-cuisine restaurant.

A shuttle also transfers guests to the private Ritz-Carlton Golf Course, which lies about sixteen miles to the east. Expensive to Very Expensive.

SIESTA KEY

Many of Siesta Key's accommodations require a minimum stay (usually one week) during season. The majority of beach accommodations are condos, villas, or homes.

(((•))) **Siesta Key Bungalows** (941-349-9025 or 888-5-SIESTA; www .siestakeybungalows.com), 8212 Midnight Pass Rd., 34242. Appealing to birders and seclusion-seekers, these ten individually decorated, one-bedroom bungalows on Heron Bay feature full kitchens (some with dishwashers), white wicker and rattan furnishings, and double pillow-top mattresses. Hand-painted murals and accents match each bungalow's fitting name, such as Hibiscus, Catamaran, and Dolphin. The living room areas contain sleeper sofas, making the bungalows convenient for families. Kayak and canoe use is complimentary, as well as a swimming pool and a makeshift sand beach. Very Expensive.

☀ (((•))) **Turtle Beach Resort & Inn** (941-349-4554; www.turtlebeachresort.com), 9049 Midnight Pass Rd., 34242. One of Sarasota's Small Superior Lodgings, this place is a real find at the southern, quiet end of the island, a three-minute walk from Turtle Beach. Ten cottages on the bay contain studio, one-bedroom, or two-bedroom accommodations, plus a private hot tub. Each cottage has its own personality, reflected in names such as Rain Forest, Montego Bay, and Southwestern. Modern designer furniture and lamps, objets d'art, and other decorative pieces carry out the themes. Ten units across the street at The Inn at Turtle Beach, designed in a Tommy Bahama mode and also with private outdoor whirlpools, are ideal for couples. Most rooms at both properties have sleeper sofas; all come with kitchen facilities. Bathrobes, TVs, and sherry are provided in each of the cottages, which spread along a lushly landscaped strip. The well-planned property provides private nooks and hammocks along waterside docks and two pools. Use of washers and dryers is free after 4 p.m., and bicycles, canoes, kayaks, rowboats, and beach gear are complimentary for guests' enjoyment. Very romantic, the original resort is nonetheless conducive to families, and pets are permitted. Expensive to Very Expensive (minimum stay required in season; housekeeping is extra).

VENICE

(((•))) **Banyan House Vacation Rentals** (941-484-1385; www.banyanhouse.com), 519 S. Harbor Dr., 34285. In the mid-1920s, architects designed Venice in accordance with its Italian name; homes and buildings are modeled after northern Mediterranean styles. The town's first community swimming pool was located in the backyard of one of the original homes, next to a fledgling banyan tree. Today that small pool, with its now-sprawling tree, resides at the same home, the red-tile-roofed Banyan House. Classic statuary, fountains, multi-hued blossoms, a waterfall stream, a sundeck, a billiard and fitness room, and a hot tub share the property. Formerly a longtime B&B, it still caters to couples. Three two-bedroom upstairs units, each with a private bath, exert their individual personalities. The Palm Room has a fireplace. The Tree House includes a sunny sitting room overlooking the pool. The Sun Deck has an outdoor deck and separate entrance. All units contain at least a small refrigerator; three are efficiencies. Two separate buildings hold five one-bedroom apartments with patios. Deluxe touches include bathrobes in the closet and wine in the fridge. Free use of bicycles allows guests to explore old Venice's nearby shopping mecca and beach. Smoking is not allowed in any of the rooms. (minimum one-week stay required). No handicapped access.

(((•))) **Inn at the Beach** (941-484-8471 or 800-255-8471; www.innatthebeach .com), 725 W. Venice Ave., 34285. This modern resort was built to include Mediterranean architectural overtones and contemporary Florida comfort and décor. Located across the street from the public access to Venice Beach, it is the closest thing Venice offers to a beach resort. The hotel has forty-nine units; many of the second-floor ones overlook the gulf. Its well-maintained rooms have a clean white, light wood, understated floral motif with plantation shutters and tile floors. All contain at least a microwave, dishware, coffee-maker, and mini fridge; efficiencies and one- and two-bedroom suites add full refrigerators, stovetops, dishwashers, and cookware. A small pool with spa and sundeck is tucked behind the hotel in the parking lot—not high on atmosphere. I'd opt for the beach. Continental breakfast is included in the rate. Moderate to Expensive.*

(((•))) **Venice Beach Villas** (941-488-1580 or 800-542-3404; www .venicebeachvillas.com), 501 W. Venice Ave., 34285. A short walk to downtown and quick drive to the beach, this refitted retro property lends itself to exploring the best of Venice. An evening walk takes you to many of the best local restaurants and around a neighborhood canopied with huge oaks carrying armfuls of Spanish moss. Its thirteen units range from studios to two-bedroom units (Expensive in season) and come complete with modern kitchen facilities. One sign of their circa-1940 age is the colorful wall tiles in the bathrooms. A pretty pool, and free use of bikes, "Florida snow shovels" for shark-toothing, and barbecue grills provide the necessaries for a Venice vacation. Its sister property at 505 Menendez holds ten more units and the same pedigree. In season, minimum stay may apply. No housekeeping. Inexpensive to Moderate.

HOME & CONDO RENTALS **Stay on Siesta Vacation Rentals** (941-346-3200 or 888-305-1790; www.stayonsiesta.com), 6604 Midnight Pass Rd., Siesta Key 34242. Condos, villas, and homes to rent on the island.

RV RESORTS **Camp Venice Retreat** (941-488-0850; www.campvenice.com), 4085 E. Venice Ave., Venice 34292, at exit 191 off I-75. This campground has full hookups and waterfront sites, plus tent sites and cabin rentals. Amenities include security gates, a heated swimming pool, shuffleboard, horseshoes, a nature trail, fishing, boat and canoe rentals, a laundry room, and a supply store.

Turtle Beach Campground (941-349-3839), 8862 Midnight Pass Rd., Sarasota 34242. Thirty-nine sites for tents and RVs near the beach. Electric and cable TV hookups.

✱ Where to Eat

Sarasota's nonchain restaurants have banded together to fight chain-restaurant homogeneity and build their promotional muscle. Look for restaurants that display the "Eat Like a Local" logo (www . dineoriginal.com). The organization hosts the annual Forks & Corks food and wine festival and participates strongly in June's two-week Savor Sarasota.

For Sarasotans, eating out is as much a cultural event as attending the opera. It is often an inextricable part of an evening at the theater or a gallery opening. Sarasotans take dining out quite seriously and keep restaurants full, even off-season. Their enthusiasm for newness makes local kitchens more innovative than those of their neighbors to the south. The town also counts one of the highest concentrations of Zagat-rated restaurants in Florida. Sarasota slides along the cutting edge of New World cuisine while maintaining classic favorites that range from rickety oyster bars to French cafés.

The following listings span the diversity of Sarasota Bay coast cuisine in these price categories:

Inexpensive	Up to $15
Moderate	$15 to $25
Expensive	$25 to $35
Very Expensive	$35 or more

Cost categories are based on the range of dinner entrée prices or, if dinner is not served, of lunch entrées.

Note: Florida law forbids smoking inside all restaurants and bars serving food. Smoking is permitted only in restaurants with outdoor seating.

ANNA MARIA ISLAND

CASEY KEY

🦐 🐟 **Casey Key Fish House** (941-966-1901; www.caseykeyfishhouse.com), 801 Blackburn Point Rd., Osprey. Casey Key Fish House does not attempt to dazzle its boat- and drive-in customers with pretensions. Everyone's happy to find good food reasonably priced, a perennially cheerful staff, fresh seafood with little fuss but lots of freshness, and a view of the water and a great blue heron or two for atmosphere. Well, to be fair, there is an aquarium and a mounted dolphinfish as "decorator touches," but this place is about the seafood. The laminated, all-day menu warns that patience is a virtue if you wish food cooked to order. It then goes on to list standard Florida fish-house fare such as baskets of crab cakes, battered shrimp, fish and chips, and grouper sandwiches. Dinners dress it up a little with such choices as diver scallops with citrus sauce or fresh grilled salmon with cucumber-dill sauce. The blackboard lists the day's catches (some in the Expensive category), which are available after 4 p.m. and are served with garlic bread and steamed veggies on a plastic plate. Don't be fooled by these simplicities. My recent luncheon affair with grilled calamari salad special resulted in lots of tender squid atop greens with a well-balanced balsamic vinaigrette—a totally unexpected pleasure. If you can't fit it in, take some Key lime pie to go, because it's way up there on the "best" scale with just the right balance of sweet to tart and a light, creamy consistency. Inexpensive to Moderate. No reservations.

LAKEWOOD RANCH

✪ **Lucky Pelican Bistro** (941-907-0589; luckypelicanbistro.com), 6239 Lake Osprey Dr. Honestly? This place feels more like an old Florida seafood house than a bistro. In any case, it's a true find on the eastern part of town that is up and coming as a shopping, dining, and recreation destination. Lucky Pelican takes its seafood pedigree cues from New England as well as Florida. It appears to always be bustling, but I was lucky to grab a seat at the counter on a recent dinnertime visit. From the counter, I could watch the fresh bread come out of the oven, kitchen staff steadily shucking oysters and preparing fresh catches from the seafood market, and servers doing an amazing job of keeping diners happy in an atmosphere of noise and chaos. The breadth of the menu equally amazes. At lunch, order a chicken Cobb or seared tuna salad, an "ocean burrito" or any number of sandwiches, or an entrée such as sautéed mussels or shrimp Veracruz. Mussels are something of a specialty, served in pots Rockefeller, Thai, or Italian style. I ordered the ocean burrito, a specialty also appearing on the dinner menu. It comes stuffed with shrimp, cod, crawfish, corn salsa, and jambalaya rice. Other specialties: bacon-wrapped swordfish marsala, Out East Lobster Bake, oyster roast, and snow and king crab. The menus also list meat and vegetarian dishes and martinis and other specialty cocktails. Inexpensive to Moderate. No reservations.

LIDO KEY

🐟 **New Pass Baithouse & Grill** (941-388-3050; www.newpassgrill.com), 1505 Ken Thompson Pkwy., Sarasota, on City Island at New Pass Bridge. Here's a place to grab a quick breakfast or lunch if you're out boating or visiting Mote Marine Laboratory Aquarium. Step up to the window; order your egg sandwich, burger, hot dog, clam basket, fish and chips, sub, or other cold sandwich; then meander off to settle onto a jumbled selection of picnic tables and dock counter space along the water at New Pass. Watch the fleets of herons, egrets, pelicans, and boats while you wait for your name to be called. The burgers are legendary and the prices are unbeatable. Afterward, troll the bait-shop tanks and shelves for fishing supplies and leave with the satisfaction that a place such as this still exists (and has since 1929!). Open daily 7–5. Inexpensive. No reservations or handicapped access.

✪ 🐟 **Old Salty Dog** (941-388-4311), 1601B Ken Thompson Pkwy., Sarasota, on City Island. A spin-off of the Siesta Key original, this one has a more properly salty setting: a tin-roofed, red stucco building tucked into a marina in the shadow of the Longboat Key bridge. If you sit outside on the breezy patios, you'll be entertained by boaters, WaveRunners, and water-skiers. The menu lists such fun casual eats as Buffalo wings, New England clam chowder, potato skins with jerk sauce and crabmeat, peel-and-eat shrimp, burgers, fish and chips, shrimp or oyster po'boys, baby back ribs, fresh catch dinners (charbroiled or deep-fried), and the trademark Salty Dog—beer-battered and deep-fried, and not for the faint of heart). We like the wide selection of beer it offers, on tap as well as bottled. Kids like that you don't have to wait long for your food. Inexpensive to Moderate. No reservations.

NOKOMIS

✪ 🐟 🐾 ♿ **Captain Eddie's Seafood Restaurant** (941-484-4372; www .captaineddiesseafood.com), 107 Colonia Ln. E. Ask anyone around the Venice-Nokomis-Osprey area where to get fresh seafood, and nine out of ten will recommend, without pause, Captain Eddie's. The restaurant began as a fish market that took over a convenience store and set up a few picnic tables to fill the space. Those picnic tables came to be in such great demand that the market eventually grew into a restaurant where the locals know they can get their money's worth in fresh fish. A few years ago, to keep up with the demand, Eddie's expanded to a new adjacent dining room and tiki bar. The renovation covered the walls in rough-hewn wood siding and added a modern look, but the long tables and casual atmosphere abide. This is a true Florida fish house—my favorite brand of dining. The hostess calls most of the patrons by name. The menu carries a lot of fried-fish items, such as shrimp, catfish, hogfish, frog legs, and oysters (but fried right and in canola oil) as well as broiled options. After an appetizer of alligator bites, I tried a broiled grouper sandwich that was the best I've tasted since my husband came home from a deep-sea fishing trip. Broiled grouper can be bland, but this was tastefully prepared, served on a yummy hoagie in a plastic basket. Moderate. No reservations.

ST. ARMANDS CIRCLE

✪ 🐾 **Café L'Europe** (941-388-4415; www .cafeleurope.net), 431 St. Armands Circle. Café L'Europe remains a shining star—after nearly forty years—that offers French classics with a New Age tweak. Dark woods and redbrick archways set an atmosphere that's warm in an inviting way, yet offers a cool, cellarlike break from Florida heat. When the weather allows, you can also sit outdoors on the patio (with your dogs, who have their own menu) to sip your French pinot blanc and sample such stunning selections as the flambéed shrimp Pernod appetizer, bourbon pecan salad, veal piccata, honey-curry sea bass, signature brandied duckling, potato-crusted grouper, or tableside chateaubriand for two. Expensive to Very Expensive. Reservations accepted for both lunch and dinner.

Surf Shack Coastal Kitchen (941-960-1122, www.surfshackkitchen.com), 326 John Ringling Blvd., St. Armands Circle. It touts "gourmet tacos"—blackened mahi mahi, filet mignon, bangin' shrimp, and such—but you won't want to miss the Catie's Corn Bread. It claims to be the "best corn bread ever," and I agree. And honestly, practically everything on the menu will wow you. Wings come with a choice of seven different sauces from Black Ale BBQ to orange ginger. You can order your guac with lobster in it and your Caesar salad with pasta. Burgers are juicy, and sandwiches include pulled chicken on brioche with cheddar, blackened ribeye, and a grilled chicken bacon wrap with pomegranate vinaigrette.

Surf Shack, with its cool vibe and street seating, is great for casual bar eats or a break from St. Armands Circle shopping, but also puts a selection of well-crafted entrees out there: grilled swordfish with shrimp and avocado, jerk-braised baby back ribs, and Mongolian chicken skillet. Moderate to Expensive. No reservations.

SARASOTA

Bijou Café (941-366-8111; www.bijoucafe .net), 1287 First St., at Pineapple Ave. Situated in the midst of the theater and arts district, the Bijou is the pick of the pre- and posttheater crowd and upper-echelon business community of Sarasota. Small and simply decorated, only modern art, some sleek floral arrangements, and lavish crown molding embellish. Linen dresses the tables, even at lunch, when the clientele is equally dressed up. The eclectic menu offers choices from Continental, New Orleans, African, and American cuisine, from fruit soup to duck liver mousse. One of my favorite dishes, shrimp Piri-Piri, is a

GRAB A BEER AND WIND DOWN AT THE SURF SHACK

classic example of how chef/owner Jean-Pierre Knaggs perfectly balances flavors to create entirely fresh taste sensations. It is mildly spicy with citrus tones, and appears on both the lunch and dinner menus. Recently I tried grilled, house-made African sausage with grits, grilled tomato, and a fruit sauce—another winner. Dinner specialties include roast duck stuffed with fruit, salmon pan roasted with fennel, lamb shank, bouillabaise, and sweetbreads. The *pommes gratin dauphinois* with Gruyère is a signature side dish, available à la carte. Desserts, made in-house, have an excellent reputation. Lunch draws a brisk crowd and can include dishes such as braised short ribs with horseradish cream, crab cakes rémoulade, and wild mushroom and grilled Gruyère cheese sandwich. Moderate to Expensive. Reservations recommended. Closed Sunday in summer, Saturday and Sunday for lunch year-round.

🍴 **Café Baci** (941-921-4848; www . cafebacisarasota.com.), 4001 S. Tamiami Trail. Affordably dressy, Café Baci has a porte cochere out front and linens on the tables (even at lunch) inside; the business clientele and older crowd wear nice clothes; and the Tuscan-Roman specialties dwell in the realm of fine cuisine. Yet its location on plebeian South Tamiami Trail, away from Sarasota's centers of chichi, allows for a reasonably priced menu. Lunch is especially popular with locals, who squeeze the parking lot full to capacity. I enjoy lunch there, too; it imparts a bit of affordable elegance in the middle of a hectic day alongside a road-rage street. Soothing and stylish in atmosphere, its food has kept it at the head of growing Italian competition since it opened in 1991. Many of the dinner entrées are available in smaller portions and prices at lunchtime. Dishes we have tried and loved include Italian wedding soup; a tasty meatball dish on special; *ravioli di funghi,* exquisite homemade half-moon pasta pockets filled with delicately creamed wild

mushrooms and topped with a buttery tomato cream sauce; *pollo* Baci, a divine version of chicken *francese* with bursts of flavor from sun-dried tomatoes and lemon wine butter sauce; and fluffy tiramisu. There are also panini and crepes. Both lunch and dinner menus touch on the four major Italian food groups: pasta, veal, chicken, and seafood. These are tended with a creative hand. Here's a taste: grilled salmon with spinach pesto risotto; a sampler of veal *piccata, marsala,* and *sarda*; and chicken parmagiana. Seasonal luncheon and early dinner specials add to the value of this experience. The extensive wine list has received the *Wine Spectator* Award of Excellence. Inexpensive to Moderate. Reservations recommended for dinner. Closed for lunch Saturday and Sunday, also all day Monday during the summer. Handicapped access in the restaurant but not the restrooms.

✪ **Libby's Café + Bar** (941-487-7300; www.libbyscafebar.com), 1917 S. Osprey Ave., Sarasota. At Libby's, I love noshing from a variety of "small" plates, such as whole grain flatbread with cauliflower, brie, and fig jam; cheesesteak egg roll; vegan tomato bisque with green soybean pesto; or salmon salad with baby kale and goji berry vinaigrette, to name a few. In the "handheld" department, you might find a Reubentarian—a wild mushroom Reuben with sweet and sour cabbage—or a truffled Kobe meatloaf club with prosciutto and roasted mushrooms. Lunchtime also brings a selection of $10 meals with choice of salad or tomato bisque and unusual sandwiches such as the deviled egg salad English muffin. Interesting dinner selections: maple and Dijon glazed salmon, four cheese and pear tortelloni, crispy shrimp and scallops, and black grouper white miso with kimchee fried rice. Both menus offer a Simply Grilled Gluten Free section listing steak, seafood, and vegetarian dishes. For dessert, I've loved Libby's Key lime pie with gummy bears and warm drunken peach crostata. Moderate. Reservations accepted.

Michael's on East (941-366-0007; www.bestfood.com), 1212 East Ave. S., in Midtown Plaza at Bahia Vista St. and Tamiami Trail. Michael Klauber is a well-respected name in Sarasota culinary circles. He created an immediate sensation when he opened Michael's back in 1987, and it remains the benchmark of cutting-edge cuisine and atmosphere. Oh so art deco, its wavy motif is devoid of square corners. You can dine around the circular bar or in two other rooms separated by scrims and etched glass (wavy, of course, and *très chic*). On the lunch menu, start with calamari or salmon crostini. If your idea of calamari has anything to do with rubber bands, try Michael's cornmeal-battered, hand-breaded version—tender to a "T" and complemented with Parma ham, Manchego cheese, olive salad, and mustard aioli. The lunch menu also features a lengthy selection of glorious salads, such as warm chicken on greens with dried cranberries, candied pecans, and goat cheese. Such are the touches that make Michael's a consistent winner. Specialties on the dinner menu include porcini-rubbed rack of lamb, lemongrass-grilled ahi tuna, and pan-roasted crab cakes with truffle-roasted potatoes. Lobster Pot Fridays serve up two Maine lobsters, mussels, clams, and the fixings for $38.95 each. For dessert, try the Chocolate Blackout Cake or malva pudding with crème anglais and mango ice cream. Michael's is also known for its extensive wine list, which features a generous selection of wines by the glass, including sparkling varieties. Moderate to Very Expensive. Reservations recommended for lunch and dinner.

Nancy's Bar-B-Q (941-366-2271; www.nancysbarbq.com), 301 S. Pineapple Ave., at Burns Square. Refreshingly, one of the newest additions to the downtown dining scene takes a detour into affordable territory. Occupying a former-life gas station, it has the casual, picnic-table air that seems to be law when it comes to good barbecue joints. Outside, an old tractor and other rural memorabilia decorate the grounds; inside you'll notice four clocks on the wall labeled "pork," "chicken," "ribs," and "brisket." That's how Nancy clocks her specialties, prepared Carolina-style smoked. Pulled pork rules the roost and tastes like almost heaven (no wait, that's West Virginia). Everything is too good to stop eating, including the ribs, beef brisket, sausages, chicken, and chilled salmon. Two squeezers of house sauce let you dress your meat sweet and tangy or spicy chipotle style. The big difference here is in the sides and desserts. Edamame succotash, baked mac 'n' cheese, Brunswick stew, sesame crunch slaw, and cool cucumber salad boost its creative factor. But don't pass up nouveau for the good old baked beans—the best I've tasted in years outside of my own kitchen. Then there are derby pie, red velvet cake, whoopee pies, and pineapple rum upside-down cake among the dessert options. Nancy is just clever enough to not mess with a good thing while somehow making it all better. Inexpensive. No reservations. Closed Sunday.

Owen's Fish Camp (941-951-6936; www.owensfishcamp.com), 516 Burns Ct., Sarasota. I couldn't decide what to eat first on my plate: the pan-fried softshell crab was tender and sweet; the collard greens, vinegary and piquant; the succotash, multidimensional and cumin-spiced. Owen's relies on the Old South style of coastal fish camps that were the progenitors of Florida's resort industry. With its quirky, deliberately distressed fish-shack décor and devotion to freshness, it has remained a downtown darling amid serious competition of late. But in contrast to the contenders, its hostess wears short shorts, chomps on gum, and gabs with her friends. Who cares when you are concentrating on whether to order pasta jambalaya, oyster po'boy, Low Country boil, cornmeal-crusted catfish, or the day's catch? Then there are the distractions: jars of boiled hot roadside peanuts or fried dill pickles, Bloody Mary oyster shooters, and bourbon pecan pie. Not to mention the menu quips, such as, "There are some days when I think I'm going to die from an overdose of satisfaction"—Salvador Dalí. I knew how he felt as I walked out of Owen's and shot a picture of the goofy retro tourist sculpture in a lawn chair out front. Inexpensive to Moderate. No reservations. Closed for lunch.

🦪 🚶‍♂️ ♿ **Phillippi Creek Village Oyster Bar** (941-925-4444; www.creekseafood .com), 5353 S. Tamiami Trail. In Sarasota they call their fish houses "oyster bars," and Phillippi Creek is one of the oldest. Combo pot appetizers are a specialty of the house and include pans full of steamed oysters, clams, or mussels, plus corn on the cob. We've eaten here on several occasions; it's my husband's first choice for casual dining when we're in town. He loves the gooey-thick clam chowder and fried oyster sandwich. I typically pick the blackened grouper sandwich, which comes with a mustardy tartar sauce. Baked or fried seafood platters feature shrimp, softshell crab, catfish, alligator, flounder, and combinations. You have your choice of settings here: either indoors, glassed-in with a boathouse motif, or out in the breeze on the dry dock. Either way, you get a backwater view and the kind of service that puts you at ease. Inexpensive to Expensive. No reservations.

✪ **Selva Sarasota** (941-362-4427; www.selvagrill.com), 1345 Main St. This downtown sensation claims Peru as its country of culinary inspiration, but the good looks of its exotic dining rooms, clientele, and kitchen art bespeak much deeper dimensions. Of course, there is the ubiquitous selection of ceviches, a signature Peruvian creation. The Triologia presents three different mixtures of fish and shrimp served in three large spoons with wisps of fried plantain and yucca. Tapas include Argentinian empanadas and Peruvian bouillabaise.

Meat and seafood get equal time on the entrées menu. The menu describes *arroz con pato* as a gourmet version of a traditional duck-breast dish of northern Peru with green pea and beer risotto, and most of the dishes are likewise Peruvian dressed up for discriminating American palates. The mirin-roasted sea bass, for instance, demonstrates both the Eastern influence with sautéed bok choy, and the prevalence of corn in the diet with a smooth, slightly sweet corn custard. The silky creaminess of the fish nearly matched that of the flan. Dessert tempts with such selections as *pastel de tres leches*, and peaches and cream bread pudding with bourbon. In the main dining room, the atmosphere is lively with the backdrop of a swirly wall that changes color thanks to the lighting. Expensive to Very Expensive. Reservations accepted.

State Street Eating House + Cocktails (941-951-1533; www.statestreetsrq.com), 1533 State St. Nestled among State Street's gallery scene in a somewhat hidden location, this smart eatery sets tables in a chic industrial atmosphere that spills out onto the street. On a rainy day, I ducked into to the small café and immediately felt welcomed as I took a seat at the gleaming bar. Soup was in order that wet afternoon, so I started with the green pea choice, which intrigued me with its promise of parmesan crema, crispy pear, and preserved lemon. It was by far the most unusual rendition I've tasted, so multi-textured in flavor. The grilled cheese sandwich, too, eschewed the ordinary with a slice of tomato built in, sea salt, and cracked pepper on nice artisanal bread. The menus are not extensive, but they make up for that with well-crafted dishes such as a House Jarred Tuna Salad—open faced with melted cheddar—and a chickpea-yellow zucchini burger with savory sumac-tomato spread for lunch. For dinner, a blue cheese plate comes with slow-poached mangos, and a veggie plate consists of roasted radish, curried garbanzo beans, marinated

MUST SEE

Yoder's (941-955-7771; www.yodersrestaurant.com), 3434 Bahia Vista St. A happy outgrowth of the Amish/Mennonite community in Sarasota, homestyle restaurants throughout the area feature comfort-food goodness. Expect farmhouse-style freshness at the table. Yoder's sits squarely in the midst of the Pinecraft Amish community, and you know it's the real thing because many of the patrons are wearing long beards and suspenders or white bonnets and full-body aprons over their plain dresses. Amish photography, art, quilts, and other handiwork decorate the dining room, which is almost always full. Although you'll find typical sandwiches and hamburgers, Midwestern comfort food predominantly makes up the all-day menu and its daily specials: fried chicken, liver and onions, turkey and dressing, pulled smoked pork, meat loaf, and roast beef. There's no replacement for homemade goodness, and even my meat loaf sandwich benefited from red juicy tomatoes and home-baked bread. At breakfast, who could resist the apple fritter French toast? Made-from-scratch pies—more than thirty varieties—are the claim to local fame here, and there's a window where fans come to pick up their whole cream or baked pies. I can vouch for the rhubarb; tart and encased in a crumbly, sugar-glazed crust, it is the perfect ending to a meal like my German mother would have made. Inexpensive. No reservations. Closed Sunday.

A SLICE OF RHUBARB PIE A LA MODE

kohlrabi, and artichoke fava bean puree. House-made meatloaf and New York strip pleases carnivores, while seafood-lovers find snapper with red and yellow pepper coulis and grilled kohlrabi or a seafood grill in tomato seafood fumet. For weekend brunch, there's sweet potato pancakes; a pork belly, sausage, potato cake, roasted kale, and egg skillet; and frosted flake crusted French toast. Moderate to Expensive. Reservations for larger parties only, but call-ahead text update waiting list is available.

SIESTA KEY

Captain Curt's Crab & Oyster Bar (941-349-3885; www.captaincurts.com), 1200 Old Stickney Point Rd. Captain Curt's complex takes up a good part of the block here near the south bridge in Siesta. Besides the blessedly air-conditioned main restaurant, there are a tiki bar, backroom saloon, and gift shop. Captain Curt's claims to be the island's oldest restaurant and to have the best clam chowder in the world. I can attest only to the latter. Besides my thumbs-up, it has won the International Great Chowder Cook-Off in Newport, Rhode Island. As for its age, it's been serving typical Old Florida–style (i.e., raw and fried) seafood since 1979. It does some nonseafood items, including a good old Midwestern pork tenderloin sandwich (try it with a dousing of Curt's hot sauce) and ribs. On the fancier side, there are grilled mahi-mahi, crab cakes, and seafood combos. The atmosphere is organized chaos,

THE TOWN THE CIRCUS BUILT

The circus comes as close to being the world in microcosm as anything I know; in a way it puts all the rest of show business in the shade. Its magic is universal and complex.
—E. B. White, Ring of Times, 1956

Legend has it that Bird Key and St. Armands Key, two of Sarasota's barrier islands, became John Ringling's possessions in a poker game. Tales of the circus master's influence on the area's development have grown to mythic proportions: elephants that built bridges, freaks who built fortunes, and an eccentric who built himself an Italian palace. However true the legends, during the twenty years after John Ringling came to Sarasota to house his circus here in wintertime, he demonstrated a three-ring influence over the city and its barrier islands.

After falling in love with the fledgling mainland village and purchasing real estate offshore, Ringling erected his lavish mansion, Cà d'Zan ("House of John" in an Italian dialect), modeled after a Venetian Gothic palazzo. He also began the construction of a causeway to Lido Key by filling and dredging, and he dreamed of a city park and a shoppers' haven on St. Armands Key. For Longboat Key he envisioned a world-class hotel. With unbridled fervor he set out during his worldwide travels to acquire a fine collection of Baroque art for public display in a museum.

The dreams Ringling failed to realize before he died in 1936 were not abandoned. The causeway was completed and donated to the state. St. Armands Circle today is famed for its shops. The steel skeleton of what was to be the world's finest hotel sat rusting on Longboat Key for years until it was reborn as a modern resort. The Ringling complex encompasses acres of bayside estate, and its collection and grounds include Baroque statuary, original Rubens masterpieces, a rose garden, the restored mansion Cà d'Zan, circus museums, and an antique Italian theater.

Aside from John Ringling's concrete legacy to Sarasota, he bequeathed an undying commitment to beauty, fantasy, art, and showmanship. The circus remains an important industry in Sarasota—in fact, at the high school, circus is an extracurricular activity, like football. Theaters and galleries thrive, thanks to Ringling's patronage of the arts. Without his influence, the entire coast might well have remained a cultural frontier for many more decades.

picnic tables, and friendly. Inexpensive. No reservations.

✪ **Ophelia's on the Bay** (941-349-2212; www.opheliasonthebay.net), 9105 Midnight Pass Rd. For twenty years and counting, this lovely spot on Little Sarasota Bay at Siesta Key's quiet southern end has meant fine dining with a creative streak. The Caesar salad, for instance, comes with buttermilk garlic dressing and pancetta. The menu changes nightly, often using a template of proteins whose preparation the kitchen varies. On my last visit, the bigeye tuna was rare-seared, sliced, arranged upon a slab of grilled watermelon, and topped with Meyer lemon pesto. The diver scallops on that occasion came with sweet corn coulis, shallot marmalade, roasted garlic and

tomato concasse, and herb risotto. Rock shrimp, Angus filet mignon, Faroe Island salmon, and duckling receive equally alluring treatments. Save room for the Key lime pie, infused with coconut and rum with mango coulis and butter cream. Sunday brunch offerings include raw bar, breakfast, and lunch items. Expensive to Very Expensive. Reservations suggested. No lunch.

VENICE

(((ᵧ))) **Cedar Reef Fish Camp** (941-451-8564; www.cedarreef.com), 4167 S. Tamiami Tr., Venice. An old-Florida style fish house was the last place I expected to find fresh flowers in a vase in the ladies' room, but there they were. Just one of many good surprises in store at Cedar Reef Fish Camp, a surfer's-theme indoor-outdoor restaurant in a South Venice strip mall. A spin-off of another in Bradenton, it knows its way around seafood and then some. The blackened shrimp in my shrimp and grits were done perfectly, and I'm a stickler about overdone shrimp. You can order a regular or New Orleans–style with andouille. New Orleans weighs in here and there throughout the wide-ranging menu: alligator chowder, rich boy (a twist on po' boy), and fried chicken with andouille sausage. The all-day menu covers baked oysters, crab legs, pasta, salads, burgers, and seafood combos. Choose the day's fresh catch along with preparation and sauce, or you can pick from the daily specials menu. Sunday's homemade lobster lasagna is $10.90. The selection of craft beers and wine is equally extensive. But whatever you do, save room for the best peanut butter pie you'll ever put in your mouth. Inexpensive to Moderate. No reservations.

✪ **The Crow's Nest** (941-484-9551; www.crowsnest-venice.com), 1968 Tarpon Center Dr. A seaworthy Venice institution, it serves the finer side of fresh seafood, including specialties such as lobster tail, walnut-crusted salmon, crab cakes, and shrimp and grits. Meat lovers can choose from grilled rib eye with Gorgonzola butter, chicken saltimbocca, and surf-and-turf selections. Service is sometimes a little off, but a lot can be forgiven when you're staring out at yachts bobbing in the harbor. The two-story, window-lined dining room has a stateroom-level nautical feel. Downstairs in the faintly lit tavern, you can order sandwiches and pub fare all day, plus meatloaf, steak, and fried seafood baskets. In season, be sure to make reservations well in advance, because this place has a big local following. Moderate to Expensive.

Made in Italy (941-488-8282), 117 W. Venice Ave. In a town named Venice, you can bet there's no shortage of Italian restaurants, but while on a recent summer day most local restaurants sat

BACK BAY VIEWS SWEETEN THE DINING EXPERIENCE AT OPHELIA'S ON THE BAY

MUST SEE

Snook Haven (941-485-7221; www.snookhaven.com), 5000 E. Venice Ave., Venice, close to exit 191 off I-75. More than a restaurant, this experience takes you to rural old Florida along the scenic Myakka River. Rent a kayak to paddle along the undeveloped river, then feed your hunger with house-smoked barbecue and Cracker specialties such as fried catfish and smoked-fried frog legs. I can personally recommend the smoked pulled pork taco with homemade chips. Combo platters give you a choice of meats: beef brisket, pulled pork, smoked turkey, smoked pork loin, kielbasa, smoked chicken, and smoked spare ribs. For non-meat-eaters, there's fried shrimp, smoked salmon taco, and even smoked vegetarian wrap. Snook Haven hosts live banjo music every Thursday afternoon and other live music Thursday through Sunday. The bar carries more than twenty craft beers—perfect for sipping as you watch for gators in the river. Inexpensive. No reservations.

TAKE A TRIP BACK IN TIME AT SNOOK HAVEN

empty, this new one was bustling. Evidently word has spread quickly about the sleek modern space that spills out onto the sidewalk with scents from its wood-fired oven. Pizzas for two come in such flavors as the signature tomato sauce, mozzarella, prosciutto, arugula, and Parmesan; or the Caprina, with sauce, goat cheese, pancetta, and basil pesto. The kitchen also does justice to its pasta dishes, as I discovered when I ordered the lasagna alla bolognese. Enough for two, its béchamel sauce had a hint of nutmeg and melded marvelously with the cheese and meat sauce. Ciabatta

sandwiches, pressed panini (one with grilled chicken, caramelized onions, tomato, smoked mozzarella, and basil pesto); veal, lamb, chicken, and seafood dishes; antipasti; and sweet temptations ensure everyone finds at least one thing to choose.

The Soda Fountain (941-488-7600; sodafountainofvenice.com), 349 W. Venice Ave. Reward yourself with a downtown shopping break at this throwback treat. Your inner and outer child(ren) will thank you. Decorated like an old-fashioned soda fountain, with black-and-white checked floors and chrome-edged swivel stools at the counter, it serves all-American sandwiches and burgers. These, however, are secondary to the main course: ice cream. Have it scooped up in a cone, slathered with syrup in a sundae, or whizzed in a canister as a shake or malted. The menu lists nine varieties of quarter-pound beef hot dogs, including the Hawaiian dog with pineapple, and the sloppy dog. Other offerings range from pizza, wraps, and hot sandwiches to chicken Caesar salad. Inexpensive. No reservations.

BAKERIES **Croissant & Co. French Artisan Bakery & Café** (941-480-1700), 323 W. Venice Ave., Venice). A wonderful sensory treat of éclairs, tartes, quiches, bread, croissants, and other French delicacies. Sandwiches come on the bakery's fresh-baked bread.

C'est La Vie (941-906-9575; www .cestlaviesarasota.com), 1553 Main St., Sarasota. This authentic French bakery holds showcases full of breads, pastries, tarts, cake, and other sweets. It also serves breakfast and lunch at sidewalk tables and inside the café, featuring crepes, quiche, and French-style sandwiches.

Der Dutchman (941-955-8007; www .derdutchman.com), 3713 Bahia St., Sarasota. Wonderful breads, cakes, pies, cookies, and pastries, plus unusual jellies, preserves, and other edibles.

Island Gluten Free Bakery (941-923-0200; www.islandgfbakery.com), 1880 Stickney Point Rd., Sarasota. Muffins, scones, cookies, cakes, pies, breads, and sandwiches all made without gluten. Also dairy- and casein-free and vegan products.

Pastry Art (941-955-7545; www . pastryartbakerycafe.com), 1512 Main St., Sarasota. Exquisite pastries, cakes in every flavor, tortes, truffles, cookies, cheesecakes, European-style fruit tarts, French-press coffees, espressos, and sandwiches and salads. A locals' favorite.

A Taste of Germany (941-346-1800; www.atasteofgermany.net), 6575 Midnight Pass Rd., Siesta Key. German breads, pretzels, and liquor cakes, plus deli sandwiches on homemade bread, homemade soups, and coffee.

BREAKFAST **Another Broken Egg** (941-346-2750; www. anotherbrokenegg.com), 140 Avenida Messina, Siesta Key. Biscuit beignets, blackberry grits, benedict Oscar, black bean benedict, muffins, omelets, and egg skillets. Also lunch.

Blue Dolphin Café (941-383-4728; www.bluedolphincafe.com), 5370 Gulf of Mexico Dr. #101, at the Centre Shops, Longboat Key; and (941-388-5586), 470 John Ringling Blvd., at St. Armands Circle, Sarasota. Stylish eatery serving banana granola pancakes, Belgian waffles, omelets (try the spinach-feta), and specials such as peach-pecan croissant French toast. Breakfast and lunch are served throughout its open hours, 7–3.

🐾 (📶) **Breakfast Cottage** (941-313-9529; www.thebreakfastcottage.com), 2301 Tamiami Trail, Nokomis. Bright, cheery, and delicious is the motto here: all true. It serves local coffee, omelets, and such unusual offerings as gluten-free French toast, bacon crumble chocolate chip pancakes, and lobster and shrimp benedict. Also lunch until 2 p.m.

♻ (📶) **Station 400** (941-906-1400; www.station400.com), 400 N. Lemon Ave., Sarasota. In the setting of a reconstructed historic train station and courtyard, struggle to choose between creative omelets, benedicts, and pancakes with a French flair—bacon and salted caramel with orange butter, coconut custard with vanilla bean syrup, and lemon curd with fresh blackberries, to name a few.

BREWERIES, WINERIES, DISTILLERIES **Drum Circle Distilling** (941-702-8143; www.drumcircledistilling .com), 2212 Industrial Blvd., Sarasota. Maker of award-winning Siesta Key rums, this distillery is tucked away on the east side of town. It conducts free forty-minute tours and tastings in an indoor tiki setting. Check the website for tour times and to make reservations.

JDubs Brewing Company (941-955-2739; www.jdubsbrewing.com), 1215 Mango Ave., Sarasota. Distributed regionally, JDubs serves exclusive small-batch brews in its taproom and patio, where food trucks provide sustenance.

Sarasota Brewing Co. (941-925-2337; www.sarasotabrewing.com), 6607 Gateway Ave., Sarasota. This longtime microbrewery sells its beer only on the premises—a working class bar serving food and six different home brews.

CANDY & ICE CREAM **Bentley's Homemade Ice Cream** (941-486-1816; www.bentleysicecream.com), 720 Albee Rd., Nokomis. Hard and soft-serve ice cream, sorbet, gelato, and ice-cream cakes.

⌐ **Big Olaf Creamery** (941-349-9392), 5208 Ocean Blvd., Siesta Key. A vintage purveyor of fresh fudge, handmade waffle cones, homemade ice cream, sugar-free ice cream, frozen yogurt, espresso, and cappuccino, this Sarasota Amish-based ice-cream operation began at this shop.

⌐ **Ciao Gelato** (941-445-5840), 317A Venice Ave. W., Venice. Gelato and sorbet by the scoop and in shakes, plus specialty coffees, cannoli, and other sweets.

⌐ **ScoopDaddy's** (941-388-1650;), 19-C N. Blvd. of the Presidents, at St. Armands Circle, Sarasota. Combines the nostalgia of a soda fountain and retro '50s entertainment; features a jukebox and reproduction gifts.

COFFEE & TEA **Burns Court Café** (941-312-6633; www.burnscourtcafe.com), 401 S. Pineapple Ave., Sarasota) A cozy corner that feels like Paris, with good coffee, cappuccino, lattes, and tea; plus fresh quiche, juices, and yogurt shakes.

Venice Wine & Coffee Company (941-484-3667; www.venicewineandcoffeecompany.com), 201 W. Venice Ave.,Venice. Buy gourmet coffee by the bag or cup at the espresso bar.

Also teas, wine, spices, and hard-to-find gourmet food items.

Kahwa Coffee Roasting (941-203-8971; www.kahwacoffee.com), 1487 Second St., Sarasota. Feeling a bit like a retro beatnik hangout, this downtown coffeehouse serves the finest signature blends of coffee roasted in Florida.

((•)) **The Local Bean** (941-870-2671;), 5138 Ocean Blvd., in Siesta Key Village, Sarasota. Espresso, lattes, more than twenty loose-leaf teas, smoothies, and bakery goods. Free WiFi access.

DELI & SPECIALTY FOODS **Columbia Gift Shop** (941-388-1026; www.columbiarestaurant.com), 411 St. Armands Circle, Sarasota. Dressings, black-beans mix, sangria mix, cookbooks, coffee, wine, humidored cigars, and other items sold in the renowned Spanish restaurant.

Geier's Sausage Kitchen (941-923-3004 or 888-743-4377; www.geierssausage.com),7447 S. Tamiami Trail, Sarasota. European-style sausage and smoked meats, prime fresh meats, imported cheeses, beer, wine, pastries, and other gourmet items.

Madison Avenue Café & Deli (941-388-3354; www.madisoncafesarasota.com), 28 N. Blvd. of Presidents, St. Armands Circle, Sarasota. Bagels, sandwiches, cookies, and wine.

The Olive Grove of Venice (941-375-8888; www.meurusimports.com), 248 W. Tampa Ave. in the Venice Center Mall, Venice. Fine olive oils, wines, and other gourmet products.

Southside Deli (941-330-9302; southsidedelisarasota.com), 1825 Hillview St., Sarasota. Popular spot for a take-out or eat-in lunch. Pressed and cold deli sandwiches, burgers, salads, cookies, and gelato.

Too Jay's (941-362-3692; www.toojays.com), Westfield Southgate, 3501 S. Tamiami Trail, Sarasota. This import from the Tampa area is the ultimate in deli food: sandwiches, hot comfort-food dishes, and the real thing in New York cheesecake.

FARMS, FRUIT & VEGETABLE STANDS For information about farms, markets, and other agricultural pursuits, stop in at the Visit Sarasota County Visitor Center (see "Info") for a copy of the *Agriculture Guide of Florida's Gulf Coast.*

Albritton Fruit (941-923-2573 or 800-237-3682; www.albrittonfruit.com), 5430 Proctor Rd., Sarasota, Albritton is a well-known name in citrus.

Sarasota Farmers' Market (941-225-9256; www.sarasotafarmersmarket.org), Lemon Ave. between First St. and Main St., downtown Sarasota. The biggest and best in the region: Florida fruits, vegetables, organic products, flowers, plants, seafood, and honey. Every Saturday, 7 a.m. to 1 p.m.

Siesta Key Farmers Market (www.siestafarmersmarket.com) Held Sundays in the village 8 a.m. to 1 p.m. Arts and crafts in addition to fresh produce and food products.

☙ **Venice Farmers Market** (thevenicefarmersmarket.com) Saturdays starting at 8 a.m. year-round. Kid's activities and Venice Youth Growing and Blooming initiatives involve the whole family.

Yoder's Fresh Market (941-955-7771; www.yodersrestaurant.com), 3434 Bahia Vista St., Sarasota. In addition to fresh produce, this Amish market sells homemade jams, jellies, meats, cheeses, and baked goods.

NATURAL FOODS Earth Origins Market (941-365-3700; www.earthoriginsmarket.com), 1279 Beneva Rd. Sarasota. A full-service mart with a juice bar, hot and cold deli, salad bar, and a large fresh produce and grains area.

Richard's Foodporium (941-966-0596; www.richardswholefoods.com), 14999 Tamiami Trail, North Port. One of several area locations, it carries a good stock of bulk natural foods and organic groceries.

PIZZA & TAKE-OUT Anna's Restaurant & Deli (941-349-4888; annasdelis.com), 6535 Midnight Pass Rd., Siesta Key. Famous for its swirled rye bread and tall stack sandwiches, such as the Surfer with ham, turkey, Swiss, and cucumber.

Main Bar Sandwich Shop (941-955-8733; www.themainbar.com), 1944 Main St., Sarasota. Find a long list of sandwiches, hot and cold, plus salads and desserts at this circa-1958 landmark. Specialties include the Aztec sandwich with roast beef, provolone, and jalapeño dressing, and the New Orleans muffuletta and Veggiletta.

✪ **Morton's Gourmet Market** (941-955-9856; www.mortonsmarket.com), 1924 S. Osprey Ave., at Southside Village, Sarasota. Wildly popular (practically legendary), Morton's sells hot prepared items, pizza, deli sandwiches, salads, bakery goods, and homemade desserts for take-out, plus fresh produce, deli and fresh meats, seafood, coffees, wine, and gourmet products.

SEAFOOD Captain Brian's Seafood Market (941-351-4492; www.captainbriansseafood.com), 8421 N. Tamiami Trail, Sarasota. Fresh local and imported seafood in a large, dine-in venue.

Admiral Jane's Seafood Market (941-484-4623), 107 Colonia Ln. E., Nokomis.

"Stone crab headquarters," this market, part of Captain Eddie's Seafood Restaurant [see "Restaurants"], proclaims. Fresh seafood of all varieties.

✳ Selective Shopping

In season, you may well be tempted, like everyone else, to save shopping and sight-seeing for rainy, cold, off-beach days. Don't. You'll lose your diligently attained good beach attitude by the time you've found your first parking spot. Go in the morning for best results and the most relaxing experience.

Sarasota's **St. Armands Circle** is known far and wide for its arena of posh shops, galleries, and restaurants. **Downtown Sarasota** has a nice mix of one-of-a-kind shops interspersed with restaurants. Nearby **Southside Village**, at Hillview Street and Osprey Avenue, has grown into an intriguing little shopping

and dining destination. On the islands you'll find fun shops and beach boutiques that blend with the sand and sun.

SHOPPING CENTERS & MALLS ✪
Downtown Sarasota (941-366-7040; www.dsasarasota.com). One of the Gulf Coast's most successful downtown restoration projects has returned Sarasota's vitality to Main Street and its environs. The area encompasses approximately 1.5 square miles and is centered at Five Points, where Main Street intersects with four other streets and Selby Five Points Park pays homage to Sarasota's World War I servicemen. Renovated old buildings house galleries, clothing boutiques, antique shops, restaurants, sidewalk cafés, clubs, and gift shops. Projects in 2012 upgraded streets and added roundabouts. Specially themed celebrations happen every first Friday from 6 to 9 p.m. Palm Avenue (www.palmavenue. org) holds a preponderance of galleries,

BRING ALONG THE SWIMSUITS FOR A SHOPPING EXCURSION IN DOWNTOWN VENICE, HOME TO CENTENNIAL PARK

while Historic Burns Square (Pineapple and Orange avenues) has its share of specialty shops and fun restaurants.

✪ **Downtown Venice** (941-484-6722), at Venice Ave. W. and adjacent streets, Venice. Down a Mediterranean-type, date palm–lined boulevard you'll find shops and restaurants to fit every budget. Wander a block to the south for more on Miami Avenue. A Third Thursday Stroll takes place every month from 5:30 to 8 p.m. Centennial Park runs along Venice Avenue across from its shops. Here musicians often entertain at the gazebo, and children splash in the interactive fountains. North of the park, Venice Centre Mall holds history and more options for shoppers.

✪ **St. Armands Circle** (941-388-1554; www.starmandscircleassoc.com), 300 Madison Dr., on St. Armands Key, Sarasota. On one of the Sarasota barrier islands that he owned, John Ringling envisioned a world-class shopping center, complete with park-lined walkways and Baroque statuary. He would be gratified by St. Armands Circle. On a scale with Palm Beach's Worth Avenue, it was named for developer Charles St. Amand (whose name was misspelled "Armand" in later land deeds, and it is this spelling that persists). Its spin-off formation is suited geographically to the pancake shape of the island. Four sections arc off the circular center drive. "The Circle," as it is known in local shorthand, is a hub of activity for the entire region, encompassing shops of the most upscale nature, galleries, restaurants, clubs, and specialty boutiques. International style is well represented. Circus plaques and a statue of Ringling recall the circus's role in this sophisticated shopping arena. People dress in finery just to shop here, but don't feel obligated. Parking is free on the street and in a garage nearby.

Siesta Key Located in the village along Ocean Boulevard, Siesta Key's shopping district has a refreshingly barefoot atmosphere with a touch of beach bawdiness. Mixed in with the shops is a generous dose of casual eateries and daiquiri bars. You'll find a more refined collection of shops around Stickney Point Road.

Southgate (941-955-0900; www.westfield.com/southgate), 3501 S. Tamiami Trail, at Bee Ridge Rd., Sarasota. Smaller than Sarasota Square, this one houses Macy's, a nice deli, boutiques and shops, plus a cinema with in-theater dining.

Westfield Sarasota Square (941-922-9609; www.westfield.com/sarasota), 8201 S. Tamiami Trail, at Beneva Rd., Sarasota. Your choice of four major department stores, movie theaters, and more than 140 specialty shops and eateries.

ANTIQUES & COLLECTIBLES Antique shops are plentiful and easy to find in and around Sarasota. Look on Pineapple Street and Fruitville Avenue, both downtown. In Venice, you will find some along Miami Avenue, parallel to the main shopping drag, Venice Avenue. Pick up a copy of the *Sarasota Antique Guide & Locator Map* from the Sarasota Visitors Center.

Antiques and Chatchkes Fine Antique Mall (941-906-1221; www.antiquesandchatchkes.com), 1542 Fruitville Rd., Sarasota. Mainly furniture and things for the home.

Burke Antiques (941-952-0042), 12 Palm Ave. S., Sarasota. Fine high-end Asian antique decorative pieces and furnishings.

Sarasota Art & Antique Center, 640 S. Washington Ave., Sarasota. This huge pink building holds a number of fine antique galleries, including **Crissy Galleries** (941-957-1110; www.crissy.com), selling quality furniture, jewelry, and art; **Sarasota Rare Coin Gallery** (941-366-2191 or 800-447-8778; www.sarasotacoin.com); and ✪ **Sarasota Estate & Jewelry** (941-364-5158), specializing in vintage diamond jewelry.

What the Dicken's (941-480-1731), 220 Tampa Ave. W., Venice, in the Venice Centre Mall. A select collection of jewelry, china, glass, books, and ladies' apparel and accessories.

BOOKS **Bookstore1Sarasota** (941-365-7900; www.bookstore1sarasota.com), 1359 Main St., downtown Sarasota. Happily, there's a new bookstore on Main Street, where two long-timers have closed in recent years. This one is lean and traditional—hold the coffee, thank you. It tends toward arts and women's books and magazines and hosts author readings and book discussions.

CLOTHING **Captain's Landing** (941-485-2329; www.captainslanding.com), 243 W. Venice Ave., Venice. High-quality Hawaiian, golf, and sporty fashions for men.

Cotton Cruise: La Casa del Quetzal Imports (941-488-1727), 246 W. Tampa Ave., Venice, in the Venice Centre Mall. Colorful and unusual women's styles.

Farmhouse Frocks (330-231-4132; www.farmhousefrocks.com), 506 S. Pineapple Ave., Sarasota. Amish seamstresses in Ohio create comfort fashions inspired by "the flowing farmhouse style," in keeping with the spirit of Sarasota's Pinecraft Amish-Mennonite community.

Dream Weaver (941-388-1974; www.dreamweavercollection.com), 364 St. Armands Circle, Sarasota. Fine woven wear—in silk, suede, and other extravagant materials—that crosses the line into fabric art.

Ivory Coast (941-388-1999; www.binjaratraders.com/ivorycol.cfm), 15 N. Blvd. of Presidents, at St. Armands Circle, Sarasota. Outstanding imported women's fashions, jewelry, and decorative items inspired by Africa.

Little Bo-Tique (941-388-1737; www.littlebotiquechildrenswear.com), 367-A St. Armands Circle, Sarasota. Adorable and stylish children's wear for boys and girls.

The Met (941-388-3991; www.themetsarasota.com), 35 S. Blvd. of Presidents, at St. Armands Circle, Sarasota.

Expensive dressy and casual designer fashions for men and women in a divine setting.

Nana's, A Children's Shop (941-488-4108; www.nanaschildrenshop.com), 223 W. Venice Ave., Venice. Quality baby and kids' clothes, books, and toys.

SunBug (941-485-7946; www.thesunbug.com), 141 W. Venice Ave., Venice. The most fun in women's fashions, from dressy to casual. Great cotton styles, swimsuits, and unusual, comfortable dresses.

CONSIGNMENT/THRIFT In Sarasota, buying secondhand is not the embarrassment that it is in some places. In fact, recycled apparel is the "in" thing among the young and artistic. Because of the wealth and transient nature of its residents, the area offers the possibility of great discoveries in its consignment shops. Fruitville Road is a good place to shop for recycled goods. Some of the stores benefit local charities.

Divine Consign (941-488-3219;), 203 W. Miami Ave., Venice. Benefits a local church. Furniture, housewares, ladies' clothing, and jewelry.

🐘 **The Elephant's Trunk Thrift Shop** (941-483-3056; www.elephantstrunkthrift.com), 595 Tamiami Trail, behind the Chamber of Commerce, Venice. Lots of furniture and other household goods, including discontinued merchandise. Operated by Hospital Volunteers of Venice.

Encore & More (941-953-4222), 1439 Main St., Sarasota, sells women's clothing and accessories, furniture, and art to benefit the Women's Resource Center.

Fifi's Fine Resale Apparel (941-312-6950; www.fifisconsignment-apparel.com), 1905 S. Osprey, Sarasota. With a number of shops around Florida, the Fifi's brand brings quality to the Sarasota consignment scene.

Tommy's Fine Men's Consignment (941-786-1850; tommysfinemensconsignment.com), 101 W. Venice Ave., Venice. New and second-hand jeans, shoes, island fashions, tuxedos, and dress wear for men.

🌿 **Woman's Exchange** (941-955-7859; www.sarasotawex.com), 539 S. Orange Ave., downtown Sarasota. Furniture, family clothing, antiques, housewares, and china. Profits support local arts.

FLEA MARKETS & BAZAARS **The Dome Flea & Farmers' Market** (941-493-6773; www.thedomefleamarket.com), 5115 FL 776, Venice. A three hundred-booth indoor market open Friday, Saturday, and Sunday 9–4.

GALLERIES **Art Uptown Gallery** (941-955-5409; www.artuptown.com), 1367 Main St., Sarasota. One of downtown's more affordable galleries, this nonprofit cooperative carries the various media of local artists. Vibrant.

Galleria Silecchia (941-365-7414 or 888-366-7414; www.galleriasilecchia.com), 20 S. Palm Ave., Sarasota. This gallery contains some of the most interesting art I've seen in all of Sarasota: large and small bronze sculptures, the exquisite glass lamp works of Ulla Darni, and gold-tinged paintings by Russian artist Yuri Gorbachev. Pieces sell in the four- to five-figure range.

Melange Fine Art (941-488-5522), 252 W. Tampa Ave., Venice. Representing more than forty-five artists, its inventory includes paintings, jewelry, clay works, clothing, and home décor.

State of the Arts Gallery (941-955-2787; sarasotafineart.com), 1525 State St., Sarasota. Short and sweet, downtown's State Street is a somewhat hidden destination for contemporary art. This gallery represents a number of fine Sarasota area artists in a wide range of media here and in its nearby Gallery C (1549 State St.).

✪ **Towles Court Artist Colony** (www.towlescourt.com), 1938 Adams Ln., off US 301, Sarasota. A charming district of restored and brightly painted bungalows has been turned into an art colony. It features the galleries and working art studios of artists in all media. The Towles Court Art Center contains several galleries and a café. It is the colony's headquarters, and other studio-galleries are scattered around it. Third Friday art walks, 6–10 p.m., include live music.

Venice Gallery & Studio (941-486-0811; www.clydebutcher.com), 237 Warfield Ave., Venice. Search out this off-the-beaten-path home to the work of Clyde Butcher, Florida's unofficial photographer laureate. Here are his darkroom and workshops, plus a collection of his limited-edition and giclée black-and-white portraits of Florida and other scenic locations. He is known for his large-format photography and is often compared to Ansel Adams.

GIFTS Some of the best gifts and souvenirs are found in attraction gift shops, especially those at The Ringling Mote Marine and Sarasota Jungle Gardens.

Artisans (941-388-0082), 301 John Ringling Blvd., at St. Armands Circle, Sarasota. Inexpensive, flirty, and unusual handbags, jewelry, and home art.

🌿 **Artisans' World Marketplace** (941-365-5994; www.artisansworldmarketplace.com), 128 S. Pineapple Ave., Sarasota. This not-for-profit has made a commitment to selling the work of below-poverty-level artisans and features such items as crèches from Peru, metal-drum sculptures from Haiti, Bali pottery, jewelry from South Africa, and carvings from Nicaragua. The resourcefulness reflected in the delightful scope of work is remarkable.

✎ **Celebration Corner** (941-484-2206), 303A W. Venice Ave., Venice. Old-fashioned toys, Green brand toys, lots of stuffed animals, wooden puzzles, kits, and kid's books.

Elysian Fields (941-361-3006; www.elysianfieldsonline.com), 1273 Tamiami Trail S., at Midtown Plaza, Sarasota. This shop's subtitle tells it succinctly enough: "Books & Gifts for Conscious Living." It's filled with wonderful New Age accoutrements, aromatherapy supplies, feng shui items, cards, candles, and lots of books.

Giving Tree Gallery (941-388-7754; www.thegivingtreegallery.com), 5 N. Boulevard of Presidents, at St. Armands Circle, Sarasota. Beautiful inset and sculpted wood art, unique jewelry, glassware, and other fine and unusual gifts.

Hurricane Rita (941-346-7712), 5212 Ocean Blvd., Siesta Key Village, Siesta Key. Island-style gifts and home décor items at affordable prices.

✈ **Toy Lab** (941-363-0064; toylab sarasota.com), 1529 Main St., Sarasota. Don't look for video games at this downtown fixture. Playmobil, yes; PlayStation, no. This tiny, tightly packed, old-fashioned toyshop has educational toys and games, puppets, stuffed animals, and puzzles.

JEWELRY **Coffrin Jewelers** (941-366-6871), 1829 S. Osprey Ave., at Southside Village, Sarasota. Fine creations in gold, silver, and platinum; specializing in original designs.

Heitel Jewelers (941-488-2720), 347 W. Venice Ave., Venice. Buy your shark's teeth jewelry, including gold tooth-shaped charms, here; also sea-motif charms, gold, diamonds, Spanish coin pendants, and other fine pieces. In business since 1903.

Jewelry by Cole (941-388-3323 or 800-572-9375; www.jewelrybycole.com), 7 N. Blvd. of Presidents, at St. Armands Circle, Sarasota. Lovely set gems; a wide variety of the usual to the unusual in sea-themed pieces; custom work.

✪ **June Simmons Designs** (941-388-4535; junesimmonsjewelry.com), 68 S. Palm Ave., Sarasota. Artistic, exclusive-edition jewelry and custom work.

Michael & Co. Jewelers (941-349-2758 or 877-349-2749; www.michaelandcojewelers.com), 5221 Ocean Blvd., Siesta Key. Specializing in create-your-own bracelets, nautical pieces, diamonds, and creative jewel settings.

Tilden Ross Jewelers (941-388-3338; www.tildenrossjewelers.com), 410 St.

Armands Circle, Sarasota. All that glitters! Calgaro, SOHO, Lombardi, and other top designers provide a showroom of exquisite sparkle, from pearls to gems to unusual gold rings.

KITCHENWARE & HOME DÉCOR **Artisans** (941-388-0082), 301 John Ringling Blvd., at St. Armands Circle, Sarasota. Fun glassworks, jewelry, art, and more.

Garden Argosy (941-388-6402; www.gardenargosy.com), 361 St. Armands Circle, Sarasota. Gifts for the home and garden: an extensive selection of candles, frames, painted wood bowls, garden statues, and fountains.

Main Street Traders (941-373-0475; mainstreettraders.com), 1468 Main St., Sarasota. "Everything for the Home" from silly cocktail napkins and art to retro and antique reproduction furnishings and women's resort wear.

The Tabletop (941-485-0319; www.thetabletop.com), 205 W. Venice Ave., Venice. Hand-painted and other fun barware, kitchen and table accessories, coffee and espresso paraphernalia, and gourmet items.

🐚 **Tervis Tumbler Outlet** (941-966-8614 or 800-237-6688; www.tervis.com), 928 S. Tamiami Trail, Osprey. Floridians know the only way to keep their drinks cool is with Tervis Tumblers, which are made locally and sold throughout Florida. You'll find the widest selection here at the original factory store. The insulated acrylic tumblers are guaranteed for life, and you can exchange defective or broken merchandise at this or any other outlet.

SHELL SHOPS **Beach Bazaar** (941-346-2995; www.beach-bazaar.com), 5211 Ocean Blvd., Siesta Key. A one-stop mart for seashells, toys, beach clothes, boogie and skimboards, sunglasses, and other vacation must-haves.

Sea Pleasures and Treasures (941-488-3510), 255 Venice Ave. W., Venice. Quantity, not necessarily quality: sea-theme gifts, shells, jewelry, shell craft supplies, shark's teeth, and the "Florida snow shovels" that shellers and shark's teeth hunters use.

SPORTING GOODS *Note:* This listing includes general sports outlets only. For supplies and equipment for specific sports, please refer to "To Do" in this chapter.

CB's Saltwater Outfitters (941-349-4400; www.cbsoutfitters.com), 1249 Stickney Point Rd., Siesta Key. Fishing gear and sportswear.

Cook's Sportland (941-493-0025; www.cookssportland.com), 4419 S. Tamiami Trail, Venice. Equipment for archery, hunting, camping, and fishing; also fishing licenses, tackle repair, sportswear, shoes, and western clothing.

✳ Special Events

January: **Sarasota Highland Games** (www.sarasotahighlandgames.com), Sarasota Fairgrounds, 3000 Ringling Blvd., Sarasota. Scottish and Celtic athletics, entertainment, and food one Saturday late in the month or early February. Admission.

February: **Forks & Corks** (941365-2800; www.dineoriginal.com/forksandcorks). This four-day festival, presented by The Sarasota-Manatee Originals group of non-franchised restaurants, includes interactive seminars, vintner and brewmaster events, and The Grand Tasting at The Ringling. **Greek Glendi Festival** (941-355-2616 or 877-355-2272; www.stbarbarafestival.org), St. Barbara's Greek Orthodox Church, 7671 N. Lockwood Ridge Rd., Sarasota. Greek food, dancing, and arts and crafts on four days near Valentine's Day. **St. Armands Circle Art Festival** (941-388-1554; www.artfestival.com), 411 St. Armands Circle. Features more than two hundred national artists for one weekend late in the month.

March: **Sarasota County Fair** (941-365-0818; www.sarasotafair.com),

Sarasota Fairgrounds, 3000 Ringling Blvd., Sarasota. Traditional county fair with midway and carnival areas, exhibits, and entertainment. **Sarasota Jazz Festival** (941-366-1552; www.jazzclubsarasota.com), Players Theatre, Sarasota. Big-name jazz players lead a slate of big bands and jazz combos at indoor and outdoor venues. Plus there are jazz appreciation lectures and a jazz trolley route. One week.

April: **Florida Winefest and Auction** (941-952-1109 or 800-216-6199; www.floridawinefest.com), various locations in the area. A prestigious event featuring food and wine seminars, tastes from the area's finest restaurants, top entertainment, a black-tie dinner, and a fine-wine auction. Four days. **La Musica International Chamber Music Festival** (941-366-8450, ext. 3; www.lamusicafestival.org), held at the Sarasota Opera House, 61 N. Pineapple Ave., Sarasota. Five classical music concerts held during two weeks in April. **Run for the Turtles** (941-388-4441; www.mote.org), Siesta Beach Pavilion, Siesta Key. One-day 5K race to benefit Mote Marine Aquarium early in the month. **Sarasota Film Festival** (941-364-9514; www.sarasotafilmfestival.com), 1991 Main St., Suite 108, Courtyard of the Stars next to Regal Cinemas on Main St., downtown Sarasota. More than two hundred film screenings, national celebrities, outdoor screenings, and live entertainment. Ten days early April. ☻ 🐟 **Shark's Tooth Festival** (941-412-0402; www.sharkstoothfest.com), Airport Festival Grounds, 610 E. Airport Ave., Venice. A bacchanal of seafood bounty, the festival gets its name also from its reputation among shark's teeth collectors. One weekend early in the month. Admission fee. **Suncoast BBQ & Bluegrass Bash** (www.suncoastbbqbash.com), Airport Festival Grounds, 610 E. Airport Ave., Venice. Live music, professionally prepared barbecue, sporting clays competition, and a kids' park for two weekend days midmonth.

May: **Sarasota Festival of New Plays** (941-366-9000; www.floridastudiotheatre.org), Florida Studio Theatre, 1241 N. Palm Ave., downtown Sarasota. Premieres the works of emerging playwrights from Florida and around the nation, launching almost seventy main stage productions. Late May through early June.

June: **Sarasota Music Festival** (941-953-3434 or 866-508-0611; www.sarasotaorchestra.org/sarasota-music-festival), Florida West Coast Symphony, 709 N. Tamiami Trail, Sarasota. Presents classical and chamber music by promising musicians from around the world. Sponsored by the Sarasota Orchestra, the program includes lectures for participants. The public is welcome at the performances. Three weeks. **Savor Sarasota** (www.savorsarasota.com), two weeks of tasting the award-winning fare of twenty-odd local restaurants with attractive discounts. Early in the month. **Suncoast Super Boat Grand Prix** (941-487-7904 ext. 103; sarasotapowerboatgrandprix.org), Sarasota Bay and other county locations. A national attraction more than twenty-five years old, it features fishing and golf tournaments, parties, a boat parade (on land), a car show, and fireworks as well as the headline powerboat races. Eleven days at month's end through July 4.

October: **Ringling International Arts Festival** (800-660-4278; www.ringling.org), The Ringling, Sarasota. Theater, dance, music, and visual arts all fall under the umbrella of this world-class festival. Four days midmonth.

November: **Bacchus on the Beach** (941-383-882; www.longboatkeyclub), Longboat Key Club & Resort, Longboat Key. A blissful weekend filled with food and wine tastings, auctions, and art. **Cine-World** (941-364-8662, box office: 941-955-FILM; www.filmsociety.org), Burns Court Cinemas, 506 Burns Ln., downtown Sarasota. Independent film screenings. Ten days early November. **Siesta Key Crystal Classic International Sand Sculpting Contest** (941-861-9930; siestakeycrystalclassic.com), Siesta Key Public Beach. A thiry-five-year competition with adult and youth divisions.

St. Armands Circle Art Festival (941-388-1554; www.artfestival.com), 411 St. Armands Circle. Features more than two hundred national artists for one weekend midmonth. **Venice Art Festival** (941-484-6722; www.artfestival.com), downtown Venice. Artisans from around the United States gather for one weekend.

CHARLOTTE
HARBOR COAST

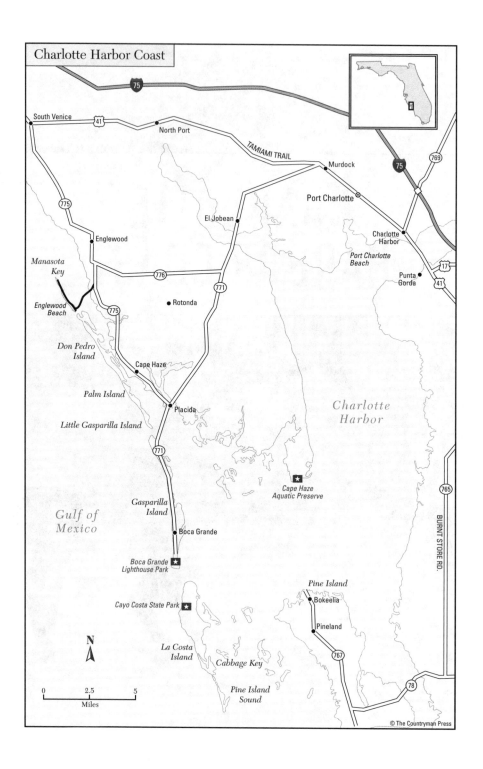

Charlotte Harbor Coast

South Venice

North Port

TAMIAMI TRAIL

Murdock

Port Charlotte

Englewood

El Jobean

Charlotte
Harbor

Manasota
Key

Port Charlotte
Beach

Punta
Gorda

Englewood
Beach

Rotonda

Don Pedro
Island

Cape Haze

Palm Island

Placida

Little Gasparilla Island

Charlotte
Harbor

Cape Haze
Aquatic Preserve

Gulf of
Mexico

Gasparilla
Island

Boca Grande

BURNT STORE RD.

Boca Grande
Lighthouse Park

Pine Island

Bokeelia

Cayo Costa State Park

Pineland

N

La Costa
Island

Cabbage Key

0   2.5   5

Pine Island
Sound

Miles

© The Countryman Press

CHARLOTTE HARBOR COAST
Wild and Watery

As one of Florida's largest bays and its second largest estuary (seventeenth largest in the United States), 270-square-mile Charlotte Harbor supplies a huge gulp of nature and a place to play on many waterfronts—a total of 830 miles of shoreline and more than seventy miles of navigable canals. No surprise that it gets rated highly by *Sail Magazine, Yachting Magazine,* and *Sport Fishing Magazine.* The region has remained the most isolated and undeveloped of any in southwest Florida, primarily because its beaches—glorious though they might be—are so far removed from main highways. The fact that 84 percent of Charlotte Harbor shoreline is preserved land ensures that the Charlotte coast will retain its quiet, natural temperament and still hold on to fishing as a way of life and livelihood.

This chapter begins where the last left off, on twisty, out-of-the-way **Manasota Key**, a refuge for wealthy isolationists at its north end and the site of the unpretentious resort community of **Englewood Beach** at its south.

On the mainland's Cape Haze peninsula—bounded by the Myakka River and Charlotte Harbor—small residential communities such as ✪ **Englewood, Grove City, Cape Haze, Placida,** and **Rotonda West** hold Amerindian mounds, fishermen, retirees, golf-course communities, and families. Placida is the jumping-off point for **Gasparilla Island**, which has built its reputation and character on one fish in particular: the tarpon. Phosphate shipping and legends of bygone buccaneers first attracted attention to the area. Later the tarpon, a.k.a. Silver King, prize of the fishing world, drew millionaires to the island community of **Boca Grande**. Privately owned **Little Gasparilla** and **Palm Islands** and mostly state-owned **Don Pedro Island** have run together with shifts of tides and time. They remain three of Florida's most pristine barrier islands.

Inland, across the harbor, **Port Charlotte** is a new city that was built around Tamiami Trail, principally as a retirement community. The town of **Charlotte Harbor** was settled shortly after the Civil War by farmers and cattle ranchers. Facing it across the Peace River's widest point, ✪ **Punta Gorda** boasts a past as deep as its harbor. The southernmost station for the Florida Southern Railroad in 1886, this deepwater port town enjoyed a bustling era of commerce and tourism before railroad builder Henry Plant decided to shut it down in favor of further developing Tampa Bay. Its heyday train depot has been restored and houses a small museum and an antique mall.

Ice making, turpentine stilling, pineapple growing, and especially commercial fishing continued to earn local citizens a living for some time. Settled by a mixed population of whites and African Americans, the town preserves an interesting chapter on black history at the Blanchard House Museum. Today Punta Gorda has recovered its past glories through downtown and riverfront restoration. Residential-retail developments replaced old shopping centers and rubble left in the wake of 2004's Hurricane Charley, which hit Punta Gorda squarely. Home of Ponce de León Park, where the explorer is believed to have met his death, Punta Gorda hosts subdivisions of modern-day youth seekers.

GETTING HERE **Punta Gorda Airport (PGD)** (941-639-1101; www.flypgd.com; 28000 A-1 Airport Rd., Punta Gorda 33982) is a small airport serving the area with low-fare Allegiant Air service. Most flyers, however, come through the Sarasota–Bradenton International Airport (SRQ) or Southwest Florida International Airport (RSW) in Fort Myers. If traveling by bus, the **Greyhound Lines'** (941-391-5843; www.greyhound.com) closest depot is located in Port Charlotte at 900 Kings Hwy. If arriving by car, take Interstate 75 or US 41 from the north and south and US 17 from Florida's East Coast. See pages 12–13 for rental car phone numbers and websites. Alamo, Avis, Budget, Dollar, National, and Thrifty have rental facilities at SRQ and RSW.

GETTING AROUND **Boca Grande Limousine** (239-964-0455 or 800-771-7433; www .bocagrandelimo.com) provides twenty-four-hour connections to all Florida airports. For a more dramatic arrival or departure, call **Boca Grande Seaplane** (941-964-0234 or 800-940-0234). **Charlotte Limousine Service** (800-208-6106 or 941-627-4494; www.charlottelimousine.com) will pick up from and deliver to all airports in the region. **Airport Limo & Car Service** (941-505-9400 or 800-954-9404; www .airportlimoandcarservice.com) has a fleet that includes Lincolns and SUVs. Lincoln Town Cars and vans. Or call **Air-Port Shuttles & Transportation** (941-505-5054 or 866-956-5054; www.air-portshuttles.com).

US 41 heads inland and I-75 run the length of the county, north to south. In these parts, getting to the gulf entails crossing several bodies of water (see "Excursions," below). A toll bridge links Gasparilla Island (Boca Grande) to the mainland; it costs $6 for cars and motorcycles to cross, $3 for bikes.

HOSPITALS & CLINICS **Bayfront Health** (Punta Gorda 941-639-3131, Port Charlotte 941-766-4122; www. bayfrontcharlotte.com), 809 E. Marion Ave., Punta Gorda; 2500 Harbor Blvd., Port Charlotte. Emergency room open twenty-four hours.

Englewood Community Hospital (941-475-6571; www.englewoodcommhospital. com), 700 Medical Blvd., Englewood. Emergency room open twenty-four hours.

Fawcett Memorial Hospital (941-629-1181; www.fawcetthospital.com), 21298 Olean Blvd., Port Charlotte. Emergency room open twenty-four hours.

VISITOR INFORMATION **Boca Grande Area Chamber of Commerce** (941-964-0568; www.bocagrandechamber.com), 471 Park Ave. #3, Boca Grande 33921.

Charlotte County Chamber of Commerce (941-627-2222; www.charlottecounty chamber.org), 2702 Tamiami Trail, Port Charlotte 33952; and (941-639-2222), 311 W. Retta Esplanade, Punta Gorda 33950.

Charlotte Harbor Visitor & Convention Bureau (941-743-1900 or 800-652-6090; www.charlotteharbortravel.com), 18500 Murdock Circle, Suite B104, Port Charlotte 33948.

Englewood–Cape Haze Area Chamber of Commerce (941-474-5511; www.englewood chamber.com), 601 S. Indiana Ave., Englewood 34223.

Punta Gorda Chamber of Commerce (941-639-3720; www.puntagordachamber. com), 252 W. Marion Ave., Punta Gorda 33950. Information center at Marion Ave. and Sullivan St.

✳ To See

The Charlotte Harbor coast is a small town—even in its larger, urban-sprawl-infected communities. Long considered a refuge for the retired, the region is not known for a

EXCURSIONS: Back-Roading

Charlotte Harbor Coast and the Island Coast boast a number of scenic back roads that bypass traffic and plunge the traveler into timeless scenes, unique neighborhoods, and beaches. To reach **Englewood** by back road from the north, cross quiet, out-of-the-way **Manasota Key** along FL 776 through **Englewood Beach**. **Dearborn Street** gets you to Englewood's charming downtown. Then follow CR 775 and CR 771 to FL 776 to get to **Gasparilla Island**. (It costs $6 to cross the causeway onto the island by motorized vehicle.) **Park Avenue** is the shopper's route in Boca; **Gulf Boulevard** takes you to the beaches. Back on the mainland, stay on 776 to get to to US 41. Or, to skirt US 41's chain-outlet anonymity in the **Port Charlotte** area, take Collingswood Boulevard off 776 to Edgewater Drive (turn left). Turn right on Bayshore Road and head back to 41.

Between Charlotte County and the Island Coast, CR 765, or Burnt Store Road, was once the locals' secret bypass, but it is becoming more clogged with developments. This connects to FL 78 (Pine Island Road), which leads to **Pine Island** and the artsy commercial fishing town of **Matlacha** when taken west. Stringfellow Road is the main Pine Island route to the small towns of **St. James City** (south), **Pineland** (west), and **Bokeelia** (north). To enter downtown **Cape Coral** the back way, follow Burnt Store Road through the FL 78 intersection to Veterans Parkway, then to Chiquita Boulevard. Turn right on Chiquita and then left on Cape Coral Parkway. Cross the Cape Coral Bridge and turn right on **McGregor Boulevard**, **Fort Myers'** prettiest street. Follow it to San Carlos Boulevard (FL 865), which takes you to **Fort Myers Beach**. Turn left on Estero Boulevard (CR 865) to travel the length of the island. It starts out a bit frenzied with activity, then carries you along at a more mellow pace as you cross into **Lovers Key** and **Big and Little Hickory Islands,** where CR 865 becomes Hickory Boulevard. Beaches along this stretch include **Lovers Key State Park** (239-463-4588; www.floridastateparks.org/park/Lovers-Key, 8700 Estero Blvd., Fort Myers Beach) and **Bonita Beach Park** (239-949-4615; www.leegov.com/parks, 27954 Hickory Blvd., Bonita Beach). (Note: Traffic creeps along CR 865 at high-season rush hours.) The road returns you via Bonita Beach Road to US 41 at **Bonita Springs**.

To get to **Sanibel Island**, turn right off of San Carlos Boulevard at Summerlin Road (CR 869). Vehicular toll at the Sanibel Causeway is $6. **Causeway Road** is lined with beaches. It takes you to Sanibel's main Periwinkle Way. (Note: Sanibel Island has no traffic or street lights; policemen direct traffic at the four-way stops.) Beaches lie along parallel Gulf drives. You can avoid rush-hour clogs on Periwinkle Way by taking "the back way" on Gulf Drive from Rabbit Road in the northwest; Tarpon Bay Road, Casa Ybel Road, or Donax Street midisland; or Lindgren Boulevard at the causeway. To reach Captiva Island, take Tarpon Bay Road (a right off Periwinkle Way or Middle Gulf Drive) to Sanibel-Captiva Road and turn left. This road takes you past many of the island's nature attractions and Bowman's and Turner Beaches. It becomes Captiva Drive once you cross the Blind Pass Bridge. Follow it to the end to get to Captiva's beach access.

---

vibrant arts scene or cultural diversity. Overall, it has a Midwestern flavor in coastal areas but is definitely Old Florida in inland rural parts. Awareness of the arts has developed slowly and on a hobby level. For information on local arts and culture, contact the Arts & Humanities Council of Charlotte County, 941-764-8100; www.charlottearts.org.

ARCHITECTURE In the smaller towns around Charlotte Harbor, single examples of historic character appear serendipitously in the midst of concrete-block homes. Downtown Englewood, a destination off the beaten path of the Tamiami Trail, holds a few such treasures that have been reincarnated as shops, boutiques, and galleries.

Punta Gorda sprinkles its architectural prizes—old homes, commercial buildings, and churches—along **Marion Avenue, Olympia Avenue, Retta Esplanade,** and side

TAMIAMI TRAIL BRIDGES CROSS THE WIDE PEACE RIVER FROM PUNTA GORDA TO PORT CHARLOTTE

streets such as **Sullivan Street** and the **Punta Gorda History Park** on Shreve Street. Along the esplanade, look for impressive newly restored homes, the jewels of the old riverfront district. In and around the town's historic section, an eclectic array of architecture ranges from old shotgun cigar workers' homes and tin-roofed Cracker shacks to Victorian mansions and a neoclassical city hall. Watch for historic murals along the way.

Boca Grande's most noteworthy examples of architecture, aside from the grande dame **Gasparilla Inn**, are four historic churches, each with their own style, located in a four-block area downtown. The Catholic church takes its inspiration from Spanish missions; the other three occupy early-twentieth-century wood-frame buildings and serve Episcopal, Baptist, and Methodist congregations.

A few blocks away, on **Tarpon Avenue**, spruced-up old Cracker homes slump comfortably in a district once called **Whitewash Alley**. For a taste of wealthy eccentricity, check out the **Johann Fust Community Library** on Gasparilla Road. It was built of native coquina, cypress, and pink stucco.

CINEMA **Regal Town Center Stadium 16** (941-623-0114; www.regalcinemas.com), 1441 Tamiami Trail, in the Port Charlotte Town Center, Port Charlotte.

GARDENS **Peace River Botanical and Sculpture Gardens** (peacerivergardens.org) 5950 Riverside Dr., Punta Gorda. On a lovely riverfront estate, Punta Gorda's newest and most elegant attraction plans to open to the public by late 2017. While the acreage of exotic fauna matures, the main attraction will be the collection of about a dozen large outdoor sculptures belonging to owners Roger and Linda Tetrault. It features important works by artists from the US to Turkey and Indonesia. A café overlooks a terraced infinity wetting pool and a couple of whimsical sculptures by Carole Feuerman. A boardwalk tunnels through mangroves where more sculptures live and to a gazebo on the Peace River.

HISTORIC HOMES & SITES ✪ **The A. C. Freeman House** (941-639-2222; www
.puntagordahistory.com), 311 Retta Esplanade, Punta Gorda. Open Monday to
Friday 10–4; seasonal docent tours Monday and Thursday 11–3. Moved to the riverfront, this house was once occupied by Punta Gorda's mayor and mortician.
Narrowly escaping the wrecking ball in 1985, the lovely clapboard Queen Anne
mansion was saved and restored by the people of Punta Gorda as a memento of
gracious pioneer lifestyles. Kids enjoy the kitchen out back, the room under the
stairwell à la Harry Potter, and the girls' room with its dollhouse and toys. Period
and nonperiod pieces furnish the home, which also houses the Charlotte County
Chamber of Commerce. ✪ **The Blanchard House Museum** (941-575-7518; www
.blanchardhousemuseum.us), 406 Dr. Martin Luther King Blvd., Punta Gorda. Open
Tuesday through Friday, other times by appointment; closed June through September. Donations suggested. The 1925 home of an African-American can steamboat
pilot and his mail-order bride, the museum displays photographs, documents, and
artifacts relating to Punta Gorda's black population and its history, which dates back
to the town's settling in 1886 by seven African Americans and eight white people. Tours
are by docent or self-guided. A garden commemorates those who gave their lives
in military service. It resides in the Trabue Woods community, a historic African-
American neighborhood.

🖈 **El Jobean Post Office & General Store** (941-627-3344) 4370 Garden Rd., El Jobean.
Adjacent to The Bean Depot Café, this museum takes a quick peek into yesteryear
in historic digs with a few exhibits and original post office accoutrements scattered
around a dining seating area.

🖈 **Ponce de León Historical Park**, 3400 Ponce de Leon Pkwy., Punta Gorda. A rock
shrine encasement, chipped-paint statues, and historic plaques commemorate Ponce
de León's supposed 1513 landing here and his subsequent death caused by an Indian's arrow. The park has a wildlife and recreational area on the harbor, plus a boat
ramp, picnic facilities, a small seawalled beach, a playground, two fishing piers, and
a nature boardwalk into the mangroves and along a creek where you'll often see herons. The park is home to the Peace River Wildlife Center rehabilitation facility (see
"Nature Preserves & Eco-Attractions.")

🖈 **Punta Gorda History Park** (941-639-1887; www.puntagordahistory.com), 501
Shreve St., Punta Gorda. So far, this
gathering of historic buildings in a
pretty two-acre park setting amounts to
three old homes and the old jail—little
more than an iron cage. Stop in first at
the old Trabue office, the oldest building in Punta Gorda (hours vary), where
Punta Gorda's founder conducted his
land sales business. Today it houses an
art gallery gift shop. Every Sunday, a
farmers' market convenes in the park.
At 2 p.m., garden tours take in the Cigar
Cottage and Price House interiors—the
only time the public can enter. In the
Cigar Cottage, the town's tobacco industry was once headquartered; you can
also learn about Punta Gorda's hibiscus-
growing fame. The fourth home is under
renovation for a youth museum. The

THE HISTORIC COURTHOUSE IN PUNTA GORDA, BUILT
CIRCA 1928, REFLECTS NEOCLASSICAL STYLE WITH GREEK
AND ROMAN INFLUENCES

MUST SEE

Boca Grande Lighthouse Museum (941-964-0060; www .barrierislandparkssociety.org), Gasparilla Island State Park, Gulf Blvd., Boca Grande. Open November through May, Monday to Saturday 10–4, Sunday noon to 4; the rest of the year closed Monday and Tuesday; closed all of August. $3 per vehicle of up to eight passengers ($2 pedestrians, cyclists, and extra passengers) for state park; donation of $1 requested. This 1890 structure—the most photographed and painted landmark on the island— was renovated in Old Florida style and put back into service in 1986 after twenty years of abandonment. You can self-tour both the lighthouse and the museum, which explores its history and Boca Grande bygones—from ancient Calusa civilizations through railroad and industrial eras to the island's modern-day reputation as a tarpon-fishing mecca. Historic cisterns, the assistant lighthouse keeper's home, and a struggling native vegetation garden compose the fenced-in complex. It overlooks the beach within Gasparilla Island State Park.

fountain from the old Punta Gorda Hotel also graces the grounds. Gardens and venerable old oak trees beautify the park.

Punta Gorda Train Depot (941-639-6774; www.puntagordahistory.com), 1009 Taylor St., Punta Gorda. Signs marked COLORED and WHITE are telltale relics of the late 1920s era when this Atlantic Coast Line station was in operation. It is the only one of six built in Mediterranean style that survives. You can see the original ticket windows and historic photographs and artifacts. On the depot's backside, an antique mall raises funds for the historical society (look under "Shopping: Antiques & Collectibles"). Across the street, one of the town's historic murals illustrates its railroad days.

MUSEUMS **Charlotte County Historical Center** (941-629-7278; www.charlotte countyfl.gov), 514 Grace St., Punta Gorda. Open Monday to Friday 9–3. $2 adults, $1 children ages twelve and younger. The center is geared toward children, with programs, signage, showcases, and interactive exhibits that illuminate facets of local history. Permanent exhibits are devoted to fishing heritage, fossils, and more. About five changing exhibits cycle through yearly to explore Calusa natives, Spanish conquistadors, turpentine camps, and the like.

Gasparilla Island Maritime Museum (941-964-GIMM), 901 First St. E. at Whidden's Marina on Harbor Dr., Boca Grande. Hours vary. Admission by donation. Some might call it a shed full of old junk, but to the citizens of Boca Grande, this museum represents Americana and a way of life that has survived in contrast with the mansions and yachts that surround it. Part of Whidden's Marina, it features photo albums that hark back to a day when the nation's top industrialists sailed here to fish and winter. Odd parts of boats and fishing gear lie strewn around the old, peeling fish shack, listed on the National Register of Historic Places. Still in operation, the marina and its store make it difficult to tell where the museum ends and the present begins.

Military Heritage & Aviation Museum (941-575-9002; www.freedomisntfree.org), 1200 W. Esplanade #48, at Fishermen's Village, Punta Gorda. Open Monday to Saturday 10–8; Sunday noon–6 (shortened hours in summer). Free admission. This collection of wartime memorabilia spans the Civil War to Desert Storm with photographs, uniforms, weaponry, documents, medals, field equipment, and more—constantly rotating to reflect the private collections of local veterans who lend their items.

Rick Treworgy's Muscle Car City (941-575-5959; musclecarcity.net), 3811 Tamiami Trail, Punta Gorda. Open 9–5 Tuesday to Sunday. Admission: $12.50 adults, $6 children ages two to twelve, free children for under age two. Lined up in orderly, glistening

THE BOCA GRANDE LIGHTHOUSE IS ONE OF THE STATE'S MOST PICTURESQUE SPOTS

rows, more than two hundred Corvettes, Camaros, Chevelles, Pontiac GTOs, Oldsmobile Cutlass 422s, Impalas, et al. pose with their hoods open, exposing gleaming, spotless engines. The museum, which opened in March 2009, claims at least one Corvette for every year from 1954 to 1975. Some of the pieces in the collection reflect the owner's nostalgic side, with older models such as the 1926 Chevrolet Roadster. Besides cars, memorabilia including the RCA dog, vintage ice coolers, gas pumps, signs, and a Budweiser racing boat and hauling rig demonstrate the breadth of Treworgy's collecting affliction. Those who share the affliction can purchase nostalgia and car-related gifts, including a $3,000 gas pump, in the impressively sprawling Speed Shop and Memorabilia Store. Even vintage cars are for sale in the Car Corral. The nostalgia theme carries over to the Muscle City Diner, a clever '50s-style diner complete with black-and-white tiled floors and a jukebox. Note: At press time, plans were being made to move the collection in Spring 2017, but no location had been decided upon.

MUSIC & NIGHTLIFE For current information about local entertainment, pick up a free copy of *The Parrot* tabloid paper.

BOCA GRANDE

South Beach Bar & Grille (941-964-0765; www.southbeachbarandgrille.com), 777 Gulf Blvd., Boca Grande. Contemporary bands play weekend nights in season. Sunset plays (almost) every evening. Even when neither of those events are happening, it's a pleasant place to hoist a few with the locals and take in the game within eyeshot of the gulf.

ENGLEWOOD

Englewood Performing Arts Series (941-473-2787; www.englewoodpas.org). Fine cultural entertainment from around the nation, mid-November through March in a local church.

ROWS OF GLEAMING CLASSIC CARS FILL MUSCLE CAR CITY

Englewood's on Dearborn (941-475-7501; englewoods.tripod.com), 362 W. Dearborn St., Englewood. Blues and other live music Wednesday through Saturday.

Cruisin' on Dearborn Street (olde englewood.com), W. Dearborn St., Englewood. Live entertainment and cruising cars augment the lively shopping experience here on the first Saturday of the month from 5–8 p.m.

White Elephant Pub (941-475-6801; www.whiteelephantpub.com), 1855 Gulf Blvd., Englewood Beach. Hosts live bands daily during season and on weekend evenings, plus karaoke some nights.

PORT CHARLOTTE

The Bean Depot Café (941-627-3344), 4370 Garden Rd., El Jobean. En route to Boca Grande, stop at this rustic little café in a setting of historic post office and general store for bluegrass jams every Wednesday and live music other select days.

Charlotte County Jazz Society (941-766-9422; www.ccjazz.org), P.O. Box 495321, Port Charlotte 33949. Sponsors several jazz concerts each year at the Cultural Center Theater (see "Theater") October through April. Call or visit the website for information on Sunday jam sessions.

Charlotte Symphony Orchestra (941-205-5996; www.charlottesymphony.com). Performs at the Charlotte Center for Performing Arts (see "Theater"), November through March.

Gatorz Bar & Grill (941-625-5000;), 3816 Tamiami Trail, Port Charlotte. Live music—jazz and Top Forty—throughout the week in an indoor-outdoor, purely Florida swamp-culture setting along the main highway.

Visani Comedy Dinner Theatre (941-629-9191; www.visani.net), 2400 Kings Highway, Port Charlotte. National comedians perform as well as tribute bands and other entertainment; Italian dinner menu available, but dining is optional.

PUNTA GORDA

Celtic Ray Irish Pub (941-916-9115; celticray.net) 145 W. Marion, Punta Gorda). Live music most days at this longstanding pub, recently expanded.

Charlotte Center for Performing Arts (941-637-0459 or 941-505-SHOW for box office; www.thecpac.net), 701 Carmalita St., Punta Gorda. This modern 869-seat facility hosts youth theater, symphony, chamber orchestra, opera, and other performances.

Downtown Punta Gorda Gallery Walk (941-391-4856; www.pgdowntownmerchants .com). Galleries and restaurants host free entertainment on the third Thursday of each month 5–8 p.m.

Fishermen's Village (941-639-8721; www.fishville.com), 1200 W. Retta Esplanade, Punta Gorda. Live entertainment most Saturday evenings and weekday afternoons.

Gilchrist Park (Retta Esplanade) Local musicians gather for impromptu jamming on Thursday nights at 5:30 p.m., and the public is invited.

The **Orange House** (941-505-8233; theorangehousewinebar.com), 320 Sullivan St., Punta Gorda. This new and welcoming wine bar serves up live pop, blues, and rock on weekends. Also tapas, beer, and coffee.

THEATER **Charlotte Players Community Theater Center** (941-255-1022; www .charlotteplayers.org), 1182 Market Circle., Port Charlotte. Home of the Charlotte Players community theater group with a youth theater component.

Lemon Bay Playhouse (941-475-6756; www.lemonbayplayhouse.com), 96 W. Dearborn St., Englewood. Home of the Lemon Bay Players community theater group. Performances September through June.

Royal Palm Players (941-964-2670; www.royalpalmplayers.com), 131 First St. W., Boca Grande. A community theater group sponsoring plays, guest-artist performances, children's performances, and concerts November through April in the Boca Grande Community House.

VISUAL ART CENTERS & RESOURCES Punta Gorda lost many of its historic and educational murals to hurricanes and development, but the Punta Gorda Historical Mural Society (puntagordamurals.org) is making headway in replacing them, and today the number is up to twenty-eight murals, four more than the prehurricane number. A listing for commercial galleries is included in the "Shopping" section of this chapter.

Arts & Humanities Council of Charlotte County (941-764-8100; www.charlottearts .org), 2702 Tamiami Trail, Port Charlotte. Hosts art displays and events.

Englewood Art Center (941-474-5548; www.ringling.edu/EAC), 350 S. McCall Rd., Englewood. Workshops and classes.

Visual Arts Center (941-639-8810; visualartcenter.org), 210 Maud St., near Fishermen's Village, Punta Gorda. Home of the Charlotte County Art Guild. Exhibit halls, gift shops, library, darkroom, state-of-the-art pottery studio, computer lab, and classes.

✳ To Do

More behind-the-scenes than the touted playgrounds of its flanking neighbors, the Charlotte Harbor coast's greatest claim to recreational fame is its fishing—particularly for that king of all sport fish, tarpon.

BEACHES You must drive way off the beaten path to find the beaches of Charlotte County. Although less convenient, that keeps them more natural, less trodden.

🐾 ♫ **Blind Pass (Middle) Beach** (941-861-5000; www.scgov.net), 6725 Manasota Key Rd., midisland on Manasota Key. Sixty acres of lightly developed shoreline attract those drawn more to seclusion than to the sports and activities of Manasota Key's other beaches. Low dunes edge wide salt-and-pepper sands. Next door you'll see one of the island's first buildings. Known as The Hermitage, it was once a nudist resort. Today it's a retreat for visiting artists. The skyline along the beach is low to the ground and unobtrusive—a great beach for long walks. From the parking lot you can follow a nature boardwalk trail into the mangroves or find a playground and picnic shelter. If there's surf to be found in the area, you'll find it here. Facilities: restrooms, showers, playground, nature trail, canoe launches, public dock.

✪ **Don Pedro Island State Park** (941-964-0375; www.floridastateparks.org/park/ Don-Pedro-Island), south of Palm Island, accessible only by boat. This secluded beach occupies a 230-acre island getaway. Once separated from Palm Island and Little Gasparilla, Don Pedro Island is now connected to the two to form one long, lightly developed barrier island. Don Pedro, the most natural component, is in the middle, with a pretty beach that attracts water birds. Contact Captiva Cruises (941-889-8000; www.captivacruises.com) for information on narrated excursions from Cape Haze Marina (6950 Placida Rd., Cape Haze). Facilities: picnic area/shelters, restrooms, showers, boat docks, nature trails. $2 per person (on honor system, correct change required).

    𝒮 **Englewood Beach at Chadwick Park** (941-681-3742; www.charlottecountyfl.com), 2100 N. Beach Rd., south end of Manasota Key at Englewood Beach. Popular with families, this beach's facilities include a boardwalk, pirate-theme playground, basketball hoop, volleyball, horseshoes, and picnic shelters. Shops and restaurants huddle around the area, which keeps activity levels high. Sunday nights bring a drum circle starting about an hour before sunset. Facilities: picnic areas/shelters, grills, restrooms, showers, beach wheelchairs. Parking: seventy-five cents per hour.

    ℰ **Lighthouse Beach/Gasparilla Island State Park** (941-964-0375; www.floridastateparks.org/park/Gasparilla-Island), along Gulf Blvd., Boca Grande, Gasparilla Island. Marked by a historic lighthouse with a museum inside, the park edges the deepwater tarpon grounds of Boca Grande Pass. Its plush sands encompass 135 acres, although in some parts the beach gets quite narrow. Swimming near the pass is not recommended because of strong currents. A historic chapel in the same park has been restored for weddings and other private functions. Facilities: picnic tables, restrooms, interpretative center/museum. Parking: $3 per car for up to eight people, $2 for pedestrians, cyclists, and extra passengers.

    🐚 𝒮 **Manasota Beach** (941-861-5000; www.scgov.net), 8570 Manasota Key Rd., north end of FL 776, Manasota Key. This lively, fourteen-acre sunning and shelling venue connects to Venice's Caspersen Beach, about 1.5 miles to the north. It also has a reputation—but not as pointed as Venice's—for shark's teeth. The sands are somewhat narrower here than to the south, and a scenic boardwalk runs along the edge. In 2012, renovations included a new facilities building. Facilities: picnic area/shelters, restrooms, showers, lifeguard, historical marker, boat ramp.

    𝒮 **Port Charlotte Beach Park** (941-627-1628, pool phone 941-629-0170; www.charlottecountyfl.com), 4500 Harbor Blvd., Port Charlotte. A highly developed recreational center that sits where the Peace River meets Charlotte Harbor along a man-made beach, this is a good place to go if you (or the children) like to keep busy at the beach. It's better for sunning than swimming, however, as bacteria levels are sometimes high. Stick to the swimming pool. A boardwalk runs along the beach and connects to the fishing pier. It looks across the way at Punta Gorda. Facilities: picnic areas and grills; restrooms; showers; concessions; bocce, basketball, volleyball, and tennis courts; playground; horseshoes; boat ramps; fishing pier; canoe and kayak rentals and launch;

THE BEACH AT BOCA GRANDE BECKONS

ARRIVE EARLY FOR A PRIME SPOT ON SANIBEL'S POPULAR LIGHTHOUSE BEACH PIER

heated swimming and kiddie pools. Open 6–9 daily; pool open Tuesday to Friday 10–4, Saturday to Sunday 11–5; pier and ramp open twenty-four hours. Swimming admission: $2.50 adults, $1.50 children ages two through fifteen. Parking: 75 cents per hour.

✪ **Stump Pass Beach State Park** (941-964-0375; www.floridastateparks.org/park/ Stump-Pass), south end of Gulf Blvd., Englewood Beach on Manasota Key. This uncrowded beach offers lovely, unspoiled seclusion. Traditionally, the 255-acre park has been a magnet for fishermen who cast into Lemon Bay. Follow the two-mile wooded trail to the south, and you'll find nice areas to spread a towel and dip your toes. The park stretches all the way to Stump Pass in a skinny strip of black-specked sand fringed by sea oats. Facilities: restrooms, shower, nature trail, picnic tables. Parking: $3 per car with up to eight passengers, $2 for bikers, pedestrians, and extra passengers (exact change required).

BICYCLING The Charlotte Coast region, with its abundance of back roads and wide-open spaces, gives cyclists an opportunity to pedal in peace. Many of its favored bike-ways are on-road or designated bike lanes, which are separated from motor traffic by only a painted white line. According to state law, bicyclists who share the road with other vehicles must heed all the rules of the road. Children under age sixteen are required to wear helmets.

Best Biking: Glimpse wild turkeys and lake views while pedaling along the thirty-seven miles of trails at **Fred C. Babcock-Cecil M. Webb Wildlife Management Area** (www.myfwc.com), 29200 Tuckers Grade, Punta Gorda.

✪ **Cape Haze Pioneer Trail** (941-681-3742; www.charlottecountyfl.com) 1688 Gasparilla Rd., Rotonda, runs 8.5 miles parallel to County Route 771 (CR771) along a former rail bed, completely off-road. A historic railroad bunkhouse sits along the trail. The county plans to restore it for use as an interpretive center.

Boca Grande bike path starts about a mile past Gasparilla Island's causeway (which can be crossed by bicycle for $3, but this is not recommended when there are high winds). Here you pedal along old railroad routes. Seven miles of pathway travel the island from tip to tip along Railroad Avenue and Gulf Boulevard. These paths are shared by golf carts, which you can rent and drive about the island as long as you are age fourteen or older. Some of Boca's downtown streets are also designated golf-cart trails.

FL 776 through Englewood and Englewood Beach is shouldered with a bike lane that ends at the Sarasota County line. Nearly eighty miles of bike routes explore **Punta Gorda** (941-575-3373; www.ci.punta-gorda.fl.us), with bike repair stations along the way. The city also has a Bicycle Loaner program for free bike use. Brightly painted bikes decorate the city and underscore its importance in Punta Gorda's identity. Bike riding on city sidewalks is legal throughout the county.

Rental Shops: **The Bicycle Center** (941-627-6600; www.bicyclecentercc.com), 3795 Tamiami Trail, Port Charlotte. Bikes fitted to your size and experience. Also schedules biking events and rides.

Bikes and Boards (941-474-2019; www.bikegoodys.com), 966 S. McCall Rd., Englewood Beach. Bike and kayak rentals, sales, delivery, and service.

Island Bike 'N Beach (941-964-0711; www.islandbikenbeach.com), 333 Park Ave., Boca Grande. Rents bikes, golf carts, and beach stuff.

BOATS & BOATING Charlotte Harbor Coast offers many waterfronts for adventure: the Gulf, harbor, Peace River, Myakka River, Lemon Bay Aquatic Preserve, and a number of creeks and canals. Charlotte Harbor has been named among the nation's top ten sailing destinations by *Sail* magazine.

Paddlesports: For information on paddling trails, contact the Charlotte County Parks and Recreation Department at 941-625-7529 or visit www.charlottecountyfl.com and request a copy of the *Blueway Trails* map and listing of fifty-seven trails covering two hundred miles. The Woolveton Trail, my favorite, takes you down small, quiet creeks tunneling under mangrove canopies.

Hooked on SUP (941-506-1699; www.hookedonsup.com), 6950 Placida Rd. at Cape Haze Marina, Englewood. Paddleboard and kayaking rentals, lessons, and tours. Guests have access to a heated swimming pool, a hot tub, showers, and barbecue facilities. Free paddlecraft launching.

Seashore Eco Tours (941-855-2PADDLE or 855-272-3353; seashoreecotours.com) 1540 S. McCall Rd., Englewood) Kayak and paddleboard tours to look for manatee and explore Don Pedro Island and Stump Pass Beach state parks. Tours led by Florida Master Naturalist certified guides.

Powerboat Rentals: **Beach Road Water Sports** (941-475-9099; www.beach roadwatersports.net), 1350 Beach Rd., on the south bridge, Englewood Beach. Rents pontoon boats, fishing skiffs, WaveRunners, kayaks, and paddleboards.

Holidaze Boat Rental (941-505-8888; www.holidazeboatrental.com), 1200 W. Retta Esplanade, at Fishermen's Village., Punta Gorda. Rents 17.5- to 22-foot fishing boats, pontoons, and deck boats plus kayaks and paddleboards by the hour, half-day, or full day.

Public Boat Ramps: **Indian Mound Park**, Englewood Recreation Center, 210 Winson Ave., downtown Englewood. Two ramps on Lemon Bay. Access to Stump Pass, picnic pavilion, restrooms, and interpretive nature trails.

Laishley Park Marina, (941-575-0142; www.laishleymarina.com), 150 Laishley Ct. at Marion Ave. and Nesbit St., Punta Gorda. A newly renovated facility with a huge, on-site restaurant. The park next door has picnic facilities and a playground with an interactive fountain.

Manasota Beach, Manasota Beach Rd., Manasota Key. One public boat ramp across the street from a county park.

Placida Park, Causeway Blvd., Placida.

Ponce de León Park, west end of Marion Ave., Punta Gorda. One boat ramp on the harbor.

Port Charlotte Beach (941-627-1628), 4500 Harbor Blvd., southeast end of Harbor Blvd., Port Charlotte. Beach recreational area, access to Charlotte Harbor. Two boat ramps.

Sailboat Charters, Rentals & Instruction: **Gulf Coast Sailing and Cruising School** (941-637-6634; www.gulfcoastsailingschool.com), 3160 Matecumbe Key Rd., Punta Gorda. An ASA sailing school with courses customizable to vacation time.

Let's Go Sailing (941-270-2827; letsgosailingenglewood.com), 1350 Beach Rd. Englewood, at the south bridge). Half- and full day sailing charters into the bay and gulf aboard thirty-one-foot sloop *Anna Lee* for two to six people.

Sight-Seeing & Entertainment Cruises: Look under "Wildlife Tours & Charters" for nature excursions.

Boca Boats Cruises (888-416-BOAT; www.bocaboat.com). Cruises depart from The Pink Elephant restaurant and public docks on Fifth St., Boca Grande. Daily Cabbage Key lunch tours and sunset cruises.

✪ **King Fisher Cruise Lines** (941-639-0969; www.kingfisherfleet.com), 1200 W. Retta Esplanade, at Fishermen's Village Marina, Punta Gorda. Excursions to Cayo Costa, Boca Grande, and Cabbage Key and along the Peace River aboard a double-decker head boat. Also sunset, harbor sight-seeing, and stop-to-dine cruises.

FISHING Tarpon reigns as the king of southwest Florida fish—the Silver King, to be exact, named for its silver dollar–like scales. ✪ **Boca Grande Pass** is one of the most celebrated spots in the world for catching the feisty fighter. But the tarpon is hardly alone on its throne: studies have reported more than 250 species of salt and freshwater fish in Charlotte Harbor. The harbor encompasses more than two hundred square miles of fishable water.

Nonresidents age sixteen and older who wish to fish must obtain a license unless fishing from a vessel or pier covered by its own license. You can buy inexpensive temporary-nonresident licenses at county tax collectors' offices and most bait shops. Check local regulations for season, size, and catch restrictions.

Fishing Charters/Outfitters: **Boca Grande Fishing Guides Association** (www.bocagrandefishing.com), P.O. Box 676, Boca Grande 33921. Organization of more than thirty qualified charter guides especially knowledgeable about tarpon.

Captain Jack's Charters (941-475-4511; www.sunstate.com/captjack), 1450 Beach Rd., at the Englewood Bait House, Englewood Beach. Half-day, full day, night, overnight, and weekend trips; party boat or private charter.

Capt. Les Hill (941-743-6622), 14482 Dahlgren Ave., Port Charlotte. Charters cover Siesta Key waters to Charlotte Harbor, Sanibel Island, and backwaters. Specialties include fly and light-tackle fishing with artificial lures.

Gasparilla Outfitters (941-964-0907 or 800-4-TARPON; www.4tarpon.com), 431 Park Ave., Boca Grande. Outfitters, fly shop, guides, and charters.

King Fisher Fleet (941-639-0969; www.kingfisherfleet.com), 1200 W. Retta Esplanade, at Fishermen's Village Marina, Punta Gorda. Deep-sea and back-bay fishing; owner Capt. Ralph Allen is the local expert on fishing and fishing conditions.

Fishing Piers: **Bayshore Fishing Pier**, 22967 Bayshore Dr., Charlotte Harbor. At the mouth of the Peace River next to the Charlotte County Historical Center.

Bayshore Live Oak Park (941-627-1628 ext, 101; www.charlottecountyfl.com), 23157 Bayshore Dr., Charlotte Harbor. Another pier extends into the river just east of the Bayshore pier in a park setting with picnic facilities and a canoe launch.

Englewood Beach (Anger) Pier, along Beach Rd. east of the drawbridge.

Gasparilla Fishing Pier South (941-627-1628), near North Village, north end of Gasparilla Rd., Gasparilla Island. An old railroad bridge.

Gilchrist Park, W. Retta Esplanade, Punta Gorda. Cast into the brackish waters where the Peace River empties into the gulf.

El Jobean Park Pier (941-681-3742), FL 776, El Jobean. Runs adjacent to a small bridge over the Myakka River.

Laishley Park Piers, 100 Nesbit St., Punta Gorda. Two quiet spots for fishing along the Trabue Harborwalk.

Ponce de León Park, 4000 W. Marion Ave., Punta Gorda. Two piers reaching into the mouth of the Peace River at Charlotte Harbor.

Port Charlotte Beach Park (941-627-1628), 4500 Harbor Blvd., Port Charlotte, southeast end of Harbor Blvd. Two boat ramps and a fishing pier are part of a beach and pool recreational center.

GOLF *Public Golf Courses & Centers:* **Deep Creek Golf Club** (941-625-6911; www .deepcreekgc.com), 1260 San Cristobal Ave., Port Charlotte. Semiprivate; eighteen holes, par seventy; driving range, putting green, and café.

Port Charlotte Golf Club (941-625-4109; www.portcharlottegolfclub.com), 22400 Gleneagles Terrace, Port Charlotte. Semiprivate; eighteen holes, par seven; full practice facilities, restaurant, and lounge.

HEALTH & FITNESS CLUBS **Punta Gorda YMCA** (941-505-0999; www.charlotte countyymca.com), 2905 Tamiami Trail, Punta Gorda. Formerly The Club Punta Gorda, this modern facility offers cardiovascular equipment, free weights, yoga, spinning, weight machines, tennis courts, baby-sitting, a coffee-juice shop, and massage. Day passes available; membership available, with access to four local YMCA facilities.

Cultural Center of Port Charlotte (941-625-4175, ext. 263; www.theculturalcenter. com), 2280 Aaron St., Port Charlotte. Full fitness facilities, classes, and personal trainers. For $30 a month, you can work out in the Fitness Salon.

✍ **Franz Ross Park YMCA** (941-629-9622; www.charlottecountyymca.com), 19333 Quesada Ave., Port Charlotte. Aerobics, body shaping, yoga, volleyball, basketball, golf tournaments, youth sports competitions, steam room, and kids' facilities and programs.

HIKING **Babcock Ranch Preserve** (800-500-5583; www.myfwc.com/viewing/ recreation/wmas/cooperative/babcock -ranch-preserve), 8000 State Rd. 31, Punta Gorda. The Footprints Trail takes you either 2 or 4.7 miles into Florida backcountry. The Eco-Trail is 1.8 miles long. On either of them, you may see deer, wild hogs, bald eagles, hawks, wood storks, and other birds.

Charlotte Harbor Environmental Center Alligator Creek Preserve (941-575-5435; www.checflorida.org), 10941 Burnt Store Rd., Punta Gorda. Six miles of nature trails depart from this center.

PASSENGERS ABOARD KING FISHER FLEET'S PEACE RIVER NATURE CRUISE POP UP AT AN ALLIGATOR SIGHTING

Charlotte Harbor Preserve State Park (941-575-5816; www.floridastateparks.org/park/Charlotte-Harbor), 12301 Burnt Store Rd., Punta Gorda. This park encompasses seventy miles of shoreline along Charlotte Harbor, spreading into two counties. In this region, three short trails delve into its diverse habitat of hammocks, pine and palmetto flatlands, and wetlands. The **Old Datsun Trail** next to the park office is 1.3 miles long—a little shorter October through May, when you must detour for nesting eagles. North of Placida off CR 771, the **Catfish Creek Trail** travels approximately 1.5 miles. Trails are open to cyclists. Paddlers see abundant bird life.

Fred C. Babcock–Cecil M. Webb Wildlife Management Area (863-648-3200; (www.myfwc.com)), 29200 Tucker Grade, Port Charlotte. The domain of endangered red-cockaded woodpeckers, this preserve attracts birders along its thirty-seven miles of unpaved hiking and biking trails, once used in logging operations. Sandhill cranes, white-tailed deer, and warblers also favor the diverse habitat found within its 79,013 acres. Avoid trails during peak of the hunting season, late October to mid-November.

✿ **Kiwanis Park** (941-627-1074; www.charlottecountyfl.com), 501 Donora St., at Victoria Ave., Port Charlotte. Here's a nice place to hike or jog while the kids entertain themselves on the playground. Nature and fitness trails thread through the woods and alongside a creek where turtles swim.

Manasota Scrub Preserve (941-861-5000; www.scgov.net), 2695 Bridge St., Englewood. A one-mile unpaved trail explores the scrubby flatwoods habitat of this 154-acre tract, home to gopher tortoises and rare scrub jays.

Myakka State Forest (941-460-1333; www.swfwmd.state.fl.us), 2000 S. River Rd., Englewood. With access off US 41 south of North Port, it opens thirteen miles of multiuse trails along the Myakka River from sunrise to sunset.

✪ **Punta Gorda Riverwalk**, downtown Punta Gorda. From Gilchrist Park to Laishley Park and the Trabue Harborwalk, 2.5 miles of pathways follow the Peace River.

HUNTING Given southwest Florida's heightened environmental consciousness, most shooting of wildlife is done with a camera. But the Charlotte Harbor coast's wilderness does provide opportunities for hunting various species. The most popular game animals are wild hogs, deer, doves, snipe, quail, turkeys, ducks, and coots.

For information on hunting licenses, permits, and seasons, visit www.myfwc.com/hunting.

Fred C. Babcock–Cecil M. Webb Wildlife Management Area (863-648-3200; myfwc .com), 29200 Tucker Grade, Port Charlotte. With some seventy-nine thousand acres, this is one of Florida's designated hunting preserves. Advance permission is required. There is a public shooting range on the property, accessible from Tucker Grade via Rifle Range Road. The range is open daily during daylight hours.

KIDS' STUFF ✐ **Captain Don Cerbone Memorial Skate Park** (941-505-8686; www .charlottecountyfl.com), 6905 Florida St., at Carmalita Athletic Park, Punta Gorda. Small park with ramps and half-pipes; playground and BMX track are part of the complex. Skate park admission is $3.

✐ **Fish Cove Adventure Golf** (941-627-5393; coralcaygolf.com/fishcove), 4949 Tamiami Trail, Port Charlotte. Two eighteen-hole putt-putt courses and a bounce house. Open Sunday to Thursday 10–10, Friday to Saturday 10–11. Admission for eighteen holes of golf is $10; $14 for thirty-six holes. Small playground and picnic facilities.

✐ **Kidstar Park** (941-235-3131; www.kidstarpark.com), 18505 Paulson Dr., at Sun Flea Market, Port Charlotte. Go-cart rides, a rock-climbing wall and giant slide, Ferris wheel and other children's rides, laser tag, motion ride, small games arcade, and snack bar and restaurant. Open weekends only.

    ⚓ **Laishley Marina Park** (941-575-0142; www.laishleymarina.com), 120 Laishley Ct., Punta Gorda. An interactive fountain next to the playground keeps kids cool and entertained at this riverfront recreational area with picnic facilities. A riverwalk path leads to the park, crossing beneath the US 41 bridge.

    ⚓ **Tringali Recreational Complex Skating** (941-681-3742; www.charlottecountyfl .com), 3460 N. Access Rd., Englewood. Weekly skate parties for elementary and middle school kids and families; also basketball, tennis, a walking trail, a gym, and a playground.

RACQUET SPORTS **Boca Grande Community Center** (941-964-2564; www.leegov .com/parks), 131 First St. W., Boca Grande. Two lighted tennis courts are located on Wheeler Street.

    McGuire Park, (941-627-1074; www.charlottecountyfl.com), 21125 McGuire Ave., Port Charlotte. Four lit hard-surface tennis courts.

    Tringali Recreational Complex (941-681-3742; http://www.charlottecountyfl. com/), 3460 N. Access Rd., Englewood. Four outdoor lit tennis courts.

SPAS **Charles of the Village** (941-639-6300; www.charlesofthevillage.com), 1200 W. Retta Esplanade, at Fishermen's Village, Punta Gorda. Facials, pedicures, manicures, and hair services. Packages available.

    Serendipity Salon & Spa (941-639-3900; www.serendipityofpuntagorda.com), 133 W. Marion Ave., Punta Gorda. Specializing in skin and body treatments: peels, skin tightening, scrubs, cellulite treatments, and facials plus salon services.

    Skintopia by Bina (941-575-0721; www.skintopiabybina.com), 208 Tamiami Trail, Suite 116, Punta Gorda. A spa carrying quality skin products and offering facials and nutritional counseling.

SPECTATOR SPORTS *Professional Baseball:* **Charlotte Sports Park** (888-FAN-RAYS; www.raysbaseball.com), 2300 El Jobean Rd., Port Charlotte. The Tampa Bay Rays play their spring training season at this state-of-the-art stadium during March. Come summer, the minor league Charlotte Stone Crabs (941-206-4487 or 866-272-9789; stone crabsbaseball.com) compete.

WATER SPORTS *Board Sports:* **Island Bike 'N Beach** (941-964-0711; www .islandbikenbeach.com), 333 Park Ave., Boca Grande. Rents stand-up paddleboards.

    Snorkeling & Scuba: The best underwater sight-seeing lies offshore some distance, where divers find a few wrecks and other man-made structures.

    Depth Finders Dive Center (941-766-7565; www.depthfinders.com), 1225 Tamiami Trail #A5, Port Charlotte. Full-service dive center, including instruction, rentals, air fills, and dive trips.

WILDLIFE SPOTTING The Charlotte Harbor coast is a haven for many of Florida's threatened·and endangered species, including Florida panthers (a relative of the mountain lion that is yellow, not black, and is characterized by a kink in its tail), bobcats, manatees, wood storks, and black skimmers. Manasota Key hosts one of the largest nesting sea turtle populations on the Gulf Coast. White pelicans migrate to the region in winter. Look for them on sandbars and small mangrove islands in the bays and estuaries. They congregate in flocks and feed cooperatively by herding fish. The Cape Haze area between Englewood and Boca Grande is known for its nesting ospreys and bald eagles. Lemon Bay Park and Cedar Point Environmental Park afford the best opportunities to see the nests. Look for sandhill cranes on golf courses and in other grasslands.

At **Babcock Ranch Preserve Eco-Tour**, a massive preserve east of Punta Gorda, you can see native sandhill cranes and a contained Florida panther along with lots of alligators. Adjacent **Fred C. Babcock-Cecil M. Webb Wildlife Management Area** shelters the endangered red-cockaded woodpecker among other species of woodpeckers, warblers, and woodland birds. It, along with **Amberjack Environmental Park, Cedar Point, Charlotte Flatwoods Environmental Park, Charlotte Harbor Environmental Center, Charlotte Harbor Preserve State Park,** and **Tippe-canoe Environmental Park** are plotted on the South Florida section of the **Great Florida Birding & Wildlife Trail** (www. floridabirdingtrail.com).

Nature Preserves & Eco-Attractions: **Audubon Pennington Nature Walk** (www .peaceriveraudubon.org), Alton Rd. at Peachland Blvd., Port Charlotte. A bit tricky to find tucked into a residential neighborhood, this eight-acre site provides a 0.75-mile loop trail with species identification signs through hardwood hammock. No facilities. Free admission.

✇ **Cedar Point Environmental Park** (941-475-0769; www.checflorida.org), 2300 Placida Rd., off FL 775, Englewood. Bald eagles, marsh rabbits, bobcats, gopher tortoises, bald eagles, and pileated woodpeckers are the stars of this 115-acre preserve, which borders the Lemon Bay Aquatic Preserve with 2.6 miles of trails. Call or visit the website for a calendar of guided nature walks and wading adventures. Free admission.

✇ **Charlotte Harbor Environmental Center (CHEC) at Alligator Creek Preserve** (941-575-5435; www.checflorida.org), 10941 Burnt Store Rd., Punta Gorda. Gates open Monday to Saturday 8–3, Sunday 11–3; trails open daily sunrise-sunset; guided trail walks, 10 a.m. Tuesday, Thursday, and Saturday. The center conducts guided tours around four miles of nature trails that wind through pine and palmetto flatlands, hammocks, and freshwater marshes where alligators and bobcats live. On one, there's a bird blind—a little shack with a picture window and field guides for watching the birds it attracts to a water feature. It hosts changing exhibits in its visitor center and grows a native plant nursery. CHEC conducts various tours and programs both on and off campus. Free admission.

🦌 ✇ **Lemon Bay Park & Environmental Center** (941-861-5000; www.scgov.net/ ParksandRecreation/Parks), 570 Bay Park Blvd., Englewood. Its more than two hundred acres of bayside forest, wetlands, shoreline, pinelands, and scrub are home to bald eagles and other creatures of the sky, woods, and water. Experience its three miles of bayside and forested nature trails (including a paved handicapped-accessible one), picnic facilities, butterfly garden with great signage, canoe launch, interactive indoor environmental displays, educational programs, kayak tours, and guided nature and birding walks. Free admission.

✇ **Peace River Wildlife Center** (941-637-3830; www.peaceriverwildlifecenter.com), 3400 Ponce de Leon Pkwy., at Ponce de León Park, Punta Gorda. Open 11–4 daily. Donations requested. You can self-tour or take a guided tour of the outdoor bird aviary. Daily feedings are fun to watch at 2:30. It accepts about two thousand orphaned, displaced, and injured creatures each year.

Wildlife Tours & Charters: ✪ ✇ **Babcock Wilderness Adventures** (941-637-0551 or 800-500-5583; www.myfwc.com/viewing/recreation/wmas/cooperative/babcock-ranch -preserve), 8000 State Rd. 31, Punta Gorda. Tours by reservation only; call for times. $22 adults, $14 children ages three to twelve (plus tax). Advance reservations required. On a ninety-minute swamp-buggy-bus ride through Crescent B Ranch and Telegraph Cypress Swamp you'll spot Old Florida wildlife, including white-tailed deer, a fenced-in panther,

FLUTED CYPRESS TREES STALK TELEGRAPH SWAMP AT BABCOCK RANCH

wild turkeys, sandhill cranes, squirrels, feral hogs, and lots of alligators. The driver gives an on-board demonstration with a live baby gator and leads a boardwalk hike through a cypress swamp. The adventure takes place on an actual ranch that dates back to the cow-hunting era. Cracker cattle are still raised here. A restaurant, live snake display, gift shop, and small history museum set in a cabin used in Sean Connery's movie *Just Cause* (filmed partly on-site) provide other activities at this, one of the Charlotte Harbor coast's finest attractions. It offers special photography and heritage tours as well.

King Fisher Peace River Nature Cruise (941-639-0969; www.kingfisherfleet.com), 1200 W. Retta Esplanade, at Fishermen's Village Marina, Punta Gorda. Timed according to the tides. You'll likely see alligators, pelicans, egrets, ibises, and cormorants on the 3.5-hour journey upriver and back in time. You may also spot manatees, roseate spoonbills, river otters, and great blue herons. Volunteers from Charlotte Harbor Environmental Center knowledgeably narrate as the double-decker boat chugs leisurely along.

✳ Lodging

Accommodations along the Charlotte Harbor coast tend to exude personality. Sure, you have your La Quinta and Budget Inn, but the remainder are either old-money polished, new-money luxurious, or money's-not-the-issue sporting. From beach cottages to the grand old Gasparilla Inn, the Charlotte Harbor coast promises something special in the way of lodging.

During high season, which begins shortly before Christmas and ends after Easter, rates may rise anywhere from 10 to 100 percent above those charged during the off-season. Some resorts schedule their rates based on as many as six different seasons, and the highest rates apply during the holidays and from mid-February through Easter.

Reservations are recommended during these months. Some resorts and rental services require a minimum stay, especially during the peak season.

The following selection includes some of the coast's greatest lodging characters. Where available, toll-free 800, 888, 877, 866, or 855 reservation numbers are listed after local numbers.

Prices are normally per person/double occupancy for hotel rooms and per unit for efficiencies, apartments, and cottages. Many resorts offer off-season packages at special rates. Pricing does not include the 6 percent Florida sales tax or Charlotte County's 1 percent sales tax and 5 percent touristist development tax. Some large resorts add service gratuities or housekeeping charges.

Rate Categories

Inexpensive	Up to $100
Moderate	$100 to $200
Expensive	$200 to $300
Very Expensive	$300 and up

An asterisk (*) after the pricing designation indicates that the rate includes at least continental breakfast in the cost of lodging; one establishment follows the American Plan, pricing all meals into the room rate.

Note that under the Americans with Disabilities Act (ADA), accommodations built after January 26, 1993, and containing more than five rooms must be usable by people with disabilities. I have indicated only those small places that do not make such allowances.

ACCOMMODATIONS

BOCA GRANDE

❀ **The Innlet** (941-964-4600; www .innletonthewaterfront.com), 1251 12th St. E., 33921. Little stepsister to the Gasparilla Inn, the Innlet is also painted yellow, to fit in with the family. Fancy lattice touches and renovations pretty up a motel remake. The name is a double entendre on its sub-inn status and its bayou location with a ramp and docking, handy for boating and fishing types. It has a nice little pool, playground, and thirty-three rooms and efficiencies (with stove top, microwave, and fridge) in modern, tasteful attire. Guests share communal porches and balconies. An on-site restaurant, The Outlet, is popular for breakfast. Moderate.

CAPE HAZE

✪ ♬ **Palm Island Resort** (941-697-0696 or 800-824-5412; www.palmisland .com), 7092 Placida Rd., 33946. A true island getaway in grand style, Palm Island occupies the northernmost point of a slab of sand above Gasparilla Island. One must boat in; a car ferry runs continuously from the mainland, where the resort also owns one-bedroom harborside condos for guests. On the island, modern Old Florida–style villas front a wide, isolated apron of sea oats-fringed beach and come with fully equipped kitchens, laundries, one to three bedrooms, casually elegant appointments, and screened porches overlooking more than two miles of deserted beach. The one hundred-plus-unit (counting the mainland accommodations, which are the only ones with handicap-accessible units) property has six pools and twelve tennis courts, plus a restaurant and bar (another on the mainland), an island store, a full-service marina, boat rentals, charter services, nature programs, kids' and other recreational programs, playgrounds, plus bicycles, golf carts (the main mode of transport on the island), kayaks, canoes, stand-up paddleboards, and beach equipment rentals—all the makings for an "I'm-never-leaving-this-island" vacation. What it doesn't have is paved roads, cars (you park outside resort gates), stress, and rigorous time schedules. Moderate to Very Expensive.

MUST SEE

✪ ♂ 🐾 (ᵩ) **Gasparilla Inn & Club** (941-964-4500 or 800-996-1913; www.gasparillainn.com), 500 Palm Ave., 33921. With subtle grandeur, the Gasparilla Inn sits on her throne of lush greenery. Dressed in pale yellow clapboard with white columns, Georgian porticos, and Victorian sensibilities, the inn has been a town anchor and social emblem since 1913. The region's oldest surviving resort, the Gasparilla first opened its doors as a retreat for such families as the Vanderbilts and Du Ponts, along with, in modern times, the Bushes and other illuminati. Not that the accommodations are ultraelegant: The 139 rooms reflect the era of their construction, with exposed pipes, tasteful cabana nuances, and fine but understated furnishings; the eighteen cottages and villas are more modern and roomy. In recent years, a renovation and menu overhaul have brought the resort into the twenty-first century. In 2016, six luxury "Sharp Houses" were added to inventory. Their three- and four-bedroom configurations and open layout with full kitchen suit families and other groups. The inn itself offers bars, lounges, libraries, a playground, generous porches, and various nooks and crannies where guests can socialize or get away. A white-linen dining room and two other restaurants, a bakery-deli, a beauty salon and spa, a top-rated eighteen-hole golf course, a croquet lawn, tennis courts, a playground, a beach club with fitness facilities, and two pools round out the amenities. It's said that the Gasparilla Inn in quiet Boca Grande is where Palm Beach socialites came to escape charity balls and the perpetual fashion show of their glittery hometown. Rates include a variety of meal, golf, and spa plans in season. Expensive to Very Expensive. Closed mid-July through mid-October (cottages available during that time).

THE GASPARILLA INN, DOYENNE OF THE GULF COAST

ENGLEWOOD BEACH

🦐 🌴 ⚲ 📶 **Weston's wannaB inn** (941-474-3431; wannabinn.com), 985 Gulf Blvd., 34223. Formerly the longstanding, old-school Weston's Resort, this inn's owners are kept the beachy, fishing vibe and brightened up the place with renovations and snappy bright paint accents on the outside of the complex's seven accommodations buildings. The rooms, though they still show their age, have transformed into a brighter interpretation of the midcentury era the original resort harkens back to. Lollipop color chairs and accents, retro chrome and dining tables, and lots of room characterize the new look. The buildings range from cottages and low-rises to three-story buildings; the eighty units from rooms to two-bedroom gulf-front suites—all with full kitchens. Two swimming pools, a laundry room, and boat docks remain. If you're looking for an affordable barefoot beach vacation or fishing getaway, here's your place, right next to Stump Pass Beach State Park. Moderate.

MANASOTA KEY

♻ ⚲ **Manasota Beach Club** (941-474-2614; www.manasotabeachclub.com), 7660 Manasota Key Rd., Englewood 34223. A tiny, low-impact sign whispers MANASOTA BEACH CLUB along a windy canopy road. And although it occupies twenty acres of Manasota Key, the resort itself is just as unobtrusive. The unadvertised property preserves the island's natural attributes with a low-key attitude, wooded paths, and an often deserted beach. Guests have reported seeing ninety-two bird species about the grounds. Fifteen beachy-woodsy-style cottages of various ages and configurations; the dining room; the bottle club (no alcohol is sold on the premises); and a library display Old

Florida charm. The fifty-five-year-old resort appeals to the "sink into oblivion" type of vacationer who wishes to hide out among natural, gnarly vegetation. The property—which has a summer-camp feel to it—also appeals to the sportsperson, with three tennis courts; a swimming pool; bocce, shuffleboard and basketball courts; a playground; croquet; bicycling; sailing, and kayaking; and a seasonal children's program. A private eighteen-hole golf course nearby is available to resort guests. During social season (February through Easter), cottage-room guests receive three meals a day on the American Plan; a Modified American Plan (two meals) is in effect Thanksgiving–January and after Easter. Mid-May to mid-November, the resort offers weekly rates on entire cottages with kitchens but no meals. Expensive to Very Expensive* (two-day minimum stay).

PORT CHARLOTTE

🦐 🌴 ⚲ 📶 **Banana Bay Waterfront Motel** (941-743-4441; www.bananabaymotel .com), 23285 Bayshore Rd., off US 41, 33980. Along Bayshore Drive in Charlotte Harbor, the feeling is Old Florida, relaxed, and fishy. Across the wide mouth of the Peace River lies Punta Gorda. A few inexpensive motels in this neighborhood serve the stay-away-from-the-crowds crowd, and Banana Bay is one of the prettiest, with banana-tree murals on its one-story stucco rooms and one-bedroom efficiencies. The thirteen rooms have a clean, perky, tropical look. All units have small fridges and microwaves; junior efficiencies throw in a stovetop and sink. Along the bay, shuffleboard courts, grills, and picnic tables put the focus outdoors on the fetching water view. Banana Bay also has its own fishing pier and a small beach. Families like the pool and, next door, the mini golf attraction. Inexpensive to Moderate.

🔌 ((•)) **Four Points By Sheraton** (941-637-6770 or 866-716-8133; www .fourpointspuntagorda.com), 33 Tamiami Trail, 33950. Four Points presents an affordable downtown stay that both business and leisure guests appreciate for its proximity to restaurants, shops, and the convention center. It has its own breakfast and dinner restaurant tucked into its open, light wood lobby, plus a riverside tiki bar and grill that's popular with guests and non-guests alike. The restaurant spills out on the terrace, where a small pool and fountain create atmosphere. The hotel's riverside location adds to the ambience, and the town's Riverwalk is steps away. A library in the lobby invites lounging or multitasking with its computers, televisions, and fireplace. The lobby's sleek, clean lines continue in the hotel's 106 rooms and suites, designed to suggest a ship's cabin with blues, portholes, nautical throw pillows, and truly original décor for a chain hotel. The nicest rooms have river views, but others on the lower floors face a condo next door. Moderate to Expensive.

WHIMSICAL MURALS ADD COLOR TO RIVERFRONT BANANA BAY

🔌 ((•)) **The Vacation Villas at Fishermen's Village** (941-639-8721 or 800-639-0020; www.fishville.com), 1200 W. Retta Esplanade #58, 33950, at Fishermen's Village. This is one of the Gulf Coast's best lodging bargains. These spacious time-share units—all forty-seven decorated in modern taste and all with a view of the water—contain two bedrooms and a loft (sleeping up to six), a living area, a full kitchen with counter bar and stools, and one bath. They are above the shops, restaurants, and courtyard hubbub of Fishermen's Village, so they can be a little noisy, especially when morning deliveries are arriving. Guests have free use of a swimming pool, tennis courts, shuffleboard, a picnic area, and bicycles, plus there are coin laundry facilities. The villas are close to all the action there is to find in Punta Gorda, on land and on water. Convenient for boat-in guests, Fishermen's Village fronts a yacht harbor and a 111-slip full-service marina. A five-year expansion plan will bring more facilities and amenities, including a sand beach and a zero-entry pool to replace the current one. Moderate.

((•)) **Wyvern Hotel** (941-639-7700; www.thewyvernhotel.com), 101 E. Retta Esplanade, 33950. Owner operated, the boutique sixty-three-room standout exerts individual style at only-in-Punta-Gorda reasonable rates. Sleek Euro-style rooms in earthy tones and dark wood are stocked with Italian linens, fine amenities, a mini-bar, and roomy marble and granite baths. Tip-top service includes free (optional) turndown service and shoe shines. In the small fitness center, some of the cardio machines have iPod hookups. Its Curve restaurant off the lobby has a baseball/sports bar theme. Rooftop, the view from the pool and its deck and bar (with tapas and other food service) takes in the Peace River and downtown Punta Gorda, whose historic district has regenerated into a dining refuge and lively nightlife scene. The rooftop lounge has become popular with the locals, but Wyvern protects guests' security and privacy with a special key-scan system that allows only them to access room floors. Moderate to Very Expensive.

HOME & CONDO RENTALS **Boca Grande Real Estate** (941-964-0338 or 866-302-0338; www .bocagranderealestate.com), P.O. Box 686, Boca Grande 33921. Large selection of vacation and seasonal accommodations.
Conch Out Vacation Rentals at Manasota Key Realty (941-474-9534 or 800-881-9534; www.englewoodfl.com), 1927 Beach Rd., Englewood 34223. Grand mansions, beachside cottages, condos, and bayside homes.
Place in the Sun Vacation Rentals (941-697-2175; www.placeinthesun.com), 8501 Placida Rd. #A3, Placida 33946. Vacation homes, condos, and villas.

RV RESORTS Most of the area's RV accommodations lie east of I-75.
((♥)) **Water's Edge RV Resort** (941-637-4677 or 800-637-9224; www .watersedgervresort.com), 6800 Golf Course Blvd., Punta Gorda 33982. Full hookups, recreation hall, pool, Jacuzzi, fishing lake and dock, convenience store, and rural setting. For adults ages fifty-five and older only.

✳ Where to Eat

Local cuisine smacks of Midwestern influence, but in recent decades Floribbean and other exotic flavors have livened things up. Fishing crews bring just-hooked seafood to the table, but that doesn't mean some restaurants won't try to pawn off frozen products. Here I've tried to include a selection of eateries that believe in freshness and fanfare at the dining table.
The following listings sample all the variety of Charlotte Harbor Coast feasting in these price categories:

Inexpensive	Up to $15
Moderate	$15 to $25
Expensive	$25 to $35
Very Expensive	$35 or more

Cost categories are based on the range of dinner entrée prices, or, if dinner is not served, of lunch entrées.
Note: Florida law forbids smoking inside all restaurants and bars serving food. Smoking is permitted only in restaurants with outdoor seating.

BOCA GRANDE

✪ **PJ's Seagrille** (941-964-0806; www .pjseagrille.com), 321 Park Ave., in the Old Theatre Building. PJ's is one of Boca Grande's most popular fine-dining experiences. Family-owned and operated for more than twenty-five years, it exudes an air of island familiarity, and regulars return year after year. Dinners offer linen and candlelight; lunch is more casual—both are served in the setting of unfinished wood and aquariums. The menus change according to fish availability and Chef Jim's creative mood swings. At lunch, you'll find standard fare with sporadic flares of imagination, such as pita chicken sandwich with pesto mayo and grilled onions, or black beans and rice with a corn muffin. At dinner, PJ's shines with an ever-changing menu featuring what the local fishermen caught that day. Some sure bets if you see them: the yellowfin tuna tartare with sesame soy vinaigrette, margarita shrimp, tomato basil bisque with lump crab, char-grilled bronzed scallops risotto, and panfried snapper with garlic, lemon, and white wine (much more complex in flavor than it sounds). The sides battle for attention. Try the regularly featured cheese grits or, when available, the curried acorn squash with almonds. Save room for homemade dessert. The Key lime pie and chocolate cake with coconut frosting are winners. Fishtales Lounge offers more casual fare and ambience. Moderate to Expensive. Reservations recommended for dinner. Closed Sunday and mid-July through September.

South Beach Bar & Grille (941-964-0765; www.southbeachbarandgrille.com), 760 Gulf Blvd., Boca Grande. Choose your level of casual: indoors with air-conditioning and a view of the beach, out on the porch under paddle fans with open windows, on a fanned porch closer to the sands and open air, or directly planted in the sand under umbrellas. This establishment screams beach shack and its food is equally salty. The Ultimate Grouper Sandwich on the lunch menu is no exaggeration, topped with roasted plum tomatoes and a tartar sauce extraordinaire. Or try the fried shrimp, ahi tuna sandwich, or shrimp wrap. There are also prime burgers, pulled pork sandwich, and baby back ribs for meat lovers. At dinner, Grouper Gaspar (piccata style with artichoke hearts and sun-dried tomatoes), pineapple rum shrimp, and seafood strudel are specialties, but the grilled ribeye just might be the ticket if you're in the mood. Fresh ingredients and gourmet touches elevate this dining experience from your typical toes-in-the-sand experience. Expensive. No reservations. (You may be turned away in season once the parking lot fills up.)

ENGLEWOOD

Farlow's on the Water (941-474-5343; www.farlowsonthewater.com), 2080 S. McCall Rd., Englewood. One of the oldest and most popular restaurants in these parts, Farlow's combines the owners' Caribbean and Southern background for a fresh approach to tropical. The extensive lunch and dinner menus prominently feature seafood, such as the mojo mahi spinach wrap and Caribbean grilled scallop salad at lunch and Jamaican jerk cobia and grouper platter at dinner. Specialties include goat tacos, seafood pie, coconut shrimp, St. Croix chicken (portabella,

wine cheese sauce, provolone), steak au poivre, and Kentucky hot brown open faced sandwich. We tried some of the night's seafood specials and loved the choice of sides (coconut risotto, corn pudding, baked sweet potato with mango rum butter), but found the fish a bit overdone. Dinners also come with a salad, and the house dressing is delish. Call an hour ahead to get on the wait list, then enjoy a cocktail at the indoor or outdoor bar. The best seating is outdoors with a view of the back bay. Live performers entertain many evenings. Moderate to Expensive.

🍴 ((ᵩ)) **Mango Bistro** (941-681-3500; www.mangobistro.com), 301 W. Dearborn. You've come to a happy place here: a dozen tables scattered among cheerful yellow walls and on the porch outside. The comforting waft of coffee greets you before you reach the attentive wait staff with their headquarters behind the coffee bar. Crepes are a specialty for breakfast, lunch, and dinner—savory bacon and eggs, portobello and spinach, ham with Brie and apples, pulled pork, and shrimp and lobster with creamy lobster sauce; and sweet caramelized apples or Reese's crepes for dessert. Try the lobster bisque, for which they seem to be famous—the menu announces they sell it by the quart. Laced with sherry and a swirl of cream on top, it couldn't be more intoxicating, and I'm not talking about the sherry. It made me want to lick the bowl; I restrained myself. There's a lot to choose from, including fresh salads, grilled wraps, pretzel bread sandwiches, a breakfast flatbread sandwich, and a gluten-free menu. If you're not in the mood for a dessert crepe, there are smoothies and fresh-made sweets, such as vanilla bean brulee cheesecake and coconut cream pie spiked with dark rum. Inexpensive to Moderate. No reservations. Open breakfast and lunch, also dinner on Friday and Saturday. Closed Sunday.

ENGLEWOOD BEACH

Gulf View Grill (941-475-3500; www
.thegulfviewgrill.com), 2095 N. Beach
Rd. In recent years, this has come to be
my favorite Manasota Key restaurant.
To start with, there's the drop-dead
view from its stilted glass-cage perch;
its sunset deck takes full advantage.
The lunch and dinner menus go heavy
on the seafood but please just about
every appetite. Seafood purists can
go for the luncheon "simply fish"
options—a choice of seven, either
grilled, sauteed, fried, or baked. Or try
the Lob-Cob salad or various grouper
sandwiches. Dinner seafood selections
include red snapper in creamy tarragon
sauce, Salmon Hoisin, and lobster mac
and cheese. Meat lovers have a choice
of steaks, veal piccata, and chicken
florentine. For a splurge, try the hot
cinnamon apple caramel sundae. Inexpensive to Moderate. Reservations
accepted.

PLACIDA

🦐 🐟 **The Fishery Restaurant** (941-697-
2451; www.thefisheryrestaurant.com),
13000 Fishery Rd., Placida. Take a side
trip to Old Florida as you drive or boat
in to this waterside shanty with a view
of mangroves, an old fishing boat, and
the dilapidated fish packing plant next
door. Scenes from Denzel Washington's
Out of Time were filmed in the restaurant, where locals and boaters belly-up
to the bar outdoors on the dock or inside
in the plain dining room where the glass
walls are the focal point. The menu
reflects what's fresh from local waters,
prepared both in Cracker style and classic Continental. Start with a coconut
shrimp appetizer or a basket of gator
bites. Choose from salads, sandwiches,
or entrées like shrimp scampi or broiled
grouper with hush puppies. It's all good,
hearty, unpretentious fare. In 2016,
new owners took over the restaurant

long held by the Albritton family, so the
menu has scaled down from what regulars had come to expect. Inexpensive to
Moderate. Closed certain weekdays in
summer.

PORT CHARLOTTE

🦐 **Golden Krust Caribbean Bakery
& Grill** (941-234-5579; www
.goldenkrustbakery.com), 1825 Tamiami Trail. Imagine my delight as a
Jamaican food junkie to have acci-
dentally stumbled upon this pocket
of authentic Jamaican cookery along
the busy strip through Port Charlotte.
No secret to the local Caribbean population, its main business seems to
come from take-out, but the pleasant,
bright dining room invites lingering
over such specialties as jerk chicken
patty, curried goat, fried snapper esco-
vitch, braised oxtail, and the Jamaican national dish, ackee and salt fish
(served normally at breakfast, but I
successfully begged for a luncheon
serving). Most dinners you can order in
small or large portions. Bright yellow
tiles and corrugated metal wainscot-
ing welcome you as you place your
order at the bakery counter. It honestly
earns the "bakery" in its name with
traditional Jamaican breads, such as
the slightly sweet coco bread, and confections the likes of rum cake, carrot
cake, and spice bun. You couldn't feel
more like you're on a mini-Caribbean
vacation from the bustle on the street.
Inexpensive. No reservations

Sunset Grill on the Harbor (941-743-
2800; www.sunsetgrilloth.com), 23241
Bayshore Rd. The view is the selling
point here, overlooking the Peace River
where it dumps into Charlotte Harbor.
Admire it from inside the second-level
dining room, or out on the usually
breezy deck around the fun-time bar.
The all-day menu touts a number of
different styles of cuisine. A Little
Italy section satisfies customers who

remember Portofino Waterfront Dining, which occupied this space for many years. Try the lobster and shrimp pasta with your choice of lobster sauce or spicy fra diavolo. From Jamaican influence comes half jerk chicken with plantains; from New Orleans, boudin-stuffed pork chops and gumbo; and from South Carolina, lowcountry boil. Generous selections of small plates, salads, flatbreads, burgers and sandwiches, and steaks populate the all-day menu. Inexpensive to Moderate. No reservations. Closed Monday.

PUNTA GORDA

Amimoto Japanese Restaurant (941-505-1515), 2705 S. Tamiami Trail, at Towles Plaza. Soothing and authentic, Amimoto satisfies the spirit as well as the stomach. The décor is simple, contemporary, and clean, decorated with tasteful Eastern art and arranged around the faux-wood Formica sushi bar. The sushi menu itself presents nearly fifty choices of sushi and rolls in four categories: raw, vegetable, cooked, and preserved (smoked)—all expertly prepared. Cooked options range from fried shrimp to Kobe beef rolls. The

steamed gyoza (dumplings) with mustard sauce are also a tasty way to start off the meal. The lunch and dinner menus list dozens more options for appetizers, such as the light miso soup with tofu and enoki, fried softshell crab, and seaweed salad for starters. Bento box combinations, a Japanese improvement on box lunches, are popular midday choices, as are rice or noodle bowls. For dinner, the menu lists grilled sea bass, breaded pork loin, and shrimp teriyaki with Asian sauces. Ginger shrimp is one of its most popular dishes, and sushi combinations are another dinner option. For a refreshing sweet, after-dinner indulgence, try the pretty plum wine ice cream. Moderate to Expensive. Reservations accepted. Closed for lunch Saturday and Sunday.

🦐 **Dean's Tex-Mex South of the Border Cantina** (941-575-6100; www.deanssouthoftheborder.net), 130 Tamiami Trail. One of the liveliest spots downtown, Dean's kicks into gear for breakfast and often jams with live music into the late-night hours. This is gringo Mexican food, no doubt, but offered with great variety and surprising quality considering its obvious bar priorities. At breakfast, for instance, the huevos rancheros step out of their comfort zone with shredded beef and fiery red and green sauces—beyond hearty! Besides all the typical tacos, burritos, quesadillas, and chimichangas, you will find burgers, wings, a nice selection of salads, plus dinners from seafood to ribs and steak. Inexpensive. No reservations.

(ᵛᵖ) **Leroys' Southern Kitchen & Bar** (941-505-2389; www.leroyssouthern kitchenandbar.com), 201 W. Marion Ave. Just what downtown Punta Gorda needed to balance its fine dining and mainstream cuisine: a salute to Southern cuisine with an emphasis on Louisiana. Barn wood, or at least barn-like wood, lines its booths, and sweet iced tea comes in wide-mouth quart Ball jars. I was tempted to nosh

MUST SEE

🦀 **Peace River Seafood & Crab Shack** (941-505-8440), 5337 Duncan Rd., 1.5 miles east of I-75 exit 164. Kelly Beall and her husband Jimmy, a crabber of twenty-some years, rescued a circa-1926 Cracker shack in the early 2000s in an attempt to also rescue the local crabbing industry, which foreign imports had just about decimated. Jimmy and other local crabbers provide the restaurant with a steady supply of its specialty—steamed blue crab. Servers cover your table with newspaper, arm you with a hammer and crab cracker, and you're ready to go. Other seafood comes from other parts of Florida, such as Apalachicola oysters, Horseshoe Beach clams, gulf shrimp, and Keys lobster. Kelly's gator gumbo is a belly buster with shrimp, sausage, crab, and rice. The menu stays the same throughout the day and includes a cheeseburger and catfish or grouper sandwich. Inexpensive to Moderate. No reservations.

PEACE RIVER SEAFOOD SEALS IN THE FLAVOR OF OLD FLORIDA WITH ITS CIRCA-1926 DIGS AND CRABBING HERITAGE

off of just small plates when I visited. The deviled eggs get a kick with pickle relish and a scab of sugared bacon. The crawfish beignets take a Creole detour from conch fritters, but are less chewy, more tasty and moist. Blackened foie gras with bourbon brioche and blueberry jam, pork belly steam buns with bourbon glaze and cucumber Tabasco kimchee, and smoked brussels sprouts with truffled goat cheese put the South in your mouth with some Asian and new-American upgrades. In the end, I decided I had to try the pulled pork with sweet corn pancakes. The pork was a tad dry, but wrapped in the pancakes with house barbecue sauce made the most interesting sort of cajun taco. The collard greens side was textbook, with a cruet of pepper vinegar to dose it up. Other specialties include charcuterie; there's a sausage board of alligator, wild boar, and andouille. Po' boys, interesting salads and burgers, steaks, seafood gumbo, scallops and succotash, and skillet apple pies use locally sourced ingredients where possible. Try the shrimp & grits with a Lowcountry

Bloody Mary (garnished with a shrimp) for Sunday brunch. Moderate. Reservations accepted.

♻ **The Perfect Caper** (941-505-9009; www.theperfectcaper.com), 121 E. Marion Ave. This local toast of connoisseurs serves fine, ingenious cuisine in a burnished bistro setting with an exhibit kitchen. Every meal I've eaten here scores A+. James Beard Award semifinalist Chef Jeanne Roland has earned a national reputation. The duck on my lunch of duck salad came medium-rare as ordered, tender and juicy, served on greens and dressed deliciously with cherry vinaigrette. A square of herbed focaccia accompanied it. Other intriguing meat-and-greens salads plus an array of entrées and sandwiches, such as arugula and Brie on ciabatta and pan-seared scallops with roasted butternut squash risotto complete the lunch menu. For dinner, a seasonally changing menu offers such delights as a crisp pork belly tacos appetizer, grilled homemade mozzarella and heirloom tomato salad with wild arugula, grilled scallops topped with brulée jumbo crab meat, Moroccan spiced lamb, and duck confit with garlic-marinated duck breast. The chef also offers a prix fixe two-course menu for an affordable $25 each. Dessert presents a tough choice, but you won't regret the chocolate bread pudding with vanilla-caramel sauce or the hand-churned ice cream, sorbet, and gelato of the day. Don't miss this place for Charlotte County's most cutting-edge cuisine. Moderate to Very Expensive. Reservations accepted. Open Monday to Saturday for dinner, Wednesday to Friday for lunch.

Trabue (941-639-0900; www.trabuerestaurant.com), 258 W. Marion Ave. Named for the town's early identity, Trabue's only resemblance to old-timey is its historic digs. Open the door, and you're swept into a scene entirely unexpected in this town largely populated by retirees: boldly painted walls; a spectacular blue-tinted, glass-fronted bar; and a magical courtyard out back where live music takes the stage certain evenings. Chef Keith Meyer has transformed the menu into "serious food but approachable." Bison meatloaf, pan-roasted sea bass, and seared sea scallops with roasted vegetable ratatouille: I believe he has achieved his goal with flying colors as bright as the walls. We stopped in for lunch in the courtyard and marveled over the attention to details: sleek, unique flatware; the cool sink in the ladies' room; the missing salt and pepper shakers (how do you vote—a sign of arrogance or seasoning mastery?). I figured the Fisherman Chowder at $11 a bowl would be a meal, with fish, snapper, mussels, and shrimp. Obviously made lovingly from scratch, it was a bit small for the price (two each mussels and clams, a small piece of shrimp, generous white fish of undisclosed species), but delicious with a nice spicy bite. And, well, that just gave me an excuse to indulge in dessert—not one but all three (sharing with friends). The Meyer lemon cheesecake with lemon curd was a clear favorite. The Key lime pie had the right amount of tartness, and the flourless chocolate cake is a must-try for any chocolate junkie. Stay tuned to the website for regularly scheduled wine dinners and other specials. Moderate to Expensive. Reservations accepted. Open Monday to Saturday for dinner, Tuesday to Friday for lunch.

BAKERIES **The Inn Bakery** (941-855-9170; www.gasparillainn.com), 384 E. Railroad Ave., Boca Grande. Brought to you by the Gasparilla Inn, this separate little shop serves up pastries, doughnuts, muffins, cookies, pie, cupcakes, sandwiches, coffee, and cold drinks.

Sugar Island Cupcakes (941-639-3030; www.sugarislandcupcakes.com), 3769 Acline Rd., Punta Gorda. Small and filled large cupcakes (think PBJ, Boston creams, and strawberry shortcake). Buy individually or by the batch.

BREAKFAST John Ski's House of Breakfast and Lunch (941-347-7645), 502 King St., Punta Gorda. Home of the "Fat Boy Breakfast Challenge" belly-stretcher. It's also known for its breakfast platters and enormous benedict plates such as Banging Shrimp and Southern Sausage.

Zeke's Uptown Bar & Grill (941-460-9353, zekesuptown.com), 115 W. Dearborn St., Englewood. Zeke's serves breakfast, lunch, and dinner in a casual indoor-outdoor venue, but I can only vouch for its wonderfully varied breakfast menu. I recommend the Zuevos Rancheros and country benedict.

BREWERIES, WINERIES, DISTILLERIES Alligator Bay Distillers (941-347-8419; www.alligatorbaydistillers .com), 25522 Marion Ave., Punta Gorda. Opened late 2015, it offers tastings of its gold, white, and pineapple rum made from Florida cane molasses.

Catania's Winery (941-475-7553; cataniaswinery.com), 524 Paul Morris Dr., Englewood. The retail operation here opened in 2011, selling its brand of tasty Cabernet Sauvignon and Sauvignon Blanc made from Italian and California grapes, as well as its own olive oil plus custom blends of coffee, vinegars, honey, other gourmet items, and home wine-making supplies. Stop in for free wine and olive oil tasting.

Fat Point Brewing (800-380-7405; www.fatpoint.com), 611 Charlotte St., Punta Gorda. Literally translating Punta Gorda, it distributes its product around town and beyond. Its ample indoor-outdoor brewery and taproom serves a variety of signature beers such as Big Boca Ale and seasonal specials, along with a small menu of eats.

CANDY & ICE CREAM Cubby's Homemade Ice Cream (941-637-9600), 264 W. Marion Ave., Punta Gorda. Sandwiches, wraps, Cuban sandwiches, and salads in addition to hand-dipped ice cream.

Good Ole Days Coffee & Ice Cream (941-655-8088; www.fishville.com), 1200 W. Retta Esplanade #28, at Fishermen's Village, Punta Gorda. Retro style café specializing in homemade ice cream and coffee.

Harborwalk Scoops & Bites (941-505-8880; www.scoopsandbites.com) 150 Laishley Ct. #111, in Laishley Park facing the river. Rated the #1 ice cream shop in America by TripAdvisor, it sells more than forty flavors of ice cream, plus shaved ice, floats, shakes, vintage sodas, coffee, "Personal Park Pizza," and homemade banana bread.

✒ **The Loose Caboose** (941-964-0440; www.loosecaboose.biz), 433 W. Fourth St., Boca Grande. Known for its homemade ice cream and smoothies in many flavors, served in the town's historic depot.

Simply Sweet (941-344-7322; www .fishville.com), 1200 W. Retta Esplanade, at Fishermen's Village, Punta Gorda. Gelato, candy, candy corn, taffy, homemade fudge, and truffles.

COFFEE 🍴 ((•)) **Mango Bistro** (941-681-3500; www.mangobistro.com), 301 W. Dearborn St., downtown in Olde Englewood Village, Englewood. There's a lot more going on here than coffee (see "Where to Eat"), but it's still a good place to stop by for your morning buzz in a pleasant setting with a free used book exchange. Besides coffee, you can quench your thirst with smoothies or a hot or iced latte.

((•)) **Mermaid Café** (941-681-2624; mermaidscaffe.com), 425 W. Dearborn St., Englewood. Organic coffee, chais, hot and cold coffee drinks, ice cream, breakfast and lunch sandwiches, and desserts.

DELI & SPECIALTY FOODS ((•)) **Kappy's Market** (941-964-2506; kappysmarket bocagrande.com), 5800 Gasparilla Rd., at North Village, Boca Grande. Freshly made deli items, plus grocery items, ice cream, and party trays.

Grapevine Gourmet & Gifts (941-964-0614; www.grapevinebocagrande.com), 321 Park Ave., in the Old Theatre Building, Boca Grande. Grapevine has a loyal following for its specialty wines, imported cheese, fish, prepared dishes, sandwiches, gourmet products, and baked goods. Closed Sunday and mid-July to mid-October.

Hudson's Grocery (941-964-2621; www.hudsonsgrocery.com), 441 Park Ave., Boca Grande. Organic and other fresh produce, fish, meats cut to order, deli, and hot meals. Look for the vintage pink gas pump outside.

Kallis German Butcher Sausage Kitchen (941-627-1413), 2420 Tamiami Trail, Port Charlotte. Wursts of every variety; also fine cuts of meat, rouladen, cheese, hams, and gourmet European imports. This place is a lot of fun for foodies.

FARMS & FARMERS' MARKETS **Englewood Farmers' Market** (941-548-7843: www.englewoodfarmersmarket.org), 300 block of Dearborn St., downtown Englewood. Every Thursday 9–2 October through May.

History Park Farmers' Market (941-639-1887), 501 Shreve St., Punta Gorda, at Punta Gorda History Park. Every Sunday October through May 8–2, June through September 8:30–1.

🍃 **Punta Gorda Farmers' Market** (941-391-4856; www.puntagordafarmersmarket.com), Taylor St. and Herald Ct., Punta Gorda. Year-round every Saturday in season 8–1, in summer 8–noon. Includes craft and artisan vendors.

Sunfresh Farmers Market 9941-475-7336 or 800-741-7340; www.sunfreshfarmersmarket.com), 3037 S. McCall Rd., Englewood. Open every day but Sunday, it stocks fresh fruit, vegetables, herbs, and specialty items such as local eggs and honey.

Worden Farm (941-637-4874; www.wordenfarm.com), 34900 Bermont Rd., Punta Gorda. Tractor-drawn hayrides tour this fifty-five-acre organic produce and livestock farm, one of the region's most highly respected. Culinary and gardening classes are also available. Check the website for dates and times.

NATURAL FOODS **Earth's Origins Market** (941-255-2179; www.earthoriginsmarket.com), 2000 Tamiami Trail #220, Port Charlotte. This small chain operates a large, clean facility with a good selection of produce and foodstuffs plus a salad bar, juice bar, deli, and bakery.

Reid's Nutrition Center (941-474-1115), 1951 S. McCall Rd. #480, at Palm Plaza, Englewood. Mostly vitamins, but also some organic products; vegetable juice and fruit smoothie bar; certified nutritionist on staff.

PIZZA & TAKE-OUT **Angelo's Pizza** (941-474-2477; www.angelospizzaenglewood.com), 2611 Placida Rd., Englewood. Pizza and Italian specialties including specialty breads in the shapes of gators, frogs, and turtles. Take-out and delivery.

Five Guys Burgers & Fries (941-764-0088; www.fiveguys.com), 1900 Tamiami Trail #100, Port Charlotte. This Washington, DC–originated chain has made a big footstep in Florida in past years, but this is the first in Charlotte County, and the first one outside of Miami that serves milk shakes. Arguably the best burgers and fries around, it has a rousing atmosphere at that.

Manatees Pizza (941-639-4400; www.manateespizza.com), 408 Tamiami Trail, Punta Gorda. Take-out and free delivery for a vast selection of pizza, stromboli, and calzones, pasta, subs, wraps, salads, and desserts.

The Philadelphian (941-766-0555), 2320 Tamiami Trail, at Midtown Plaza,

Port Charlotte. Famous, it claims, for its cheesesteaks and hoagies, the latter of which come in eight varieties.

SEAFOOD **Twin Lobsters** (941-698-8945), 2700 Placida Rd., Englewood; (941-766-8989), 3762 Tamiami Trail, Port Charlotte. Colorful New England–style fish market including live Maine lobster.

✻ Selective Shopping

SHOPPING CENTERS & MALLS **Boca Grande (Park Ave.).** Despite the millionaires and power brokers who make Boca Grande their winter home, shopping here is low-key and affordable, with shades of historic quaintness. The restored railroad depot houses gift and apparel boutiques; there's more in back at Railroad Plaza. Across the street you'll find an eccentric general store and a department store that's been there forever, both of which set a somewhat funky tone. Sam Murphy Park presents a serene place to rest alongside a gentle waterfall pool and under shade trees. Don't visit in August and September, when the town literally closes down.

((ᵧ)) **Fishermen's Village** (941-639-8721 or 800-639-0020; www.fishville .com), 1200 W. Retta Esplanade, Punta Gorda. More than thirty-five shops and restaurants occupy a transformed fish-packing plant that dates back to the 1930s. This is Punta Gorda's most hyper center of tourism activity and the site of festivals and social events since 1980. Starting in 2015, it underwent a $40 million renovation and redevelopment that includes a new, open center court with a new restaurant and entertainment area and connection with the city's Harborwalk. A second phase will add another multi-use building with stores and restaurants, plus a sand beach and a new pool with a zero-entry. There are docking, lodging, charter boats, and fishing from the docks, along with shopping, entertainment, and dining geared

FISHERMEN'S VILLAGE COMBINES THE PLEASURES OF WATER SPORTS AND SHOPPING

Downtown Punta Gorda (941-639-3720; www.pgdowntown merchants.com). Centered around Marion and Olympia Avenues, both one-way streets, between Nesbit Street and Tamiami Trail South, you'll find a quiet historic downtown that underwent a recent renaissance. Restaurants and galleries occupy many of the old buildings. Streetscaping includes old-fashioned streetlamps, alley arcades, historic murals, and park benches. A new major residential-retail development taking up a city block was recently completed. Every third Thursday from 5 to 8 p.m. the theme is **gallery walk** with live music, demonstrations, art, food, and a chance to meet local artists. Farmers Market convenes every Saturday with more than twenty-five vendors.

generally toward seniors. A preponderance of nautical clothing and gifts reflect the motif.

Olde Englewood Village (941-473-9795; www.oldeenglewood.com). Dearborn Street is downtown Englewood's main drag despite the fact it has no traffic lights; its historic buildings hold fun-to-browse galleries, gift shops, and restaurants, although several stood bare in 2016. The first Saturday of the month, classic cars and music fills the street during Cruisin' on Dearborn Street.

Port Charlotte Town Center (941-624-4833; www.portcharlottetowncenter .com), 1441 Tamiami Trail, Port Charlotte. An indoor megamall with movie theaters and more than 90 commercial enterprises, including Burdines, Sears, and other chain outlets and specialty shops.

ANTIQUES & COLLECTIBLES **Train Depot Antique Mall** (941-639-6774; puntagordahistory.com), 1009 Taylor St., Punta Gorda. Sales of this mall's wide range of memorabilia benefit the Punta Gorda Historical Society. It also holds flea markets. Closed Sunday.

BOOKS **Copperfish Books** (941-205-2560; www.copperfishbooks.com), 103 W. Marion Ave., Punta Gorda. A light and cheerful shop with new, used, and antique books plus coffee, puzzles, cards, and other gifts. Look online for literary events.

CLOTHING **Captain's Landing** (941-637-6000 or 866-463-1643; www

.captainslanding.com), 1200 W. Retta Esplanade #24, at Fishermen's Village, Punta Gorda. Men's casual clothing with a nautical, tropical, and fishing flair.

Courtyard Boutique & Gift Shop (941-637-1226; www.fishville.com), 1200 W. Retta Esplanade #9, at Fishermen's Village, Punta Gorda. Kicky women's fashions and accessories for both casual and dressy occasions.

Elizabeth Bryant Boutique (941-475-0785; www.bryantboutique.com), 200 W. Dearborn St., downtown Englewood. Contained in a charming historic cottage, it sells the Oh My Gauze line of clothing, but the custom-made jewelry is one-of-a-kind.

Giuditta (941-639-8701), 252 W. Olympia Ave., downtown Punta Gorda. This boutique is stuffed with fashions in exotic patterns and finely tailored styles for the sophisticated woman.

Hip Notique (941-347-7250; www .hipnotique.net), 111 W. Marion Ave., Punta Gorda. Colorful, original, casual women's fashions, bags, and accessories.

Holly's Island Shop (941-964-2767; hollysislandshop.com), 383 Park Ave., Boca Grande. Beachy styles for women and kids, sandals, jewelry.

Little Minnows (941-505-5437; www .little-minnows.com), 1200 W. Esplanade #D5 at Fishermen's Village, Punta Gorda. Adorable clothing for babies and tots, plus toys and other gifts.

Nichole's Collections (941-575-1911; www.fishville.com), 1200 W. Retta Esplanade #12, at Fishermen's Village, Punta Gorda. Fine cotton and casual women's fashions.

CONSIGNMENT Back on the Rack (941-655-8172; www.botrflorida.com), 208 Tamiami Trail, Punta Gorda. Upscale fashions for women including brands such as White House Black Market and Chico's.

Ivy's Attic Resale Shoppe (941-915-9734; www.ivysatticresale.com), 446 W. Dearborn St., Englewood. Women's clothing and accessories plus home décor and furnishings.

Sandy's Clotheshorse (941-473-7400), 2670 S. McCall Rd., Englewood. Women's clothing, mostly casual, resort wear.

FLEA MARKETS & BAZAARS Sun Flea Market (941-255-3532; www.sunfleamarket.com), 18505 Paulson Dr., Port Charlotte. Open weekends, the indoor, air-conditioned space holds some fifty-five vendors, plus there is a family amusement park on-site. Friday to Sunday 9–4.

GALLERIES Artisan's Atelier (941-637-8484), 117 Herald Court Centre #113, Punta Gorda) A mini-mall of local artists who are often on hand, creating their work and interacting with guests. Photography, paintings, pottery, jewelry, art clothing, and other media.

Arts Alliance of Lemon Bay (941-475-7141; www.artsallianceoflemonbay .org), 452 W. Dearborn St., Englewood. A wonderfully varied collection of local co-op art, including painted furniture, bronze sculpture, photography, jewelry, oil paintings, ceramics, and wood vases. Also offers art classes.

Creations at the Village (941-639-6363; wwwfishville.com), 1200 W. Retta Esplanade #C46, at Fishermen's Village, Punta Gorda. More than fifty local artists create the unusual sculptures, collages, watercolors, baskets, and mixed media works of art that fill this small, colorful spot.

The Hatch Gallery (941-697-9531; jon-hatch-originals.com), 13060 Fishery Rd., Placida. Housed in an old clam farming shack, it displays the whimsical wildlife art of Jon Hatch made from driftwood art; also antiques and collectibles.

History Park Art Gallery Gift Shop (941-391-4446), 501 Shreve St., Punta Gorda, at the Punta Gorda History Park. A small shop but packed with interesting photography, jewelry, art, and gifts created by local artists.

Old Florida Outdoor Center and Gallery (941-468-1447; www.oldflorida outdoorcenter.com), 463 W. Dearborn St., Englewood. A large facility with big and small original pieces of yard and home art made from wooden pallets, driftwood, clay, silk, and glass.

Sea Grape Artists Gallery (941-575-1718; www.seagrapegallery.com), 113 W. Marion Ave., Punta Gorda. Displays and sells the fine art and affordable paintings, pottery, jewelry, beadwork, and other three-dimensional art of more than twenty co-op members, who staff the gallery, so you have a chance to meet the artists.

Smart Studio & Art Gallery (941-964-0519; www.smart-studio-fl.com), 370 Park Ave., Boca Grande. Shows and sells paintings of prolific wintering artist Wini Smart and her daughter, Gail Cleveland, as well as other one-of-a-kind jewelry and decorative arts. Closed in the off-season.

GIFTS Beach Road Boutique (941-474-6564), 1350 Beach Rd., on the causeway, Englewood Beach. Everything you're looking for in tasteful high-end beach souvenirs—from nice T-shirts to jewelry, bags, and home accessories. A cool wine and beer bar serves food indoors or outside, overlooking the water.

Havana Tranquility (941-347-8177; havanatranquility.com/puntagorda) 25139 Marion Ave., Punta Gorda) A plush, masculine club selling fine cigars with both public and member domains.

Laff Out Loud (941-505-2067; www .fishville.com), 1200 W. Retta Esplanade

#14, at Fishermen's Village, Punta Gorda. Whimsical toys and novelties for all ages: stuffed animals, dolls, puppets, lava lamps, and other nostalgic memorabilia and tropical souvenirs.

Margaret Albritton Gallery (941-698-0603), 13020 Fishery Rd., Placida. After lunch at The Fishery (see "Where to Eat"), browse this delightful shop for everything from kitschy pink flamingo gifts to fine art.

Open Studio (941-474-4060; www .theopenstudio.org), 380 Old Englewood Rd., Englewood. This indoor-outdoor complex includes an Artists' Gallery in addition to art classes, community gardens and market, yoga and massage, and a juice bar.

Pirate's Ketch (941-637-0299; www .piratesketch.com), 1200 W. Retta Esplanade #E44, at Fishermen's Village, Punta Gorda. Tasteful nautical clocks and lamps, weather vanes, seashell kitsch, framed sea charts, original art and prints.

✿ **Pomegranate & Fig** (941-205-2333; www.pomegranateandfig.com), 117 W. Marion Ave. #111, Punta Gorda. Unusual accessories for the home, women, and little girls—jewelry, ballet skirts, ceramic crosses, textiles, and rugs.

JEWELRY **Bijoux** (941-639-1676), 1200 W. Retta Esplanade #L31, at Fishermen's Village, Punta Gorda. Jewelry, candles, scarves, women's clothing, and gifts.

Dearborn Street Jewelry & Repair (941-460-1750; www .dearbornstreetjewelryandrepair.com), 480 W. Dearborn St., Englewood. Small but well-stocked with affordable and interesting silver and gold charms, bracelets, toe rings, necklaces, and earrings.

Fine Things Jewelry (941-964-2166), 321 Park Ave., at Serendipity Gallery, Old Theater Building, Boca Grande. Designer jewelry and fine art.

Mermaid's Caché (941-460-8135; www.sadiegreens.com) 405 W. Dearborn St., Englewood. Sea glass and other

handmade, affordable jewelry, plus gifts, antiques, collectibles, and clothing.

Paradise Jewelers (941-475-2396), 3700 N. Access Rd., Englewood. Custom designs, nautical pieces, diamonds, gems, and repair.

KITCHENWARE & HOME DÉCOR **The Caged Parrot** (941-637-8949; www .fishville.com/shops), 1200 W. Retta Esplanade #A57, at Fishermen's Village, Punta Gorda. Garden accessories, woodblock models of Punta Gorda buildings, fanciful wall hangings, tin sculpture wall animals, ceramic hibiscus tiles, and wind chimes.

Holly's Island Shop (941-964-2767; hollysislandshop.com), 383 Park Ave., Boca Grande. Vintage-looking custom signs and other fun, beachy decorative items, plus toys, jewelry, and clothing.

Salt (941-855-9037), 433 W. Fourth St. #3, Boca Grande. A fun boutique with a sense of place for gifts such as candles, rugs, and beach and nautical décor.

✳ Special Events

February: **Charlotte County Fair** (941-629-4252; www.thecharlottecountyfair .com), Charlotte County Fairgrounds, 2333 El Jobean Rd., Port Charlotte. Rides, games, food, concerts, and shows for ten days starting early in the month. **Charlotte Harbor Regatta** (941-206-1133; charlotteharborregatta.com). Races in various boat classes with up to one hundred participating boats and more than four hundred sailors. Spectators can watch the action either from land or aboard a special sightseeing boat. Four days early in the month. **Florida Frontier Days** (941-629-7278; www .charlottecountyfl.com), Bayshore Live Oak Park, Charlotte Harbor. Reenactors, artisans, storytelling, old-time games, music, and hands-on activities. Last weekend of the month. **Lemon Bay Festival & Cracker Fair** (941-474-551 or 800-603-7198; www.lemonbayfest.com). One week of historical programs and nature cruises culminating in an all-day Cracker Fair at Pioneer Park on Dearborn Street. **Wine & Jazz Festival** (941-639-3720; www.puntagordachamber.com), Laishley Park, Punta Gorda. One day of local and national artists plus food from local restaurants and, of course, wine.

March: **Peace River National Arts Festival** (941-639-8810; visualartcenter.org), Laishley Park, Punta Gorda. Waterfront art show with food, beverages, entertainment, and kids' activities. One weekend. **Spring Fine Arts Festival** (941-286-3870; www.englewoodrotary.com), W. Dearborn St., downtown Englewood. A late-month weekend of art from around the United States, live entertainment, and refreshments.

April: **Pedal and Play in Paradise** (941-637-8326; pedalandplayinparadise .com) Besides bike tours for all levels, there's yoga, wine and cheese, beer, and music for two days early April. **Taste of Punta Gorda** (puntagordarotary.com) takes place in Laishley Park for one Sunday early in the month. Some twenty-five restaurants serve food samples, plus there is live entertainment, several demos, a rock-climbing wall, bounce houses, and other family activities.

May: **Emancipation Day Celebration** (941-575-7518; blanchardhousemuseum .us), Blanchard House Museum, 406 Martin Luther King Blvd., Punta Gorda. Celebrating freedom from slavery with barbecue and chicken dinners one day midmonth. ✐ **Punta Gorda Hibiscus Festival**, Laishley Park. Celebrates the town's reputation as "City of Hibiscus," with an evening concert, plant show and sale, kids' activities, secret garden trolley tour, and bike rides. One weekend

midmonth. **World's Richest Tarpon Tournament** (941-964-0568; worlds richesttarpon.com). One of five Boca tarpon tournaments with two days of competition and a street party.

June: **Blues, Brews & BBQ Fest** (941-639-3720; puntagordachamber.com), Four Points by Sheraton, 33 Tamiami Trail, Punta Gorda. Local craft brewers and barbecue aficionados provide the "brews & BBQ" quotient, national blues performers bring the music for one entire weekend late in the month.

July: **Charlotte Harbor Freedom Swim** (941-661-5622),.Independence Day in Charlotte County means swimming across the Peace River from Port Charlotte to Fishermen's Village in Punta Gorda.

September: **The Punta Gorda Sullivan Street Craft Festival** (www .artfestival.com; 561-746-6615), brings craft artisans from across the country, a twenty-year-tradition, for one weekend midmonth.

October: **Florida International Air Show** (941-639-1101; www.floridaairshow .com), Punta Gorda Airport. A thrilling display of aerial feats, including the Blue Angels. One weekend midmonth.

November: **Englewood Beach Waterfest** (941-473-9795; englewoodbeach waterfest.com). The one-day event consists of three components: Paddlefest (paddleboard competition), Racefest (World Championship for the Offshore Powerboat Association), and Ecofest (a family friendly exhibition).

December: **Christmas Peace River Lighted Boat Parade** (941-639-3720; www.puntagordachamber.com). A procession of vessels in holiday attire. Saturday evening midmonth.

SANIBEL ISLAND &
THE FORT MYERS
COAST

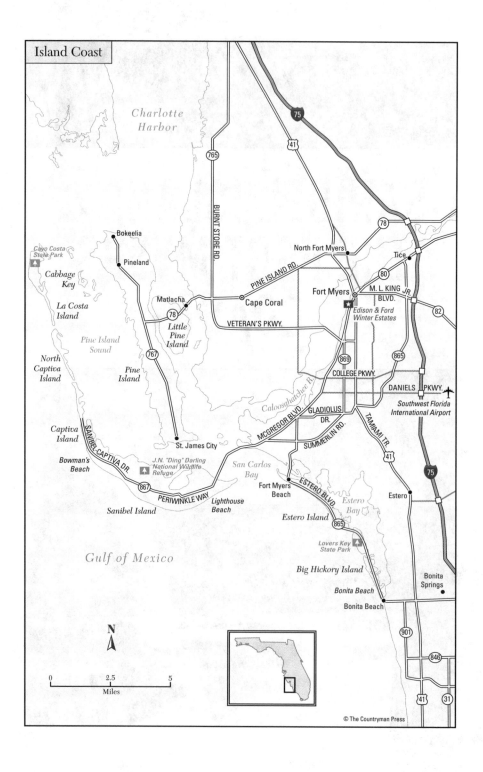

Island Coast

Charlotte Harbor

Cayo Costa State Park

Cabbage Key

La Costa Island

North Captiva Island

Captiva Island

Bowman's Beach

Sanibel Island

Gulf of Mexico

Bokeelia

Pineland

Matlacha

Pine Island Sound

Little Pine Island

Pine Island

St. James City

J.N. "Ding" Darling National Wildlife Refuge

Lighthouse Beach

PERIWINKLE WAY

SANIBEL-CAPTIVA DR

767

78

765

BURNT STORE RD.

PINE ISLAND RD.

Cape Coral

VETERAN'S PKWY.

867

San Carlos Bay

Fort Myers Beach

ESTERO BLVD.

Estero Island

Lovers Key State Park

Big Hickory Island

Bonita Beach

Bonita Beach

North Fort Myers

Fort Myers

Edison & Ford Winter Estates

Caloosahatchee R.

McGREGOR BLVD.

GLADIOLUS DR.

SUMMERLIN RD.

COLLEGE PKWY.

869

865

Tice

80

M. L. KING JR. BLVD.

82

DANIELS PKWY.

Southwest Florida International Airport

TAMIAMI TR.

41

75

Estero

Estero Bay

Bonita Springs

901

846

41

31

75

41

N

0   2.5   5
Miles

© The Countryman Press

SANIBEL ISLAND & THE FORT MYERS COAST

Sand, Shells, and Serenity

A dreamy, tropical land adorned with a necklace of islands, this stretch of coastline resembles, more than any of its neighboring regions, the laid-back islands of the Keys, Bahamas, and Caribbean. Tourism pundits brand it "The Beaches of Sanibel and Fort Myers" to capitalize on its most reputable parts. More developed than its Charlotte Harbor neighbors and more relaxed than what lies to the south and at the Sarasota end of things, the Island Coast gives us the leafy greenery for the southwest Florida sandwich. It is considered one of Florida's most ecology-minded resort areas. How it balances its dual roles as wildlife preserver and tourism mecca has served as a model for statewide eco-tourism.

At their northern extreme, the islands are mired in an Old Florida time frame. **Cabbage Key, Useppa Island, Cayo Costa,** and **Pine Island** gave birth to the Gulf Coast's legacy of fishing lifestyles, back when the Calusa lived off the sea. On Pine Island, fishing, crabbing, and shrimping are still a way of life and survival. Many commercial fishermen have turned to charter captaining in the wake of net-ban legislation. *Field & Stream* editors once named Pine Island among the twenty-five hottest American fishing destinations. Protected from rampant resort development by its lack of beaches, Pine Island clings to an older way of life like a barnacle to a mangrove prop. **Cayo Costa**, mostly state-owned, and **North Captiva** remain the uncut jewels in the Fort Myers coast necklace. **Useppa Island** and **Cabbage Key** preserve another era of island bygones, days graced by celebrity sporting types in search of escape, adventure, and tarpon.

Out in San Carlos Bay, to the south, the islands of **Sanibel** and **Captiva** developed quietly but steadily through the years. At various times in the past, the islands have supported a government lighthouse reservation, citrus and tomato farms, communities of fishermen (who sometimes dealt in rum-smuggling on the side), and a coconut plantation. From 1910 to 1940, wealthy notables made their way to the islands, intent on the relative anonymity that the wilds afforded them. Teddy Roosevelt discovered Captiva Island in 1914. Charles Lindbergh and his wife, Anne Morrow Lindbergh, visited often, inspiring her to pen her well-loved essays in *Gift from the Sea*, which uses seashells as a metaphor for the different stages in a woman's life. In more recent years, maverick artist the late Robert Rauschenberg called Captiva home; his estate has been turned into an artist-in-residence collective. Pulitzer Prize–winning cartoonist and conservationist Jay N. "Ding" Darling gained national attention for Captiva and Sanibel Islands by fighting for the preservation of their natural attributes during his 1930s winter visits. His efforts sparked the development of Sanibel's environmental conscience, which eventually led to a grassroots movement to incorporate in 1974 to stymie development.

Fort Myers Beach, on San Carlos and Estero Islands, is synonymous with gulf shrimp, beach bustle, and spring breakers. Most of the bustle happens around Times Square, a pedestrian zone where retail meets the beach with an uber-casual vibe.

Southward, the maze of islands that includes **Lovers Key** and **Mound Key** is reminiscent of the coast's earliest times, with primeval estuaries, intact shell mounds, whispers of buried pirate treasure, and fishing lifestyles. To their south, **Bonita Beach** continues the island parade. Part of Bonita Springs (see the South Coast chapter), it is included here because of its physical connection to Lovers Key.

On the mainland, **Cape Coral** once served as a hunting refuge for steel magnate Ogden Phipps, who vacationed in Naples. The fifth-largest Florida city by area, it was something of a developer's folly. The young city was cleared, canalled, and platted in 1970 and is slowly growing into itself. A downtown revitalization effort is currently under way, and a huge new marina, housing developments, and resorts have recently appeared on its horizon. **North Fort Myers**, rural in character, borders it on the east, and the Caloosahatchee River defines it on the south.

Across the river from North Fort Myers and Cape Coral, **Fort Myers** has evolved from its fort status during the Seminole Wars into the hub of communications, government, and transportation for the region. Cattle barons gave the community its early wild temperament; Thomas Edison and his class of successful entrepreneurs elevated it above its cow-trail streets. Downtown underwent a recent renovation that sharpened its appeal, including an expansion of its riverfront real estate.

Most unusual circumstances created the growing town named **Estero,** along Tamiami Trail south of Fort Myers. The nineteenth-century religious cult that called itself the Koreshan Unity first settled there, led by Cyrus Teed, or Koresh (the Hebrew version of his name). The Koreshans believed that the earth clings to the inside of a hollow globe like coconut meat to its shell. Members practiced celibacy and communal living. They also experimented with tropical gardening, bringing the mango and the avocado to southwest Florida. The site of their brief stay has been preserved and re-created by the state, together with their buildings and the natural Florida they discovered there.

Between Fort Myers and Estero, **San Carlos Park** escalated to booming status with the genesis of a state university more than a decade ago. On its shirttails came massive shopping centers, restaurants, and other commercial enterprises that fill in the gap that once existed between quiet towns.

GETTING HERE Fly into **Southwest Florida International Airport (RSW)** (239-590-4800; www.flylcpa.com; 11000 Terminal Access Rd. #8671, Fort Myers 33913) via Air Berlin, Air Canada, American, Delta, Frontier, JetBlue, Silver, Southwest, Spirit, Sun Country, United, or WestJet. See pages 12–13 for rental car phone numbers and websites. Alamo, Avis, Budget, Dollar, National, and Thrifty have facilities at RSW. If traveling by bus, the Greyhound Lines (941-334-1011; www.greyhound.com) depot is located in Fort Myers at 2250 Widman Way.

GETTING AROUND From Southwest Florida International Airport in Fort Myers, **Aaron Airport Transportation** (239-768-1898 or 800-998-1898; www.aarontaxi.com) makes pickups and deliveries throughout the region. For lifts from the islands, call **Sanibel Taxi** (239-472-4160 or 888-527-7806; www.sanibeltaxi.com). **Pine Island Taxi** (239-283-7777) provides twenty-four-hour service anywhere with advance notice.

In the area's northern regions, Pine Island Road, FL 78, diverges from the major arteries and crosses North Fort Myers and Cape Coral to reach Pine Island. Del Prado Boulevard and Cape Coral Parkway, which intersect, are Cape Coral's main commercial routes; downtown Cape Coral, which city officials are intent on defining these days, runs along Cape Coral Parkway north of Del Prado. Stringfellow Road, which lies at the end of Pine Island Road, is Pine Island's principal north–south artery.

On the south side of the Caloosahatchee Bridge, Fort Myers's main east–west connectors are Martin Luther King Jr. Boulevard, Colonial Boulevard (which feeds into the Mid-Point Toll Bridge—$2 toll to Cape Coral), College Parkway (which also crosses the river between Fort Myers and Cape Coral at Cape Coral Parkway with a $2 toll), Daniels Parkway/Gladiolus Drive, and Alico Road. The last two are also airport exits. Traveling roughly from north to south, historic and royal-palm-lined McGregor Boulevard (FL 867) follows the river past old homes. Summerlin Road (FL 869) and Metro Parkway run parallel, to the east. The Tamiami Trail, also parallel and sandwiched between Summerlin Road and Metro Parkway, becomes Cleveland Avenue.

Take McGregor or Summerlin west (they eventually merge) to get to Sanibel and Captiva Islands, the land of no traffic lights. There's a $6 toll for crossing the bridge to Sanibel without a transponder gate-pass, so stay in the right lanes unless you have one. Motorists who wish to purchase a Sun Pass, which works on the Sanibel Causeway and the bridges to Cape Coral, as well as all Florida toll roads, can do so in advance at www .sunpass.com. Periwinkle Way is Sanibel's main drag and connects to Sanibel-Captiva Road via Tarpon Bay Road. Policemen direct traffic at the main intersections during high-traffic hours. Sanibel-Captiva Road turns into Captiva Drive at the pass between the two islands.

San Carlos Boulevard, off Summerlin Road, takes you to Fort Myers Beach and the islands that lie to its south along County Route 865 (CR 865), known as Estero Boulevard in Fort Myers Beach, Hickory Boulevard in Bonita Beach. Alico Road, exit 128 off of I-75, takes you to San Carlos Park; Corkscrew Road (FL 850) exit 123, to the south, goes to Estero.

On the Island Coast, city buses follow routes around Fort Myers, Cape Coral, and south Fort Myers. Call **Lee Tran** (239-533-8726; www.leegov.com/leetran) for schedules and information about trolley rides to and around Fort Myers Beach's beach accesses, including Lovers Key.

HOSPITALS & CLINICS **Cape Coral Hospital** (239-424-2000; www.leememorial.org), 636 Del Prado Blvd., Cape Coral. Emergency room open twenty-four hours.

Gulf Coast Medical Center (239-343-1000; www.leememorial.org), 13681 Doctor's Way, Fort Myers. Emergency room open twenty-four hours.

HealthPark Medical Center (239-343-5000 or 800-936-5321; www.leememorial. org), 9981 S. HealthPark Dr., Fort Myers. Home of Children's Hospital of Southwest Florida. Emergency room open twenty-four hours.

Lee Memorial Hospital (239-243-2000; www.leememorial.org), 2776 Cleveland Ave., Fort Myers. Emergency room open twenty-four hours.

VISITOR INFORMATION **Cape Coral Chamber of Commerce** (239-549-6900 or 800-226-9609; www.capecoralchamber.com), 2051 Cape Coral Pkwy. E., Cape Coral 33904.

Estero Chamber of Commerce (239-948-7990; www.esterochamber.org), 22050 S. Tamiami Trail, Estero 33928.

Greater Fort Myers Beach Chamber of Commerce (239-454-7500; www .fortmyersbeachchamber.org), 1661 Estero Blvd. #8, Fort Myers Beach 33931.

Greater Fort Myers Chamber of Commerce (239-332-3624 or 800-366-3622; www.fortmyers.org), 2310 Edwards Dr., Fort Myers 33901. Welcome center located downtown.

Greater Pine Island Chamber of Commerce (239-283-0888; www.pineislandchamber .org), 3640 Pine Island Rd., Matlacha 33993.

Lee County Visitor & Convention Bureau (239-338-3500 or 800-237-6444; www
.fortmyers-sanibel.com), 2201 Second Street, 6th Floor, Fort Myers 33901.

North Fort Myers Chamber of Commerce (239-997-9111; nfmchamber.org), 2787 N.
Tamiami Trail #10, North Fort Myers 33903.

Sanibel-Captiva Islands Chamber of Commerce (239-472-1080; www.sanibel-
captiva.org), 1159 Causeway Rd., Sanibel Island 33957. Information center located
shortly after the causeway approach to Sanibel.

Southwest Florida Hispanic Chamber of Commerce (239-418-1441; www
.hispanicchamberflorida.org), 1400 Colonial Blvd. #250, Fort Myers 33907.

❋ To See

For many years the region was considered a cultural limbo, void of strong artistic
or regional identity except for a certain retiree/Midwestern influence. Still lagging
behind Sarasota and Naples in that department, the region nonetheless is making
inroads toward "artsification." The population, furthermore, is diversifying in terms
of ethnicity and age.

The residents of Cape Coral and North Fort Myers include many nationalities that
share their customs at social clubs, restaurants, festivals, and other venues. Throughout Fort Myers, African Americans, Asians, East Indians, Europeans, Latinos, and
other ethnic groups heighten the cosmopolitan flavor. Flashes of Southern and Cracker
spirit survive in the less resortlike areas of North Fort Myers and Pine Island.

The islands along the coast have inspired their share of creativity. Singer Jimmy
Buffett has frequented Cabbage Key and Captiva Island. His brand of beachy folk
song is the closest thing the Gulf Coast has to homegrown music. A Sanibel musician
named Danny Morgan affects that same style and has been entertaining the islands
for decades.

One of the few arts that residents can truly call their own is shell art, a form that
flourishes on Sanibel Island, Florida's ultimate shell island. In its highest form, shell art
can be stunning and delicate; its lowest can result in some pretty tacky shell animals.

Wealthy visitors to Sanibel and Captiva have exerted an influence on the fine arts
through the years. The illustrious roll call began in the 1920s with Charles and Anne
Morrow Lindbergh. Edna St. Vincent Millay's original manuscript for *Conversation
at Midnight* burned in a Sanibel Island hotel fire, and the late Robert Rauschenberg,
a pioneer in the field of photographic lithography, lived for many years on Captiva
Island before his death in 2008. His protégé, Darryl Pottorf, continues his legacy.
World-renowned painter Marcus Jansen is based in Fort Myers.

ARCHITECTURE **Fort Myers** is home to some lovely architecture downtown and
along McGregor Boulevard. Thomas Edison's home was perhaps Florida's first prefab
structure: Because wood and materials were scarce (many newcomers made do with
palmetto huts), Edison commissioned a Maine architect to draw up plans and construct
sections of the home to be shipped down and pieced together on-site. Downtown, the
Richard Building, circa 1924, boasts an Italian influence, while the courthouse annex
superbly represents Mediterranean Revival. So do the Miles Building, built in 1926 by
Dr. Franklin Miles, the "Father of Alka-Seltzer"; **Patio De León**, a restored entertainment and shopping complex; and the **Franklin Building**, now home to local retailers.
The newer Harborside Convention Center and other more recent constructions echo
the motif.

Pine Island possesses the best, most concentrated collection of preserved vernacular architecture, especially in ❂ **Matlacha**. In **Bokeelia**, the entire Main Street is designated a historic district. Notice especially the Captain's House, a fine example of slightly upscale folk housing of the early 1900s, with French Provincial elements. Nearby Turner Mansion represents a higher standard of living and is reminiscent of New England styles. The club at **Useppa Island** exhibits another prime collection of Old Florida styles, both traditional and revival.

CINEMA **Beach Theater** (239-765-9000; www.fmbtheater.com), 6425 Estero Blvd., Fort Myers Beach. A theater with four screens, serving a full-meal (and slightly overpriced) menu, beer, and wine.

Gulf Coast Town Center Stadium 16 (230-454-4731; www.gulfcoasttowncenter. com), 10028 Gulf Center Dr., at I-75 and Alico Rd., Fort Myers. Sixteen theaters, plus an IMAX.

Hollywood Theaters Coconut Point 16 (239-498-8706 or 844-462-7342), 8021 Cinema Way, Estero. Complex of sixteen theaters.

Island Cinema (239-472-1701; www.islandcinema.com), 535 Tarpon Bay Rd., at Bailey's Shopping Center, Sanibel Island. A two-screen theater showing first-run films.

Marquee Cinema Coralwood 10 (239-458-2543; www.marqueecinemas.com), 2301 Del Prado Blvd., at Coralwood Shopping Center, Cape Coral. Ten screens for first-run films.

Regal Bell Tower Stadium 20 (239-590-9696; www.regmovies.com), 13499 Bell Tower Dr. at Daniels Pkwy. and US 41, Fort Myers. A modern megacomplex of theaters in the form of an airport hangar.

DANCE **Gulfshore Ballet** (239-590-6191; gsballet.org), 2155 Andrea Ln., Suite C 5–6, Fort Myers. Ballet instruction.

GARDENS ❂ ♂ **Edison & Ford Winter Estates** (239-334-7419; www.edisonford winterestates.org), 2350 McGregor Blvd., Fort Myers. Open 9–5:30 daily; guided and self-guided multi-lingual audio tours. Guided garden tours at 10:30 Tuesday. $20 adults, $11 children ages six to twelve; laboratory and museum tour only $12 adults, $5 children. Guided garden tours $30 adults, $16 children. A stand of bamboo sold Thomas A. Edison on this piece of property in the late 1800s. He was convinced the plants would be useful in his experiments with light bulb filament. From there, the inventor expanded his research gardens around his home to include plants he might use in tire making and other inventions for friends and fellow Fort Myers winterers Henry Ford and Harvey Firestone. After a 2004 hurricane, estates staff set about restoring the twenty-six-acre property to its original look, including historic landscaping. Mina's Moonlight Garden, named for Edison's wife, is a serene highlight of the lovely riverside grounds, originally designed by a famous landscape architect from New York named Ellen Biddle Shipman, America's

THOMAS EDISON PUT FORT MYERS ON THE MAP WHEN HE BUILT HIS WINTER HOME THERE IN THE LATE 1880S

foremost landscaper at the time and the first woman landscaper of renown. Rows of stately royal palms, like those Edison had planted along McGregor Boulevard around his home, are eye-catchers, along with gushes of flowering foliage such as bougainvillea and angel trumpets. Botanical signs identify the 320 varieties of plants, and special botanical tours further explore the different collections, including cycads, orchids, and exotic fruit trees. The newest gardens include the Heritage Garden, which reflects the estates' original landscape plan, and a propagation garden like the one Edison maintained to start his seedlings.

Fragrance Garden of Lee County (239-533-7575; www.leegov.com/parks), 7330 Gladiolus Rd., in Lakes Regional Park, Fort Myers. Open daily 7–dusk. Parking: $1 per hour or $5 per day. The garden was designed primarily for the visually and physically impaired, although the general public will also enjoy this attraction that features cactus and succulents and native vegetation. For the visually impaired

AT THE HISTORIC CAPTIVA CEMETERY, VISITORS ARE MORE LIKELY TO LEAVE SHELLS THAN FLOWERS AT HEADSTONES

there are pungent herbs and fragrant plants, such as frangipani, jasmine, and gardenias. Paved paths with vegetation planted at wheelchair height accommodate the physically challenged. Gazebos were built wide enough for easy wheelchair access, too.

HISTORIC HOMES & SITES **Calusa Heritage Trail** (239-283-2062; www.flmnh .ufl.edu/rrc), 13810 Waterfront Dr., Pineland, on Pine Island. Open daily sunup–sundown; guided tours January to April, Wednesday, Friday, and Saturday 10 a.m. and 1 p.m. Suggested donation $7 adults, $5 seniors, $4 children (younger than school age). Archaeologists from Gainesville's Florida Museum of Natural History meet here at the time-stilled village of Pineland to discover the lifestyles of the lost Calusa tribes. The 3,700-foot trail with modern interpretative signage tells of Pineland's importance as a center of Calusa culture for more than 1,500 years. It climbs to the top of an ancient shell mound. The site's newest addition is a burial mound, currently behind a chain-link fence and under vegetation restoration. On certain days archaeologists are digging at the site. Volunteers are welcome, but call in advance.

♂ 🌿 **Chapel-by-the-Sea** (239-472-1646; www.captivachapel.com), 11580 Chapin Ln., Captiva Island. This quaint church, once a schoolhouse that subbed as a place of worship on Sundays, is a popular spot for interdenominational services (during season), weddings, and seaside meditation. Many of the island's early pioneers are laid to rest in its cemetery. Visitors typically leave seashells in lieu of flowers at gravesites.

Fishing shacks, Pine Island Sound at Captiva Rocks, east of North Captiva. The last artifacts of the region's early commercial fishing enterprises have braved weather and bureaucracy to strut the shallows along the Intracoastal Waterway. The shack at the mouth of Safety Harbor on North Captiva is the most noticeable. It once served as

MUST SEE

✪ ♂ **Edison & Ford Winter Estates** (239-334-7419; www.edisonfordwinterestates.org), 2350 McGregor Blvd., Fort Myers. Open daily 9–5:30; guided and self-guided, multi-lingual audio tours. $20 adults, $11 children ages six to eleven; laboratory and museum tour only $12 adults, $5 children. Daily Historian Tours are $25 for adults and $15 for children. Nowhere in the United States will you find the homes of two such important historical figures sitting side by side. This site is so much more than some preserved houses, however; it's a slice of Floridiana, Americana, and Mr. Wizard, all rolled into twenty-six riverside acres. The one-hour, one-mile tour begins across the street under the nation's largest banyan tree, a gift from tire mogul Harvey Firestone. The tree, four hundred feet around, poses outside a museum that contains many of Edison's 1,093 inventions—including the phonograph, the movie camera, the light bulb, children's furniture, and cement—as well as the 1907 prototype Model T Ford his friend and wintertime neighbor, Henry Ford, gave him. The newest exhibit chronicles the inventor's quest for a domestic source of natural rubber. His laboratory, full of old bottles and other ancient gizmos, sits behind the museum. Edison's late-1880s home hides in a tangle of tropical flora with which the inventor experimented. (Special garden tours are available—see "Gardens.") Actually Edison had two homes, identically built and connected with an arcade. One contained the Edisons' living quarters; the other, guest quarters and the kitchen. A picket fence separates Edison's estate from Ford's. The Mangoes, as it was called in honor of the fruit orchards the car manufacturer so loved, seems humble compared to its neighbor. Its furnishings are true to the era and the Fords' simple tastes. An outbuilding holds three vintage model Fords. In 2006, the estates reopened after a massive, three-year, $9 million overhaul, which included the debut of the Caretaker's House, the oldest building on the property, dating to the 1860s. Improvements are ongoing, including restoration of one of the region's first swimming pools, which is on the property, and a propagation garden designed according to Edison's own specifications, near the banyan tree.

an icehouse. If you look east, you'll spot several others where fishermen and their families used to live. Privately owned and maintained as weekend fishing homes for local enthusiasts, most are listed in the National Register of Historic Places and serve as picturesque reminders of days gone by.

✪ 🦐 **Koreshan State Historic Site** (239-992-0311; www.floridastateparks.org/park/Koreshan), 3800 Corkscrew Rd., Estero. Open daily 8 a.m. to sunset. Narrated tours 10 a.m. and 2 p.m. daily, January to March; 10 a.m. Saturday and Sunday only the rest of the year. $5 per vehicle with up to eight passengers; $4 per single-occupant vehicle; $2 per cyclist, pedestrian, or extra passenger; tours $2 adults, $1 children. Contained within a state park, this site has restored the customs and ways of a turn-of-the-last-century religious cult that settled on the banks of the Estero River. Under the leadership of Cyrus Teed, whose Hebrew

ONCE A ONE-ROOM SCHOOLHOUSE, CAPTIVA'S CHAPEL-BY-THE-SEA HOSTS INTERDENOMINATIONAL SERVICES AND MANY A WEDDING

KORESHAN'S HISTORIC VILLAGE PRESERVES AND RE-CREATES A TIME WHEN A RELIGIOUS COMMUNITY GREW UP ALONG THE BANKS OF THE ESTERO RIVER

name was Koresh, members of Koreshan Unity were well versed in practical Christianity, speculative metaphysics, functional and aesthetic gardening, art, occupational training, and cellular cosmogony. The latter, their most unusual theory, held that the earth lined the inside of a hollow globe and looked down into the solar system. Teed and his followers envisioned an academic and natural utopia of ten thousand followers. They planted their settlement (home for only 250 at its peak—it didn't help that they practiced celibacy) with exotic crops and vegetation. Before losing their momentum upon the death of their charismatic leader in 1908, the Koreshans built a theater, an art hall, a communal mess hall, a store, and various homes and workshops, all of which have been restored or reconstructed to tell their strange story. Demonstrations in season and other special events throughout the year illuminate the times. Camping, hiking, and kayaking count among the recreational activities.

Mound Key State Archaeological Site (239-992-0311; www.floridastateparks.org/park/Mound-Key), 3800 Corkscrew Rd., Estero. The only way to reach this adjunct of the Koreshan State Historic Site (see above), where Calusa and Spanish missionaries set up camp in eras past, is by boat. Many do it by canoe or kayak from Koreshan, Lovers Key State Park, or Estero River Outfitters (see "Paddlesports"). An interpretative hiking trail weaves through the native shell mounds, one of which reaches 32 feet high, qualifying as the county's highest geologic elevation. The 133-acre island built up from years of shellfish eating as the Calusa piled the discarded shells on a sandbar that grew into the seat of their kingdom. Farmers settled years later, and modern-day explorers can find remnants of the centuries' habitation. It is illegal to take any artifacts from the island, which is under excavation by archaeologists.

Sanibel Cemetery, off the bike path on Middle Gulf Dr. (not accessible by car). No signs direct you to this site. Just follow the path and you'll come across a fenced plot with wooden signs and headstones announcing the names of early settlers—a wonderful, quiet place to ponder times past.

Sanibel Lighthouse, southeast end of Periwinkle Way, Sanibel Island. Built in 1884, the lighthouse was the island's first permanent structure. Once vital to cattle transports from the mainland, it still functions as a beacon of warning and welcome. The lighthouse and Old Florida–style lightkeeper's cottage were renovated in 1991, and there is talk of restoring the tower so visitors can climb it.

KIDS' STUFF ✍ **Broadway Palm Children's Theatre** (239-278-4422; www.broadwaypalm.com), Royal Palm Square, 1380 Colonial Blvd., Fort Myers. Each year, Broadway Palm Dinner Theatre puts on two or three plays geared toward families and served up with kids'-fare lunch.

MUST SEE

✪ ✑ **Imaginarium Science Center** (239-321-7420; www.i-sci.com), 2000 Cranford Ave., Fort Myers. Open Tuesday to Saturday 10–5, Sunday noon to 5. $12 adults, $10 seniors, $8 for children ages three to twelve (includes 3-D show). I have visited many of the interactive science museums that have hit Florida in the past couple of decades, and I'm happy to say this is among my favorites. It is not overwhelmingly huge, like some, but it is colorfully attractive and varied in its approach to teaching about everything from Florida environment to the world of sports. Emphasis is on weather and water (the museum occupies a former city water plant). You can feel a cloud, tape yourself on location broadcasting a tornado, and walk through a thunderstorm. Aquariums, a touch tank, a fish and fowl lagoon, and stingray feedings acquaint visitors with Florida's water creatures. The animal lab exhibits dramatic critters, such as a Madagascar hissing cockroach, a bearded dragon, snakes, and lionfish. Other displays appeal to all ages with gadgets, toys, and computers; special 3-D movies and hands-on shows are part of the fun.

MUSEUMS ✑ **Cape Coral Historical Museum & Rose Gardens** (239-772-7037; www.capecoralhistoricalmuseum.org), 544 Cultural Park Blvd., Cape Coral. Open Wednesday and Thursday 1–4, and Saturday 10–2; closed July. $5 adults, $2 children. Exhibits in three buildings include a Native American Room, a Cracker kitchen model to complement the existing Cracker house model, seashell and model boat collections, a military exhibit, a replicated burrowing owl nest, and changing exhibits. A mural depicting Cape Coral's old rose gardens brightens up the spot. Outside, a blossoming garden continues the link between the town and roses, while butterfly, herb, and Florida-friendly yards fill the grounds.

Museum of the Islands (239-283-1525; www.museumoftheislands.com), 5728 Sesame Dr., Pine Island Center. Open November through April, Tuesday to Saturday 11–3, Sunday 1–4; May through October, Tuesday, Thursday, and Saturday 11–3. $2 adults, $1 children. Occupying the old Pine Island library at Phillips Park, the museum concentrates on the area's Calusa and fishing heritage. Highlights include a historic horse-drawn buggy and seashell collection.

✪ ✑ **Sanibel Historical Museum & Village** (239-472-4648; www.sanibelmuseum.org), 950 Dunlop Rd., near City Hall, Sanibel Island. Open mid-October through April, Tuesday to Saturday 10–4; May through July, Tuesday to Saturday 10–1; closed August through mid-October. $10 adults (ages eighteen and older). The village began with a historical Cracker-style abode, once the home of an island pioneer. The museum inside the historic home uses photos and artifacts to focus on Sanibel's ancient and modern history of native Americans, Spanish settlement, homesteading, steamboating, and tourism. The island's original Bailey's General Store, circa 1927, was moved to the site in 1993 as a kickoff to establishing a pioneer village on the grounds. Since then, a 1920s post office, a teahouse, the old one-room schoolhouse for whites, and other vintage buildings have been added. One houses a lens that outfitted the Sanibel Lighthouse in the 1960s. Newest: The 1924 Shore Haven home, moved in 2012, now serves as a welcome center. Its accompanying Caretakers' Cottage is home to a Black History Museum.

✑ **Southwest Florida Museum of History** (239-321-7430; www.swflmuseumofhistory.com), 2031 Jackson St., Fort Myers. Open Tuesday to Saturday 10–5. Admission: $9.50 adults, $8.50 seniors, $5 students, free for children under age five. Walking tours of downtown January to April, 10 a.m. Wednesday and Saturday; $12 . The displays in this museum—housed in a handsome Spanish-style railroad depot—take you back to the days of prehistoric mammals and ancient civilizations, and up through the eras of the

MUST SEE

✪ ✍ **Bailey-Matthews National Shell Museum** (239-395-2233 or 888-679-6450; www.shellmuseum.org), 3075 Sanibel-Captiva Rd., Sanibel Island. Open daily 10–5. $11 ages eighteen and up, $5 children ages five to seventeen, free for ages four and younger. The only one of its kind in the United States, this museum reinforces Sanibel's reputation as a top shell-collecting destination. It uses nature vignettes and artistically arranged displays to demonstrate the role of shells in ecology, history, art, economics, medicine, religion, cuisine, and other fields. The centerpiece of the museum is a dramatic, two-story globe surrounded by shells of the world. The Children's Learning Lab provides games and hands-on experiences in colorful reef-motif surroundings, but oddly with a touch tank you can't touch. One diorama explores the role of shells in the lives of the Calusa, and an interactive exhibit scans the menu of edible mollusks. The newest exhibits explore shell anatomy and advise visitors on enhancing their shell collecting experience. The museum holds about a million specimens in the Great Hall of Shells and scientific collection upstairs, representing a large fraction of the world's 150,000 species of living mollusks.

Calusa, commercial fishing, cattle driving, gladiolus farming, and local World War II training. Well-arranged scale and life-size models, graphic depictions, videos, changing exhibits, and interactive historical games illuminate the past. Changing traveling and original exhibits have a national and international scope. Outdoors, tours examine a replica of a local Cracker house from the early 1900s and the world's last and longest Pullman private railcar, circa 1930. (Don't miss the Pullman tour; it's truly a highlight if you have a good guide.) Call in advance to participate in the museum's downtown walking tours.

Barbara Sumwalt Historical Museum (239-283-9600; http://useppahs.org), Useppa Island Club, Bokeelia. Open daily 12–2 (open until 3:30 in March and April, closed most Mondays in September). $5 donation requested for visitors older than age eighteen, which includes audio tour. The wee island of Useppa is stuffed to the gills with history, a fact that calls for a historical museum all its own. This one is exceptionally well presented for such a small place. (It helps that wealth outmeasures square footage on the island.) Dioramas are interpreted via taped presentations that you can listen to on personal players as you tour. They describe the island's Calusa history, its fishing and resort eras, and its role in training revolutionaries for the Cuban Bay of Pigs confrontation in 1960. Its newer exhibits deal with damage the island suffered in 2004's Hurricane Charley. Because the island is owned by a private club, visitors must be island guests or guests aboard the *Lady Chadwick* luncheon cruise to the island (see Captiva Cruises under "Boats & Boating: Sight-seeing & Entertainment Cruises").

MUSIC & NIGHTLIFE Downtown Fort Myers is trying to metamorphose into a hot entertainment district featuring jazz bars, bistros, nightclubs, and street festivals, including a first Friday Art Walk and third Friday Music Walk. As for the islands, Fort Myers Beach is definitely the most hopping. On Sanibel and Captiva you'll find a quieter brand of partying; nightlife there is focused on theater and more highbrow forms of music, with a couple of bars featuring contemporary live music. Friday's *Gulf Coasting* supplement to the *News-Press* covers the region's entertainment scene.

CAPE CORAL

✪ **Dixie Roadhouse** (239-541-7900), 1023 SE 47th Terrace. A spacious indoor-outdoor venue known for its big-name country music concerts and line-dancing lessons.

Jimbob's Pub (239-574-8100), 1431 SE 16th Place. Live music on weekends, karaoke on Thursdays.

CAPTIVA ISLAND

✪ **Crow's Nest Beach Bar & Grille** (239-472-5161; www.tween-waters.com), 'Tween Waters Inn Island Resort & Spa, 15951 Captiva Rd. Live contemporary dance bands weekends and some weekdays; entertaining crab races on Monday and Thursday, except during September. The island's hottest spot, it is undergoing a style transition to beachier and more casual.

FORT MYERS

Point Ybel Brewing Company (239-603-6535; www.pointybelbrew.com), 16120 San Carlos Blvd. Near Fort Myers Beach and Sanibel Island, this craft brewery hosts live music on a regular basis in season, and once or so a week in off-season.

    Fort Myers Community Concert Association (239-693-4849; fortmyerscommunity concerts.org), P.O. Box 606, 33902. Highbrow musical entertainment—from brass ensembles to ballet—at the Barbara B. Mann Performing Arts Hall (see "Theater").

    ((•)) **The Lodge** (239-433-2739; www.thelodgefl.com), 2278 First St. Live music Friday and Sunday; also Wednesday, when ladies drink free.

    The Ranch Concert Hall & Saloon (239-985-9839; theranchfortmyers.com), 2158 Colonial Blvd. Open Wednesday, Friday, and Saturday nights for live music and dancing in a Western-style saloon. Line and other dance lessons are available.

    Sandy Parrot Tiki Bar & Grill (239-454-8454; www.thesandyparrot.com), 17200 S. Tamiami Trail, Fort Myers. Live music nightly starting around 6 with a big indoor dance floor and outdoor tiki bar setting.

    Southwest Florida Symphony (239-418-0996; www.swflso.org), 8290 College Pkwy. #103. Performs classical and pops series November through May at the Barbara B. Mann Performing Arts Hall in Fort Myers, BIG ARTS on Sanibel Island, and local churches.

FORT MYERS BEACH

If you can't find nightlife in Fort Myers Beach, better check your eyes and ears.

    The Beached Whale (239-463-5505; www.thebeachedwhale.com), 1249 Estero Blvd. Party from the rooftop to live music nightly in the heart of Times Square.

    Dixie Fish Co. (239-233-8837; www.dixiefishfmb.com), 714 Fisherman's Wharf. The newest addition to the Fort Myers Beach dining and entertainment scene, it hosts live music most nights in the open-air setting of a historic wholesale seafood operation.

    Junkanoo (239-463-6139; fortmyersbeachrestaurants.com), 3040 Estero Blvd. You don't have to wait until dark to party in Fort Myers Beach. Here's a popular spot "where the party never ends," and young people headquarter their day at the beach with drinks, food, pool tables, water sports, volleyball, music, and dancing, indoors and out.

    Lani Kai Island Resort (239-463-3111 or 800-237-6133; www.lanikaiislandresort .com), 1400 Estero Blvd. *The* premier collegiate party spot on the beach, with live entertainment nightly and during the day on weekends in the rooftop Island View Restaurant.

    Ugly's (239-463-8077; www.nervousnellies.net), 1131 First St., at Nervous Nellie's Restaurant. Upstairs overlooking the bay, with live music nightly, free boat docking, and all-day happy hour.

PINE ISLAND

Bert's Bar & Grill (239-282-3232; www.bertsbar.com), 4271 Pine Island Rd., Matlacha. Florida funk at its finest, with a salty attitude, good munchies, waterfront stance, and live music year-round.

Ragged Ass Saloon (239-282-1131; www.raggedasssaloon.com), 3421 Stringfellow Rd., St. James City. Check the website for who's playing this weekend at this casual island spot.

Tarpon Lodge (239-283-3999; www.tarponlodge.com), 13771 Waterfront Dr., Pineland. Live music Tuesday, Thursday, and Friday.

SANIBEL ISLAND

BIG ARTS (239-395-0900; www.bigarts.org), 900 Dunlop Rd. Hosts classical musical quartets, trios, and orchestras November through April.

George & Wendy's Sanibel Seafood Grille (239-395-1263; sanibelseafoodgrille .com), 2499 Periwinkle Way. Currently the hippest place on Sanibel for nightlife, with live music or karaoke most nights.

Jacaranda (239-472-1771; www.jacarandaonsanibel.com), 1223 Periwinkle Way. Lively nightlife dancing on Sanibel with top-40 hits, reggae, and island music performed live.

SPECIALTY LIBRARIES For Lee County libraries reference information by phone, call 239-479-INFO.

((ʸ)) **Sanibel Public Library** (239-472-2483; www.sanlib.org), 770 Dunlop Rd., Sanibel Island. Contains an identification collection of seashells, wireless Internet access, and Internet access computers by reservation. In season, this library hosts big-name authors, such as Clive Cussler and Sue Monk Kidd, for free talks.

Talking Books Library (239-995-2665 or 800-854-8195; www.leegov.com/library/ about/branches/tb), 1651 Lee St., Fort Myers. This library for the visually and physically impaired has books on tape that patrons can receive by postage-free mail.

FLORIDA REPERTORY THEATRE PERFORMS PROFESSIONAL PRODUCTIONS IN A HISTORIC MOVIE THEATER

THEATER **The Arcade Theatre/Florida Repertory Theatre** (239-332-4488 or 877-787-8053; www.floridarep.org), 2267 First St., downtown Fort Myers. The glory of the 1920s, this Victorian playhouse has been restored and advanced to the twenty-first century. Home to an energetic professional company that brings new life to old boards on two stages.

○ **Barbara B. Mann Performing Arts Hall** (239-481-4849 or 800-440-7469; www.bbmannpah.com), Florida South-Western State College, 8099 College Pkwy. SW, Fort Myers. Hosts major Broadway shows, musical performers, and dance troupes. Broadway season runs December through late April.

BIG ARTS Strauss Schoolhouse Theater (239-472-6862; www.bigarts.org/ theater.html), 2200 Periwinkle Way,

BARBARA B. MANN PERFORMING ARTS HALL CREATES
DRAMA EVEN IN ITS LOBBY SPACES

Sanibel Island. Represents a professional troupe that concentrates on comedies, musicals, and musical revues.

Broadway Palm (239-278-4422; www .broadwaypalm.com), 1380 Colonial Blvd., at Royal Palm Square, Fort Myers. Lunch and dinner musical performances starring professional actors in a made-over grocery store that seats and serves 448. Each year, a few of the shows (and their buffets), such as *Rapunzel*, are geared toward families. Its Off-Broadway Palm Theatre presents cabaret-style shows in an adjacent, intimate, one hundred-seat playhouse. You can buy tickets for lunch and dinner shows or shows only. Both theaters are closed Mondays year-round and Tuesdays May through October.

Cultural Park Theatre Company (239-772-5862; www.culturalparktheater.com), 528 Cultural Park Blvd., Cape Coral. A 184-seat facility that hosts community theater. The Broadway season performances run from mid-September through mid-May. The theater also has a concert and summer season and acting classes for kids and adults.

Foulds Theater (239-936-3239; www.artinlee.org), 10091 McGregor Blvd., at Lee County Alliance for the Arts headquarters, Fort Myers. An indoor and outdoor stage for recitals, concerts, and workshops. Various community groups perform family and adult theatrical and musical shows.

Germain Arena (239-948-7825; www.germainarena.com), 11000 Everblades Pkwy., Estero. Home of the Everblades hockey team, this venue also hosts big-house touring entertainers.

VISUAL ART CENTERS & RESOURCES Flocks of wildlife-art and other eclectic galleries make a name for Sanibel Island in cultural circles, while smaller communities support their own offbeat galleries and art associations. On Pine Island, national artists come to hide out and nourish their souls, creating an art colony of sorts that's centered in Matlacha. Downtown Fort Myers, too, is developing a bright arts culture. The following entries introduce you to opportunities for experiencing art as either a viewer or a practicing artist. A listing of commercial galleries is included in the "Shopping" section.

Alliance for the Arts (239-939-2787; www.artinlee.org), 10091 McGregor Blvd., Fort Myers. This not-for-profit center conducts classes and workshops, and it operates a public gallery, members' gallery, 150-seat indoor theater, outdoor stage, and Saturday green market. It is home base for many local arts and cultural groups and annual festivals.

BIG ARTS (239-395-0900; www.bigarts.org), 900 Dunlop Rd., Sanibel Island. Home of an energetic multidisciplinary organization that includes the Phillips Gallery. Art shows and classes are scheduled regularly at the facility.

Bob Rauschenberg Gallery at FSW (239-489-9313; www.bobrauschenberggallery .com/), Florida SouthWestern State College, 8099 College Pkwy. SW, Fort Myers. Hosts exhibits and lectures by nationally and internationally renowned artists.

SANIBEL ISLAND'S BEACHES ARE KNOWN NOT ONLY FOR THEIR SEASHELLS BUT ALSO FOR THEIR BIRDING OPPORTUNITIES

Cape Coral Arts Studio Rubicond Park (239-574-0802; www.capecoral.net), 4533 Coronado Pkwy., Cape Coral. Classes, exhibitions, and sales.

Fort Myers Beach Art Association (239-463-3909; www.fortmyersbeachart.com), 3030 Shell Mound Blvd. at Donora St., Fort Myers Beach. Member and other exhibits; workshops and classes. Host of the annual Paint the Beach plein-air art festival in November.

✳ To Do

Shelling, island-hopping, fishing, sailboarding, and warming chilled bones on hospitable beaches: These are a few of the favorite things to do in the Fort Myers–Sanibel area.

BEACHES The region's fifty miles of local beaches are known for their natural state and abundance of shells. *Family Fun* magazine recently rated this stretch of beach the "#1 Beach in the Southeast U.S." Red algae drift periodically washes up on the beaches. It is not pretty and is often smelly, but it poses no risk to your health. Red tide, however, is a different problem, causing dead fish to wash up on the beach from time to time and people to have allergic respiratory reactions to the algal blooms. For current beach conditions, visit www.mote.org/beaches or call 941-BEACHES.

Most beaches charge for parking. Sanibel Island beach stickers, which can be purchased from the recreation center, allow you to park for free at most accesses. Along the Gulf Drives you'll see signs at beach accesses designating resident sticker-only parking. Cyclists and walk-ins, however, can take advantage of these accesses without stickers. Lee County also sells parking stickers for free access (www.leegov.com/parks/parking).

BONITA BEACH

⚓ **Barefoot Beach Preserve County Park** (239-591-8596; www.colliergov.net), Barefoot Beach Rd., Naples (entrance at Hickory Blvd. and Bonita Beach Rd., south end of Little Hickory Island). Actually within neighboring Collier County but accessible from Bonita Beach, the 342 acres in this preserve contain a coastal hammock and 8,200 feet of beach with low dunes. A four-time top-ten placer in the annual Dr. Beach American beaches ratings, it's known for its natural vegetation—sea grapes, cabbage palms, and other native plants. Gopher tortoises often lumber across the road and footpaths. Rangers give nature walks and shell talks at the chikee learning center. Facilities: restrooms, showers, nature learning center, aquatic butterfly garden, snack bar, and beach rentals. Parking: $8 per day.

✪ ⚓ **Bonita Beach Park** (239-949-4615; www.leegov.com/parks), 27954 Hickory Blvd., south end of Little Hickory Island. The largest public park on Bonita Beach, this becomes lively during the high season and on weekends. Water sports and volleyball, plus a hamburger joint and bar, create a youthful spirit. Vegetation is sparse; there's nothing hidden about this beach. Parking fills up early in season and on weekends year-round. Eight other accesses with free but limited parking line Hickory Boulevard to the north, marked by bright signs. Facilities: picnic table shelters, restrooms, showers, nearby water-sports and beach rentals, volleyball, playground, nearby restaurant. Parking: $2 per hour.

Little Hickory Island Beach Park (239-949-4615; www.leegov.com/parks), 26082 Hickory Blvd., north end of Little Hickory Island. The #10 public access on the island, tucked between high rises, sees lighter traffic. Its parking lot is small, but a city park across the road has more spaces. Facilities: picnic table shelters, restrooms, and showers. Parking: $2 per hour.

CAPE CORAL

⚓ **Yacht Club Community Park** (239-574-0806; www.capecoral.net), 5819 Driftwood Pkwy. The man-made beach on the Caloosahatchee River is part of a large park that sponsors recreational and other programs, and it exudes a true sense of community. The groomed beach is better for sunning than swimming, for which the pool fills the void. The first Wednesday of every month, the park hosts Sunset Celebration on the Pier with live music and entertainment, food, and arts and crafts. Facilities: restrooms, showers, picnic shelters, barbecue grills, swimming pool, kiddie pool, marina, shuffleboard, outdoor racquetball courts, tennis, playgrounds, fishing pier, boat ramps, bait shop, food concession. Swimming pool (239-542-3903) open daily 10–5. Park admission free; pool admission $5.25 ages eighteen and older, $4.50 ages ten to seventeen, $3 ages nine and younger.

CAPTIVA ISLAND

⚓ **Alison Hagerup Beach Park** (239-472-2472; www.leegov.com/parks), 14790 Captiva Rd., north end Captiva Rd. Only early arrivals get the parking spots for this prime spread of deep, shelly sand, formerly known as Captiva Beach. It's a good place to watch a sunset, and Travelocity named it the nation's most romantic beach. Facilities: portable restrooms. Open dawn to dusk. Parking: Minimum $5 for two hours.

FORT MYERS

⚓ 🚲 📶 **Lakes Regional Park** (239-533-7575, 239-267-1905 for train; www.leegov.com/parks), 7330 Gladiolus Dr., Fort Myers. This land of freshwater lakes features a small sand beach and marina, but no swimming. Landscaped with all native vegetation, this is a great place for the family to spend the day. The 279-acre park offers a splash pad playground, kayaking, pedal boating, fishing, nature and bike trails, a miniature train ride (fee), bike rentals, and two fun playgrounds, one with a railroad theme. Facilities: picnic areas, restrooms, showers, playgrounds, climbing wall, fitness trail, bike path, water-sports rentals, snack concession, gardens. Parking: $1 per hour or $5 per day.

A SCULPTURE AT LAKES REGIONAL PARK CAPTURES CHILDHOOD ABANDON

FORT MYERS BEACH

Bowditch Point Park (239-765-6794; www.leegov.com/parks), 50 Estero Blvd., at the north end of the island. This pretty, green, seventeen-acre park fronts Estero Bay and the gulf. It's a nice, quiet beach, unspoiled, and a favorite of boat-ins. Drivers also frequent it, and its seventy-five parking spaces fill up quickly in season, so you may want to consider taking one of the beach's tram shuttles to get there. Hiking and biking trails take you along the waterfront and into native vegetation, habitat for gopher tortoises. Facilities: picnic shelters, grills, restrooms, showers, nature trails, boat docks, food concession, bike rentals, kayak and stand-up paddling rentals and tours, paddlecraft launch. Parking: $2 per hour.

🐾 🚲 **Bonita Beach Dog Park** (239-707-1874; www.leegove.com/parks), 8800 Estero Blvd., south of Lovers Key State Park. A small strip of hard-packed beach makes dogs and their owners happy at New Pass between Lovers Key and Bonita Beach. Plan on crossing some wetland areas to get to the beach, where birds abide offshore despite the running and thrashing of pooches. Lee County's only off-the-leash dog beach (most beaches on Sanibel Island allow pets on a leash) requires proof of license and immunization. People are allowed no more than two dogs each, and children younger than age five are not allowed in the off-leash area. Facilities: bag and disposal stations, portable people restrooms, doggy shower, leash-free beach. Free parking.

🚲 **Crescent Beach Family Park** (239-765-6794; www.leegov.com/parks), 1100 Estero Blvd., Fort Myers Beach The newest beach on Estero Island, it is still developing at Times Square. For now, there's a small handicapped parking lot, and two volleyball courts, at the small stretch along the sands. More parking and picnic shelters are in its future. Facilities: portable restrooms, picnic tables, volleyball. Handicap parking only.

✪ 🚲 **Lynn Hall Memorial Park** (239-765-6794; www.leegov.com/parks), 950 Estero Blvd., in the Times Square vicinity. Part of the pedestrian Times Square plaza, this park attracts college students in the spring and families the rest of the year. A rocking, rollicking place, it appeals to beach barhoppers, crowd watchers, and those interested in water sports. It features a fishing pier, beachwear stores, restaurants, ice cream shops,

MUST SEE

♂ ♦ **Lovers Key State Park** (239-463-4588; www.florida stateparks.org/park/Lovers-Key), 8700 Estero Blvd., FL 865 between Fort Myers Beach and Bonita Beach. The area between Estero and Little Hickory Islands consists of natural island habitat populated by birds, dolphins, and crabs. On the barrier island of Lovers Key, Australian pines provide shaded picnicking along a narrow, natural stretch of sand. Walk or ride a truck-pulled tram through the natural mangrove environment to South Beach, the park's main beach. A gazebo provides a group picnic shelter and a popular wedding venue. To the north, a boardwalk bridge takes you to a beach with no facilities that borders Big Carlos Pass. Or you can reach it from the North Beach parking lot just south of the pass bridge. Away from the beach, nature trails invite hiking and biking, shaded picnic grounds line estuarine inlets; there are rentals and launches for canoes and kayaks, a playground, and a path that accommodates hikers and cyclists. Facilities: picnic area, restrooms, showers, boat ramps, fishing, food concession, beach shop, bike and paddlecraft rentals. Admission: North Beach, $2 per person; South Beach, $8 per vehicle with up to eight passengers, $4 per single-occupant vehicle, $2 per extra passenger, bicyclist, or pedestrian.

beachside drinks, parties, parasailing, and Jet Skiing. Sunset celebrations often bring out musicians and other performers. For thinner crowds, hit public accesses, marked with banners, on the south end of Estero Boulevard. Facilities: picnic areas, grills, restrooms, showers, playground, fishing pier, water-sports rentals; nearby restaurants, bars, and shops. Parking in lot for $2 per hour. (Warning: Park only in designated areas, or your car will be towed at great expense.)

SANIBEL ISLAND

✪ **Bowman's Beach** (239-472-6397, www.leegov.com/parks) 1700 Bowman's Beach Rd. off Sanibel-Captiva Rd., Sanibel Island. Bowman's is Sanibel's most natural beach. Long, coved, and edged by an Australian pine forest, it's on a stretch of land that can be reached by footbridges from the parking lot (a rather long walk, so go lightly on the beach paraphernalia). Shells are plentiful here—in some places, a foot or more deep along the high-tide mark. Facilities: picnic area, restrooms, fitness trail, playground. Parking: $4 per hour.

🐚 **Causeway Islands Park** (239-765-6794; www.leegov.com/parks), 19931 Sanibel Causeway Rd. Historically, windsurfers and fishermen favor this packed-sand roadside beach. Beach lovers in RVs or campers often pull up here to picnic and spend the day in the sun. Arrive early on weekends and holidays to claim a spot. Facilities: picnic areas, grills, restrooms. It is the only beach in the county with no parking fees—only the $6 toll to get on it from the mainland.

Lighthouse Park Beach (239-472-6397; www.mysanibel.com), 112 Periwinkle Way, east end of the island, Sanibel Island. Skirting Sanibel Island's historic lighthouse is an arc of natural beach fronting both the Gulf and San Carlos Bay. One of Sanibel's most populated beaches, it features a nature trail and a popular fishing pier. Strong currents inhibit swimming off the point. The wide beach gives way to sea oats, sea grapes, and Australian pine edging. I like the neighborhood around it, because it is historic and more laid-back than other parts of the island. Facilities: picnic area, restrooms, nature trail, fishing pier. Parking: $4 per hour.

♦ **Tarpon Bay Beach** (239-472-6397; www.mysanibel.com), Middle Gulf Dr. at Tarpon Bay Rd., Sanibel Island. Another popular beach, this one is characterized by sugar sand and a nice spread of shells. It's a bit of a hike from the parking lot to the beach, but

SANIBEL'S LIGHTHOUSE PARK BEACH FEATURES A HISTORIC STRUCTURE, A FISHING PIER, AND BEACHES ON TWO
WATERFRONTS

there is a dropoff spot. The area gets congested on busy days. RVs can park here. Great for swimming. Facilities: restrooms, outdoor showers. Parking: $4 per hour.

Turner Beach (239-472-6397; www.mysanibel.com), south end Captiva Rd., Captiva Island. A pretty beach with wide, powdery sand, Turner tends to get crowded and parking is limited. The entrance is on a blind curve, which can be dangerous. More bad news: Riptides coming through the pass make this taboo for swimming. Park your beach towel far north or south of the pass for calmer, swimmable waters. We like to come here in the evening to watch the sunset and walk the beach. Surfers like the waters to the north in certain weather. It's also a hot spot for fishermen, who line bayside shores and the bridge between Sanibel and Captiva. Facilities: restrooms, foot shower; nearby restaurants, water sports, and store. Parking: $4 per hour.

UPPER ISLANDS

✪ **Cayo Costa State Park** (941-964-0375; www.floridastateparks.org/park/Cayo-Costa), La Costa Island; accessible only by boat. The Lee County coast is blessed with some true getaway beaches, untamed by connection to the mainland. On these, one can actually realize that romantic fantasy common to beach connoisseurs: sands all your own. Cayo Costa stretches for nine miles and is most secluded at its southern extremes. A larger population of beachgoers congregates at the north end, where docks, a picnic and camping ground, and primitive cabins attract those who seek creature comforts with their sun and sand. A tram transports boaters from docking on the bay side to facilities on the beach side. Or you can walk the short distance on a path that is part of a 5.5-mile trail system. Shelling is superb in these parts, particularly at Johnson Shoals, which surfaces at the island's north end during low tide. Charters and water taxis from Captiva Island and Bokeelia provide transportation to the island. Facilities: picnic grounds, restrooms, showers, nature trails, camping, cabins. Admission: $2 per person.

EXCURSIONS: Sanibel Island By Bike

Sanibel Island boasts more than twenty miles of paved shared-use paths in addition to another ten or so miles of off-road paths for bicycling. In season, by-bike is often the best way to get around when traffic clogs the main roads. Follow this route for a good half-day or more tour of the island. Start at **Lighthouse Park Beach** (239-472-6397; www.mysanibel.com; 112 Periwinkle Way) at the island's southeast end. Ride your bike to the fishing pier and lighthouse, spend some time walking and shelling on the beach, then head west along **Periwinkle Way**, the island's main road. Turn right at the four-way stop on **Lindgren Boulevard/Causeway Road** and stay on its shared-use path until you reach the crosswalk at the **Sanibel-Captiva Islands Chamber of Commerce** (239-472-1080; www.sanibel-captiva.org, 1159 Causeway Rd.). Cross into the parking lot. To the far left of the lot, you will see signs to unpaved **Pond Apple Trail**. (It can get muddy with summer rains.) Follow it to the large retention pond, where you will usually see a lot of birds and possibly an alligator or two. On the other side of the pond, follow the shell trail through the woods via the **Shipley Trail** and boardwalk, past the historic **Bailey Homestead**, which is not yet open to the public, but where you can see some exhibits and artifacts. The trail empties into **Roadside Park**, where there is a crosswalk back to the Periwinkle Way shared-use path. Go right and continue to **Casa Ybel Road**. Take a left after about a mile on **Middle Gulf Drive** and another right to **Gulfside Beach Park** when the path forks. On the way to the beach, you'll pass the **Sanibel Cemetery**, accessible only by path. When you reach a dirt road (**Algiers Lane**), head left on it. Have a rest at the beach and a picnic if you so desire, then return to Casa Ybel Road via Algiers Lane. Take the crosswalk on **West Gulf Drive** and head left. Follow it for 2.5 miles past **Rabbit Road** to the path on the back side of its homes; pedal over the **Sanibel River** to Sanibel-Captiva Road crosswalk, about a mile. Take a left and ride about a mile to **J. N. "Ding" Darling National Wildlife Refuge** (239-472-1100; www.fws.gov/refuge/jn_ding_darling; off Sanibel-Captiva Dr. at Mile Marker 2). Visit the free Visitor & Education Center to learn more about the refuge, then head to paved **Wildlife Drive** ($1 admission per cyclist older than 15). This is a 4-mile ride past habitats for birds and other wildlife—a five-mile loop back to the visitor center. Or you can take an unpaved shortcut at the **Cross-Dike Trail**. Back on San-Cap Road, take a left and head back to Sanibel's commercial area along the shared-use path, about four miles away. Along the way, stop at the **Sanibel-Captiva Conservation Foundation (SCCF) Nature Center** (239-472-2329; www.sccf .org, 3333 Sanibel-Captiva Rd.) and the **Bailey-Matthews National Shell Museum** (239-395-2233 or 888-679-6450; www.shellmuseum.org, 3075 Sanibel-Captiva Rd.) if your schedule allows.

North Captiva, across Redfish Pass from South Seas Island Resort and Captiva Island; accessible only by boat. Like Cayo Costa, here's a place to go for private beaching. Though it's narrow at the south end, the sand is like gold dust. You'll find no facilities unless you venture across the island to the bay, where restaurants and civilization inhabit the north end.

BICYCLING The bikeways of the Fort Myers–Sanibel region come in two varieties. Bicycle (or shared-use) paths, the more common, are separated from traffic by distance and, ideally, a vegetation buffer. Bicycle lanes are a designated part of the roadway. Cyclists also take to the road in rural areas, where no bikeways exist but traffic is light. By law they must abide by the same rules as motor vehicles. Children under age sixteen are required to wear helmets.

Best Biking: More than two miles of bike trails run through **Lakes Regional Park** (239-533-7575 www.leegov.com/parks), where bike rentals are also available. Long stretches of bike path in **Fort Myers** follow **Daniels Parkway, Metro Parkway, Colonial Boulevard,** and **Summerlin Road**. The **Summerlin path** leads to the Sanibel causeway (cyclists cross for $1) to connect with island paths. **McGregor Boulevard's** sidewalk provides another popular and scenic circuit. The **John Yarbrough Linear Park** (239-707-3164; www.leegov.com/parks), follows Ten Mile Canal for about six miles from north Colonial Boulevard to Six Mile Cypress Road. Far-reaching plans could eventually hook up the system with the West Coast Greenway extending from Tampa to Naples. More than five miles of bike paths also wind through **Lovers Key State Park**, and a ranger leads guided bike tours; call 239-463-4588 or visit www.floridastateparks.org/park/Lovers-Key for a schedule.

Many of **Cape Coral's** city streets designate bike lanes.

✪ **Sanibel's** twenty-three-mile path covers most of the island and occasionally leaves the roadside to plunge you into serene backwoods scenery. Cyclists also

A CAST OF RABBIT SCAT AT 'DING' DARLING REFUGE'S WILDLIFE EDUCATION BOARDWALK—ONE OF ABOUT A DOZEN SUCH LEARNING TOOLS

pedal four-mile, paved Wildlife Drive through J. N. "Ding" Darling National Wildlife Refuge (see page 200) and its unpaved but hard-packed Indigo Trail.

The seventeen-mile **Pine Island** bike path stretches along Stringfellow Road from St. James City to Bokeelia. Cape Coral has a dedicated BMX park.

Rental/Sales: ⚐ **Billy's Bikes & Rentals** (239-472-5248 or 800-575-8717; www.billysrentals.com), 1470 Periwinkle Way, Sanibel Island. Bicycles, surrey bikes, and equipment for family biking. Also scooters and Segway tours. Rentals by the hour, day, or week.

Fun Rentals (239-463-8844; www.funrentals.org), 1901 Estero Blvd., Fort Myers Beach. Rentals start at $13 for two hours. Per-day to per-week rates are available. Scooter and motorcycle rentals, too.

Lovers Key Adventures & Events (239-765-7788; www.loverskeyadventures.com), 8720 Estero Blvd., Fort Myers Beach. Rents bikes at Lovers Key State Park.

YOLO Watersports (239-472-1296 or 239-472-9656; yolowatersports.com), 11534 Andy Rosse Ln., Captiva Island. Rentals by the half-day, full day, twenty-four-hour period, and week. Also, motor scooters, golf carts, and water-sports equipment.

BOATS & BOATING With its procession of unbridged islands and wide bay, the region begs for outdoor types to explore its waters. Island-hopping constitutes a favorite pastime of adventurers.

Paddlesports: In addition to the following outlets, many resorts and parks rent canoes, kayaks, and stand-up paddleboards.

Adventure Sea Kayak & SUP (239-822-3337; www.captivaadventures.com), 15951 Captiva Dr. at 'Tween Waters Inn Marina, Captiva Island. Rentals and tours by kayak and paddleboard.

CGT Kayaks (239-212-8218; www.cgtkayaks.com), 27313 Old 41 Rd., Bonita Springs. This operation rents single and tandem kayaks and paddleboards.

Estero River Outfitters (239-992-4050; www.esteroriveroutfitters.com), 20991 S. Tamiami Trail, opposite Koreshan Historic Site, Estero. Rents and sells quality new and used kayaks, canoes, and paddleboards for a four-mile adventure down the natural Estero River to Estero Bay.

GAEA Guides (239-694-5513 or 866-256-6388; www.gaeaguides.com). Naturalist-guided kayaking tours that include sunset, full moon, manatee, and bat tours. Also teaches kayak clinics on the Orange River and conducts archaeological kayak tours for Randell Research Center from Pine Island.

✪ **Great Calusa Blueway** (239-461-7400; www.calusablueway.com). This paddling trail along the island Intracoastal Waterway extends more than 190 miles, from Cayo Costa to Bonita Springs and up the Caloosahatchee River. Using GPS technology, it takes paddlers to Mound Key, Lovers Key State Park, Bunche Beach, Tarpon Bay, Cayo Costa, and other dynamic birding, archaeological, and beaching destinations. You can view maps or request a free map at the site or by calling the phone number listed above.

Gulf Coast Kayak (239-283-1125; www.gulfcoastkayak.com), 4120 Pine Island Rd., Matlacha, Pine Island. Guided kayak and paddleboard tours into ✪ **Matlacha Aquatic Preserve** and other local natural areas; full moon and mangrove maze ventures. All guides are naturalists and kayak instructors. Rentals available for self-guided tours.

Holiday Water Sports (239-765-4FUN; www.holidaywatersportsfmb.com), 200 Estero Blvd., at Pink Shell Beach Resort; (239-765-2252), Diamondhead Beach Resort, 2000 Estero Blvd., Fort Myers Beach; and (239-463-6778), Best Western Beach Resort, 684 Estero Blvd., Fort Myers Beach. Kayak and stand-up paddleboard rentals for use on-site, plus sailboats, Waverunners, and parasailing.

Lakes Regional Park (239-332-2453; www.leegov.com/parks), 7330 Gladiolus Dr., Fort Myers. Kayak and pedal boat rentals for paddling on a freshwater lake.

Lovers Key Adventures & Events (239-765-7788; www.loverskeyadventures.com), 8720 Estero Blvd., Fort Myers Beach. Rents canoes, kayaks, and paddleboards for use within Lovers Key State Park.

✪ **Manatee Park** (239-690-5030; www.leegov.com/parks), 10901 FL 80, Fort Myers. Paddle among the manatees along the Orange River with a kayak or canoe rental any day (weekends only April through October). Clinics available seasonally. Parking fee.

✎ **Tarpon Bay Explorers** (239-472-8900; www.tarponbayexplorers.com), 900 Tarpon Bay Rd., Sanibel Island. Rents canoes and kayaks for use in ✪ **Tarpon Bay** and on the "Ding" Darling refuge's Commodore Creek Canoe Trail; stand-up paddleboards for bay use only. Also guided tours. *Canoe & Kayak* magazine has rated Tarpon Bay among the top ten places to paddle in the United States.

Tropic Star Cruises (239-283-0015; www.tropicstarcruises.com), 16498 Tortuga St., Bokeelia, Pine Island. Rents single and double kayaks for half- and full-day trips or twenty-four hours from Bokeelia.

Dining Cruises: **J. C. Cruises** (239-334-7474; www.JCCruises.com), 2313 Edwards Dr., Fort Myers Yacht Basin, downtown Fort Myers. Lunch, dinner-dance, and sight-seeing cruises up the Caloosahatchee River and in the Intracoastal Waterway and gulf aboard the *Capt. J. P.*, a three-deck, five-hundred-passenger paddle-wheeler.

Sanibel Harbour Marriott Princess (239-466-4000; www.marriott.com), 17260 Harbour Pointe Dr., at Sanibel Harbour Resort off Summerlin Rd. before Sanibel Island causeway, Fort Myers. Two-hour sunset dinner buffet and Sunday brunch cruises aboard a sleek, elegant luxury yacht.

Personal Watercraft Rentals/Tours: **Holiday Water Sports** (239-765-4386; www .holidaywatersportsfmb.com), Pink Shell Beach Resort, 200 Estero Blvd., Fort Myers Beach; (239-765-2252), Diamondhead Beach Resort, 2000 Estero Blvd., Fort Myers Beach; and (239-463-6778), Best Western Beach Resort, 684 Estero Blvd., Fort Myers Beach. Wave-Runner rentals and ninety-minute dolphin-spotting tours.

Powerboat Rentals: All Around Boat Rentals (239-257-3329; www.aaboatrentals .com), Cape Coral. Fully equipped twenty-two-foot pontoon boat rentals with ninety horsepower engines. Boats hold up to twelve passengers and will launch for your Cape Coral marina location of choice.

Beach Bums Boat Rentals (239-472-6336; www.beachbumsboatrentals.com), 15951 Captiva Dr. at 'Tween Waters Inn Marina, Captiva Island. Rents center consoles and deck boats by four-, six-, and eight-hour intervals.

The Boat House (239-472-2531; www.sanibelmarina.com/rentals.html), Sanibel Marina, 634 N. Yachtsman Dr., Sanibel Island. Center consoles and cruisers for trips into intracoastal waters only.

Fish-Tale Marina (239-463-3600; www.thefishtalemarina.com), 7225 Estero Blvd., Fort Myers Beach. Rents Grady Whites, pontoons, deck boats, and skiffs.

Four Winds Marina (239-283-0250 or 800-523-9223; www.fourwindsmarina.com), 16501 Stringfellow Rd., Bokeelia, Pine Island. Rents twenty-one- to twenty-four-foot fishing and deck boats.

Jensen's Marina (239-472-5800; www.gocaptiva.com), 15107 Captiva Dr., Captiva Island. A colorful, locals' corner where fishermen hang out to tell lies. Rent a skiff, center console, or pontoon boat for half- or full-day rates. Water taxi transportation to the upper islands is also available.

Snook Bight Yacht Club & Marina (239-765-4371; www.snookbightmarina.com), 4765 Estero Blvd., Fort Myers Beach. Quality pontoons (twenty-one- to twenty-five-foot), deck, and fishing boats by the half or full day.

Southwest Florida Yachts (239-656-1339 or 800-262-7939; www.swfyachts.com or www.flsailandcruiseschool.com), 6095 Silver King Blvd. at Westin Cape Coral, Cape Coral. Offers power-yachting lessons and rentals in the thirty-two- to fifty-foot range.

Public Boat Ramps: Lavender's Landing (239-283-0015), 7290 Barrancas Ave. NW, Bokeelia. Newly renovated, it has two ramps.

Yacht Club Boat Ramp (239-574-0806; www.capecoral.net), 5819 Driftwood Pkwy., Cape Coral. Two public ramps on the Caloosahatchee River, with bait shop, marina, and recreational facilities.

Lovers Key State Park (239-463-4588; www.floridastateparks.org/park/Lovers -Key), 8700 Estero Blvd., at County Road 865 (CR 865) between Fort Myers Beach and Bonita Beach. Access to Estero Bay and the gulf with picnicking facilities and bait and snack shop.

Matlacha Park (239-283-4110; www.leegov.com/parks), 4577 Pine Island Rd. NW, Matlacha, Pine Island. Playground, fishing pier, and two ramps.

Punta Rassa (239-765-6794), 15001 Punta Rassa Rd. before the Sanibel causeway, Fort Myers. Two double ramps, picnic facilities, historic marker, and restrooms.

Sanibel, Causeway Rd. Two ramps at the west end of the Sanibel causeway.

Sailboat Charters: New Moon (239-395-1782; www.newmoonsailing.com), 'Tween Waters Inn Marina, 15951 Captiva Dr., Captiva Island. Up to six passengers aboard a thirty-nine-foot sloop. Sailing lessons for kids and adults, three-hour cruises, and extended custom sails.

Sailboat Rentals & Instruction: ✪ Offshore Sailing School (239-454-1700 or 888-454-7015; www.offshore-sailing.com), 16731 McGregor Blvd., at South Seas Island Resort Marina on Captiva Island and Pink Shell Beach Resort on Fort Myers Beach. Weeklong and three-day certification (US SAILING) instruction offered, from beginning women's-only and mixed sailing courses to family learning vacations, advanced racing, coastal navigation, and performance racing. Operated by an Olympic and America's Cup veteran. Course instructors are knowledgeable, experienced, and easygoing ("no yelling" is the rule). Accommodation packages with resorts available.

CAPE CORAL YACHT CLUB IS A RECREATIONAL HUB WITH EVERYTHING FROM A MARINA AND FISHING PIER TO A SWIMMING POOL AND RACQUETBALL COURTS

Southwest Florida Yachts/❂ Florida Sailing & Cruising School (239-656-1339 or 800-262-7939; www.flsail andcruiseschool.com), 6095 Silver King Blvd. at Westin Cape Coral, Cape Coral American Sailing Association (ASA) certification courses and bareboat charters provide excellent adventures into Charlotte Harbor for live-aboard experiences. Also powerboat courses.

Sight-Seeing & Entertainment Cruises: Look under "Wildlife Tours & Charters" for nature excursions.

❂ ✍ **Captiva Cruises** (239-472-5300; www.captivacruises.com), P.O. Box 580, Captiva Island 33924, at McCarthy's Marina. Offers a complete menu of upper island sight-seeing, beach, and luncheon trips aboard the finely fitted 150-passenger *Lady Chadwick* and a 48-passenger pontoon; guides share history and lore along the way. These cruises are the only way for nonguests of the inn and club to see private Useppa Island and enjoy lunch at the Collier Inn restaurant. New cruises include transportation to Don Pedro Island State Park in Charlotte County and a lunch cruise to Pineland on Pine Island.

J. C. Cruises (239-334-7474; www.jccruises.com), 2313 Edwards Dr., Fort Myers, at Fort Myers Yacht Basin. Sight-seeing and dining cruises on the river and into the Intracoastal Waterway and gulf aboard a five-hundred-passenger paddleboat.

CAPTIVA CRUISES' LADY CHADWICK ANCHORS AT USEPPA ISLAND

Sanibel Thriller Cruises (239-472-2328; www.sanibelthriller.com), 634 N. Yachtsman Dr., at Sanibel Marina, Sanibel Island. Offers zippy narrated tours that circle Sanibel and Captiva.

Stars & Stripes (239-472-2723; www.sanibelmarina.com/charters.html), 634 N. Yachtsman Dr., at Sanibel Marina, Sanibel Island. Ninety-minute sight-seeing and wildlife tours depart four times daily.

Tropic Star Cruises (239-283-0015; www.tropicstarcruises.com), 16499 Porto Bello St., Bokeelia, Pine Island at Knight's Landing. Full-day nature and Boca Grande cruises and ferry service to Cayo Costa (ferry/kayak package available).

FISHING Snook and tarpon are the prized catch of local anglers. Snook, which is a game fish and can't be sold commercially, is valued for its sweet taste, but recreational pressures have led to recent restrictions, so check before you keep one.

Redfish is another sought-after food fish. More common catches in back bays and waters close to shore include mangrove snapper, spotted sea trout, shark, sheepshead, pompano, and ladyfish. Deeper waters offshore yield grouper (red and the more valued black and gag), red snapper, amberjack, mackerel, and dolphinfish. Most fish, including tarpon, are released in these days of environmental consciousness. Check local regulations for season, size, and catch restrictions.

Nonresidents age sixteen and older must obtain a license unless fishing from a vessel or pier covered by its own license. Inexpensive, temporary, nonresident licenses are available at county tax collectors' offices and most K-marts, marinas, and bait shops.

Deep-Sea Party Boats: **Getaway Deep Sea Fishing** (239-466-3600 or 800-641-3088; www.getawaymarina.com), Getaway Marina, 18400 San Carlos Blvd., Fort Myers Beach. All-day, half-day, and nighttime party boat excursions plus charters and boat rentals.

Fishing Charters/Outfitters: Competent fishing guides work out of the region's major marinas. If it's your first time fishing these waters, I recommend hiring someone with local knowledge.

Captain Pat Hagle Charters (239-283-5991), P.O. Box 245, Pineland 33945. Fish excursions into Pine Island Sound; also nature, history, shelling, beachcombing, and water-taxi cruises.

Sanibel Marina (239-472-2723; www.sanibelmarina.com), 634 N. Yachtsman Dr., Sanibel Island. Several experienced fishing guides operate out of the marina.

Fishing Piers: **Yacht Club Community Park** (239-574-0806; www.capecoral.net), 5819 Driftwood Pkwy., Cape Coral. The 620-foot lit fishing pier is part of a boating/recreational complex that includes a bait and tackle shop.

Centennial Park, Edwards Dr. near Yacht Basin, downtown Fort Myers. Complete park with playgrounds and other facilities.

✪ **Fort Myers Beach Pier**, 1000 Estero Blvd., at Lynn Hall Park (www.leeparks.org), Fort Myers Beach. The concrete T-pier with wooden railings, recently renovated, offers lots of casting room and hungry pelicans. It holds a tin-roofed bait shop (rudystreasurechest.com/find.html) that also rents rods.

Lighthouse Park Beach (239-472-6397; www.mysanibel.com),112 Periwinkle Way, southeast end of Periwinkle Way, Sanibel Island. A T-dock into San Carlos Bay.

✪ **Manatee Park** (239-690-5030; www.leegov.com/parks), 10901 FL 80, Fort Myers. A great place for visitors to learn more about the endangered West Indian manatee that is native to the region, while they fish from the pier on the Orange River.

Matanzas Bridge Fishing Pier (239-229-1610; www.leegov.com/parks), 700 Fishermen's Wharf Dr., Fort Myers Beach. Free pier that runs underneath the Sky Bridge.

Matlacha Park (239-283-4110; www.leegov.com/parks), 4577 Pine Island Rd. NW, Matlacha, Pine Island. Playground, picnicking, and boat ramps.

GOLF Home of such golfing greats as Patty Berg and Nolan Henke, the region keeps pace with the growing popularity of golf.

Public Golf Courses: **Alden Pines Country Club** (239-283-2179; www.aldenpinesgolf .com), 14261 Clubhouse Dr., Bokeelia, Pine Island. A public, eighteen-hole, par-seventy-one course with affordable rates year-round. Snack bar.

Dunes Golf & Tennis Club (239-472-2535; www.dunesgolfsanibel.com), 949 Sandcastle Rd., Sanibel Island. Semiprivate, eighteen-hole, par-seventy course. Restaurant and bar. Lush, Audubon-preserve links. High rates, especially in season.

🐾 **Eastwood Golf Course** (239-321-7487; www.cityftmyers.com/225/Eastwood-Golf -Course), 4600 Bruce Heard Ln., Fort Myers. One of the region's favorites; eighteen holes, par seventy-two, located away from traffic. Restaurant and bar.

🐾 **Fort Myers Country Club** (239-321-7488; www.cityftmyers.com/227/Fort-Myers -Country-Club), 3591 McGregor Blvd., Fort Myers. Fort Myers's oldest, it opened in 1917 and was recently renovated; eighteen-hole, par-seventy-one course. Restaurant and lounge.

Sanibel Island Golf Club (239-472-2626; www.sanibelislandgc.com), 1100 Parview Dr., Sanibel Island. Semiprivate, eighteen-hole, par-seventy course with restaurant, pro shop, rentals, and lessons.

Coral Oaks Golf Course (239-573-3100; www.capecoral.net/coraloak), 1800 NW 28th Ave., Cape Coral. eighteen-hole, par-seventy-two course championship course designed by Arthur Hills around eight lakes and an old oak hammock. Driving range, chipping area, putting green, pro shop, and restaurant.

HEALTH & FITNESS CLUBS **Gulf Coast Fitness** (239-549-3354; www.gulfcoastgym capecoral.com), 1013 Cape Coral Pkwy. E., Cape Coral. Smoothie bar, cardio and strength-building equipment, spinning classes, personal training, tanning, and child care.

Around the Clock Fitness (239-931-6664; www.aroundtheclock.fitness), 1755 Boy Scout Dr., Fort Myers. More than one hundred cardio machines, a separate women's-only facility, classes, smoothie-juice bar, a spa-salon next door, kids supervision and fitness classes, and club-style locker rooms with free towel service. Twenty-four-hour full-service fitness center with staffed Kids' Zone and healthy café. Short-term passes and memberships available.

Sanibel Health Club (239-395-2639; www.sanibelhealthclub.com), 975 Rabbit Rd., Sanibel Island. Full cardiovascular and weight-training equipment, yoga and Pilates classes, and personal training. Short-term memberships (day, week, month) available.

Sanibel Recreation Center (239-472-0345; www.mysanibel.com), 3880 Sanibel-Captiva Rd., Sanibel Island. Short-term memberships allow visitors to take advantage of all this complex has to offer: a kids' play pool with fountains and slide, a lap pool, a nicely equipped fitness center, tennis, and aerobic and other classes.

HIKING **Cayo Costa State Park** (941-964-0375; www.floridastateparks.org/park/ Cayo-Costa), on Cayo Costa. Six miles of trails take you through barrier island ecology, a pioneer cemetery, and remnants of a circa-1904 quarantine station.

Corkscrew Regional Ecosystem Watershed (CREW) Marsh Trail (239-657-2253; www.crewtrust.org), 4600 Corkscrew Rd., Estero, eighteen miles east of I-75, exit 123. Five miles of hiking trails through peri-Everglades environment—pine flatwoods, oak and palm hammock, and sawgrass marsh—to a twelve-foot observation tower. The

CALUSA SHELL MOUND TRAIL AT J. N. "DING" DARLING NATIONAL WILDLIFE REFUGE PROVIDES A QUIET BOARDWALK STROLL INTO A HARDWOOD HAMMOCK AND THE PAST

Cypress Dome Hiking trailhead is four miles west of the Marsh Trails. Free guided tours the second Saturday and the first and third Tuesday of each month, November through April. Full-moon hikes, too.

✪ ☗ ✧ **J. N. "Ding" Darling National Wildlife Refuge** (239-472-1100; www.fws.gov/refuge/jn_ding_darling/ or ding darlingsociety.org), 1 Wildlife Dr., off Sanibel-Captiva Rd., Sanibel Island. Its longest hike, the Indigo Trail, travels for more than four miles from the refuge education center, across a boardwalk and along bird-rich ponds. In 2013, the Wildlife Education Boardwalk through freshwater habitat extended its length and added cool scat (animal poop) and tracks interpretation. A shorter refuge trail takes you to a protected Calusa shell mound.

Estero Bay Preserve State Park (239-992-0311; www.floridastateparks.org/park/Estero-Bay), off W. Broadway in Estero; mailing address: 3800 Corkscrew Rd., Estero 33928. Provides about six miles of sand nature trails through scrubland along the Estero River and bay marshes. Wildlife you might see in the ten-thousand-acre tract and from its observation decks include gopher tortoises, hawks, woodpeckers, eagles, and manatees. There's a second trailhead at the south end of Winkler Road (off Summerlin Road) in Fort Myers, leading to three loops equaling six miles and to two observation decks.

✧ **Sanibel-Captiva Conservation Foundation** (239-472-2329; www.sccf.org), 3333 Sanibel-Captiva Rd., Sanibel Island. Nearly five miles of trails through natural habitat to an observation tower along the Sanibel River. The majority of wildlife consists of birds, lizards, alligators, and insects. At its new Bailey Homestead Preserve campus on Periwinkle Way, Shipley Trail connects to a boardwalk and Pond Apple Trail, for more than two miles of forested hiking. Check SCCF's website for other island trails.

KIDS' STUFF ✧ **Eagle Skate Park** (239-573-0206; www.capecoral.net), 315 SW Second Ave., Cape Coral. Ramps, half- and quarter-pipes, grind boxes and rails; outfitted for skaters and BMX bikers. Admission: $6.

✧ **Fort Myers Beach Pool** (239-463-5759; www.fortmyersbeachfl.gov), 2600 Oak St.(at School St.), Fort Myers Beach. Not your ordinary city pool, this one at the Bay Oaks Recreational Complex has a two-story slide and the toddler Tad Pool with a smaller slide. Admission: $5 ages thirteen and older, $3 ages one to twelve. Closed Tuesday and Thursday in winter.

✧ **Fort Myers Skate Park** (239321-7558; www.cityftmyers.com), 2277 Grand Ave., downtown Fort Myers behind the Skatium. Skateboarders and in-line skaters love this YMCA outdoor facility with its cool ramps and half-pipes. Skate and pad rentals are available. Admission is $5 per day. On Monday evenings the park is open for BMX riders.

✧ ⟨⟨ᵠ⟩⟩ **Skatium** (239-321-7510; www.cityftmyers.com), 2250 Broadway, Fort Myers. Hours vary for indoor ice skating. Cost for public ice skating sessions is $7, plus $3 for skate rental. Skating classes available.

✐ **Germain Arena** (239-948-7825; www.skateeverblades.com), 11000 Everblades Pkwy., exit 123 off I-75, at Corkscrew Rd., Estero. The public can ice skate at this indoor rink. Admission is $7 for a regular session. Skate rental is $3. Sunday evening family skating costs $5 each, including rentals, plus there are special late skate and pizza-and-pop sessions. The arena also offers learn-to-skate classes, an ice-hockey league, and a figure-skating club and clinics. A video arcade and hockey pro shop complete the amenities.

✪ ✐ **Greenwell's Bat-A-Ball and Family Fun Park** (239-574-4386; www .greenwellsfamilyfunpark.com), 35 NE Pine Island Rd., Cape Coral. Named after the city's favorite sports son, former Red Sox player Mike Greenwell, this facility contains batting cages, a miniature golf course, a small playground, a maze, a video arcade, six go-cart tracks, kiddie rides, a fish pond and feeding dock, and snack concessions. Kids really love it here, but be prepared to lay out a lot of money if you spend much time—especially in the arcade room.

✐ **Happy's Family Fun Center** (239-800-3192; www.happysfamilyfuncenter.com), 616 NE 15th Ave., Cape Coral. Indoor climbing structures, slides, bounce houses, a video arcade, obstacle courses, and a "5D" rollercoaster simulator.

✐ **HeadPinz Entertainment Center** (239-574-8353; headpinz.com), 1899 Del Prado Blvd., Cape Coral; and (239-301-2155), 14513 Global Pkwy., Fort Myers. Deluxe and spacious bowling alley and video arcade facilities with food and special events. The Fort Myers complex also offers laser tag and an aerial ropes course.

✐ **Periwinkle Park** (239-472-1433; www.sanibelcamping.com), 1119 Periwinkle Way, Sanibel Island. The owner of this trailer park raises and breeds exotic birds and waterfowl. He daddies roughly four hundred birds of ninety species, specializing in African and Asian hornbills. Flamingoes, parakeets, cockatiels, cockatoos, and others occupy the park and its fifteen aviaries. During the off season, visitors can drive through; in season, biking is recommended. A few of the birds raised here can be seen more easily at Jerry's Shopping Center (1700 Periwinkle Way). Take the children in the evening, when the birds are most talkative.

✐ **The Shell Factory** (239-995-2141; www.shellfactory.com), 2787 N. Tamiami Trail, N. Fort Myers. A shell shop on steroids, this longtime attraction has grown into a megacomplex. Although still old-fashioned, it now includes restaurants, a fun park, a new climbing wall and zip line, a nature park, a pirate attraction, a money museum, a mining slough, aquariums, video games, restaurants, daily live music, a dog park with water and a diving pier, a playground, and gifts from fine to tacky. Admission to the Shell Factory is free; admission to the nature park is $12 for adults, $10 for seniors, and $8 for children ages four to twelve. Bumper boat rides, water wars, and miniature golf are $5. Attraction hours are 10–5 daily; retail 10-6 daily. Special events, such as Gumbo Fest, are fun for the whole family and feature live entertainment.

✐ **Strausser BMX Sports Complex** (239-573-3128; www.capecoral.net), 1410 SW Sixth Pl., Cape Coral. A bicycle motocross track is provided for practice and weekly races. Also picnic grounds, a playground, and softball fields.

✪ ✐ **Sun Splash Family Waterpark** (239-574-0558; www.sunsplashwaterpark.com), 400 Santa Barbara Blvd, Cape Coral. This spot offers wet fun in a dozen varieties and includes pools, slides, flumes, a log roll, cable drops, a river ride, volleyball, food, lockers, and special events. Admission: $19.95 ages thirteen and older, $17.95 children ages two to twelve and senior citizens (plus tax). Admission prices drop after 5 p.m. Parking is $5. The park is open early March through September, but the schedule varies according to time of year and day; it is open daily, mid-June through mid-August.

✐ **Zoomers Amusement Park** (239-481-9666; www.zoomersamusementpark.com), 17455 Summerlin Rd., Fort Myers. The complex includes Midway rides, three go-cart tracks, mini-golf, bowling, bumper boats, an arcade, a café, and other family attractions. Admission per activity.

Sky Zone Trampoline Park (239-313-5448; www.skyzone.com/fortmyers), 14181 Tamiami Trail. An indoor facility with multiple trampolines, jumps, a foam pit, and special programs such as Toddler Time and GLOW ZONE. Fun for all ages.

RACQUET SPORTS **Fort Myers Racquet Club** (239-931-0015; www.cityftmyers.com), 1700 Matthew Dr., Fort Myers. Newly renovated, eight clay courts and two hard courts (eight lit total), lessons, and tournaments. Admission.

Rutenberg Community Park (239-707-0584; www.leegov.com/parks), 6500 S. Pointe Blvd., Fort Myers. Eight lit tennis and two handball courts.

Sanibel Recreation Center (239-472-0345; www.mysanibel.com), 3880 Sanibel-Captiva Rd., Sanibel Island. Four lit courts; admission.

Signal Inn Resort (239-472-4690; www.signalinn.com), 1811 Olde Middle Gulf Dr., Sanibel Island. One racquetball court. Admission fee for nonguests.

STARS Complex (239-321-7545; www.cityftmyers.com), 2980 Edison Ave., downtown Fort Myers. Two lit tennis courts.

Yacht Club Community Park (239-574-0808; www.capecoral.net), 5819 Driftwood Pkwy., Cape Coral. Five lit tennis courts, two outdoor racquetball courts, and a pro shop. Admission.

SHELLING Welcome to shelling heaven. Sanibel Island, in particular, is known for its great pickings. Be aware that a state law prohibits the collection of live shells on Sanibel Island, to preclude the possibility of dwindling populations. Collecting live shells is also prohibited in state and national parks. Elsewhere in the county, live collecting is also discouraged. Any shell with a creature still inside is considered a live shell. Shellers who find live shells washed up on the beach—a common occurrence after storms—are urged to gently return (no flinging!) the shell to deep water.

Hot Shelling Spots: **Big Hickory Island**, northwest of Little Hickory Island, accessible only by boat. An unhitched crook of beach favored by local boaters and shellers.

✪ **Bonita Beach**, Little Hickory Island. Look north of the public beach.

✪ **Cayo Costa State Park**, between North Captiva and Boca Grande, accessible only by boat. Because it takes a boat ride to get here, these sands hold caches of shells merely by virtue of their remoteness. North-end Johnson Shoals provides a thin strip of sandbar for good low-tide pickings.

Sanibel Island. Known as the Shelling Capital of the Western Hemisphere, the island even has its own name for the peculiar, shell-bent stance of the beach collector: the Sanibel Stoop. Unlike the other Gulf Coast barrier islands, Sanibel takes an east–west heading. Its perpendicular position and lack of offshore reefs allow it to intercept shells that arrive from southern seas. Its fame as a world-class shelling area has made Sanibel a prime destination for shell collectors for decades. With shell-named streets, store shelves awash in shells and shell crafts, an annual shell festival, and a shell museum, one risks suffering shell shock just by visiting. Best gulfside shelling spot: Bowman's Beach, midisland, away from the paths leading to the parking lot.

Shelling Charters: **Adventures in Paradise** (239-472-8443; www.adventure inparadiseinc.com), 14341 Port Comfort Rd., at Port Sanibel Marina, east of Sanibel toll booth, Fort Myers. Shelling and lunch excursions to Cayo Costa and North Captiva Island aboard power catamarans.

Captiva Cruises (239-472-5300; www.captivacruises.com), P.O. Box 580, Captiva Island 33924, at McCarthy's Marina. Full and half-day shelling trips, with experienced instruction, to Cayo Costa.

SANIBEL HARBOUR MARRIOTT RESORT & SPA MAKES AN ELEGANT WATERFRONT STATEMENT

SPAS **Aquagene** (239-463-8648; www.pinkshell.com), Pink Shell Resort, 275 Estero Blvd., Fort Myers Beach. This resort spa takes its cues from the sea in design. Spa treatments include an algae wrap, Sea of Life Facial, and a coconut-mango massage. A waterfall fountain at the entrance begins the relaxation process.

Esterra Spa & Salon (239-463-0887; www.sunstream.com), 6231 Estero Blvd. Fort Myers Beach. A day spa but affiliated with the three Sunstream Resorts (Diamond-Head, Gull Wing, and Pointe Estero) on Fort Myers Beach; complete services include massage, body treatments, nail and hair services, and facials.

Sanibel Day Spa (239-395-2220 or 877-695-1588; www.sanibeldayspa.com), 2075 Periwinkle Way #24, upstairs at Periwinkle Place, Sanibel Island. Long-established and well-reputed place of pampering offers extensive à la carte and spa package services, including hair care, manicures, pedicures, men's treatments, facials, oxygen therapy, Ayurvedic wellness treatments, scrubs, and massages.

Sanibel Harbour Marriott Resort & Spa (239-466-2156 or 800-767-7777; www.sanibel-resort.com), 17260 Harbour Pointe Dr., directly before the Sanibel causeway, Fort Myers. Sanibel Harbour was a spa before it became a resort (see "Lodging"). Guests, members, and day visitors can take advantage of the swimming pool, whirlpools, training room, fitness classes, saunas, steam rooms, and racquetball courts. The spa offers special services including interactive couples treatments, herbal wraps, aromatherapy massage, personal training, facials, and the unique BETAR musical and sound relaxation system.

Spada (239-482-1858; spadaspa.com), 13161 McGregor Blvd., Fort Myers. Full line of Aveda body and skin care treatments, including prenatal and couples massages, facials, cranberry spa manicure, and microderm-abrasion.

Touch Spa Salon (239-454-9933; www.touchspasalon.com), 15245 S. Cleveland Ave., Fort Myers. Facials are its strong suit and come in flavors of European, pumpkin chiffon, pearl and ginseng, and more. Also waxing, hair, and nail services.

SPECTATOR SPORTS *Crab Races:* ✪ ✎
Crow's Nest Beach Bar & Grille (239-472-5161; www.tween-waters.com), 15951 Captiva Dr., at 'Tween Waters Inn Resort & Spa, Captiva Island. Participate or watch at 6 and 9 every Monday and Thursday night (except September). The early session is geared toward families.

Pro Baseball: **Hammond Stadium,** (239-533-7695; www.leegov.com/parks), 14100 Six Mile Cypress Pkwy., Fort Myers. Hosts the Minnesota Twins (239-768-4270 or 800-33-TWINS; http://minnesota.twins.mlb.com) for spring training in March. April through August, the Miracle Professional Baseball team (239-768-4210; www.miraclebaseball.com), a member of the Florida State League, competes here.

JetBlue Park at Fenway Park South (239-334-4700), 11500 Fenway South Dr., Fort Myers. For the Boston Red Sox's (877-RED-SOX9; boston.redsox.mlb.com) 2012 spring training season, this new $77.9-million stadium opened in south Fort Myers, complete with its own Green Monster fence. The complex also includes ten thousand seats, six practice fields, and state-of-the-art training facilities.

THE BOSTON RED SOX PLAY THEIR SPRING TRAINING SESSION AT JETBLUE PARK AT FENWAY PARK SOUTH

Pro Hockey: **Florida Everblades** (239-948-7825; www.floridaeverblades.com), Germain Arena, 11000 Everblades Pkwy., Estero, exit 123 off I-75. Southwest Florida's professional ice hockey team plays its October through April season at Germain Arena. The public can skate at the rink daily (times vary) for a fee. (See "Kids' Stuff.")

WATER SPORTS *Dive Shops & Charters:* **Scubavice** (239-481-4733; www.scubavicedivers.com), 12600 McGregor Blvd., Fort Myers. National Association of Underwater Instructors (NAUI) certification courses and equipment, plus dive trips out of the region.

Parasailing & Waterskiing: **Holiday Water Sports** (239-765-4FUN; www.holidaywatersportsfmb.com), 250 Estero Blvd., at Pink Shell Beach Resort; (239-765-2252), DiamondHead Beach Resort, 2000 Estero Blvd., Fort Myers Beach; and (239-463-6778), 684 Estero Blvd., at Best Western Beach Resort, Fort Myers Beach. Parasailing plus Hobie Cat, ocean kayak, paddleboard, aquacycle, and WaveRunner rentals available.

Ranalli Parasail (239-565-5700; www.ranalliparasail.com), 2000 Estero Blvd., Fort Myers Beach, at DiamondHead Beach Resort. Rides along Fort Myers Beach for up to six people and twelve thousand feet.

YOLO Watersports (239-472-9656 or 239-472-1296; yolowatersports.com), 11534 Andy Rosse Ln., Captiva Island. Parasailing rides from six hundred to eight hundred feet high with dips, plus water-sport rentals.

Sailboarding & Surfing: Winter and summer storms bring the sort of waves that surfers crave, but in general, gulf waves are too wimpy for serious wave riders.

Strong winds, however, provide excellent conditions for sailboarders at several locations throughout the region. Sanibel Causeway is the most popular windsurfing and kite-surfing spot.

Ace Performer (239-565-4860; www.aceperformer.com), 16842 McGregor Blvd., Fort Myers. Rents equipment and gives lessons for windsurfing, kite boards, and kayaks. Free delivery to the Sanibel Causeway.

YOLO Watersports (239-472-9656; yolowatersports.com), 11534 Andy Rosse Ln., Captiva. Rents surfboards and stand-up paddleboards.

Snorkeling & Scuba: Florida's west coast has no natural reefs, but several have been built to provide homes for marine life and make divers and fishermen happy. More than twenty of these artificial reefs lie along the Sanibel Island–area coast. The latest, the USS *Mohawk*, allows divers to explore an intact WWII battleship in ninety feet of water twenty-eight nautical miles off Captiva Island. It lies near the Captiva Blue Hole site, a.k.a. The Crack, and attracts great marine life, including whale sharks. The Edison Reef, one of the largest, was created from the sinking of a former Fort Myers bridge in forty-two feet of water fifteen nautical miles off the Sanibel Lighthouse. The Belton Johnson Reef, constructed of concrete culvert, lies about five nautical miles off Bowman's Beach on Sanibel. Other popular sites include the Redfish Pass Barge, lying in twenty-five feet of water less than a nautical mile from Redfish Pass between Captiva and North Captiva, and the Doc Kline Reef, a popular tarpon hole less than eight nautical miles from the Sanibel Lighthouse. Cayo Costa State Island Preserve offers snorkelers nice ledges in two to five feet of water alive with fish, sponges, and shells.

WILDERNESS CAMPING **Cayo Costa State Park** (941-964-0375; www.florida stateparks.org/park/Cayo-Costa), P.O. Box 1150, Boca Grande 33951, La Costa Island. You'll need boat transportation to reach this unbridged island (see Tropic Star Cruises

ON FLORIDA'S GULF COAST, WHERE SURFING WAVES ARE RARE, SKIM-BOARDING APPEALS TO YOUNG BEACHGOERS

and Jensen's Marina under "Boats & Boating"), which is home to myriad birds. Bring your own fresh drinking water and lots of bug spray. And don't expect to plug in the smartphone. There are showers, picnic grounds, boat docks, nature trails, a tram that runs cross-island, tent sites, and some very primitive cabins to rent. Call ahead to reserve the latter.

Koreshan State Historic Site (239-992-0311; www.floridastateparks.org/park/Koreshan), 3800 Corkscrew Rd., Estero 33928. Koreshan's sixty campsites circle a volleyball court and are built fairly close together; a few face the Estero River. The park contains a nature trail, paddling trail, boat ramp, playground, and eleven buildings in the historic compound. For reservations, call 800-326-3521 or visit www.reserveamerica.com.

WILDLIFE SPOTTING Loggerhead turtles lumber up on local beaches each summer to lay their cache of eggs. (Only vigilant night owls actually see them, but you can find their tracks in the morning light and see their nests, which patrols stake off.) Brown pelicans swarm fishing piers for handouts. Roseate spoonbills dress wetlands in pink. Black skimmers nest on uninhabited sandy islands, while hundreds of other birds visit or stay in local habitats. The Fort Myers–Sanibel area is a vital area for wildlife, and many opportunities exist to spy on animals in their natural habitat.

Alligators: Once endangered, the alligator population sprang back in recent decades, only to be decimated in past years by fear gone overboard. Thanks to organizations and laws that fought to protect the prehistoric reptiles, the jawsome creatures have been taken off endangered lists. Sanibel Island paved the way by pioneering a no-feeding regulation that later became state law. (Hand-fed alligators lose their fear of people.) Then, in 2004, after a couple of deadly attacks on Sanibel, the city began open harvesting of the creatures; when a gator trapper is called, he is allowed to take as many gators as he wishes at that outing. Now the alligator, once a common sight, especially at J. N. "Ding" Darling National Wildlife Refuge, is more rarely seen. Concerned citizens and naturalists continue to cry for reform, but for now the slaughter continues.

Innate homebodies, alligators usually leave their home ponds only during spring and summer mating. That's when you're most likely to spot them. You will hear the bellow of the bull gator in the night and sometimes see both males and females roaming from pond to pond in search of some midsummer night's romance. They can do serious damage to a car, so be alert. And never approach one on foot.

When it's cold, alligators stay submerged to keep warm. When they're in the water, you first spot their snouts, then their prickly, tire-tread profiles. Once your eye becomes trained to distinguish them from logs and background, you'll notice them more readily. On sunny days throughout the year you may spot them soaking up rays on the banks of freshwater rivers and streams.

Birds: Roseate spoonbills are the stars of the J. N. "Ding" Darling National Wildlife Refuge, but hundreds of other species live among the sanctuary's wiry mangrove limbs and shallow estuarine waters, including ibises, brown and white

ONE OF THE COLORFUL LOCALS

pelicans, tricolored herons, red-shouldered hawks, snowy and reddish egrets, anhingas, mangrove cuckoos, and ospreys.

Dolphins: Playful bottle-nosed dolphins cruise the sea, performing impromptu acrobatic shows that it's hard to believe aren't staged. When the next performance will be is anybody's guess, but if you learn their feeding schedules you have a better chance of catching their act. They often like to leap out of the wake of large boats. Out in the gulf I've been surrounded by their antics to the point where I suffered minor whiplash from spinning around to keep track of them all. Don't expect them

BIRDERS OF ALL AGES GET SERIOUS ON SANIBEL ISLAND

to get too close—take some binoculars—and forget seeing them in captivity around here. Locals once staged a protest in Pine Island Sound when collectors tried to take some of their dolphins. And when a swim-with-the-dolphins facility was proposed near Sanibel Island, citizens again rose up in arms against animal exploitation.

Manatees: In east Fort Myers—where warm waters discharged from the Florida Power & Light Company have always attracted the warm-blooded manatees to so-called Yankee Canal in the winter months—♂ ♫ **Manatee Park** (see "Nature Preserves & Eco-Attractions") provides a manatee viewing area, exhibits, and other recreational and educational assets along the wild and natural Orange River.

Pine Island's backwaters offer a good venue for manatee spotting. Check out the bay behind Island Decor & More, a popular sea-watch site, just before the Matlacha Bridge. If you're around South Seas Island Resort on Captiva Island, watch the marina waters for surfacing manatees. On Sanibel, look in the summer around Tarpon Bay in the J. N. "Ding" Darling National Wildlife Refuge, where you can paddle among them.

Nature Preserves & Eco-Attractions: ♂ ♫ **Butterfly Estates** (239-690-2359; http://thebutterflyestates.com), 1815 Fowler St., Fort Myers. Open Tuesday to Sunday 10-5; summer hours 10-3. $7 ages thirteen and older, $4 ages two to twelve, $6 seniors and Florida residents. A recent addition to downtown's cultural scene, this greenhouse structure gives wing to thousands of butterflies, moths, and the imagination. Lush plants and trickling waterfalls add to the beauty of the small but lively butterfly house. A gift shop, café, and gastropub occupy charming, renovated, historic cottages at the estates.

♫ **Calusa Nature Center & Planetarium** (239-275-3435; calusanature.org), 3450 Ortiz Ave., Fort Myers. Open Monday to Saturday 10–4, Sunday 11–4. Call or go online for astronomy and laser show times. Museum, trails, and planetarium $10 adults and teens, $5 children ages three to twelve, children under three free. This multifaceted environmental center offers three wildlife trails with a butterfly aviary, a native plant garden, a caged bobcat and foxes, a touch tank, and an injured-bird aviary. Indoors you can see more live animal exhibits—snakes, tarantulas, alligators, turtles—and demonstrations. The Insectarium crawls with live bugs and offers interactive fun, such as dressing up like an insect. Daily programs allow visitors to get up close and personal with some of the fascinating creatures of Southwest Florida, plus the center hosts special nature programs for children and adults every month. The planetarium uses telescopes, laser lights, and astronomy lessons in its presentations (usually at 1:30 and 2:30).

Cayo Costa State Park (941-964-0375; www.floridastateparks.org/park/Cayo -Costa), P.O. Box 1150, Boca Grande 33951. Located on Cayo Costa Island; accessible only by boat. $2 per person. A wildlife refuge occupies about ninety percent of this 2,225-acre island. Cayo Costa preserves the Florida that the Native Americans tried to protect against European invasion. Besides the occasional feral hog that survives on the island, egrets, white pelicans, raccoons, ospreys, and black skimmers frequent the area. The path across the island's northern end features a side trip to a pioneer cemetery. Blooming cacti and other flora festoon the walk, which is sometimes a run when the weather turns warm and uncontrolled mosquito populations remind us of the hardships of eras gone by. Campsites and cabins accommodate overnighters.

C.R.O.W. (239-472-3644; www.crowclinic.org), 3883 Sanibel-Captiva Rd., Sanibel Island. Open Monday to Saturday 10–4 December 15–April 30; Monday to Friday 10–4 May 1–December 14. $7 adults, $5 teens ages thirteen to nineteen, free for children twelve and younger,. C.R.O.W. is the acronym for forty-year-old Clinic for the Rehabil-itation of Wildlife. It opened the impressive Healing Winds Visitor Education Center in 2009 to great acclaim. Among its state-of-the-art hands-on exhibits, visitors can watch recovering patients via critter-cam and learn what it takes to be a wildlife vet from exhibits such as "Peek at a Pelican" and "Radiographs." The hospital tends to sick and injured wildlife: more than four thousand birds, bobcats, raccoons, rabbits, and otters a year.

Four Mile Cove Ecological Preserve (239-549-4606; www.capecoral.net), at the end of SE 23rd Terrace, north of Midpoint Memorial Bridge in Cape Coral (follow the signs off Del Prado Blvd. north of Coralwood Mall at SE 21st Ln). Open daily 8–sunset. An urban preserve runs parallel to the bridge and allows exploration of 365 acres of wetlands along a 1.25-mile nature trail that takes you away from the bustle of traffic into bird and gopher tortoise habitat. A number of monuments honor World War II, Korean, Vietnam, and Iraqi soldiers in the Veteran's Memorial Pavilion. Interpretative center and restrooms, picnicking and guided nature walks. Kayak rentals (239-574-7395) are available on the weekends (November through May only). The kayak trail into Alligator and Deerfly Creeks becomes shallow and narrow, requiring portage. Children under age six are not allowed in kayaks.

Lakes Regional Park (239-533-7580; www.leegov.com/parks), 7330 Glad-iolus Dr., Fort Myers. Open daily 7–dusk; train village open Monday to Friday 10–1:45, Saturday 10–3:45, Sunday noon–3:45 (10–3:45 in season). Parking $1 per hour, $5 per day; fifteen-minute mini train rides $5 ages five and older, $1 for ages one to five (includes admission to the railroad museum, $1 for museum only). Lakes Regional Park excels as a family picnic-and-play park, but also as a prime birding spot. For the fam-ily: a sand beach on the lake (a former quarry; no swimming allowed), water fountain play areas, playgrounds with a climbing wall, a miniature train and a railroad museum (239-267-1905; www.rrmsf.org), a fragrance garden, walking and biking trails, and rentals for pedal boats, hydrobikes, and kayaks. The park's concession also sells ice cream and rents bikes for its more than two miles of trails that reach across the lake.

Manatee Park (239-690-5030; www.leegov.com/parks), 10901 FL 80 (Palm Beach Blvd.), Fort Myers. Open daily dawn-dusk Parking $1 ($2 in season December–March) per hour, $5 per day. A well-kept, seventeen-acre recreational park feeds our fas-cination for the lovable manatee, teddy bear of the water world. In addition to a manatee viewing area with a hydrophone to hear their underwater "singing," it provides polar-ized filters for peeping underwater, habitat exhibits, a nature boardwalk, a canoe and kayak launch (and rentals and clinics in winter), nature programs (in winter), wildlife

MUST SEE

♻ 🐾 🐚 **J. N. "Ding" Darling National Wildlife Refuge** (239-472-1100; www.fws.gov/refuge/jn_ding_darling or dingdarlingsociety.org), 1 Wildlife Drive, off Sanibel-Captiva Rd., Sanibel Island. Wildlife Drive open sunrise to sunset (closed Friday); Visitor & Education Center open January to April 9–5, May through December 9–4. Visitor & Education Center free; Wildlife Drive entrance $5 per car, $1 per cyclist or pedestrian over age fifteen. More than 6,300 acres of pristine wetlands and wildlife are protected by the federal government, thanks to the efforts of Pulitzer Prize–winning cartoonist and politically active conservationist Jay N. "Ding" Darling, a regular Captiva visitor in the 1930s. A four-mile drive takes you through the refuge, once a satellite of the original Everglades National Wildlife Refuge. To really experience "Ding," get out of the car. At the very least follow the easy trails into mangrove, bird, and alligator territory. If you have a smart mobile device, you can scan codes to watch interpretative videos or download a free GPS-driven game app. Look for roseate spoonbills, yellow-crowned night herons, white pelicans, reddish egrets, painted buntings, and dozens of other life-list prizes. Narrated tram and guided paddling tours are available (239-472-8900; www.tarponbayexplorers.com). The free education center holds hands-on wildlife displays, realistic habitat vignettes, bird sculptures, manatee and crocodile exhibits with articulated skeletons, and a peek into the world of the refuge's namesake. Free naturalist programs take place throughout the week in season and during the summer.

habitat areas (including a butterfly garden), an Ethnobotany Trail that explains how the Calusa used certain plants, an information center, a playground, and picnic facilities. Best times to see manatees fall between late December and the end of February.

🐾 **Matanzas Pass Preserve** (239-765-6794; www.leegov.com/parks), 199 Bay Rd., Fort Myers Beach. Open daily 7 to dusk. A quiet respite from vacationland action, this fifty-nine-acre preserve provides 1.25 miles of wooded hiking on two loop trails and boardwalks through mangroves and the island's last maritime oak hammock. The Historic Cottage at the trailhead is open free to the public every Wednesday and Saturday 10–noon.

🐚 **Ostego Bay Foundation's Marine Science Center** (239-765-8101; www.ostegobay.org), 718 Fisherman Wharf, Fort Myers Beach. Open Monday to Saturday 10–4 Suggested donation $5 per adult, $2 per child ages seven to twelve. Primarily a marine-science education and research facility, Ostego Bay maintains a showroom of local sea life for visitors to tour. Aquariums hold local species in various habitats, such as sea grass, estuarine, and gulf. Call to ask about feeding times (typically around 1:30), when reclusive creatures come out of hiding for optimal viewing. Manatee, loggerhead, and other kiosks explain the plight of endangered species and the workings of the local shrimping industry. Interactive displays include a touch table, microscopes, and a touchable shark skin and teeth. The foundation has built a boardwalk along the bay where the shrimp boats dock off Main Street. Here you can learn still more about shrimping, estuaries, and local maritime heritage. A

VISIT MANATEE PARK NOVEMBER THROUGH APRIL TO SEE ITS EPONYMOUS, LOVABLE, BLUBBERY SEA MAMMALS LIVE

three-hour Wednesday working waterfront tour starts at the science center and takes you along the boardwalk beginning at 9 a.m. October through May; the cost is $15 per adult, $10 per child over age six. Reservations required.

♠ ♂ ♿ **Rotary Park** (239-549-4606; www.capecoral.net), 5505 Rose Garden Rd., Cape Coral. Known for its population of pint-sized burrowing owls, it is site of the Burrowing Owl Festival every February. It is also home to a butterfly garden and house, an environmental center (open 8–4), a dog park, a playground, a handicap-accessible boardwalk and other trails, gardens, and wetland habitat. Free butterfly house tours happen at 10:30 a.m. Monday, Friday, and Saturday. The park is open daily during daylight hours.

♂ **Sanibel–Captiva Conservation Foundation Center** (239-472-2329; www.sccf.org), 3333 Sanibel-Captiva Rd., Sanibel Island. Open during summer, Monday to Friday 8:30–3; October to May, Monday to Friday 8:30–4;. Nature Center admission is $5 for visitors ages seventeen and older. This research and preservation facility's main campus encompasses more than 1,800 acres. A guided or self-guided tour introduces you to indigenous flora and natural bird habitats and leads to an observation tower. Indoor displays and dioramas further educate and include a touch tank. Guest lecturers, seminars, and workshops address environmental issues during winter. The weekly beach walk is fun and informative. A native plant nursery and butterfly house also share the premises.

Six Mile Cypress Slough Preserve (239-533-7550; www.leegov.com/parks), 7751 Penzance Blvd., on Six Mile Cypress Pkwy., Fort Myers. Trails open daily dawn to dusk; interpretive center Tuesday to Sunday 10–4. Parking $1 per hour or $5 per day. Egrets, herons, ibises, bald eagles, and belted kingfishers come to feed at this shallow waterway, its cypress forest, and ponds. Alligators also take up residence. Take a guided or self-guided tour around the more than mile-long boardwalk through cypress stands and wetlands. Guided ninety-minute walks start at 9:30 daily in season; see the website for off-season schedules. The interpretative center's display room holds engaging interactive displays and short video clips that explain relevant topics such as cypress knees, bird migration, and flora and fauna. The center also hosts special monthly events such as nature photography classes, wet walks into the slough, and full-moon hikes.

Wildlife Tours & Charters: ♂ **Adventures in Paradise** (239-472-8443; www .adventureinparadiseinc.com), 14341 Port Comfort Rd., at Port Sanibel Marina off Summerlin Rd., before the Sanibel Causeway, Fort Myers. Sea-life-encounter excursions led by a marine biologist, where guests net sea creatures in the shallows for identification and education. Also shelling and dolphin quests.

Manatee Guides (239-247-4955; www.manateeguides.com). A certified Florida master naturalist leads wildlife-sighting kayaking tours from the launching point at New Pass south of Lovers Key.

Manatee & Eco River Tours (239-693-1434; manateeandecorivertours.com), 16991 State Rd. 31 at Sweetwater Landing Marina, Fort Myers. Specializes in one-hour tours at 11 a.m. up the Orange River to spot manatees, available November through April. Also river and sunset tours.

Sanibel-Captiva Conservation Foundation Center (239-472-2329; www.sccf.org), 3333 Sanibel-Captiva Rd., Sanibel Island. Hosts guided nature trail, beach walk, and island boat tours.

♂ **Tarpon Bay Explorers** (239-472-8900; www.tarponbayexplorers.com), 900 Tarpon Bay Rd., Sanibel Island. Naturalist-guided kayak, stand-up paddleboarding, pontoon boat, and tram tours through J. N. "Ding" Darling National Wildlife Refuge and ✪ **Tarpon Bay**. The sunset nature cruise to watch birds come in to roost is most popular. Also canoe and kayak rentals, bike and boat rentals, and free lunchtime wildlife talks.

✳ Lodging

Maine may boast its bed & breakfasts; Vermont, its historic inns; and Colorado, its ski lodges. But when vacationers envision Florida, it's the beachside resorts that flash first through the mental slide projector. The Fort Myers/Sanibel coast has perfected this image of sun-and-sand abandon. Megaresorts are designed to keep guests (and their disposable income) on property. Not only can you eat lunch, rent a bike, and get a tennis lesson, you can hire a masseuse, charter a boat for a sunset sail, play golf, and enroll your child in Sandcastle Building 101. These destination resorts are in business to fulfill fantasies, and they spare no effort to achieve that goal.

Side by side with the resorts, you'll also find homey little cottages that have held their ground against buyouts and takeovers. Existing between the two extremes are a wide variety of high-rise condos, funky hotels, mom-and-pop motels, fishing lodges, and inns. Privately owned second homes and condominiums provide another source of upscale accommodations along the coast. For families and other groups, these can often be a better value than hotel rooms. Time-share rental was practically invented on Sanibel Island, and you'll find plenty of these options still around. Vacation brokers who match visitors with such properties are listed under "Home & Condo Rentals" at the end of this section.

The highlights of Lee County hospitality listed here—alphabetically by town—include the best and freshest in the local industry. While spanning the range of endless possibilities, this list concentrates on those properties that break out of the skyscraping, wicker-and-floral mold. Toll-free 800, 888, 855, 866, or 877 reservation numbers, where available, are listed after local numbers.

Prices are normally per unit/double occupancy. The range spans low- and high-season rates and standard to deluxe accommodations. Many resorts offer off-season packages at special rates and free lodging for children. Pricing does not include the 6 percent Florida sales tax. Some large resorts add service gratuities or maid charges, and Lee County imposes a 5 percent bed tax as well, which goes toward beach and environmental maintenance.

Rate Categories

Inexpensive	Up to $100
Moderate	$100 to $200
Expensive	$200 to $200
Very Expensive	$300 and up

An asterisk (*) after the pricing designation indicates that the rate includes at least a continental breakfast in the cost of lodging and occasionally other meals as described in the listing.

Note that under the Americans with Disabilities Act (ADA), accommodations built after January 26, 1993, and containing more than five rooms must be accessible to people with disabilities. I have indicated only those small places that do not make such allowances.

ACCOMMODATIONS

CABBAGE KEY

✪ **Cabbage Key Inn** (239-283-2278; www .cabbagekey.com), P.O. Box 200, Pineland 33945. Cabbage Key appeals to vacationers seeking an authentic Old Florida experience. Built on an unbridged island atop an ancient shell mound, the inn and its guest accommodations are reminiscent of the 1930s, when novelist Mary Roberts Rinehart commissioned a home made from native cypress and pine for her son and his bride. Six cypress-paneled guest rooms in the inn and six cottages (two of them historic) accommodate overnighters. Four of the cottages have kitchens, and four have their own private docks. A couple of the cottages date back to the Rinehart era; the others are modern homes that accommodate up to eight. The restaurant and its currency-papered bar attract boaters and water tours for lunch, but the island shuts down to a whisper come sundown. The inn can give you a list of boat charters from Captiva or Pine Island for transportation to and from the island. Boat rentals are available for day use. Moderate to Very Expensive (two-night minimum stay required).

CAPE CORAL

🦐 (((ψ))) **Casa Loma Motel** (239-549-6000 or 877-227-2566; www.casalomamotel .com), 3608 Del Prado Blvd., 33904. If you're looking for a place to stay while enjoying the town's family attractions or somewhere less costly than the beaches, this tidy little property has its own charm—and canal-front views and docks in the bargain. Its 49 efficiencies are each stocked with a kitchenette containing a microwave, mini fridge, and stove top. Reclining chairs in some rooms and stylish motel furnishings provide comfort. Some porches and balconies overlook the canal and docks. Nicely landscaped grounds complement the Spanish villa architecture, with its red roof and arched balcony openings. A canalside pool with waterside tables, loungers, and a tiki-covered deck offer scenic places to relax. A small fitness center and laundry facilities complete the property's amenities. Inexpensive to Moderate.

🐬 🛥 (((ψ))) **The Westin Cape Coral Resort at Tarpon Point Marina** (239-541-5000; http://www.westincapecoral .com/), 5951 Silver King Blvd., 33914. Step through the sliding glass doors onto a stunning lobby, where a magical, tubular waterfall and marble passage to the view of yachts, mangroves, and blue water of the marina welcome you. Cape Coral's first luxury resort and Southwest Florida's first Westin rises nineteen stories high at the edge of mangrove estuary in the southwest part of town.

Its inventory of 262 units includes studio accommodations and condos from one to three bedrooms. They showcase the finest furnishings in neutral tones with signature Westin beds, showers, and other trademarks. Built to green lodging standards, the resort's room key system turns on lights and air-conditioning. The studios come with mini fridges and have access to communal laundry facilities. The condos have their own washer and dryer (full-size in the two- and three-bedroom units) in addition to a full kitchen and dining area. Adjoining condos and studio formats are also available. Sweeping balconies, many with views of the water, extend the living space. Although one could feel content just getting comfy and gazing at the panorama, the resort offers plenty of enticement to go out and enjoy its amenities. Water sports, a lagoon pool, tennis courts, restaurants, a spa, and a kids' club engage guests in the outdoors. Expensive to Very Expensive.

CAPTIVA ISLAND

✪ **Jensen's Twin Palm Cottages & Marina** (239-472-5800; www.gocaptiva .com), 15107 Captiva Dr., 33924. One of Captiva's most affordable lodging options is also one of its homier places. You get an immediate sense of neighborliness on the grounds. Perhaps it has to do with its partiality to fisherfolk, demonstrated by its bayside docks, fishing charters, boat rentals, and bait supplies. I expected to find the accommodations in that same vein, where what's out in the water matters more than what's indoors. The fourteen units look plain enough from the outside: white stucco cottages with tin roofs and a splash of blue trim. Each screened-in porch holds a plain picnic table. Inside, the one- and two-bedroom cottages are entirely cheery, with immaculate white board-and-bead walls, perky curtains, and simple, sturdy wooden furniture. The full kitchens are modern and spotless—nothing fishy about 'em. Just charming old-island style dressed up comfortably. Owners David, John, and Jimmy Jensen are known to make some music and entertain the local fishermen in the evenings, sometimes with impromptu "Mullet Parades." Moderate to Expensive.

✪ ♂ ♪ **South Seas Island Resort** (239-472-5111 or 866-565-5089; www .southseas.com), 5400 Plantation Rd., 33924. South Seas is historically one of the great destination resorts of Florida, where you can enter through the security gates and leave one week later without ever having gone off property. Celebrities have always craved its privacy and discretion, but families love it, too. South Seas offers any type of getaway dwelling you could imagine, from tennis villas to beach cottages to harborside hotel rooms—nine different types of accommodations in all. Rooms are furnished with stylish, high-quality pieces, thirty-two-inch LCD televisions, pillow-top beds, and other luxury appointments. The property monopolizes a third of the island, with about 475 guest units—mostly privately owned; six eateries; formal lounges; shops; a gorgeous gulfside, nine-hole golf course; a fitness center and spa; a yacht harbor; nineteen swimming pools, including a mini waterpark with two slides; eleven tennis courts; boating; fishing; water-sports equipment rentals and lessons; excursion cruises; a recreation program and nature center for children; and 2.5 miles of beach. A free trolley takes guests around the 330-acre property, which water embraces on three sides. Expensive to Very Expensive.

♂ ♪ (ᵗ) **'Tween Waters Inn Island Resort & Spa** (239-472-5161 or 800-223-5865; www.tween-waters.com), 15941 Captiva Rd., 33924. 'Tween Waters spans the gap between beach cottage lodging and modern super resort. Built early in the 1930s, when wildlife patron Jay N. "Ding" Darling kept a cottage there, the National Register of Historic Places property shows glints of Old

ONE OF THE HISTORICAL COTTAGES AT 'TWEEN WATERS INN

Florida architecture (some of it rather unglamorous) and easygoing attitudes. Compact but complete, it holds 149 newly renovated rooms, restored historic cottages efficiencies and apartments as well as restaurants, a bustling marina, tennis courts, a fitness center, a spa, and a swimming pool and bar. Named for its location between two shores at Captiva's narrowest span, the inn lies across the road from a length of beach that is usually lightly populated because it lacks nearby public parking. Its marina, one of its best features, is the island's top water-sports center, with charters, tours, and boat and kayak rentals. The Crow's Nest lounge provides the island's best nightlife. Continental breakfast is included in the rates. Expensive to Very Expensive.*

FORT MYERS

(ᵗ) **Crowne Plaza Fort Myers** (239-482-2900 or 877-227-6963; www.ihg.com/crowneplaza), 13051 Bell Tower Dr., 33907. Close to the airport, shopping, dining, and movie theaters, one of this property's best features is the relaxation factor of the rooms, which provide sleep masks, lavender spray, nightlights, and massage showerheads. As part of the bustling Bell Tower entertainment area, Shoeless Joe's, the hotel's sports bar/restaurant, draws a lively crowd to its outdoor porch area and indoor pool-table scene off the spacious marble-floored lobby. Abstract metal and glass sculptures, a shiny black player piano, and black-and-white checkered marble and granite flooring add touches of highbrow elegance to the entryway. Priority Club guests on the third and fourth floors enjoy complimentary refreshments and snacks in the fifth-floor concierge lounge and microwaves in the rooms. All 226 rooms have mini fridges. Airport transportation is free to all guests. A waterfall outdoor pool and small cardio fitness center complete the amenities. Moderate.

✪ ♂ ✍ ((ͱ)) **Sanibel Harbour Marriott Resort & Spa** (239-466-4000 or 800-767-7777; www.marriott.com), 17260 Harbour Pointe Dr., 33908. Stunningly beautiful for a property its size, the Sanibel Harbour Marriott Resort capitalizes on Florida style and a spectacular location. Not actually on Sanibel Island as the name suggests, the resort's 347 rooms and suites are located on a chin of land across San Carlos Bay from the island, on an inlet known as Sanibel Harbour. Half the units have water views of either the bay or nearby estuaries. The concierge-style Captiva Tower holds 107 of the rooms and suites, which are decorated in European style and shiny brass, and are more intimate and away from the bustle than the Sanibel Tower accommodations. Suites feature comfy beds, pull-out sofas, and oversize jetted bathtubs. The property encompasses four restaurants, a coffee bar-bistro, a buffet-dining yacht, three outdoor swimming pools, five lit Har-Tru tennis courts, a complete spa, and a small bayside beach. Charley's Cabana Bar has a 280-degree view of the sea and a lovely, breezy cocktail patio. Dining is better-than-average hotel food and runs the gamut from a coffee and pastry stand to a steakhouse. The fitness center, canoe/kayak trail, and water-sports charters and rentals provide guests with a well-rounded menu of fitness and recreation options. Moderate to Very Expensive.

FORT MYERS BEACH

((ͱ)) ♨ **Harbour House** (239-463-0700 or 866-998-9250; www .harbourhouseattheinn.com), 450 Old San Carlos Blvd., 33931. Prices here are surprisingly affordable for attentively decorated condos a short walk from the beach. All of its thirty-four studios and one- and two-bedroom condos are individually owned, but decorated with basically the same starfish-and-rattan motif. Their most outstanding feature is their paint job, mixing many bright colors within one unit, all behind hot pink doorways. The rooms have kitchen facilities (some without ovens), flat-screen TVs, WiFi access, and balconies or lanais. The views are not equal in all, but not great in any. With only three floors, you can't see the gulf, but some give glimpses of Matanzas Pass or the second-floor swimming pool and Jacuzzi. A community room with a full kitchen at the pool gives guests a cozy place to pour a cup of coffee, read the paper, get out of the sun, read e-mail, and hold gatherings. Two restaurants are across the street, with more en route to the beach. Moderate to Expensive.

✍ ((ͱ)) **The Outrigger Beach Resort** (239-463-3131 or 800-657-4967; www .outriggerfmb.com), 6200 Estero Blvd., 33931. The Outrigger Beach Resort occupies the quiet south end of Fort Myers Beach, where the sand flares wide and gorgeous and is protected by a sandbar that's a bird hangout. The fifty-year-old, 144-room resort boasts a casual, unstructured vacationing style that works well for families. Activity centers around its white-fenced pool and tiki bar deck area, where guests can sun and mingle. Or you can rent water-sports equipment through the front desk. Rooms are compact, modern, and furnished simply. Five types of accommodations range from the traditional to efficiencies with full kitchens. Prices also depend on whether they're on the first or second floor and on the quality of the view. Beach volleyball, a little café, a full-service restaurant across the street, and live entertainment keep the place vivacious. Moderate to Very Expensive.

♂ ♂ (ŵ) **Pink Shell Beach Resort & Spa** (239-463-6181 or 888-222-7465; www.pinkshell.com), 275 Estero Blvd., 33931. Set between bay waters and 1,500 feet of beach, the twelve-acre property encompasses high-rise accommodation towers, an Octopool fantasy water feature with an underwater theme, a marina, and a world-class spa. The central reception area boasts a mammoth stylized banyan tree "growing" through it. Older Sanibel View Villas holds sixty gulfside kitchenette suites and Beach Villas twenty-eight two-bedroom condos. Newer White Sand Villas has ninety-two one- and two-bedroom units with floor-to-ceiling gulf-facing windows. Captiva Villas, the fourth and newest building, contains another forty-three units. All accommodations are privately owned and decorated in tasteful tropical style with a view of the wide, powdery beach and gulf. Three restaurants, a coffee shop/deli, three pools, a kids' program, and a slew of water-sports rentals and tours complete Pink Shell's reputation as a barefoot but stylish destination resort at the northern tip of Fort Myers Beach, away from the bustle of the Times Square area. Moderate to Very Expensive.

♣ ☀ **Silver Sands Villas** (239-463-6554 or 800-603-0501; www.silversandsvillas.com), 1207 Estero Blvd., 33931. In Fort Myers Beach, not much can be found that one could describe as charming, but here's a notable exception. Its assemblage of twenty-one one- and two-bedroom (Expensive), circa-1935 cottages with pale yellow paint jobs and tin roofs make a strong personality statement. Inside they are simple in character, with fresh paint and hardwood floors, full kitchens in all but three units (all of which have refrigerators and microwaves), and old Florida–style porches. The compact, pet-friendly property, bordered by a canal and within walking distance of the beach, holds complimentary docking for guests, a small pool, a fountain courtyard, a huge shady banyan tree, canal-front views, outdoor tables, gas grills, and laundry facilities—all behind a picket fence and hibiscus hedge right on the happening strip of Estero Boulevard, from where you hardly notice it. It's very congenial and convenient while feeling deliciously hidden away. Inexpensive to Moderate.

PINE ISLAND

☀ **BridgeWater Inn** (239-283-2423 or 800-378-7666; www.bridgewaterinn.com), 4331 Pine Island Rd., Matlacha 33909. In fish-frenzied Pine Island, Matlacha has its share of fishing cottages where what matters is what's biting. Fishing types will also like this tropically bright, eight-unit (plus one cottage) roadside lodge because its wraparound covered deck hangs over the water. Rooms and efficiencies, decorated with distinct style and comfort, open up onto the deck, so you can step right out the door and cast. Suites Two and Three have the best views. With leather furniture and eye-catching colors (check out the hanging tropical bird planters made in Colombia from recycled tires), Bridge Water is a step up from other Matlacha accommodations. Restaurants, fish markets, shops, and galleries are within walking distance. Moderate to Expensive.

♂ (ŵ) **Tarpon Lodge** (239-283-3999; www.tarponlodge.com), 13771 Waterfront Dr., Pineland. Refashioned from a circa-1926 sportsman's inn, it retains that bare-bones, fish-fanatic feel but with a measure of Victorian charm. Operated by the same family as Cabbage Key Inn, it's a different kind of getaway that revolves around fishing by day and dining in its fabulous restaurant (see "Restaurants"), listening to live music, and sleeping in a lodge room or water-view cottage by night. The two-bedroom Boathouse (Very Expensive in season) has a kitchenette and Jacuzzi, and that's about as luxurious as it gets. Continental breakfast is included in all rates. It features a swimming pool, boat docking, and a sweeping green lawn spreading to lovely bay waters. The lodge lies within easy walking distance to the Calusa Heritage Trail and the local golf course. Moderate to Expensive.*

SANIBEL ISLAND

✪ 🐚 ((·)) **Gulf Breeze Cottages and Motel** (239-472-1626 or 800-388-2842; www .gbreeze.com), 1081 Shell Basket Ln., 33957. The address is Shell Basket Lane, and this place is just that delightful and seashell oriented. A dozen classic cottages, efficiencies, and duplexes make for the ideal barefoot beach vacation. Shuffleboard, a picnic pavilion with barbecue grills, and a station where you can clean your shells and fish provide outdoor-time amenities. This property blends old island with new, holding its ground amid low-rise, concrete neighbors. Sea grapes, bougainvillea, Bahama shades, carved balustrades, lattice, and fish-scale siding add a fairy-tale quality. Moderate to Very Expensive (for up to six people).

✪ ((·)) 🐚 **Island Inn** (239-472-1561 or 800-851-5088; www.islandinnsanibel .com), 3111 W. Gulf Dr., 33957. Sanibel's only historic lodging—more than one hundred years old—displays all the refinement of Florida's great old inns and hotels but without the snobbery. It has the same congenial and relaxed atmosphere that Granny Matthews, a Sanibel matriarch of renown, created at the turn of the twentieth century when she entertained the whole island (including guests from other resorts) at Saturday night barbecues. She also initiated the Sanibel Shell Fair as a way to keep guests busy; she hosted it in the lobby, where white wicker, French doors, a windowed dining room, a fireplace, a windowed restaurant, and shell displays now give an immediate impression of immaculate spaciousness and island graciousness. Rates include continental

ISLAND INN WEARS ITS 100-PLUS YEARS GRACIOUSLY

breakfast. The lodging options comprise seven cottages, which have one to three bedrooms, and forty-nine rooms. Rooms have either full kitchens or refrigerators only and can be combined into suites. The resort doesn't pretend to furnish extravagantly; all is done in uncontrived old-island style. That does not translate into shoddiness, however. The Island Inn is owned by shareholders who reinvest profits for constant upgrading. Décor is cheerful, comfortable, and impeccably maintained. Outside of the lodge room doors there sits a wooden table where guests display their shell finds for others to peruse and admire. It's an Island Inn tradition. The atmosphere is saturated with conviviality. Outdoors, native vegetation landscapes tin-roofed structures. A butterfly garden frames a croquet court, a swimming pool sits squarely on the beach, and volleyball, tennis, and shuffleboard provide recreation. Moderate to Expensive* (minimum stay for cottages).

((ꞥ)) **Sanibel's Seaside Inn** (239-472-1400 or 866-565-5092; www .theinnsofsanibel.com/seaside-inn), 541 E. Gulf Dr., 33957. I recommend this place to visitors looking for intimacy on the beach without great extravagance. A measure of Key West—banana yellow tints, tin roofs, and gingerbread-trimmed balconies—creates Seaside Inn's old-island charm. It's the kind of place where you kick off your shoes the first day and don't find them again until you're packing to leave. Kitchen facilities and DVD players come in every studio, beach cottage, and one-, two-, and three-bedroom suite, of which there are thirty-two in all. A swimming pool, brick-paved deck, complimentary continental breakfast (delivered to your room the day prior), video- and book-lending library, complimentary bike and kayak use, shuffleboard, and tropical appointments complete the picture of seaside coziness. Use of facilities and amenities at Seaside Inn's sister resorts, including Sundial Beach Resort and Sanibel Inn, is

KIDS LOVE THE SHELL-SHAPED SLIDE AT SUNDIAL BEACH RESORT'S POOL

available free of charge to guests. Expensive to Very Expensive.*

♻ ♪ ((ꞥ)) **Sundial Beach Resort** (239-472-4151 or 866-565-5093; www .sundialresort.com), 1451 Middle Gulf Dr., 33957. Sundial promises the perfection of a worry-free vacation. Sanibel's fine shelling beach is the focus of the twenty-acre resort, which takes its name from a species of shell. In the stunning lobby, a sundial shell mosaic is inset in a marble floor. The resort provides extensive recreation, with twelve HydroGrid and clay tennis courts, five heated swimming pools, beach cabanas, bike and beach rental concessions, a fitness center, a game room, recreation programs, and an eco-center complete with touch tank. The lavish main building houses a Japanese restaurant and one of two bar-and-grills; the second is located poolside. Less stylish, low-rise condo buildings are camouflaged by well-maintained vegetation and hold four hundred fully equipped, privately owned studio suites and one-to three-bedroom units, of which about half are in the rental program. Decorated in tropical array and natural rattan, the units take advantage of gulf or garden views. Given its high level of service, the Sundial is one of the area's least pretentious and most comfortable properties, especially for families, who can take advantage of its sea camp. Expensive to Very Expensive.

○ (((•))) **West Wind Inn** (239-472-1541 or 800-824-0476; westwindinn.com), 3345 W. Gulf Dr., 33957. "Friendliness and cleanliness" is its motto—old-fashioned values for a Sanibel resort that started in the late 1960s. But this casual favorite looks anything but worn-out. The four lodging buildings of the two-story low-rise cluster beachside, and most of its 103 rooms have at least a glimpse of the gulf. Many overlook the pool and its fun-time pool bar, which, like the rest of the buildings, shows a bit of Mediterranean flair with tile embellishments and a red barrel-tile roof. The pool bar serves lunch, or guests can get out of the weather and dine in the Normandie Seaside Pub for breakfast, lunch, and, when in season, dinner. Rooms, decorated demurely in plantation prints, come with a kitchenette or small refrigerator and microwave oven. All rooms have DVD players and free access to wireless Internet service. Moderate to Very Expensive.

USEPPA ISLAND

○ **Collier Inn & Cottages** (239-283-1061; www.useppa.com), P.O. Box 640, Bokeelia 33922. Used to be that only club members could enjoy the delicious privacy and historic elitism of Useppa Island. Once an escape for turn-of-the-twentieth-century celebrities, the island remains exclusive and aloof from the world. Now, if you can afford the price, you can be admitted onto the carefully guarded island by taking advantage of the island's get-acquainted program with a stay at the Collier Inn. The one-hundred-year-old building, the original circa-1900 home of Barron Collier's Izaak Walton Club, holds seven elegant rooms and suites individually designed for classic mood and comfort; historic cottages and the marina reception building add another four units. Plus, there are privately owned two- and three-bedroom cottages with kitchens available.

THE COLLIER INN HAS BEEN WELCOMING BY-BOAT TRAVELERS SINCE THE EARLY 20TH CENTURY

Guests have access to the Useppa Island Club's full-service marina, Har-Tru tennis courts, swimming pool, man-made beach, croquet, outdoor chess, and fitness center. The pink-paved walkway around the island takes you past historic cottages, bounteous gardens, an ancient shell mound, and the one-hundred-acre island's intriguing historical museum. Collier Inn Restaurant serves daily meals; a continental breakfast buffet is included for accommodations without kitchen facilities. Price: Moderate to Very Expensive* (minimum stay for cottages and homes; for all accommodations on weekends and holidays).

HOME & CONDO RENTALS **Leisure American Vacation Rentals** (239-463-3138 or 800-741-5694; www .leisureamerican.com), 19050 San Carlos Blvd., Fort Myers Beach 33931. Condos, cottages, and homes in the Fort Myers Beach area.

Island Vacations of Sanibel & Captiva (239-472-7277 or 888-451-7277; sanibel islandvacations.com), 1101 Periwinkle Way, Sanibel 33957. Condos and homes for short-term rental on the islands. Note: Home rentals on Sanibel require a one-month stay.

RV RESORTS  **Fort Myers–Pine Island KOA** (239-283-2415 or 800-562-8505; koa.com/campgrounds/fort-myers), 5120 Stringfellow Rd., St. James City 33956. Resort has 363 sites, cabins and cottages, a pool, saunas, hot tub, exercise room, tennis court, shuffleboard, horseshoes, lake fishing, and free daily bus in season to the beach, shopping, and other attractions.

Red Coconut RV Resort (239-463-7200 or 888-262-6226; www.redcoconut.com), 3001 Estero Blvd., Fort Myers Beach 33931. Right on the beach but packed in a bit tightly; 250 full hookup sites, on-site trailer rentals, laundry, shuffleboard, and cable TV. Call for reservations.

✳ Where to Eat

The Island Coast is home to two of the nation's shellfish capitals. Shrimp—that monarch of edible crustaceans—reigns in Fort Myers Beach, where a fleet of shrimp boats is headquartered and an annual festival pays homage to America's favorite seafood. The sweet, pink gulf shrimp is the trademark culinary delight of the town and its environs. The fish markets of Pine Island, an important commercial fishing and transshipment center, sell all sorts of fresh seafood—oysters, shrimp, scallops, snapper, catfish, mullet—but the signature seafood is the blue crab and stone crab that come from local waters.

The following listings cover the variety of Island Coast feasting in these price categories:

Inexpensive	Up to $15
Moderate	$15 to $25
Expensive	$25 to $35
Very Expensive	$35 or more

Cost categories are based on the range of dinner entrée prices, or, if dinner is not served, of lunch entrées.

Note: Florida law forbids smoking inside all restaurants and bars serving food. Smoking is permitted only in restaurants with outdoor seating.

CAPE CORAL

Cork Soakers Deck & Wine Bar (239-542-6622; www.corksoakers.net), 837 SE 47th Terrace. As quirky as its name sounds, this is Cape Coral's new hot spot for casual dining on the generous porch or inside when summer's heat bears down. Its Mothers Punch and Bitchslap Mary (over-garnished Bloody Mary served only on Sunday) are legendary, as are its cheddar-chive bacon biscuits with chipotle honey butter, deviled eggs du jour, shrimp and grits with Cajun barbecue sauce, and Big Ass Burger—a half pound on a ciabatta bun. Not crazy enough for you? Try "The Hangover," fried bologna sandwich with a fried egg, bacon, arugula, and roasted poblano aioli. The menu may be small but it packs a powerful punch. Bands add to the liveliness Thursday through Sunday. Inexpensive to Moderate. No reservations. Closed Monday.

🦎 **Iguana Mia** (239-945-7755 or 866-639-3287; www.iguanamia.com), 1027 E. Cape Coral Pkwy. This, the original

ORDER YOUR SHRIMP USING THE COUNT-PER-POUND DESIGNATION

MUST SEE

✪ **Cabbage Key Inn** (239-283-2278; www.cabbagekey.com), P.O. Box 200, Pineland 33945. Accessible only by boat and still funky after all these years, Cabbage Key has a reputation among boaters as a safe haven for a beer, a cheeseburger, and all-around friendliness inside walls covered with dollar bills. Everyone's in a good mood at Cabbage Key, particularly the bartender and wait staff (despite their sassy T-shirts that answer all the questions they get asked daily). Lunch—the most popular meal—consists of shrimp, salads, stone crab in season, burgers, sandwiches, and Key lime pie. Tour boats bring in crowds, so it can get crazy, and waits for a table are often a beer-sodden affair. (If you're driving the boat, you may wish to opt for a walk around the nature trail instead.) Dinner is much quieter, and the local fish couldn't get any fresher. I recently had grouper with a chipotle sauce drizzle and nearly swooned; it ruined me for grouper anywhere else. The shrimp scampi on pasta is another good bet. So are the Bloody Marys. The restaurant also serves breakfast. Moderate to Expensive. No handicapped access. Reservations requested for dinner.

Iguana Mia, spawned others in Fort Myers and Bonita Springs, but we like this one best, even if it means we have to cross the bridge to Cape Coral and pay a toll to get there. It's the most down-to-earth of the three. Sure, it's just as flashy, with its electric-green exterior paint job and nicely rendered interior Mexican frescos, but it retains some of the unpretentious lunchroom ambience it started out with. Stacked cases of Mexican beer still count as décor elements. And most important, the food is flat-out better. Things seem more rushed at the newer places; here it's mañana paced. My husband invariably orders the sour cream chicken chimichanga, a specialty. I—usually already half full from shoveling huge

RUMRUNNERS CATERS TO BOAT- AND DRIVE-IN GUESTS LOOKING FOR CREATIVE CUISINE AND FINE VIEWS

gobs of the salsa with warm, crunchy tortilla chips—like the tortilla soup, nachos, quesadilla, carnitas, or tamales. You're bound to find something you like on the menu—it's huge and lets you do some of your own meal engineering. Inexpensive to Moderate. No reservations.

Rumrunners (239-542-0200; rum runnersrestaurant.com), 5848 Cape Harbour Dr., at the Cape Harbour Marina. Good news: Rumrunners boasts an imaginative style and a view of a mangrove waterway in the midst of an upmarket development. Even better: Prices are surprisingly affordable for such specialties as seafood potpie—chock-full of shrimp, scallops, and crab with a creamy lobster sauce and a flaky pastry sitting atop it. We've sampled a wide variety of starters, main courses, and desserts besides the potpie and have had no complaints except for one order of rather limp calamari. In the "loved it" category: Salmon BLT at lunch; Buffalo chicken tossed with Gorgonzola crema; spinach and blue cheese salad; vodka penne; angel hair pasta generously decorated with shrimp, scallops, mussels, and torn basil; and warm chocolate bread pudding (did I detect a splash of rum in there?). Pasta dishes are available in full and half portions. Four cuts of beef please steak-lovers. The building at first seems cold and oversized, but once you're sitting in the glassed room or on the deck overlooking the water, you immediately warm to the location. Inexpensive to Moderate. Dinner reservations accepted.

Siam Hut (239-945-4247), 4521 Del Prado Blvd. A long-standing favorite in Cape Coral, Siam Hut's affordability is matched by its versatility and authentic goodness. You basically can design your own meal from the noodles, stir-fried, curry, and fried rice sections. For instance, I've tried the *pad kee mao*, a stir-fried rice-noodle dish of basil, colorful and crunchy veggies, and chili paste. I had a choice of tofu, beef, pork, chicken, shrimp, or squid to centerpiece that, and I chose the last—tender, tasty rings set afire by the seasonings. (You also get to pick your degree of spiciness.) The coconut milk green curry also turned out to make a flavorful, filling, and bargain lunch with the inclusion of the day's soup and a small romaine and carrot salad dressed in a tasty peanut vinaigrette. Dinners, which do not come with soup and salad, include specialties such as fried-crispy frogs' legs with garlic and black pepper, fried whole tilapia in a variety of preparations, and Thai entrée salads. Go traditional and sit in a floor table pit, or choose one of the more plentiful booths or standard tables and chairs. Inexpensive. No reservations. Closed Sunday and lunch Saturday. Minimum $10 charge for credit cards.

CAPTIVA ISLAND

In recent years, one owner has bought up the majority of restaurants in downtown Captiva, resulting in lack of competition and growing mediocrity. Luckily a few individually owned and resort restaurants that reach further remain.

✑ **The Bubble Room** (239-472-5558; www.bubbleroomrestaurant.com), 15001 Captiva Dr. Okay, so this is tourist food, but the Bubble Room is so Captiva—something you have to experience once. It's especially fun to take kids there. The quirkiness begins outside, where bubbles bedeck the kitsch-cottage structure and lawn gnomes greet you. Inside, the tables are glass-topped showcases filled with jacks, Monopoly money, comic books, dominoes, and assorted toys from the past. A Christmas elves scene, circus plaques, Betty Boop, celebrity photos, a plaster hippo's mouth, and other nostalgic memorabilia fill every wall, phone booth, bathroom door, nook, and cranny. A toy train runs under the ceiling in one of its five rooms, and servers—Bubble Scouts—wear goofy hats. So that's the atmosphere—and you've gotta see it for yourself. The menu continues the frivolity. At lunch, the Mae West is a grilled chicken breast sandwich; the Louis Armstrong is a muffaletta. Dinner's Duck Ellington is a tasty rendition of roasted duck with orange and banana glaze. Other snappily titled dishes include Guy "Lamb" ardo (mint-glazed lamb chops), Some Like It Hot Hot Hot (Louisiana-style shrimp), and Pasta-blanca. The service is exceptional, considering the tight quarters and volume of business. Other things for which the Bubble Room is known are its basket of bubble bread (yum! cream cheesy), its sticky buns with dinner, and its fabulous desserts. You must leave room to share a huge slab of moist and delicious red velvet cake, the rich almond-studded orange crunch cake, or any of the other tempting selections. Moderate to Expensive. Limited handicapped access. No reservations.

✑ **Mucky Duck** (239-472-3434; www.muckyduck.com), 11546 Andy Rosse Ln. A Captiva dining landmark since 1976, its name is a parody of English pubs, and the goofy attitude and gags don't end there. Despite its name, there's little British influence other than fish-and-chips. At lunchtime, it's wise to plan on spending some beach time while you wait for your name to be called, especially in season. The fried grouper sandwich is huge and crunchy, and the Captiva Sandwich (smoked turkey, prosciutto, and cheeses on focaccia) a tasty alternative to fish. At dinner, come early for sunset and expect an hour or so wait in season for indoor or outdoor seating. Barbecue shrimp with bacon is a signature dish, demonstrating the importance of seafood at this popular beachside spot. If the name makes you crave duck, there is a roasted duckling à l'orange dish on the dinner menu, along with some other landlubber options. Seafood-lovers should go for the crab cakes, grouper in wine sauce, salmon en croute, or shrimp sampler. The Key lime pie comes frozen, which is especially refreshing in the summer. Mostly beer and wine service, the bar does serve vodka drinks, made with forty-proof liquor. Moderate to Expensive. Handicapped access difficult; some steps to negotiate, and tight quarters inside. No reservations.

ESTERO

✪ **Blue Water Bistro** (239-949-2583; www.bluewaterbistro.net), 23151 Village Shops Way, Suite 109, at Coconut Point Center. Successful Naples restaurateur Skip Quillen (Chops City Grill, Pazzo! Cucina Italiana and Yabba Island Grill) opened Blue Water Bistro with an old concept, but one new for him: seafood. He has put his thumbprint on it by using sauces and products with zing. A global selection of fish, burgers, and steaks offer enough diversity to satisfy the whims of the restaurant's large indoor and outdoor capacity. Begin with the long, tall drink menu, filled with the expected to the unexpected in beers, wines, tequilas, martinis, mojitos, shots, and other fun quaffs. The bar dominates the modern, semicircular space, so it's no surprise that drinking is as much a priority here as dining—everything from a bubble gum martini to a passion fruit mojito. Start off with a three crab-lobster cake, tequila-roasted oysters, or "morning after" mussels steamed Bloody Mary style (the alcohol infusion doesn't end with the drink menu here). For an entrée, I recently opted for the grilled swordfish off the Fresh Catch menu, which changes

with a half-dozen or so selections of what's fresh in the swimming world. You then have your choice from seven sauces and about a dozen sides. Our server pointed out the macadamia and panko–crusted mahi as the most popular entrée, followed by grouper scampi and blackened salmon with bourbon and brown sugar glaze. The latter sounded sweet, but I was pleasantly surprised at the subtlety of the flavors, particularly when combined with the buttery jalapeño-pecan sauce. Early dining and all-night bar menus are available and affordable. Inexpensive to Expensive. Reservations accepted.

✪ **Blu Sushi** (239-334-2583; www .blusushi.com), 10045 Gulf Center Dr., at Gulf Coast Town Center. Started in Fort Myers, Blu Sushi has spun off into this location in Estero, where it has become even more popular than its original location. The restaurant is as blue and cutting edge as its name. Outdoor seating, great people watching, and fun martinis (in blue-stemmed glasses, of course), sakes, and saketinis are part of the adventure. Try the mango X-rated martini or the Asian pear saketini for something exotic. Appealing to even the less-than-enthusiastic sushi fan, the specialty rolls fuse Japanese and American favorites for tasty, creative sushi. The Lava Drops are a hit: chopped crab and spicy mayo with cream cheese, deep-fried and brushed with eel sauce. Other recommendations from the more than twenty varieties of specialty rolls: the Christie (tuna, sriracha sauce, flying fish roe, cucumber, avocado, and tamago), the Bahama (spicy conch, cucumber, and smelt roe), and the Fire Dragon (spicy tuna inside out with tilapia and avocado on top). The seaweed salad is tasty and proportioned to share as an appetizer; the king miso soup adds crabmeat to the traditional. Or try the tuna tataki, carpaccio-thin slices of lightly seared top-quality tuna wading in a pool of ponzu sauce. Moderate. No reservations.

FORT MYERS

🍴 ((📶)) **The Lodge** (239-433-2739; www
.thelodgefl.com), 2278 First St. Just in
case you came to Florida to sit in a ski
lodge—yes, as in *snow*-skiing—this relatively new downtown restaurant sets
the scene. A miniature ski lift circles, a
fireplace dominates one room, while in
the other the bar and an open kitchen
with a sign reading "Go Pig or Go Home"
are central. The pig reference is a clue
that barbecue and wild hogs conspic-
uously occupy the menu—as big as the
great Northwest itself. Besides the usual
ribs, pulled pork, brisket, and chicken
platters, it describes some creative
sandwiches with barbecued meat such
as the brisket wrap I tried on my visit.
A tad dry, as brisket can be, a creamy
horseradish sauce and squirts from the
four sauces on the table helped it along.
Other unusual offerings include smoked
chicken and apple salad, pan-seared
rainbow trout, Colorado lamb ribs, osso
buffalo, and BBQ shrimp and pork belly.
Desserts range from salted caramel
crunch skillet cookie a la mode to Amish
bread pudding with honey pecan glaze.
The bar offerings are equally ambitious:
sports TVs galore including one covering an entire wall, a beer station where
you self-serve from twenty-eight varieties of craft and other brews, creative
craft cocktails, and live music three
nights a week.

🍴 **Nomiki's Plakka** (239-433-5659),
12901-3 McGregor Blvd. The food and
atmosphere here are genuinely Greek.
The owners recently remodeled, doing
away with a lot of the Greek kitsch and
clutter for a cleaner, more modern look.
(Is it crazy that I miss the old *Big Fat
Greek Wedding* look?) Paintings and
murals depict Greece and the beautiful
Mediterranean Sea. With a few nods
to American palates, most of the menu
describes Greek specialties such as
spanakopita (baked spinach and feta
pie), Greek and souvlaki salads, gyros,
pastitsio, moussaka, *dolmathes*, roast leg
of lamb, pan-fried smelt, octopus, and
shrimp sautéed in tomato-ouzo sauce
with melted feta. Desserts sound like
Greek to me—except for the baklava
and rice pudding: *yalaktobouriko, kataif,
melfr*. They look yummy. There's even a
baklava sundae. Beer and wine also come
from Greece, along with American selections. Inexpensive to Moderate. Restaurant has handicapped access; restrooms
do not. No reservations.

Origami (239-482-2126; www
.sushiorigami.com), 8911 Daniels Pkwy.
#5. Once the area's foremost and few
places with a sushi bar, Origami, opened
1994 in a different location, remains
a favorite, despite the fact that it is
Korean by birth. Like its name, Origami's
menu is as multilayered and beautiful
as a work of folded paper art, and that
wins me over every time. Origami was
also first to dabble in Korean barbecue
locally. For this, you sit at a special table
with a gas grill in the center. We ordered
the spicy pork, which our server tossed
on the small grill with fresh sweet onions
and mushrooms. Nicely seasoned and
exceedingly tender, it made a marvelous
climax to a dinner that started with sushi
and Korean kimchee soup and ended
with green tea crème brûlée. At lunch,
the menu offers rice and noodle dishes,
vegetarian selections, bento boxes, and
sushi specials. One favorite sushi roll,
the Crazy Dragon, treats the mouth to
a texture tango with faux crab , cooked
eel, and avocado inside; crispy tempura
flakes, spicy mayo, and eel sauce on
the outside. The regular menu covers
Japanese familiars, such as tempura
and teriyaki, but then takes taste buds
into less familiar Asian territory. For
instance, Korean seafood pancake and
marinated Korean short ribs are on the
long list of appetizers. House specials
range from Chilean sea bass with sweet
pepper sauce and pineapple rice to spicy
Thai chicken. Moderate to Expensive. No
lunch Sunday.

🍴 ♿ **El Patio Restaurant** (239-278-
3303; www.elpatiorestaurants.com), 4444
Cleveland Ave., at Regency Square. This

strip-mall place packs 'em in—Peruvians, gringos, families alike—for an exotic taste of Peruvian cuisine, known for the invention of ceviche, its great variety of corn, and its Asian influence. El Patio's extensive menu sweeps the country's specialties, starting with exotic soups, such as hen soup with noodles, potatoes, and eggs; and shrimp chowder. Appetizers include tamales, avocado stuffed with chicken or seafood, Peruvian big corn with white cheese, and mashed potatoes stuffed with seafood. Ceviche—seafood marinated in lime juice, which causes a chemical reaction that seems to cook the fish—comes as an entrée or appetizer. Varieties include fish, shrimp, and combinations thereof. I chose the fish and, when given a choice by our charming Peruvian waiter, asked for it hot (as in spicy; the dish itself is always served chilled). It came with two cold, yamlike vegetables and a lettuce leaf filled with corn fries—roasted and salted large-kernel corn, somewhat akin to corn nuts but starchier and not as hard. They're a favorite bar snack in Peruvian eateries. The ceviche, garnished simply with red onion slices, was outstanding. Another of my favorite dishes, hearty *tacu tacu*, has a fried rice base that you can customize with choice of fish, beef, chicken or seafood. I did beef, which came served with toppings of sautéed onions and chunks of tomatoes. Other entrées span seafood and beef realms, and include stir-fried *chaufas*, a specialty marinated fish dish with spicy cream sauce, paella, and Peruvian-style spaghetti with beef. For dessert, there are Peruvian versions of doughnuts, flan, and other treats from the bakery. Inexpensive. No reservations.

Gloria's Trattoria Café Napoli (239-931-0050; www.latrattoriacafenapoli.com), 12377 S. Cleveland Ave. An empanada and small plate of linguine for starters. An "Espanol Tavern-Galician style" panino (pork, chorizo, ham, mozzarello, and aioli) and chicken with salsa verde on focaccia for our luncheon

main course. And a choice between flan and cannoli for dessert. My head was a little confused, but my palate was delighted by the fusion of Spanish, Italian, and more. Granite tabletops, saltillo tiling, and metal chairs give this café the feel of elsewhere—somewhere perhaps frequented by artists, writers, and others of bohemian intrigue. Service wasn't always polished, but that seemed right, too. If our pasta taster was any indication, Gloria has mastered the art and even makes some of her own pasta, according to the dinner menu. The napoletana sauce—light roasted tomato sauce—on the linguine demonstrated the excellence of simplicity. Sounding particularly sexy on the dinner menu, the truffle cheese sacchetti filled with ricotta, mozzarella, and black truffles would be my first choice. The menu pronounces paella—one with seafood, the other with meat—and arroz con pollo as house specialties. For lighter, more experimental appetites, the dinner-time tapas menu lets you dabble further among sunny culinary landscapes: Gorgonzola-stuffed plums wrapped with prosciutto, pork ribs in mojo, lightly fried string beans in truffle oil, and chicken empanadas drizzled with salsa verde. Moderate. Reservations accepted.

Osteria Celli (239-267-1310; www.osteriacelli.com), 15880 Summerlin Rd. #308 at Winkler Rd., Publix Shopping Center, Fort Myers. Fairly new, this gem of an Italian restaurant remains a bit of a secret that loyal fans cherish. While its seasonal menu does not try to cover every Italian staple as is often typical in Italian eateries, it presents comfort food with the imagination of a talented chef. The pillowy gnocchi, for instance, bears little resemblance to the smaller pebbly norm, with a silky blanket of gorgonzola and strips of speck to elevate it yet more. And the pappardelle! You expect wide noodles, but this homemade pasta was almost lasagna sized, with just the right elasticity, and tangled around the most delicious braised lamb ragout possible.

MUST SEE

✪ ♂ **The Veranda** (239-332-2065; www.verandarestaurant.com), 2122 Second St. My husband and I had our first "big" dinner date at the Veranda, so it will always be one of my favorites—but not solely for sentimental reasons. Victorian trappings and Southern charm create an atmosphere of romance in a historic-home setting. Occupying two early twentieth-century houses, the Veranda is a place for business lunches and special-occasion dinners. The dining room huddles around a two-sided redbrick fireplace and looks out on a cobblestone garden courtyard, separated from traffic by showy greenery and a white fence. Historic Fort Myers photos and well-stocked wine cases line the dark-wood bar. Start with something unusual from the Veranda's appetizer board—perhaps the artichoke fritters stuffed with blue crab and topped with béarnaise sauce, or Southern grit cakes with pepper jack cheese and grilled andouille sausage. Entrées are traditional but exceed the ordinary. Tender medallions of filet mignon are dressed Southern style in a rich, smoky, sour-mash whiskey sauce. Rosemary merlot sauce complements the rack of New Zealand lamb. Champagne beurre blanc tops basil and parmesan crusted snapper. Daily specials typically include fresh seafood catches, and the menu changes to reflect the seasons. Lunches span the spectrum from specialties such as chicken piccata or salmon to a grilled portobello sandwich or fried green tomato salad. Desserts wilt willpower with such temptations as chocolate pâté on raspberry coulis, peanut butter fudge pie, and Baileys cheesecake. Expensive to Very Expensive. Reservations recommended. Closed for Saturday lunch, Sunday lunch and dinner.

THE VERANDA INFUSES CREATIVITY INTO SOUTHERN CUISINE

It's a place where true Italian connoisseurs can celebrate the simplicity of fine product and kitchen mastery in a clean, bright, modern setting (a born-again Blockbuster store, but you'd never know) with a display kitchen. We recently tried a breaded swordfish special with an amazing tomato and onion sauce and beef cannelloni slathered in a creamed ricotta cheese. A lesson: pay close attention to the night's specials. Other regular (but seasonally changing) menu items that have excited our taste buds: the chicken liver pate and charred octopus appetizers, Frenched lamb chops with yogurt sauce, and entirely original presentations of tiramisu and lemon panna cotta. Moderate to Expensive. Reservations accepted. No lunch.

FORT MYERS BEACH

Locals go to Fort Myers Beach expecting fresh seafood and reasonable prices. It's known more for fun dining and waterfront views than for culinary innovation, and menus are fairly predictable.

Bayfront Bistro (239-463-3663; www .bayfrontbistro.com), 4761 Estero Blvd., at Snook Bight Marina behind Publix. To break away from Fort Myers Beach's typical fried shrimp mold, this one takes you to a higher level of culinary daring. Literally, the new waterside restaurant sits elevated at the second level overlooking the marina's boats and unadulterated mangroves across the bay. Opt for patio seating or air-conditioning. Its indoor seating huddles around a handsome bar with a snook sculpture centerpiece. Outdoors is no more casual with its wave-motif chairs and cobalt tableware. Views from both effectively soothe the soul. The food dwells on the same upper echelon—from a half lobster melt with lobster bisque at lunch to snapper with sundried tomato basil risotto and Guinness-braised short ribs on the dinner menu. Most recently, I went with what our server pointed out as a signature—Bayfront butterfish. So multidimensional

it thrilled with every bite, it is marinated in *miso yaki* and served aboard a sweet chile veggie stir-fry and wasabi mashed potatoes underpinned with swirls of slightly sweet wasabi cream and flavored oils. Outstanding! Key lime pie snob that I am, I can unequivocally recommend Bayfront's rendition as the best I've tasted on Fort Myers Beach. The restaurant also serves weekend brunch on Saturday and Sunday mornings. Moderate to Expensive. Reservations accepted.

🦐 🐚 ♿ **Matanzas Inn** (239-463-3838; www.matanzasonthebay.com), 416 Crescent St. When I think of Fort Myers Beach, I think of three things: shrimp, boats, and water. Matanzas Inn embodies the laid-back, free-spirited soul of the "the Beach" with its ramshackle look and landmark position in the shadow of the high bridge, where boat traffic, dolphin antics, and aerial bird shows provide entertainment whether you're sitting inside the glassed dining room or outside it. I invariably order fried shrimp when I sit down to a meal here, despite the fact that the menu comprehensively stretches beyond Fort Myers Beach's trademark dish, using mostly locally sourced seafood and other products. I can depend on on the shrimp dish's crunch and freshness. It appears on both the lunch and dinner menu. Other worthy considerations: blackened chicken Alfredo, flounder stuffed with shrimp and scallops and baked with garlic cream, crunchy grouper (coated with cornflakes), seafood chimichanga, and baby back ribs. Or choose to customize your choice of seafood and preparation. The Key lime pie is well worth the calories—creamy, and, like Fort Myers Beach, just tart enough. In May, the restaurant throws an annual Bluegrass, Brew, and BBQ festival. Moderate to Expensive. No reservations.

🦐 ♿ **Zushi Zushi** (239-463-9874; www .zushizushi.com), 201 Old San Carlos Blvd. We had low expectations for sushi in a bar setting at this beach-party haven. Surprise! Not only did we find great variety and creativity, but polished crafting. It entirely devotes itself, unlike a lot of the newer Thai-sushi hybrids, to Japanese, and its multipage menu is almost entirely given to rolls. Its partner operation in the same building, House of Brewz, does serve American munchies, however. Zushi's main list gives you a choice of regular or cone-shaped hand rolls and indicates whether they are wrapped in nori (seaweed) or sushi rice. That makes it somewhat easier to sift through all the selections. We ordered the regular caliente roll (fried white fish, avocado, cucumber, masago roe, and spicy mayo); spicy tuna topped with an excellent kimchee sauce; and crunchy tuna, where the tuna was raw, but the roll itself was lightly battered and fried. Each delivered delightful mouth joy of varying textures and wide-spectrum flavors. The menu dedicates one section to the "dragon roll family," but we made our fourth selection from the house specialty rolls. The Deep Z Roll was a magnificent masterpiece—fat with shrimp tempura, avocado, cream cheese, and *masago*. This roll, too, was deep-fried and topped with eel sauce and spicy mayo. Beautifully presented in a boat with a sculptured mound of wasabi and pickled ginger, the rolls sailed our doubts into the sunset. Not only serious, this sushi, but it is overall more affordable than most. Inexpensive to Moderate. No reservations.

PINE ISLAND

Blue Dog Bar & Grill (239-558-4970; www.bluedogfl.com), 4597 Pine Island Rd., Matlacha. Pine Island's new favorite for lunch and dinner (and weekend breakfast in season), it is typically island casual, but the food rises a step or two from the same-old fried seafood fare. Start with conch fritters or a bowl of homemade soup—three-day black bean or whatever the day's special might be. Then segue into the all-day menu's sandwich or entrée divisions to satisfy all meat and seafood cravings. We love the TNT shrimp tacos, named for the

restaurant's own spicy sauce. The half-pound burgers come juicy and sided with sea salt fries. Build up your burger with ingredients from feta cheese to a fried egg. The menu also lets you customize your seafood, whether you choose the island's iconic mullet or "catch of the moment." Pick the method of preparation and mango salsa, curry sauce, lemon caper, or one of the other five topping choices. For meat-eaters, there's a hand-cut New York strip steak or grilled chicken smothered in onions, mushrooms, and provolone cheese. Eighteen beers on tap and a small wine list covers the "bar" part of this good-time spot with character. And characters. Inexpensive to Moderate. No reservations.

Tarpon Lodge Restaurant (239-283-2517; www.tarponlodge.com), 13771 Waterfront Dr., Pineland. Before there was Tarpon Lodge, Pine Island dining projected an Old-Florida-meets-the-Midwest image. Since then, there's a creative, gifted force to reckon with. Set in a 1926 fishing lodge, banked with vintage wavy-glass windows looking out on the water, the restaurant brings on the freshness in every sense of the word. For lunch, bronzed shrimp tortilla wrap, crab cake sliders or Cuban sandwich. Imaginative dressings and sides make the dishes. Try the hearty and fresh-tasting crab and roasted corn chowder for lunch or dinner. The succinct menu's dozen dinner entrées include vegetarian pasta, housemade crab tortellini, and filet mignon with brandy peppercorn or béarnaise sauce or caramelized pearl onions (Very Expensive), plus the day's fresh catch and nightly specials. Here in this seafood kingdom, with its steep fishing heritage, you can't go wrong ordering the catch, or—thanks to the chef's savvy—anything else, for that matter. Moderate to Expensive. Reservations suggested.

SANIBEL ISLAND

Bleu Rendez-Vous French Bistro (239-565-1608; bleurendezvous.com), 2430

Periwinkle Way. In an open-kitchen setting, French-trained Chef Christian Vivet produces classics with his signature touches—a well-mapped balance of France's fine and folk foods. True to French tradition, the escargots are butter-swamped and heavy on the garlic. The tender sweetbreads come with a light calvados sauce (available in appetizer and entrée portions). Other starters include blood sausage and bone marrow canoe. Entrees, too, demonstrate chef's commitment to authentic French cuisine: beef bourguignon, rabbit in wine sauce, roasted sea bass with beurre blanc, and crispy duck with orange sauce. Try the Rustic Apple Galette or chocolate profiteroles for sweet culmination. Expensive to Very Expensive. No lunch.

✪ **Gramma Dot's Seaside Saloon** (239-472-8138; www.sanibelmarina .com/gramma.html), 634 N. Yachtsman, at Sanibel Marina. I have finally found it: the island's (perhaps all of Lee County's) best Key lime pie. Flecks of lime zest give this creamy version its pucker power, and now I'm afraid I'm addicted. That's not all that makes this place popular among locals, boaters, and other visitors. Take in the view of luxury yachts in the harbor and savor the freshness of the seafood dishes to get the full picture. The curried lobster salad and fried grouper sandwich are top choices on the lunch menu, which is available until the little screened-porch eatery closes at 7:30 p.m. (After 5 p.m., lunch items go up $1 in price.) Salad-lovers can choose from a variety of different Caesars—fried oyster, grouper, shrimp, and popcorn shrimp. Winning entrées include the spinach boursin grouper, coconut shrimp, bacon-wrapped shrimp with BBQ sauce, and fried oysters. Portions are generous and accompanied by a tasty potato croquette, the house tartar sauce, fresh sautéed veggies, and fruit. Inexpensive to Expensive. No reservations.

🦩 🍴 **Lazy Flamingo** (239-472-5353; www.lazyflamingo.com), 6520-C Pine Ave., at Blind Pass. This is the original Lazy Flamingo, which has spawned another on Sanibel's southeast end and others in the region. Look for a Pepto-Bismol pink building at Blind Pass, just before the bridge to Captiva. Neighborhood and nautical are the concepts behind this first Flamingo, where you order and pick up your own food at the counter, eat off plastic plates in the shape of scallop shells, and wipe your hands with paper towels from a roll at the table or bar. The menu and ambience have an essence of the Florida Keys, including the popular ring-and-hook game that originated in a bar down there and started a trend here. Conch fritters, clam pot, mesquite-grilled grouper, wings, prime-rib sandwich, and Caesar salad are some of the most popular menu items. Avoid the Dead Parrot Wings; they are inedibly searing to all but the most calloused, but the regular chicken wings rank highest on the island. Most of the meals come with fries, but you can substitute a small Caesar salad, which is usually crisp and tasty. The place is small: about a dozen counter seats and a few booths plus some outdoor tables. For the same food but more room, shrimp-boat décor, and table service, try the Lazy Flamingo at 1036 Periwinkle Way (239-472-6939). Inexpensive to Moderate. No handicapped access. No reservations.

Timbers Restaurant & Fish Market (239-472-3128; www.prawnbroker.com), 703 Tarpon Bay Rd. Glancing at the restaurant's regular daily menu might not convince you there's anything special going on here. But take a look at the nightly specials; that's undoubtedly where you want to be. Regular specialties include crunchy grouper; king crab legs; scallops broiled or fried; steak; peel-and-eat steamed shrimp appetizer; and the triple shrimp platter with scampi, baked and stuffed with seafood, and crunchy varieties. The crunchy style is best, so you may want to skip the other tasters and sink your teeth into some of the finest, crispiest fried shrimp around. Daily specials showcase what's fresh in the market with your choice of preparation and sauce. The sesame tuna and yellowtail snapper with citrus beurre blanc are winners, when available. Dinners come with a choice of soup or salad (the Manhattan clam chowder rocks (add crab bisque for $1), and a starch. Desserts are homemade at a Fort Myers bakery. The Key lime pie is just the right amount of tart, and the moist coconut cake? Plan to share or take half of it home. Moderate to Expensive. No reservations. No lunch.

Sweet Melissa's Café (239-472-1956; sweetmelissascafe.com) 1625 Periwinkle Way. It's fortuitous that Chef Melissa Talmage prepares courses in appetizer and full portions: all the more reason to try more of the powerful dishes that come from her kitchen. The menu changes with the seasons, but the grilled romaine Caesar salad never leaves the menu, thank the culinary gods! Another standard (if you don't see it on the menu, you can usually order it regardless), the fish stew explodes with the goodness of mahimahi or redfish, scallops, shrimp, clams, mussels, chorizo, fennel, and a tomato saffron broth. Order a half-portion, then mix and match it with small dishes such as crawfish ravioli, pork belly and clams, and pulled chicken crepe. Or go for full entrées, such as smoked beef tenderloin or grilled pompano with Creole Crushed Potatoes. If there's steamed mussels and frites on the lunch menu, don't skip it. Sandwiches range from crawfish po' boy to pork belly taco. Expensive. Reservations accepted. Closed Sunday, no lunch Saturday.

Traders Gulf Coast Grill & Gifts (239-472-7242; traderssanibel.com), 1551 Periwinkle Way. Here you become a part of the store as you sip and dine in the restaurant and bar. Over the years, it has become *the* place for islanders to meet for lunch, with its succinct menu of sandwiches, pastas, and small plates. The soup of the day is usually a good bet, the white gazpacho legendary, and the seafood gumbo, fortified with rice,

could be a meal. I also can recommend the spinach salad with grilled portobello and Gorgonzola and pancetta dressing and the passion berry iced tea for lunch. The dinner menu describes such complex masterworks as macadamia-crusted grouper with Thai peanut sauce, lollipop pork chops with fig au jus, panko-crusted salmon with lemon-caper dill vinaigrette and avocado salsa, and Parmesan-crusted chicken breast with lemon-caper beurre blanc. Nightly specials—such as the pan-seared grouper with lobster ravioli and sauce we recently enjoyed—dazzle. Cutting edge aside, Traders is also known for its burgers and barbecued baby back ribs. Moderate to Expensive. Reservations accepted. Closed August and September.

BAKERIES **European American Baking Co.** (239-225-0450; www.eabake.com), 12450 Metro Pkwy., Fort Myers. Wholesale, retail, and café operation with the most tempting international treats: éclairs, scones, strudel, Italian butter cookies, cheesecake, napoleons, tarts, turnovers, and artisan breads. Also sit-down breakfast and lunch space and menus.

Mon Paris Bakery (239-437-1988; www.monparisbakery.com), 13550 Reflections Pkwy., Fort Myers. In addition to wonderful French pastries and breads, it seduces customers with fine coffee, crepes, quiche, and sandwiches.

BREAKFAST ✪ ✿ **CRaVE** (239-466-4663; cravemenu.com), 12901 McGregor Blvd., at the Bridge Plaza, Fort Myers. Highly acclaimed for its creative comfort food breakfast, lunch, and dinner, Crave's morning menu (available until 4 p.m.) describes incredible pancakes and omelets, such as one with seafood, asparagus, shiitake mushrooms, broiled tomato, and hollandaise. Other unusual offerings include salmon and eggs with creamed horseradish, shrimp and grits, hash eggs Benedict, and specials such as bourbon-glazed filet mignon and meat loaf omelet with bacon, shrimp, and cheese.

Heavenly Biscuits (239-463-7600), 110 Mango St., Fort Myers Beach. Known for its cinnamon rolls and lovely biscuit sandwiches, this ten-table indoor-outdoor establishment has a loyal following. Each day brings a special egg bake and sandwiches du jour plus design-your-own breakfast and lunch sandwiches.

Mermaid Garden Café (239-425-3480; www.mermaidgardencafe.com), 8695 College Pkwy. at the Atrium lower level, Fort Myers. A well-kept secret, this adorable little place adds homey style, global influences, and good health to breakfast dishes such as guava pastries, lentil organic bowl, and *huevos rotos florentini*. Also serves lunch. Closed Sunday.

Over Easy Café (239-472-2625; www.overeasycafesanibel.com), 630–1 Tarpon Bay Rd., Sanibel Island. Islanders are happy to have an alternative (and a better one at that!) to breakfast at Lighthouse Café, a tourist favorite long touted for its breakfasts. Over Easy's menu does standard along with unusual dishes, such as my favorites: egg Reuben sandwich, vegetarian Benedict (ask for extra hollandaise on the side because it tends to run off), and portobello and spinach omelet. Also lunch.

((ᵖ)) **The Tuckaway Bagel and Wafel Café** (239-463-5398; www.tuckawaycoffeefmb.com), 1740 Estero Blvd., Fort Myers Beach. Steamed bagel sandwiches, such as the Sammy with banana, cinnamon sugar, Nutella, and cream cheese or Sunrise with egg, bacon, ham, and pepper Jack cheese, are the specialty. Liege *wafels* and gourmet coffee are another, plus it offers four lunch sandwiches and smoothies.

BREWERIES, WINERIES, DISTILLERIES **Bury Me Brewing** (239-332-2337; www.burymebrewing.com), 4224 S. Cleveland Ave. #7, Fort Myers. Small craft brewery near Edison Mall with tasting room and foosball. Sample Creamation Honey Cream Ale, From My Cold Dead Hands IPA, and similarly ghoulish brews.

Cape Coral Brewing Company (239-257-1033; capecoralbrewing.com), 839 Miramar St., Cape Coral. One of the area's newest breweries, its taproom creates a congenial pub atmosphere for playing darts or life-sized Jenga and tossing back a Burrowing Owl Brown Ale or Bad Buoy IPA.

Fort Myers Brewing Company (239-313-6576; www.facebook.com/FMBrew), 12811 Commerce Lakes Dr. #28, Fort Myers. Fort Myers' first and largest craft brewery, its tasting facilities are indoor-outdoor. Check its Facebook page for live music and food truck schedule.

Point Ybel Brewing Company (239-603-6535; www.pointybelbrew.com), 16120 San Carlos Blvd.) A popular spot for craft beer tastings which often features live music.

Wicked Dolphin Artisan Rum (239-242-5244; www.wickeddolphin.com), 131 SW Third Pl., Cape Coral. Free one-hour tours start with a free rum punch and end with a rum tasting. Call or go online to make a reservation. Made from Florida sugarcane and other local products, its craft products include five core rums—crystal, gold, black, spiced, and coconut—plus six other specialty and seasonal blends.

CANDIES & ICE CREAM **Cape Creamery** (609-668-3791), 1715 Cape Coral Pkwy. W., Cape Coral. All homemade ice cream in many tempting flavors, plus shakes and sundaes.

🍦 **Love Boat Ice Cream** (239-466-7077; www.loveboaticecream.com), 16229 San Carlos Blvd., Fort Myers. Homemade ice cream at a longtime favorite at the crossroads leading to Fort Myers Beach and Sanibel Island. Watch for news of an expanded facility.

Norman Love Confections (239-561-7215 or 866-515-2121; www.normanloveconfections.com), 11380 Lindbergh Ave., Fort Myers. Treat yourself or a loved one to chocolates and pastries that have won kudos and awards throughout the country. Love's specialties are locally flavored truffles such as passion fruit, coconut, and Key lime. Next door, get your ice cream fix at Artisan Gelato by Norman Love (239-288-4333). Love operates another chocolate and dessert salon at Miromar Outlets (see "Shopping") and at press time announced plans to open a second Fort Myers location at 13211 McGregor Blvd.

🐚 **Pinocchio's Ice Cream** (239-472-6566; www.pinocchiosicecream.com), 362 Periwinkle Way, Sanibel Island. Homemade Italian ice cream and sundaes. Try the Dirty Sand Dollar–caramel ice cream with malted milk balls and chocolate flakes.

🐚 **Royal Scoop** (239-992-2000; www.royalscoop.com), 15 Eighth St., Bonita Springs. Close enough to the beach to cool down, this local tradition feels retro and hosts community events including tours of their homemade ice cream–making operation. Recommended flavors: royal turtle and cookie dough.

Scoops on First (239-226-0450), 2250 First St., Fort Myers. Thirty-two flavors of hand-packed ice cream and all the goodies it goes into plus coffee, cookies, and other ways to catch a sugar buzz.

COFFEE **Bennett's Fresh Roast** (www.bennettsfreshroast.com) Its two locations, downtown Fort Myers (239-332-0077, 2011 Bayside Pkwy.) and on Sanibel Island (239-312-4651; 1020 Periwinkle Way), are known as much for their from-scratch donuts and cinnamon rolls as for their fine coffee, including cold brew. Also, breakfast and lunch items such as the donut hot dog and lobster roll.

Latté Da (239-472-0234; www.captivaislandinn.com), 11508 Andy Rosse Ln., Captiva Island. Sells Seattle's Best brand coffees and espresso, plus locally homemade Queenie's Real Ice Cream.

✪ **Sanibel Bean Island Coffees** (239-395-1919; www.sanibelbean.com), 2240-B Periwinkle Way, Sanibel Island; also at

Southwest Florida International Airport. Sanibel's popular buzz shop serves the usual espresso, cappuccino, and latte selections, plus fresh-squeezed juice, smoothies, ice cream, bagels, breakfast, sandwiches, and salads.

((•)) **The Tuckaway Bagel and Wafel Café** (239-463-5398; www.tuckawaycoffeefmb.com), 1740 Estero Blvd., Fort Myers Beach. Serving hot and iced gourmet coffee, lattes, espresso, and smoothies, this café is also known for its steamed bagel sandwiches and authentic Liege *wafels* (not to be confused with waffles). Try one with mango jam or stop in for a vegetarian or deli lunch sandwich.

DELI & SPECIALTY FOODS **Sand Castle Gifts & Gourmet** (239-472-2201), 2075 Periwinkle Way #20, Periwinkle Place, Sanibel Island. Fudge, gourmet hot sauces, preserves, and other bottled items.

European Food Market (239-332-7200), 12901 McGregor Blvd., at Bridge Plaza, Fort Myers. Eastern European specialties from Poland, Romania, and the Slavic countries including pierogi, fresh and smoked kielbasa and other meats and sausages, beers, bread, candy, and jarred salads and pickled vegetables.

Francesco's Italian Deli and Pizzeria (239-463-5634; www.francescosfortmyersbeach.com), 7205 Estero Blvd., at Santini Marina Plaza, Fort Myers Beach. Homemade breads, calzones, deli and breakfast sandwiches, pizza whole or by the slice, Italian dishes for reheating, homemade Royal Scoop ice cream and Italian gelato, and gourmet cheeses and groceries.

India Bazaar (239-939-0797; www.indiavijaya.com), 5228 Bank St., Fort Myers. A shop filled with exotic smells, foods, and gifts from India, Thailand, the Middle East, and Britain. Packaged and frozen ethnic ingredients plus premade meals. Also Indian jewelry, clothing, and fabrics.

Leaf Asian Market (239-288-5368) 4300 S. Cleveland Ave., Fort Myers) Across from the Edison Mall, this Asian supermarket stocks fresh mushrooms, fruits, and vegetables; sushi; seafood; processed sauces and spices; kitchen implements; and frozen goods. Made-to-order lychee and other flavored iced teas.

✪ **Mario's Italian Meat Market & Deli** (239-936-7275; www.mariosmeatmarket .com), 12326 Cleveland Ave., Fort Myers. Fresh homemade sausage, braciola, and other meats; fresh produce; delicious homemade Italian cheeses, butchery wares, sauces, pastas, soups, and sandwiches; and hot and frozen prepared Italian specialties—excellent lasagna and eggplant rollatini. Limited seating.

Petra's Mediterranean Middle Eastern Food (239-939-3090), 1916 Boy Scout Dr., Fort Myers. Stop here for feta cheese, flat breads, gyros, and unusual processed items such as rose jam, stuffed eggplant, and exotic candies. A luncheon counter sells inexpensive gyros, stuffed grape leaves, shish kebabs, and more, plus there are refrigerated prepared dishes for take-home.

✪ ((•)) **Sanibel Deli & Coffee Factory** (239-472-2555; www.sanibeldeli.com), 2330 Palm Ridge Rd., Sanibel. Breakfast sandwiches, pastries, salad, pizza, sandwiches; free WiFi access; free "earth-friendly" delivery.

FARM, FARMERS MARKETS, FRUIT & VEGETABLE STANDS For the freshest produce, visit the farms and roadside stands throughout the region. Some feature U-Pick options, especially for tomatoes and strawberries. Farmers Markets have sprouted in locations throughout the area, many of them in season from November through May.

Buckingham Farms (239-206-2303, buckinghamfarmsonline.com), 12931 Orange River Blvd., Fort Myers. Organic, hydroponic farm that sells its crops and honey, plus farm eggs and homemade farm-to-table meals.

Downtown Farmers' Market (www .cityftmyers.com), under the bridge near Centennial Park, Fort Myers. Look for fresh fruit, vegetables, flowers, herbs, live plants, and arts and crafts year-round every Thursday, 7–1, at this traditional market, the region's oldest.

The Farm (239-768-2767; www .thefarm-estero.com), 9050 Corkscrew Rd., Estero. U-Pick and produce stand options. Also free-range, organic eggs.

GreenMarket (239-939-2787; www .artinlee.org), Alliance for the Arts, 10091 McGregor Blvd., Fort Myers. More than thirty food and arts vendors congregate every Saturday from 9 a.m. to 1 p.m. Live entertainment and kids activities.

Pair-A-Dice Produce (239-466-4464; m.guerrillamarketinginc.com/pair-a -diceproduce), 16758 McGregor Blvd., Fort Myers. My personal favorite for locally grown tomatoes, citrus, and other fresh fruit, vegetables, and preserves. It also ships fruit.

Sanibel Farmers' Market, Sanibel City Hall, 800 Dunlop Rd., Sanibel Island. Runs from November through May, every Sunday 8–1.

Sun Harvest Citrus (239-768-2686 or 800-743-1480; www.sunharvestcitrus .com), 14810 Metro Pkwy. S., at Six Mile Cypress, Fort Myers. Part tourist attraction, part citrus stand, Sun Harvest offers free samples, tours, demonstrations, a playground, and a gift shop.

NATURAL FOODS **Chef Brooke's Natural Café** (239-332-2433; chefbrooke online.com), 1850 Boy Scout Dr. #A106, Fort Myers. Organic smoothies and juices; breakfast and lunch,; hot and cold entrées; gluten-free and health-food products; cooking classes. Nonvegans may be put off by the funky curry smell that permeates. Take out or eat in.

((•)) **Pizza Fusion** (239-337-7979; www .pizzafusion.com), 12901-5 McGregor Blvd., at Bridge Plaza, Fort Myers. Everything from the pizza to the wine and the art on the wall is sustainability-oriented. Besides pizza, there are creative salads,

FRUITFUL ISLANDS

For those in the know, Pine Island is synonymous with exotic fruit. Guavas once grew wild throughout the island, brought to this subtropical land from the tropical Caribbean. Later, mangoes flourished. The only other place in Florida where tropical fruits grow in such abundance is Homestead, on the east coast, at a latitude some ninety miles south of Pine Island.

What makes Pine Island so nearly tropical? The warm waters of Charlotte Harbor run wide at the island's north end, around Bokeelia. They insulate the land, warming cold air before it reaches fragile fruit groves. Longans, sapodillas, carambolas, lychees, and other rare treats thrive as a result of this pocket of climate. Fructose freaks from miles around make a pilgrimage to roadside stands along Pine Island and Stringfellow roads throughout the summer and fall. To celebrate its fruity reputation, Pine Island throws MangoMania Tropical Fruit Fair each summer (see "Special Events").

sandwiches, and desserts. Signature pizzas include organic eggplant and fresh mozzarella, and Philly steak, plus there are gluten-free choices. Delivery available (via hybrid car).

Sanibel Sprout (239-472-4499), 2463 Periwinkle Way at Bailey Center. Juice and smoothie bar; menu of healthy soups, sandwiches, and pasta; limited inventory of health-food packaged products plus fresh veggies.

PIZZA & TAKE-OUT **Grimaldi's** (239-432-9767; www.grimaldispizzeria.com), 13499 S. Cleveland Ave. #201, at Bell Tower Shops, Fort Myers. Straight from New York, its coal-fired brick ovens render thin crust pizzas to the very standard of crispiness. The love is in the details: silky mozzarella handmade from the milk of free-range cows, a killer secret-recipe tomato sauce, and quality toppings.

Little Lilly's Island Deli (239-282-9264; www.littlelillysislanddeli.com), 10700 Stringfellow Rd., Bokeelia. Locals rave about the homemade soup du jour, plus there is crab cake croissant, tropical chicken sandwich, sausage and peppers sub, and build-your-own options.

Lobster Lady Seafood Market & Bistro (239-471-0136; www.lobsterladyseafood .com), 1715 Cape Coral Pkwy., Cape Coral. Homemade fish dips, soups, and seafood sandwiches and dishes to go; also fresh seafood and live lobsters.

🦞 **El Mambo Cuban Restaurant** (239-542-9995), 4716 Del Prado Blvd. S., Cape Coral. Serving Cape Coral's Latino population and those who love the food, it sells Cuban bread, desserts, fresh fruit juices, empanadas, Cuban and other sandwiches, and Cuban specialties.

Hickory Bar-B-Q (239-481-2626; hickory-bbq.com), 15400 Old McGregor Blvd. Its secret-recipe vinegary barbecue sauce and creamy coleslaw are reason enough to keep faithful customers coming back. Then there's the smoked pulled pork, ribs, and coconut cream pie.

Plaka I on the Beach (239-463-4707), 1001 Estero Blvd., Fort Myers Beach. Gyros, spinach pie, moussaka, and baklava to go or eat in a screened-in dining room near the beach.

Rosati's (239-221-3706; www .myrosatis.com), 21301 S. Tamiami Trail #400, Estero. The best Chicago-style pizza around, plus pasta, wings, and sandwiches. Take-out only.

Starz Restaurant & Pizzeria (239-482-7827; www.starzpizzeria.com), 16681 McGregor Blvd., Fort Myers. Close to the islands, its pizzas, calzones, subs, and Italian specialties have a faithful following. Take-out only at this store, but it operates another with sitdown service in Fort Myers (239-482-3105; 8750 Gladiolus Dr.).

SEAFOOD **Lobster Lady Seafood Market & Bistro** (239-471-0136; www

.lobsterladyseafood.com), 1715 Cape Coral Pkwy., Cape Coral. Tanks of huge live lobsters, plus fresh and frozen seafood and butcher meats.

Skip One Seafood (239-482-0433), 15820 S. Tamiami Trail, Fort Myers. Fresh and fairly priced wild shrimp, stone crab (in season), lobster tails, clams, and fish. Join the crowds who have discovered the quality and value of its food for lunch and dinner.

Timbers Fish Market (239-472-3128; www.prawnbroker.com), 703 Tarpon Bay Rd., Sanibel. Located inside a popular seafood restaurant, Timbers has the best selection, prices, and freshness on the island for all types of seafood—fresh, steamed, and smoked.

✳ Selective Shopping

SHOPPING CENTERS & MALLS **Bell Tower Shops** (239-489-1221; www .thebelltowershops.com), 13499 S. Cleveland Ave. at Daniels Pkwy., Fort Myers. Saks Fifth Avenue anchors this alfresco, Mediterranean-style plaza of one-of-a-kind shops, comfy seating coves, upscale chains (Victoria's Secret, Brookstone, Williams-Sonoma), good restaurants, and movie theaters.

Captiva Island. Like Captiva in general, the shopping scene here is quirky, pricey, and beach-oriented.

Coconut Point (239-992-9966; www .simon.com/mall/coconut-point), 23106 Fashion Dr., Tamiami Trail and Coconut Point Rd., Estero. The fashionable mall within a planned community includes big-box stores, major chains such as Victoria's Secret, Brookstone, and Haagen Dazs, along with some local venues, including Blue Water Bistro (see "Dining").

Coralwood Shopping Center (239-333-4372; coralwoodcenter.com), 2301 Del Prado Blvd., Cape Coral. An outdoor mall of restaurants and chain stores, including Bealls Department Store, Home Goods, and J.C. Penney.

Downtown Fort Myers, First Street. Downtown is looking up after a redevelopment project that put utility lines underground and paved streets and sidewalks with recycled brick. More business- and government-minded than commercial, it does harbor some interesting galleries and shops selling one-of-a-kind clothing, jewelry, and accessories. Street parking is free.

Edison Mall (239-939-5464; shop edisonmall.com), 4125 Cleveland Ave., Fort Myers. An entirely retail, enclosed, and air conditioned mall with major department stores such as Macy's, Dillard's, J. C. Penney, and Sears, plus about 150 smaller clothing and gift shops and a food court.

Fort Myers Beach. Shop in your bikini, if you wish, at Times Square, a hub of ultracasual island activity. You'll find a profusion of swimsuit boutiques, surf shops, and food outlets at this open-air pedestrian mall. At the island's south end, Santini Marina Plaza has some interesting shops and food stops.

The Franklin Shops (239-333-3130; www.thefranklinshops.com), 2200 First St., Fort Myers, took over a historic building with art, clothing, jewelry, and other local vendors occupying floor and showcase space.

🐾 📶 **Gulf Coast Town Center** (230-267-0783; www.gulfcoasttowncenter .com), 9903 Gulf Coast Main St., at I-75 and Alico Rd., Fort Myers. The Market Plaza serves as a family entertainment hub (there's live music every Friday and Saturday), and the University Plaza caters to university students with free WiFi access. Among its 120-plus stores and restaurants is a Bass Pro Shops outlet (239-461-7800; www.basspro.com).

Sanibel Island. Periwinkle Way and Palm Ridge Road constitute the shopper's routes on Sanibel, which is known for its galleries (specializing in wildlife art), shell shops, and resort-wear stores. These are clustered in tastefully landscaped, nature-compatible outdoor centers, the largest being Periwinkle Place (periwinkleplace.com) on Periwinkle Way.

ANTIQUES & COLLECTIBLES **Albert Meadow Antiques** (239-472-8442), 15000 Captiva Dr., Captiva Island. High-quality, turn-of-the-twentieth-century decorative arts by Tiffany and Gallé, plus antique jewelry, lamps, silver, Navajo weavings, and art deco and art nouveau pieces. Closed mid-April through mid-December.

Judy's Antiques and Jewelry (239-481-9600), 12710-3 McGregor Blvd., Fort Myers. One of the oldest in the McGregor Antiques District, this establishment is well organized and sells quality sterling, porcelain, and crystal, specializing in estate jewelry.

McGregor Antique Mall (239-433-0200), 12720 McGregor Blvd., Fort Myers. In the same neighborhood as Judy's but more folksy and nostalgic in its considerable offerings—household goods, books, toys, country-style furnishings, and more.

The Swap Shop (239-432-0906; www.swapshopantiques.com), 17851 Pine Ridge Rd., Fort Myers Beach. Stop at this big red barn for affordable housewares, fine ceramics, '50s furnishings and décor, and carved tiki statues.

Vamped Up Vintage (239-936-4888; vampedupvintage.com), 1400 Colonial Blvd. #21 at Royal Palm Square, Fort Myers. This off-the-beaten-path shop is fun any time of the year, but especially when prepping for Halloween or June weddings. It deals entirely in vintage clothing, carrying everything from tuxes and wedding gowns to gaudy bell-bottom jumpsuits and fur-trimmed hats.

BOOKS **Annette's Book Nook** (239-463-3999), 7205 Estero Blvd., at Santini Marina Plaza, Fort Myers Beach. New and used paperback exchange; a nice selection of new local guides, adult books, and kids' books.

MacIntosh Books & Paper (239-472-1447; www.macintoshbooks.com), 2330 Palm Ridge Rd., Sanibel Island. A small shop packed full of books of local and general interest; a selection of cards earns it the "Paper" in its name.

CLOTHING **C.J.'s Boutique** (239-395-3733), 2359 Periwinkle Way, Sanibel Island. Select, flowing fashions for upscale hippy types.

Francesca's Collections (239-267-5050; www.francescascollections.com), 13499 Cleveland Ave. #19, at Bell Tower Shops, Fort Myers. Young, fun, affordable women's fashions, accessories, and gifts.

Giggles (239-395-0700; www.gigglessanibel.com), 5400 Plantation Rd., Captiva Island. Cute and whimsical Florida-appropriate clothing for kids, particularly little girls.

H2O Outfitters and Footloose Sandals & Shoes (239-472-4717; www.beachstuffinc.com/h2o.html), 1700 Periwinkle Way, at Jerry's Shopping Center, Sanibel Island. Name-brand men's and women's beach and marina fashions, shoes, and quality souvenir T-shirts and sweatshirts.

Jos. A. Bank Clothiers (239-454-3543; www.josbank.com), 13499 Cleveland Ave. #181, at Bell Tower Shops, Fort Myers. Fine sporting, casual-tropical, and formal wear for men.

Palmettos (239-463-1515), 7205 Estero Blvd. #712, at Santini Marina Village,

Fort Myers Beach. Fine casual, Florida-fit fashions for men and women.

Pier Peddler (239-765-0660), 1000 Estero Blvd., Fort Myers Beach. At the base of the Fort Myers Beach Fishing Pier, it carries beach and tropical fashions for men and women at a higher price point and sophistication than the surrounding beach marts and surf shops.

Savvy on First (239-265-1591; www .savvyonfirst.com), 2263 First St., Fort Myers. The work of more than four hundred artists includes art, crafts, trendy clothing, handbags, jewelry, and fun and unusual gifts.

Trader Rick's (239-489-2240; www .traderricks.com), 13499 US 41 #217, at Bell Tower Shops, Fort Myers; and (239-472-9194), 2075 Periwinkle Way #38, at Periwinkle Place, Sanibel. Creative-casual Florida wear for "the artful woman," plus unusual and handmade jewelry, toiletries, and other accessories.

CONSIGNMENT Buying secondhand on the Island Coast is not the embarrassment it is in some places. Because of the wealthy and transient nature of its residents, the area offers the possibility of great discoveries in its consignment shops.

Classy Exchange (239-931-4006; www.classyexchange.com), 12791 Kenwood Ln. #B1, Fort Myers. Designer women's fashions and accessories.

Cecilia's Elite Repeat (239-437-1222; www.elite-repeat.com), 12995 S. Cleveland Ave. #130, at Pinebrook Park, Fort Myers. Formal, career, and casual wear, including shoes and jewelry, for women.

Once Again Consignment (239-482-5445; www.shoponceagainboutique .com), 12721 McGregor Blvd., Fort Myers. Nicely arranged women's clothing and shoes with brand names, including a rack of Chico's.

FACTORY OUTLET CENTERS ❧ **Miromar Outlets** (239-948-3766; www

.miromaroutlets.com), 10801 Corkscrew Rd. #199, at exit 123 off I-75, Estero. An above-average assortment of more than 140 factory shops, eateries, and designer outlets, including Bloomingdale's, Adidas, Nike, Reebok, Coach, and Talbots. Listen to live music on Saturday and Sunday in season, take the kids to Playland, or replenish (so you don't drop) at one of several restaurants.

Sanibel Outlets (239-454-1974; www .sanibeloutlets.com), 20350 Summerlin Rd., at McGregor Blvd., Fort Myers. Sitting at Sanibel's doorstep are more than forty-five outlets for Samsonite, Maidenform, Gap, Reebok, OshKosh, Polo Ralph Lauren, Bass Shoes, and other popular brands.

FLEA MARKETS **Fleamasters Fleamarket** (239-334-7001; www.fleamall.com), 4135 Dr. Martin Luther King Jr. Blvd., Fort Myers. Some four hundred thousand indoor square feet of produce, souvenirs, and novelties in more than nine hundred shops and eateries; open Friday to Sunday. An amphitheater hosts live country and doo-wop concerts and dances.

GALLERIES In season, hit Pine Island's Matlacha, a thriving artists' community, for Creative Coast weekends the second weekend of the month November through April. Besides gallery tours, visitors get entertainment, food, and Pine Island's special brand of fun. Fort Myers throws a monthly Art Walk the first Friday year-round.

Arts for ACT Gallery (239-337-5050; www.artsforactgallery.com), 2265 First St., Fort Myers. Local artists and traveling exhibits to benefit abused women. Prices range from one to four figures for original paintings, jewelry, pottery, painted furniture, artistic clothing, and more.

Crossed Palms Gallery (239-283-2283), 8315 Main St., Bokeelia, Pine Island. A delightful gallery facing the sea, it occupies two restored 1950s fishermen's cottages built around a cistern, which has become part of the gallery. Its rooms are filled with original fine art, glasswork, pottery, and jewelry by local and national artists. Closed summers.

Jungle Drums (239-395-2266; www .jungledrumsgallery.com), 11532 Andy Rosse Ln., Captiva Island. On the outside, dolphins and birds are carved into the stair rail and floor studs. Inside, local and national artists depict wildlife themes in various media, much of it whimsical, all of it delightfully creative.

Lovegrove Gallery & Gardens (239-282-1244; www.leomalovegrove.com), 4637 Pine Island Rd., Matlacha. Spend some time with the irrepressible, energetic Leoma Lovegrove, whose art has gotten her into the White House and beyond. Her colorful, lively art spans many media into the realm of performance art. She may be most famous for her Beatles art and painted coconuts, which has started a Florida trend.

Space 39 Gallery (239-690-0004; www.spacethirtynine.com), 39 Patio De León, Fort Myers. One of downtown's leading galleries for national traveling and permanent exhibitions, it is part bar, part gallery with live jazz music most nights.

Tower Gallery (239-472-4557; www .towergallery-sanibel.com), 751 Tarpon Bay Rd., Sanibel Island. In its charming Caribbean-motif old-beach-house digs, this cooperative specializes in fine tropical art by twenty-three area artists: masterful black-and-white photography by the late Charles McCullough, Sanibel scenes, pottery, and glass.

Unit A Studio (239-240-1053; www .unitaspace.com), 1922 Evans Ave., Fort Myers. One of America's most important artists, Marcus Jansen lives in Fort Myers and maintains a studio where he displays his work and hosts art exhibitions from around the world.

WildChild Gallery (239-283-6006; www.wildchildartgallery.com), 4625 Pine

LOVEGROVE GALLERY & GARDENS CREATES ITS OWN MICROCOSM OF FANTASY

Island Rd. NW, Matlacha. Part of Pine Island's quirky art scene, it has wares ranging from jewelry and pottery to original oils and sculptures by local artists. On weekends, you can sometimes find artists at work or demonstrating.

GENERAL STORES **Bailey's General Store** (239-472-1516; www.baileys -sanibel.com), 2477 Periwinkle Way, at Bailey's Shopping Center, Sanibel Island. An island fixture for ages, this stocks mostly hardware and fishing and kitchen supplies. It also has an attached grocery, bakery, coffee counter, and deli.

Island Store (239-472-2374; www .captivaislandstore.com), 11500 Andy Rosse Ln., Captiva Island. Here's where you can buy those necessities you forgot, including deli products and liquor. But try not to forget too much, because the prices reflect the location, here at the end of the earth. A seafood wagon pulls up to sell its wares most days.

GIFTS **Bubble Room Emporium** (239-472-5558; www.bubbleroomrestaurant .com), 15001 Captiva Dr., Captiva. Find some of the same zany buttons and hats that the Bubble Room servers wear (see "Where to Eat"), plus toys and baubles for you and your home.

✄ **Cheshire Cat Toys** (239-482-8697; www.cheshirecatfinetoyshop.com), 13499 S. Cleveland Ave., at Bell Tower Shops, Fort Myers. Playmobil sets, stuffed animals, puppets, fine dolls, books, arts and crafts, and learning toys.

Discovery Bay (239-463-4715), 7205 Estero Blvd., at Santini Marina Plaza, Fort Myers Beach. Whimsical, tasteful nautical and tropical gifts and home accessories.

Local Color (239-463-9199), 1021B Estero Blvd., at Times Square, Fort Myers Beach. This tiny shop packs in a little of everything—clothing, jewelry, tableware, toiletries, cards, and more—all with an artistic, mature flair.

Pandora's Box (239-472-6263), 2075 Periwinkle Way #1, at Periwinkle Place,

Sanibel Island. Delightful decorative items, creative jewelry, potpourri, specialty children's gifts, soaps, yard art, and the best selection of greeting cards on the island.

✄ **Sailor's Toy Shoppe** (239-312-8144), 1989 Periwinkle Way, at Tahitian Gardens, Sanibel. Beach toys, novelty items, comic books, party favors, and candy.

Sanibel Surf Shop (239-472-8185), 1700 Periwinkle Way, at Jerry's Shopping Center, Sanibel Island. Collections of T-shirts, beach toys and necessities, jewelry, and shells all under one roof, selling affordable mementos of the island.

A Swedish Affair (239-275-8004 or 888-867-9567; www.swedensfinest .com), 1400 Colonial Blvd., at Royal Palm Square, Fort Myers. Scandinavian gifts from funny to fine: amusing cards, old-fashioned toys, lingonberry preserves, folk art, candles, glassware, Christmas ornaments, and fine pewter serving pieces.

Toys Ahoy (239-472-4800), 2075 Periwinkle Way, at Periwinkle Place, Sanibel Island. Old-fashioned and learning-focused toys, puppets, books, stuffed toys, and more.

JEWELRY ✪ **Congress Jewelers** (239-472-4177; www.congressjewelers.com), 2075 Periwinkle Way #35, at Periwinkle Place, Sanibel Island. Dolphin, mermaid, bird, sandals, sand bucket, and shell pendants, plus other fine jewelry.

Enjewel Boutique (239-332-0293; enjewelboutique.com), 2266 First St., Fort Myers. Artistic sterling silver pieces, turquoise and glass jewelry, sparkly bags, ladies' clothing, and shoes.

Island Jewel (239-463-0500), 7205 Estero Blvd. #30, at Santini Marina Plaza, Fort Myers Beach. I like this shop for its interesting fused glass and other handmade, affordable pieces in addition to gold, handbags, and other gifts.

KITCHENWARE & HOME DÉCOR **Beach Pottery Etc.** (239-437-4211; www.fortmyersbeachpottery.com),

17980 San Carlos Blvd., Fort Myers Beach. You can't miss the colorful front yard at this cottagelike shop, filled with tiki carvings, pots, Mexican statues, metal sculptures, plants, and all manner of large home and yard décor.

Cargo Trading Co. (239-472-8111; cargosanibel.com), 2075 Periwinkle Way, at Periwinkle Place, Sanibel Island. Artisan crafts, whimsical gifts, and stylish beach- and nautical-themed home accents and décor.

Island Decor & More (239-283-8080), 4206 Pine Island Rd., Matlacha. Affordable decorative home art and accessories and other gifts with an islandy appeal.

Island Style (239-472-6657; www.islandstylegalleries.com), 2075 Periwinkle Way #6, at Periwinkle Place, Sanibel Island. Whimsical, artistic, and one-of-a-kind decorative elements with a Sun Belt motif: hand-painted chairs, carved wooden and glass mobiles and stabiles, brightly colored dishware, and Caribbean-inspired pieces.

Miromar Design Center (239-390-5111; www.miromardesigncenter.com), 10800 Corkscrew Rd., Suite 382, at I-75 across from Miromar Outlets, Estero. This ultrasophisticated facility gathers forty-five high-end furniture showrooms, flooring, kitchen designs, art galleries, and a bistro under one elegant roof. Guest speakers, seminars, and one complimentary hour of designer-on-call service.

Sand Castle Gifts & Gourmet (239-472-2201), 2075 Periwinkle Way #20, at Periwinkle Place, Sanibel Island. Fun and tropical place mats, towels, and dishware; also gourmet food items, including a selection of hot sauces and other cooking products.

Sanibel Home Furnishings (239-472-5552; www.sanibelhomefurnishings.com), 1618 Periwinkle Way, Sanibel. Sophisticated and tasteful island-style furnishings and decoration ideas.

Traders (239-395-3151), 1551 Periwinkle Way, Sanibel Island. This restaurant-and-store combo excels at both (see

"Where to Eat"). Warehouse size, the shop brims with objets d'art, candles, hats, scarves, and imported gifts.

Wilford & Lee (239-395-9295; www.wilfordandlee.com), 2009 Periwinkle Way, at Tahitian Gardens, Sanibel. Affordable (for Sanibel) and distinctive home decorations, including lamps, marine-life wall sculptures, and tableware.

SHELL SHOPS **Island Decor & More** (239-283-8080), 4206 Pine Island Road, Matlacha. The focus at this longtime shell shop has changed to home décor (see above), but it still carries an aisle of specimen shells. Bonus: a good location for spotting dolphins and manatees.

🦑 **Sanibel Seashell Industries** (239-472-1603; www.seashells.com), 905 Fitzhugh St., just off Periwinkle Way, Sanibel. Serious shell junkies and shell artisans should head here for the best specimens at the best prices. The same family has opened a smaller, more gifty shop in front of the warehouselike outlet at 1544 Periwinkle Way.

The Shell Factory (239-995-2141 or 800-282-5805; www.shellfactory.com), 2787 N. Tamiami Tr., North Fort Myers. A palace of Florida souvenirs, tacky to fine, The Shell Factory is built like a bazaar. In addition to shells, it sells jewelry, art, clothes, Christmas decorations, and knickknacks. More than 350 taxidermy animals from all over the world reside inside the Quonset hut that makes up the original core of the attraction. Also at the complex (can't miss it; look for the giant conch shell on the sign) are restaurants, an arcade, a kids' entertainment center, a dog park, and a nature park with wild animals and a petting zoo.

She Sells Seashells (239-472-6991; www.sanibelshellcrafts.com), 1157 Periwinkle Way, Sanibel; and (239-472-8080), 2422 Periwinkle Way, Sanibel. The island's oldest shell dealer has everything you need for shell crafts and displays.

✱ Special Events

January: Caloosahatchee Celtic Festival (239-321-7530; www .celticheritageproductions.com/ caloosahatchee.htm), Centennial Park, downtown Fort Myers. One day at the end of the month devoted to Irish and Scottish music, dance, and food. **Cape Coral Festival of the Arts** (239-699-7942; www.capecoralfestival.com), Cape Coral Pkwy., Cape Coral. This main thoroughfare closes down for a street festival the second weekend of the month.

February: ✿ ✍ **Edison Festival of Light** (239-334-2999; edisonfestival.org), Fort Myers. Commemorates the birthday of Thomas Edison and culminates in a spectacular lighted night parade. Two weeks early in the month.

March: ✍ **Fort Myers Beach Lions Club Shrimp Festival** (239-463-6986; www.fortmyersbeachshrimpfestival .com), Lynn Hall Memorial Park, Fort Myers Beach. Kids' run, 5K run, parade, and shrimp boil. One weekend mid-month. **Greek Fest** (239-481-2099; www .greekfestfortmyers.com), Greek Orthodox Church, 8210 Cypress Lake Dr., Fort Myers. Ethnic food and music. Three days early in the month. Admission. **Sanibel Music Festival** (239-344-7025; www .sanibelmusicfestival.org), Sanibel Island. Features concerts by classical artists from across the nation. Most events held at Sanibel Congregational Church, 2050 Periwinkle Way. Month-long. **Sanibel Shell Show and Festival** (239-472-2155; www.sanibelcommunityhouse.net), Sanibel Community House, 2173 Periwinkle Way, Sanibel Island. Showcases sea life, specimen shells, and shell art. Three days in early March. Admission fee for show. **Southwest Florida Reading Festival** (239-479-4636; www.readfest.org), Centennial Park, downtown Fort Myers. One day midmonth to celebrate literacy; features prominent authors and related activities.

April: **Earth Day at the Refuge** (239-472-1100; www.dingdarlingsociety.org), J. N. "Ding" Darling National Wildlife Refuge, 1 Wildlife Dr., Sanibel Island. Green giveaways, nature arts and crafts, lectures, and free admission to Wildlife Drive for cyclists and pedestrians.

May: **"Ding" Darling & Doc Ford's Tarpon Tournament** (239-292-0566; www .dingdarlingtarpontourney.com), Doc Ford's Rum Bar & Grille, Fort Myers Beach Weekend event early in the month.

July: ✿ **MangoMania Tropical Fruit Fair** (239-283-4842; mangomaniafl.net), German-American Social Club, 2101 SW Pine Island Road, Cape Coral. Celebrates Pine Island's favorite fruit with music and stands selling mangos, mango trees, mango drinks, mango cookies, and other local delicacies. Good, honest community fun. One weekend in mid-July. Admission.

September: **Island Hopper Songwriter Fest** (www.islandhopperfest.com) National songwriters perform at venues throughout the islands.

October: 🐾 ✍ **"Ding" Darling Days** (239-472-1100), J. N. "Ding" Darling National Wildlife Refuge, Sanibel Island. One week in mid-October is devoted to birding, exploring the refuge, and celebrating conservation art. ✍ **Haunted Walk and Friendly Forest** (239-275-3435; www.calusanature. org), Calusa Nature Center, 3450 Ortiz Ave., Fort Myers. Scary trail for the older kids and family-friendly trick-or-treating for the little ones around Halloween. **Oktoberfest** (239-283-1400; www.capecoraloktoberfest.com), German-American Social Club, Cape Coral. Cape Coral celebrates its strong German heritage with Oktoberfest music, food, and activities. Two weekends. Admission. ✍ **Pirate Festival** (239-454-7500; www.fortmyersbeach.org/piratefest), Old San Carlos Blvd., Fort Myers Beach. Treasure hunts, a walking pub-crawl, and pirate look-alike contests. A weekend early in the month.

November: **American Sandsculpting Championship** (239-454-7500; www.fmbsandsculpting.com), Wyndham Garden, Fort Myers Beach. This thirty-year-old tradition features amateur and masters divisions, entertainment, and workshops. One week in mid-November. ✑ **Cape Coral CoCoNut Festival** (239-573-3121; www.cocofest.com), Sun Splash Family Water Park, Cape Coral. Tropical food, live music, and a carnival. One weekend midmonth. Admission. **Captiva Holiday Village** (239-579-1462; www.captivaholidayvillage.com). A month-long celebration on Captiva Island that begins with tree lightings the day after Thanksgiving and carries on through the holidays with lighted boat and décorated golf cart parades, holiday strolls, and a Mullet Band Parade.

December: **Cape Coral Boat-a-Long** (239-573-3123; www.capecoral.net), Four Freedoms Park, Cape Coral. Decorated boat parade with live entertainment, Santa, Christmas crafts, food, and more. **Christmas Luminary Trail** (239-472-1080; www.sanibel-captiva.org), Sanibel and Captiva Islands. More than three miles of luminary candles line the main roads of Sanibel's and Captiva's commercial areas, where businesses stay open and dole out free drinks and food. One weekend early in the month. ✑ **Holiday Nights** (239-334-7419; www.edisonfordwinterestates.org), Edison & Ford Winter Estates, 2350 McGregor Blvd., Fort Myers. Period and seasonal exhibits and miles of light strings draw crowds to this popular monthlong attraction. Admission.

NAPLES &
THE SOUTH COAST

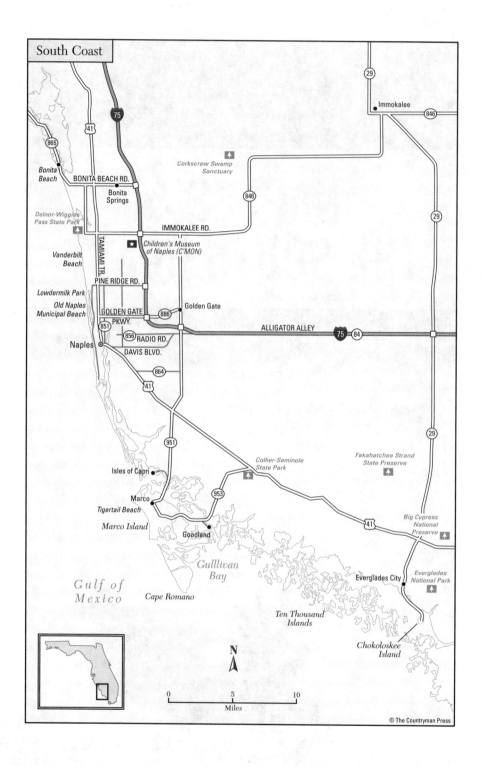

South Coast

NAPLES &
THE SOUTH COAST

Precious Commodities

erched on alabaster sands at the edge of Florida's Everglades, meticulous Naples transcends its wild setting like a diamond in the rough. Settled by land developers late in its life, this cultural oasis historically has appealed to the rich and the sporting. Today the state's final frontier is known for its million-dollar homes, superb golfing, art galleries, posh resorts, world-class shopping, and fine dining. In the spirit of its Italian namesake, Naples underwent a sort of renaissance in the 1990s that included a highly successful urban renewal project on Fifth Avenue South and various cultural venues, including Sugden Community Theatre, von Liebig Art Center, and the world-class Baker Museum of art. In 2012, a children's museum debuted, and in 2015, Naples Botanical Garden expanded its offerings with a gift shop and café.

In its northern reaches the city spreads into the quiet residential district of **North Naples**, seaside **Vanderbilt Beach**, and the town of **Bonita Springs**, and it continues to grow now eastward to **Immokalee** and the Catholic college community of **Ave Maria**.

Bonita Springs looks back on an early agricultural heritage, with a reputation for tomatoes, citrus, and other cash crops. Citrus freeze-outs farther north, plus the town's navigable Imperial River, created the community, first called Survey, in 1893. Here Henry Ford maintained a hunting lodge to which he and his Fort Myers friends, including Thomas Edison, traveled by horseback. Today, the tomato fields have morphed into upscale golfing communities, all surrounding a neighborly little town left frozen in time by dint of the Tamiami Trail's rerouting. These days, Bonita Springs starts to blend in with north Naples, both physically and in its character. New residential, hotel, and shopping developments boost it upward like an overachieving tomato vine climbing above its stake.

At the South Coast's southern and eastern extremes, the civility is balanced with swamp-buggy mud races, agriculture, Native American villages, fishing

THE CHILDREN'S GARDEN AT NAPLES BOTANICAL GARDEN

EVERGLADES CITY'S RIVERFRONT—FESTOONED WITH CRAB TRAPS, NETS, AND BUOYS—STILL REFLECTS ITS FISHING ROOTS

lodges, Florida panthers, and the unvarnished wilderness of the Everglades.

Neighboring **Marco Island** introduces the labyrinthine, mysterious land of Ten Thousand Islands. It was once an important center of the ancient Calusa culture, and the carved Key Marco Cat archaeological find (now exhibited at the Smithsonian) stands as an island icon. Tempered in a rough-and-tumble history, the island also boasts contemporary upscale resorts and good manners. Ancient Indian mounds, clam canneries, and pineapple plantations color the past of its three communities: **Isles of Capri, Marco,** and ✪ **Goodland.** First settled by the clan of William Collier (no relation to Barron Collier) in 1871, Marco Island has done most of its growing in modern times. Between 1960, when plans for a modern bridge were being formed, and 1980, the population increased by 755 percent. Goodland, so named because its land provided fertile soil for avocado farming, purposely kept itself behind the times—giddily stuck in a good-time, catch-fish mode—for most of its life. But these days signs of gradual upscaling appear on the laid-back horizon.

✪ **Everglades City**—the county seat until Naples took over—languishes in its wilderness setting at the doorstep to Big Cypress Swamp, Everglades National Park, and Ten Thousand Islands. Its settlers have always kept a step ahead of the law, doing what they must to survive, whether it was fishing, alligator poaching, or pot smuggling. Today, with a population of about four hundred, commercial fishing restrictions have channeled the town's orientation toward stone crabbing and tourism. Across a long, narrow causeway, **Chokoloskee Island** remains relatively untouched by change—a haven for RV campers and fishermen.

GETTING HERE The South Coast has two small airports. At **Naples Municipal Airport (APF)** (239-643-0733; www.flynaples.com; 160 Aviation Dr. N., Naples 34104), Elite Airways provides scheduled service from Newark. Private aircraft also land and depart from here. The terminal hosts the Museum of Military Memorabilia. **Marco Island Executive Airport (MKY)** (239-394-3355; www.colliergov.net; Collier County Airport Authority, 2005 Mainsail Dr. #1, Naples 34114) sees only private aircraft traffic. Most people arriving to the South Coast fly into **Southwest Florida International Airport (RSW)** (239-590-4800; www.flylcpa.com; 11000 Terminal Access Rd. #8671, Fort Myers 33913) via Air Berlin, Air Canada, American, Delta, Frontier, JetBlue, Silver, Southwest, Spirit, Sun Country, United, or WestJet. See pages 12–13 for rental car phone numbers and websites. Alamo, Avis, Budget, Dollar, National, and Thrifty have rental facilities at RSW. If traveling by bus, the **Greyhound Lines** (941-774-5660; www.greyhound.com) depot is located in Naples at 2669 Davis Blvd.

GETTING AROUND Call **Naples Transportation Shuttle** (239-262-7300; www.naples eventplanningandtours.com) for airport or other transportation needs. There's also **Checker Cab** (239-455-5555) or, on Marco Island, **Classic Transportation** (239-394-1888 or 800-553-8294; www.classicluxurytransportation.com).

Bonita Beach has the closest sands to I-75 in this area. US 41 distances itself from its modern counterpart to take you into downtown business districts and past upscale golfing communities. in Bonita Springs. Old US 41 branches off toward the town's business district. Bonita Beach Road (exit 116) crosses US 41 to travel to Bonita Beach. In Naples, US 41 (also known as Ninth Street) closes in on the sea once again as it travels through town. I-75 exit 111 (Immokalee Road/CR 846) gets you to the Vanderbilt Beach/North Naples area; exit 107 dumps into Pine Ridge Road, which leads to the north end of Naples. Exit 105 at Golden Gate Parkway (CR 886) gets you closest to downtown. I-75 then swings east, so that CR 951 at exit 101 distances you from downtown but is the fastest route to Marco Island.

Parallel to US 41 in Naples, major city dissectors include Goodlette-Frank Road (CR 851), Airport-Pulling Road (FL 31), and Livingston Road near the interstate. East–west trunks are, from north to south, Immokalee Road (CR 846) at the north edge of town, Pine Ridge Road (CR 896), Golden Gate Parkway (CR 886), Radio Road (CR 856), and Davis Boulevard (FL 84) in town; and Rattlesnake Hammock Road (CR 864) at the southeastern extreme.

CR 951 (interstate exit 101) will take you to the main high bridge at Marco Island's north end. CR 951 becomes Collier Boulevard and continues through the island's commercial section and along the gulf front. Bald Eagle Drive (CR 953) heads north–south to Olde Marco and mid-island. It connects to San Marco Drive (CR 92), which gives access to the community of Goodland then crosses the south bridge. The south-end bridge is a better access if you're approaching from the east along US 41. Turn southwest off US 41 onto CR 92 to cross the south bridge.

FL 29 takes you from US 41 and I-75 to Everglades City. Once in Everglades City, take a right onto Camellia Street to get to School Drive along the river, lined with old fishing boats, stacks of crab traps, and fish houses. Copeland Avenue crosses the causeway to Chokoloskee Island.

The **Naples Trolley** (239-262-7300; www.naplestrolleytours.com), 1010 Sixth Ave. S., Naples conducts two-hour narrated sightseeing tours in the Naples area, with twenty scheduled stops. Board and deboard at will. **Collier Area Transit (CAT)** (239-252-7777; www.colliergov.net) travels throughout Naples and Marco Island.

HOSPITALS & CLINICS **Marco Health Center** (239-624-8540; www.nchmd.org), 40 S. Heathwood Dr., Marco Island. Medical care and rehab on an outpatient basis.

Naples Downtown Hospital (239-624-5000; www.nchmd.org), 350 Seventh St. N., Naples. Heart and cancer institutes; emergency room open twenty-four hours.

North Naples Hospital (239-552-7000; www.nchmd.org), 11190 Health Park Blvd., off Immokalee Rd., Naples. Emergency room open twenty-four hours.

VISITOR INFORMATION **Bonita Springs Area Chamber of Commerce** (239-992-2943 or 800-226-2943; www.bonitaspringschamber.com), 25071 Chamber of Commerce Dr., Bonita Springs 34135.

Everglades Area Chamber of Commerce (239-695-3941 or 800-914-6355), 32016 Tamiami Trail, Everglades City 34139. Welcome center corner of US 41 and County Route 29 (CR 29).

Greater Naples Chamber of Commerce (239-262-6376; www.napleschamber.org), 2390 Tamiami Trail N., #201, Naples 34103.

Marco Island Area Chamber of Commerce (239-394-7549 or 800-330-1422; www .marcoislandchamber.org), 1102 N. Collier Blvd., Marco Island 34145.

Naples Marco Everglades Convention & Visitors Bureau (239-252-2384 or 800-688-3600; www.paradisecoast.com), 2660 Horseshoe Blvd., Naples 34104.

✳ To See

The affluent residents of Naples—many of them transplanted CEOs and captains of industry from lands to the north—share their county with impoverished migrants who work in Immokalee, the nearby agricultural center. The influences of Haitian, Puerto Rican, Jamaican, and other Caribbean cultures are finding their way into the mainstream, while flashes of Southern spirit and Cracker charm surface in Goodland, Everglades City, and Chokoloskee. North Naples is experiencing a burgeoning population of a younger demographic and families, thanks to its close proximity to Florida Gulf Coast University.

Miccosukee and Seminole inhabit reservations in the Everglades. They celebrate their culture each year at the Green Corn Ceremony during the first new moon in June. They also contribute the South Coast's only authentic, indigenous art: thatched chickee roof construction, colorful weaving, stitching, jewelry, dolls, basketware, and other age-old handicrafts.

Highbrow art has become a trademark of Naples and its long roll of galleries and performance spaces. For information on cultural events, contact the United Arts Council of Collier County at 239-254-8242 or visit www.collierarts.com.

ARCHITECTURE In Naples, commercial architecture is marked by style and panache, not to mention the architectural beauty of homes and resorts. Banks and insurance companies seem to compete for virtuosity. It's truly a land of visual allure. Pelican Bay developments provide examples of a new residential style and provide a contrast with old-money Port Royal.

Old Naples, that neighborhood in the vicinity of the pier and Fifth Avenue South, has held on to some real treasures, including the tabby-mortar **Palm Cottage**, the old **Mercantile**, and the **Old Naples building** at Broad Avenue and Third Street. In the same neighborhood, on **Gordon Drive**, pay attention to the charming board-and-batten Cracker survivors.

In **Everglades City** and **Chokoloskee Island**, recreational vehicles and cement-block boxes typify the fishing-oriented community's traditional style, though that is changing with a gradual trend toward gentrification. The **Rod & Gun Club**, built in 1850, stands out and dresses the town in Southern flair. The style of thatch housing, perfected by the Indians and known as chikee (pronounced *chi-KEY*), prevails in the Everglades and serves as a trendy beach-bar motif at the ritziest resorts throughout the coastal region.

CINEMA **Marco Movies** (239-642-1111; www.marcomovies.com), 599 S. Collier Blvd., at Marco Walk, Marco Island. Four screens with first-run movies, food, beer, and wine service.

Paragon Pavilion Cinema (239-596-0008; www.paragontheaters.com), 833 Vanderbilt Beach Rd., at Pavilion Shopping Center, Naples. Featuring reclining seats, reserved seating, beer and wine service, and a 3-D theater.

Regal Hollywood Cinema 20 Cinemas (239-597-4252), 6006 Hollywood Dr. at Pine Ridge Rd., Naples.

Silverspot at Mercato (239-592-0300; www.silverspot.net), 9118 Strada Pl. #8205, Tamiami Trail at Vanderbilt Rd., Naples. The first in a line of luxury cinemas, this theater opened in 2009 and features oversize leather seats, reserved seating, an elegant lounge, and above-typical theater food. Some of its eleven screens show indie films.

MUST SEE

⚛ **Naples Botanical Garden** (239-643-7275 or 877-433-1874; www.naplesgarden.org), 4820 Bayshore Dr., Naples. Open daily 9–5 (8–5 on Tuesdays). $13.95 adults, $9.95 children ages four to fourteen. Highlights of these beautifully designed 170 acres include a Children's Garden with a butterfly house, rolling hill, tree house, waterfall, Cracker house, and hidden garden; a Caribbean Garden with a traditional re-created chattel house; an amazing waterfall feature with giant lily pads in the Brazilian Garden; an orchid garden; and preserved natural wetlands with a birding tower. The Lea Asian Garden adheres to the property's mission to showcase the plants and culture of subtropical climates. "Gardens with Latitude" is its tagline. In addition to a 250-variety plumeria collection, a rice paddy, and typical Asian water elements and foliage, it incorporates a re-created fifteenth-century Hindu temple and other exotic shrines and structures. The Florida Garden takes an educational path with an enabling garden designed for physically impaired visitors, a section devoted to eco-gardening, a boardwalk and birding tower, and—my favorite—the Naples Garden Club's Idea Garden, where Southwest Florida gardeners can glean helpful knowledge to put to use at home. In 2015, a new gift and plant shop, video presentation, and Fogg Café opened.

GARDENS ⚛ **Naples Zoo at Caribbean Gardens** (239-262-5409; www.napleszoo .com), 1590 Goodlette-Frank Rd., Naples. Open daily 9–5 (last ticket sold at 4). $19.95 adults, $18.95 seniors, $14.95 children ages three to twelve. These tropical gardens, today the setting for a nicely proportioned zoo (see "Kids' Stuff"), were planted in 1919 by Dr. Henry Nehrling, a botanist who brought his private collection to Naples. After he died, Julius Fleischmann, a developer, restored and expanded the doctor's three thousand-plus specimens and opened the gardens to the public in 1954. Besides native vegetation, exotics such as magnificent creeping figs, birds of paradise, and monkey-puzzle, calabash, mango, and kapok trees flourish in wetlands and on hammocks.

⚛ **Palm Cottage's Norris Gardens** (239-261-8164; www.napleshistoricalsociety. org), 137 12th Ave. S., Naples. Open Tuesday to Saturday 1–4. $10 for garden and cottage tour; free for children ages ten and younger. The Norris Gardens, which opened in 2007, encircle a green oval lawn next to the historic Palm Cottage. Circular residential-scale theme gardens grow at the quadrangle's corners to reflect horticulture at the turn of last century. They include the Pioneer Garden, Edible Garden, Palm Garden, Water Garden, Garden of the Senses, and Shade Garden. A genuine Seminole pole-and-thatch chikee structure provides space for community programs at the gardens. Self-guided garden tours are included with the cost of admission to Palm Cottage. Docents conduct one-hour tours of the gardens; a self-guided tour of Palm Cottage is included.

HISTORIC HOMES & SITES **Indian Hill**, Indian Hill Dr. off Scott Dr., Goodland. Marco Island is rich in natural and historic heritage, but hides it well among twentieth-century trappings. Witness Indian Hill. On your own you'll have to search to find it, and when you do, you'll know it only by the way the road peaks, leaving you unable to see what's on the other side. Southwest Florida's highest elevation at fifty-eight feet above sea level, built up by ancient Calusa shell mounds, it now holds a ritzy neighborhood called the Heights, which feels the tiniest bit like San Francisco.

⚛ **Liles Hotel** (239-992-6997; www.bonitaspringshistoricalsociety.org), Riverside Park, 27300 Old 41, Bonita Springs. Open Monday to Friday 8–4. Free admission. Built in 1926, this is one of the town's oldest buildings. City workers occupy office space within, but visitors are welcome to peruse its historic exhibits, a bedroom decorated with 1930s furnishings, and two-story hallways. The Bonita Springs Historical Society maintains and changes the exhibits, which deal with everything from Indian mounds

A DRAMATIC WATER FEATURE IS CENTERPIECE OF THE BRAZILIAN GARDEN AT NAPLES BOTANICAL GARDEN

to homemade dolls. From January through April, docents are on hand to answer questions and interpret on Thursdays 1–3. Later in its life, the hotel became the Imperial River Court tourist camp, and the six historic fishing shacks next to it survive from that mid-twentieth century era. Part of Riverside Park's Historic Plaza, a lovely fountain and old water tower complete this flashback.

🦦 **Otter Mound Preserve** (239-252-2961; www.colliergov.net), 1831 Addison Ct., Marco Island. This Calusa archaeological site and its short interpretative trail along a

PREVIOUS OWNERS OF OTTER MOUND PRESERVE USED WHELK SHELLS LEFT OVER FROM CALUSA FEASTING TO CREATE EDGED TERRACES

mulch pathway tell the story of the Native Americans who once inhabited this area. The land's later owner, Ernest Otter, used the hundreds of whelk shells they left behind, evidence of their shellfish diet, to line terraces around the property starting in the 1940s.

Palm Cottage (239-261-8164; www.napleshistoricalsociety.org), 137 12th Ave. S., Naples. Open Tuesday to Saturday 1–4; $10 for garden and cottage tour; free for children ages ten and younger. Land was selling for $10 a lot in 1895 when Naples founder Walter N. Haldeman built a winter home for fellow worker Henry Watterson. Haldeman, publisher of the *Louisville Courier-Journal*, had discovered the exotic beaches and forests of Naples in 1887 and proceeded to buy up land and sing its praises. His enthusiasm persuaded winter escapees from Kentucky and Ohio, including Watterson, his star editor, to visit. The cottage Haldeman built for his friend was made of Florida pine, tidewater cypress, and a certain type of tabby mortar made by burning seashells over a buttonwood fire. It was one of the first permanent buildings in southwest Florida to be constructed of local materials and is Naples's oldest house. Before reaching its current museum status, the cottage—rather spartan by modern standards—knew many lives. If the walls could talk at Palm Cottage, as it eventually came to be known, they would tell of wild parties with the likes of Gary Cooper and Hedy Lamarr in attendance. A theater shows oral history films telling more stories about Naples. The renovated cottage is the headquarters of the Collier County Historical Society, which conducts guided tours. In the cottage's adjacent historic garden (see "Gardens"), visitors can view vegetation like early settlers used and planted. Every Wednesday from November to April, ninety-minute walking tours of Naples's historic district depart from Palm Cottage at 9:30 a.m. (arrive by 9:15, reservations and prepayment are required); cost is $16 per person. It includes an added thirty-minute tour of the cottage.

🏵 **Smallwood Store** (239-695-2989; smallwoodstore.com), 360 Mamie St., south of Everglades City, Chokoloskee Island. Open November 1–May 1, daily 10–5; May 2–October 31, daily 11–4. $5 adults, free for children under age twelve. A historic throwback to frontier days in the 'Glades, this museum preserves a Native American trading post of the early 1900s. Splintery shelves hold ointment containers, FlyDed insect killer, livestock spray, a sausage-making machine, Seminole cloth work, and hordes of memorabilia. Post office and bedroom vignettes recall life in the pioneer days and look pretty much the same as they did at that time. One of the best features is the view from the back porch. This was the site of a Jesse James–era murder immortalized in Peter Matthiessen's novel *Killing Mr. Watson*.

SCULPTURES AND AN AUTHENTIC SEMINOLE CHIKEE HUT ADD TO THE INTEREST OF THE GARDENS AT PALM COTTAGE

MUST SEE

✪ ✑ **Golisano Children's Museum of Naples (CMON)** (239-514-0084; www.cmon.org), North Collier Regional Park, 15000 Livingston Road, Naples. Open Tuesday to Saturday 10–5 (closed Wednesday), Sunday 11–4 p.m. Admission $10, free for children under age one. The museum opened in 2012 next to Sun-n-Fun Lagoon and was essentially designed by focus groups of kids and parents. The Naples Trolley is the centerpiece as you enter the thirty-thousand-square-foot hall of the colorful ship-shaped building. Inside the trolley, kids get their picture taken for a driver's license and punch buttons to go to some of the museum's twelve different galleries. A computerized graffiti wall, a touchable art exhibit, and hands-on painting and drawing heighten kids' interest in art. A mammoth, very real-looking banyan tree has its 350 branches filled with stuffed animals. Inside the tree, kids can step into a virtual pond and watch the fish flit away and water plants grow. The Journey through the Everglades exhibit's boardwalk winds up into the tree and overlooks a mangrove maze of twenty or so pods with hands-on learning experiences,. At the Beach, kids can fish with poles and magnetic bait, then measure the fish they caught. At the Farm & Market, conveyor belts take sorted fruits and vegetables to the grocery store next door, where the checkout person runs functioning machinery to ring up what customers have taken off the shelves. One exhibit teaches about seasons in other parts of the country and kids can rake leaves and climb into a chilly igloo. Different special areas engage tots (ages three and younger) and the age eight-to-fourteen set. In Backyardville, water play, a hedge maze, rolling hill, and chalkboard wall provide outdoor fun. Garden Café sells healthy drinks and snacks.

THE NEW CHILDREN'S MUSEUM OF NAPLES (CMON) ENGAGES KIDS' IMAGINATIONS AT THE DOORWAY

KIDS' STUFF ✑ **Naples Zoo** (239-262-5409; www.napleszoo.com), 1590 Goodlette-Frank Rd., Naples. Open daily 9–5 (last ticket sold at 4). $19.95 adults, $18.95 seniors, $14.95 children ages three to twelve. Primates, big cats, and other carnivores are specialties of this small, neighborhood zoo. Among its newest exhibits are a herd of giraffes you can hand-feed; Black Bear Hammock, the largest such accredited exhibit east of the Mississippi; fossas from Madagascar; a venomous snakes exhibit; a Florida panther exhibit; and Leopard Rock. Live animal presentations and feedings educate and advance a conservation mission. A boat ride takes a close-up look at the zoo's monkey and lemur population, which is sequestered on nine islands. Play areas amuse toddlers. Shaded, meandering, chirp-orchestrated paths take you past other fenced animals. The fifty-two-acre grounds are attractively maintained with the lush vegetation of the zoo's once-called Caribbean Gardens (see "Gardens"). To take in all the sights and shows requires about four hours.

A GIANT SLOTH SKELETON GREETS GUESTS AT COLLIER COUNTY MUSEUM

MUSEUMS ✪ 🐾 ✎ **Collier County Museum** (239-252-8476; www.colliermuseums .com), 3331 Tamiami Trail E., Naples. Open Monday to Friday 9–5, Saturday 9–4. Donations accepted. The unique aspects of this village of history include typical Seminole chikee huts, a vintage swamp buggy that kids can climb into, the skeleton of an Ice Age giant ground sloth, a working archaeological lab, a replicated Seminole war fort, and a 1910 steam locomotive from the county's cypress-logging era. State-of-the-art exhibits of prehistoric fossils, vignettes, and artifacts up to the 1960s include a video of a Gary Cooper movie filmed in the area. It also hosts changing exhibits.

Holocaust Museum of Southwest Florida (239-263-9200; www.holocaust museumswfl.org), 4760 Tamiami Trail N., #7, at Sandalwood Square, Naples. Open January to April Tuesday to Friday 12:30–5, Saturday to Sunday 1–4; May to December Tuesday to Sunday 1–4. Admission: $10 per adult, $5 children ages twelve to eighteen. This museum began as a student project, and today its photos, written materials, and artifacts take visitors chronologically through the Jewish experience from pre–World War II through post-Nazi liberation. One exhibit is devoted to local Holocaust survivors and their families. An authentic, two-ton, World War II–era railway boxcar sits in the parking lot for visitors to see, when it's not traveling as an educational outreach tool. The facility also hosts traveling exhibits related to war and the Holocaust. Opt for a one-hour audio tour or ninety-minute guided tour (1 and 2:30 Tuesday to Friday and 1:30 Saturday to Sunday in season, 1:30 in off-season).

KIDS CAN PLAY IN A RE-CREATED SEMINOLE WAR FORT AT COLLIER COUNTY MUSEUM

Marco Island Historical Museum (239-642-1440; www.colliermuseums.com), 180 S. Heathwood Dr., Marco Island. Open Tuesday to Saturday 9–4. Admission free. The experience begins when you leave behind your car and twenty-first century Marco Island for a time thousands of years ago when the Calusa built an important religious center on the island. The grounds of the museum represent a Calusa village built upon an elevation of shells, riddled with canals, and decorated with native vegetation and a thatched roof and pole structure modeled after Calusa buildings. The main museum building also imitates Calusa building style with thatch and tabby mortar. It displays an eight-by-four-foot exterior tile wall mural by local artist Paul Arsenault that depicts a Calusa shell-fishing expedition into the mangroves. The importance of Marco Island to Calusa civilization was established in 1896 by archaeologist Frank Hamilton Cushing in what has been called one of the most significant archaeological discoveries in North America. The most famous of his excavation finds was a 6-inch wooden effigy that's come to be known as the Key Marco Cat, an island icon. The original currently resides in the Smithsonian Institution, but museum planners hope to someday bring it and other Cushing discoveries back home. In the meantime, a supersize bronze Key Marco Cat replica presides over the courtyard. The inside devotes extensive exhibit space to Calusa culture. The Calusa and Their Legacy exhibit revolves around life-size vignettes exploring Calusa pottery-making, fishing, spirituality, and other lifestyle facets of the vanished tribe. Wood carved replicas and excavated pottery shards represent some of the finds Cushing found preserved in muck. The Modern Marco Room details in images the island's modern-day development. A Pioneer Room and outdoor "Windows & Doors to History" exhibit are scheduled to debut in late 2016. The museum also hosts traveling exhibits.

Museum of the Everglades (239-695-0008; www.colliermuseums.com), 105 W. Broadway, Everglades City. Open Monday through Saturday 9–4. $2 suggested donation. This facility occupies a renovated historic laundry started by developer Barron Collier to serve the community of road builders during the construction of the Tamiami Trail in the 1920s and exhibits some old-time laundry equipment. The museum explores the tremendous feat of blazing a trail through the swampy, buggy Everglades, the region's Calusa and Seminole and fishing heritage, pioneer life, and other aspects of local history. Take your pick of four excellent video documentaries to watch. It also hosts special changing exhibits.

Naples Depot Museum & Naples Lionel Train Museum (239-262-6525; www.colliermuseums.com for Depot Museum and for Lionel Train Museum, 239-262-1776; www.naplestrainmuseum.org), 1051 Fifth Ave. S., corner Tamiami Trail and 10th St. S., Naples. Depot museum open Monday to Friday 9–5, Saturday 9–4; Lionel open Tuesday to Saturday 10–2, May- August Saturday 10-2, closed September. Admission free for Depot Museum; $7 for adults, $4 for children six to fourteen for Lionel including train ride. Gary Cooper, Hedy Lamarr, and other illuminati of yore once arrived at this circa-1927 depot. The new museum has made great strides in recent years, focusing on the history of the railroad and transportation in the region—from dugout canoes to mule wagons to swamp buggies. A highlight of the exhibits is the movie that plays every seven minutes in the museum's windows, giving visitors the virtual experience of watching the circa 1927 Orange Blossom Special train pulling into the station. Two historic, tourable rail cars—a caboose and a lounge car—sit alongside the depot. Lionel has set up an elaborate display of eight operating model trains, including Thomas the Tank, which circulate through a model town. It also operates a scale train outside for kiddie rides.

MUSIC & NIGHTLIFE ✪ **7th Avenue Social** (239-231-4553; www.7thavenue social.com), 839 Seventh Ave. S., Naples. Downtown Naples' newest hot spot, with late-night hours, live music, craft cocktails, and craftier food.

✪ **The Continental** (239-659-0007; damicoscontinental.com), 1205 Third St. S., Naples. A classy late-night spot for craft cocktails, live music, food, and dancing. Also known for its fine steaks and seafood for lunch and dinner.

Little Bar (239-394-5663; www.little barrestaurant.com), 205 Harbor Dr., Goodland. Hosts live music weekend and some weekday nights. Site of the annual summertime Spammy Jammy, where partici-

CAMBIER PARK BRINGS GREEN SPACE TO DOWNTOWN NAPLES

pants in pajamas bring their crazy Spam sculptures and creations.

Naples Concert Band (239-263-9521; www.naplesconcertband.org), P.O. Box 31, Naples 34106. For some forty-five years this band's ninety volunteer musicians have been performing free Sunday concerts once a month, October through April, at Cambier Park in Old Naples.

Off the Hook Comedy Club (239-389-6901; www.offthehookcomedy.com), 2500 Vanderbilt Beach Rd. #1100, Naples. Transplanted from the longtime Marco Island operation by the same name, it brings national acts to North Naples. Row restaurant makes it a dinner-and-a-show experience.

Snook Inn (239-394-3313; snookinn.com), 1215 Bald Eagle Dr., Marco Island. Live local bands play contemporary and island music in the open-air, waterfront chikee bar.

Southwest Florida Performing Arts Center (239-389-6901; www.swflpac.com), 11515 Bonita Beach Rd. SE #101, Bonita Springs. Opened in summer 2016 by the Off the Hook Comedy Club team, this entertainment complex includes a restaurant and stage for major acts including comedians, tribute bands, and musical groups. It also offers classes for kids and adults in art and music.

Stan's Idle Hour (239-394-3041; www.stansidlehour.net), 221 Goodland Dr. W., Goodland. Live music, often of a comical nature, happens throughout most days. Sunday celebrations are packed with drinkers and dancers doing the trademark Buzzard Lope. The upstairs Gator Bait is a sports bar.

Weekend Willie's (239-597-3333; weekendwillies.com), 5310 Shirley St., Naples. A neighborhood, working class bar with live music and karaoke, sports TVs, and a full food menu.

THEATER **Gulfshore Playhouse** (239-261-7529 or 866-811-4111; www.gulfshore playhouse.org), Norris Center Theater, 755 Eighth Ave. S., Naples. Naples's newest professional company performs October through May.

Gulfshore Opera (239-529-3925; www.gulfshoreopera.org, 3281 Golden Gate Blvd. W., Naples. Committed to regional engagement, it tours its productions in Charlotte (Punta Gorda), Lee (Fort Myers), and Collier (Naples) counties, with special programs and shows for children.

Marco Players (239-642-7270; www.themarcoplayers.com), 1055 N. Collier Blvd., at Marco Town Center Mall, Marco Island. Nonprofit community theater that produces comedies and musicals November through April.

Opera Naples (239-963-9050; www.operanaples.org), 2408 Linwood Ave., Naples. Four annual presentations at the Wang Opera Center, late December through March.

✪ **Artis–Naples** (239-597-1900 or 800-597-1900; artisnaples.org), 5833 Pelican Bay Blvd., Naples. Formerly the Philharmonic Center for the Arts, it is home to the eighty-five-piece Naples Philharmonic and the Miami City Ballet (miamicityballet.org). It hosts audiences of up to 1,425 for Broadway shows, touring orchestras, opera, comedians, modern dance, and more than four hundred events yearly. It also has a two-hundred-seat black-box theater and four art galleries, plus the adjacent Baker Museum (see "Visual Art Centers").

Sugden Community Theatre (239-263-7990), 701 Fifth Ave. S., Naples. The home of the Naples Players (www.naplesplayers.org), a community theater troupe that has been entertaining October through May for more than fifty years. The complex features a main stage, plus a more experimental black-box theater, and plays host to the Naples Jazz Society, ballet, opera, and other performance art. Every Sunday to Tuesday at 6 p.m., a local band gathers outside for a twenty-minute "Naples Patriotic Moment" featuring the national anthem and "Taps" in honor of those serving in the military.

TheatreZone (888-966-3352; www.theatrezone-florida.com), G&L Theatre at Community School of Naples, 13275 Livingston Rd., Naples. Dramas, comedies, and musical revues late November through mid-May.

VISUAL ART CENTERS & RESOURCES Like its Italian namesake, Naples serves as the region's aesthetic pacesetter. Gallery-lined streets host artists of local, national, and international stature. The following entries introduce you to opportunities for experiencing art as either a viewer or a practicing artist. A listing for commercial galleries is included in the "Shopping" section.

A MODERN SCULPTURE MARKS THE ENTRYWAY TO ARTIS–NAPLES

MUST SEE

✪ **The Baker Museum** (239-597-1900 or 800-597-1900; artis-naples.org), Artis–Naples, 5833 Pelican Bay Blvd., Naples. Open Tuesday to Saturday 10–4, Sunday noon–4; closed Monday and the month of August. Complimentary guided tours available in season at 11 and 2 Tuesday to Saturday and 1 on Sunday. $10 adults, $5 students free for youth under age eighteen. Permanent exhibits include a collection of modern American masters from 1900 to 1955, including Alexander Calder, Jackson Pollock, and Hugh Breckenridge. World-renowned glass sculptor Dale Chihuly created one of his famous Persian Ceilings and two magnificent chandeliers for the museum: one that hangs in the performance hall building and another suspended in a three-story stairwell. The museum also displays on a rotating basis two monumental sculptures by Louise Nevelson. The museum's fifteen galleries elegantly showcase world-class traveling exhibitions.

Centers for the Arts Bonita Springs (239-495-8989; www.artcenterbonita.org), Visual Arts Campus: 26100 Old 41 Rd., Bonita Springs; performing arts campus: 10150 Bonita Beach Rd., Bonita Springs. The Visual Arts Campus comprises an impressive ten-acre complex of galleries, a gift shop with art supplies and works, and photography, pottery, sculpture, and other studios that host classes, children's programs, lectures, dance performances, and exhibitions. Opened in 2014, the Performing Arts Campus consists of two buildings, one devoted to film. The other hosts improv, music, dance, and theater.

Art League of Marco Island (239-394-4221; marcoislandart.org), 1010 Winterberry Dr., Marco Island. Workshops, lectures, two galleries with monthly changing exhibits, and a gift shop. The league also sponsors an annual arts and crafts festival in January and other cultural events.

United Arts Council (239-263-8242; www.uaccollier.com), 2335 Tamiami Trail N., Suite 504, Naples. A central clearinghouse for culture, music, dance, theater, and visual arts in the Naples area.

✪ 🖼 **The von Liebig Art Center** (239-262-6517; www.naplesart.org), 585 Park St., Naples. Home of the Naples Art Association, the center holds classes, workshops, and showings for children and its members, and presents other special exhibitions. The library, which features a skylight, contains arts information.

✳ To Do

The Ten Thousand Islands are the meat of the South Coast's recreational banquet. Here, the old-fashioned sports—fishing, paddling, hiking—are most in style. The beaches of Naples and Marco Island serve up the newer, exhilarating side dishes, everything from parasailing to Jet Skiing.

BEACHES Naples beaches have been winning awards for their beauty for ages. In 2015, two of its beaches made the Dr. Beach top ten US beaches list.

Parking fees are levied at most beaches; county residents can purchase stickers that allow them to park for free. For information on county beaches, contact Collier County Parks and Recreation Department (239-252-4000; www.collierparks.com), 15000 Livingston Rd., Naples 34109.

🏖 **Clam Pass Park** (239-252-4000; www.collierparks.com), 410 Seagate Dr., at the Naples Grande Beach Resort, Naples. This beach, used by guests of the Naples Grande Beach Resort but open to the public, is reached by a tram that follows a nearly mile-long boardwalk over a tidal bay and through mangroves. Boat and cabana rentals are available

SEASIDE SERENITY AT CLAM PASS PARK

at this county facility. The sand is fine and fluffy and, once past the resort crowd, leads to preserve lands to the south and a pass to the north. You can kayak or sail into the sea or paddle along a trail among the mangroves, which are frequented by ospreys, hawks, and a variety of other feathered creatures. Facilities: restrooms, showers, food and beach concessions. Parking: $8 per day.

✪ ✎ **Lowdermilk Park** (239-213-7120; www.naplesgov.com), 1301 Gulf Shore Blvd., Naples. Beach headquarters for the South Coast: There are lots of special activities at this gulfside spot and its thousand feet of sandy beach. Families love its little duck pond, and tiki umbrellas provide shaded picnicking on the beach. Facilities: picnic area, restrooms, showers, volleyball, playground, concessions, special handicapped access, wheeled surf chairs. Parking: metered, twenty-five cents per six minutes, $2.50 per hour.

Naples Municipal Beaches, Gulf Shore Blvd. south of Doctors Pass, Naples. The historic pier on 12th Avenue South, where facilities and a parking lot are located, anchors stretches of natural beach. Smaller lots lie to the north and south. Facilities: restrooms, showers, concessions, fishing pier. Parking: metered, twenty-five cents per ten minutes, $1.50 per hour.

South Marco Beach (239-252-4000; www.collierparks.com), S. Collier Blvd. at Swallow Ave., south end of Marco Island. Parking is on the east side of Collier Blvd., half a block away. A paved brick path beneath palm trees leads to this patch of public beach between giant high rises. No facilities, but there's a restaurant next door. Parking: $8 per vehicle. The lot fills early in season. Another lot to the north called Turtle Lot ($9) is a short walking distance from a different public access path to the beach.

✎ **Sugden Regional Park** (239-252-4000; www.collierparks.com), 4284 Avalon Dr., Naples. On the east side of town, it is most famous for sailing in its freshwater lake. A sand beach edges it on the side opposite bleacher stands, and here you can rent a

MUST SEE

🏖 **Delnor-Wiggins Pass State Park** (239-597-6196; www .floridastateparks.org/park/Delnor-Wiggin), 11135 Gulf Shore Dr. N., at CR 846, Vanderbilt Beach, Naples. This highly natural, low-key beach, named among America's Forty Certified Healthy Beaches and a 2015 placer in Dr. Beach's top ten beaches in the US (#9), extends for a mile south from the mouth of the Cocohatchee River. The lush white sands are protected during loggerhead turtle nesting season (summer) and support stands of natural maritime vegetation, such as cactus, sea grape, nickerbean, and yucca. A nature trail leads to an observation tower at the beach's north end. This is a popular park, but you can usually find parking in one of the many lots if you arrive early enough. (There's extra parking about a half-mile away.) Restrict your swimming to south of the pass's fast-moving waters, which are a boon to fishermen. Facilities: picnic areas, grills, pavilion, restrooms, showers, boat ramp, volleyball, lifeguard. Admission: $6 per car, up to eight passengers; $4 per single-occupant vehicle; $2 per pedestrian, cyclist, or extra passenger.

DELNOR-WIGGINS PASS STATE PARK: A HAVEN FOR BIRDS, BEACHERS, SHELLERS, SEA TURTLES, AND FISHERMEN ALIKE

canoe, paddle boat or sailboat; or swim in a guarded, roped-off area. A biking/walking path loops the lake, plus there are cool playgrounds, picnic areas, and a fishing pier. Water-skiing and sailing lessons are available. Parking is free.

🏖 **Tigertail Beach** (239-252-4000; www.collierparks.com), 430 Hernando Dr., north end of Marco Island. This county-owned beach is a good place for shelling and sunning. In season, arrive early to find a parking spot. Wooden ramps cross dunes to thirty-one acres of wide, marvelous beach. The south end fronts high rises, but the north end stretches into wilderness. The fun playground is divided for two different age groups. Tidal pools separate the main beach and a fronting sandbar known as Sand Dollar Spit, which attracts shellers, kayakers, and feeding and nesting birds. (You can walk to it from the beach's south end.) In 2016, the park got a new observation tower. Facilities: picnic area, restrooms, showers, water-sports rentals, restaurant, playground, volleyball. Parking: $8.

Vanderbilt Beach Park (239-252-4000; www.collierparks.com), 280 Vanderbilt Dr., north of Naples, Vanderbilt Beach. This stretch of sand runs alongside resorts and is well suited to those who like sharing the beach with a lot of people and enjoy bar- and restaurant-hopping along the beach. Facilities: restrooms, showers; water-sports rentals available at nearby resorts. Parking: $8 per vehicle at nearby parking ramp on Vanderbilt Dr.; metered on the street.

BICYCLING City and country biking paths are available to those who prefer this slow, intimate mode of exploration. Sidewalks, bike paths (marked with white diamonds), and roadsides accommodate cyclists. By state law, cyclists must conduct themselves as pedestrians when using sidewalks. Avoid cycling on crowded downtown walks. Where they share the road with other vehicles, cyclists must follow all the rules of the road. Children under age sixteen must wear helmets.

Best Biking: Naples has laid out a sporadic system of metropolitan bike paths. A favorite route of local cyclists loops through ten miles of pathway in the north-end Pelican Bay development. Within it, a 580-acre nature preserve provides a change of scenery from upscale suburbia.

A bike path runs the length of **Bonita Beach,** nearly three miles long. At its south end it connects to another, which leads to **Vanderbilt Beach.**

Naples Bicycle Tours (239-825-6344 or 800-979-3370; www.naplesbicycletours. com) conducts two- to three-hour excursions, with transportation, in Naples and the Everglades.

Marco Island's bike paths parallel main drives such as Collier Boulevard and Barfield Drive.

Skinny bike paths traverse **Everglades City** and cross the causeway to **Chokoloskee Island.** Back-road bikers take to the twelve-mile (one-way) ✪ **W. J. Janes Memorial Scenic Drive** through Fakahatchee Strand Preserve State Park, off CR 29 north of Everglades City. Royal palms, cypress trees, and air plants provide pristine scenery and bird habitat (ten miles in you'll find a popular bird-feeding pond). Morning or sunset riders may spot wild turkeys, alligators, raccoons, snakes, otters, bobcats, and deer. Rangers at **Everglades National Park** (239-695-3311; www.nps.gov/ever) lead two-hour bike tours every Thursday in season (mid-December–Easter). A 3.5-mile mountain bike trail at ✪ **Collier-Seminole State Park** travels through a cabbage palm hammock.

Rentals/Sales: Many resorts rent bikes or provide bike use to guests.

Bonita Bike Rental (239-947-6377; www.bonitabikeandbaby.com). It delivers a variety of bikes, including kids' bikes, and trailers for kids.

Island Bike Shop (239-394-8400; www.islandbikeshops.com), 1095 Bald Eagle Dr., Marco Island. Rents scooters and bikes in various sizes and styles; also offers bike tours. Rates by the hour, day, week, and month. Delivery available.

Naples Cyclery (239-566-0600; www.naplescyclery.com), 813 Vanderbilt Beach Rd., at Pavilion Shopping Center, Naples. Rents a wide variety of speed bikes, surreys, and equipment for kids.

BOATS & BOATING Naples, Marco Island, and Everglades City are lousy with marinas. These are headquarters for boat rentals, tours, and charters to serve every interest, from shelling and fishing to gaping at mansions.

Paddlesports: The ultimate paddling experience, Everglades National Park has marked a ninety-nine-mile ✪ **Everglades Wilderness Waterway** (www.everglades -wilderness-waterway.com) trail that extends from Everglades City to Flamingo, the park's main eastern access. Platform campsites accommodate overnighters. There are also good canoeing trails near the Oasis Visitors Center in ✪ **Big Cypress National Preserve.** Outfitters in Everglades City provide rentals, supplies, tours, and shuttle service. In addition to the following outlets, many resorts and parks rent canoes and kayaks.

Collier County is working on developing the ✪ **Paradise Coast Blueway** (www .paradisecoastblueway.com), a system of paddling trails throughout the county that provide GPS-marked trail routes. Phase I, the Ten Thousand Islands section, was completed in 2009. Seventy-three miles long, it includes one long trail from Everglades

City to Goodland and six shorter day-trip trails. Phase II will extend to north Naples and Bonita Springs.

✪ **Collier-Seminole State Park** (239-394-3397; www.floridastateparks.org/park/Collier-Seminole), 20200 E. Tamiami Trail, between Naples and Everglades City. Rents canoes for use on the park's 13.6-mile canoe trail into mangrove wilderness preserve. Guided tours available some Sundays in season by reservation.

Conservancy of Southwest Florida Nature Center (239-262-0304; www.conservancy.org), 1495 Smith Preserve Way, Naples. Kayaks are available to rent for use in the Gordon River.

Everglades Area Tours (239-695-3633 or 800-860-1472; www.evergladesareatours.com), 238 Mamie St., Chokoloskee Island. Knowledgeable naturalists take you on paddling adventures deep into the Everglades by transporting you and your kayak via a "mother" powerboat. Some excursions involve camping, fishing, biking, hiking, and photography.

✐ **Everglades National Park** (239-695-3311; www. evergladesnationalparkboat-toursgulfcoast.com), Gulf Coast Visitor Center, 815 Oyster Bar Ln., Everglades City. Free ranger-led two- and four-hour canoe trips in season (mid-December–Easter). Times vary. Canoe use is included. Rentals and launch also available for self-guided tours (239-695-2591).

Everglades Adventures (239-695-3299 or 877-567-0679; www.evergladesadventures.com), 107 Camellia St., Everglades City. Rents seventeen-foot aluminum canoes, high-quality touring and fishing kayaks, and equipment with complete outfitting and shuttle service. Guided excursions into the Everglades are typically four hours.

Naples Kayak Company (239-262-6149; www.napleskayakcompany.com), 2360 Shadowlawn Dr., Naples;. Kayak and stand-up paddleboarding rentals, instruction, nature tours, and sales from several locations throughout Collier County. Delivery and pickup available to some areas.

Florida Excursions (239-592-1200; cruisefishdive.com), 28651 N. Diesel Dr., Bonita Springs. Rents kayaks, canoes, and stand-up paddleboards fat various drop-off points in Naples and Marco Island.

Old Naples Surf Shop (239-262-1877; www.oldnaplessurfshop.com), 1311 Third St. S., Naples. Rents stand-up paddleboards and offers lessons and eco-tours. Delivery included. Also rents surfboards and skim boards.

Paddlecraft Park (239-530- 5940; www.rookerybay.org), Collier Blvd., Isles of Capri. A new launch into bay waters, with a freshwater rinse station, picnic pavilions, and restrooms. Launch fee.

✐ **Rookery Bay National Estuarine Research Reserve** (239-530-5940; www.rookerybay.org), 300 Tower Rd., Naples. Naturalist-led kayak tours of the mangroves in Henderson Creek and Rookery Bay weekly November through May for ages twelve and older. Fee includes admission into the Rookery Bay Environmental Learning Center (see "Nature Preserves & Eco-Attractions").

Dining Cruises: Marco Island Princess (239-642-5415; www.themarcoislandprincess.com), 951 Bald Eagle Dr., at Rose Marco River Marina, Marco Island. Daily narrated lunch cruises, and sunset dinner excursions. Two full-service bars on board.

Naples Princess (239-649-2275; www.naplesprincesscruises.com), Port O Call Marina, 550 Port O Call Way, on US 41 across the river from Tin City, Naples. Excursions include a sightseeing cruise, buffet lunch, sunset sight-seeing or hors d'oeuvres, and sunset buffet dinner. Full-service cash bar.

Personal Watercraft Rentals/Tours: **Marco Island Ski & Water Sports** (239-642-2359; www.marcoislandwatersports.com), 400 S. Collier Blvd., at the JW Marriott

Marco Island Beach Resort, Marco Island. Rents WaveRunners and conducts Wave-Runner excursions into Ten Thousand Islands. Also parasailing.

Powerboat Rentals: **Pure Naples** (239-263-4949; www.cruisenaplesflorida.com), 1200 Fifth Ave. S., at Tin City, Naples. Deck boats with Bimini tops, plus Jet Ski rentals and tours.

Big Hickory Fishing Nook Marina (239-992-3945), 26107 Hickory Blvd., Bonita Beach. Rents pontoon boats, kayaks, and stand-up paddleboards for two, four, or eight hours.

Port of Naples Marina (239-774-0479; www.portofnaplesmarina.com), Port O Call Marina, 550 Port O Call Way, off US 41 E., Naples. Rents deck boats and pontoons to accommodate up to ten people.

Rose Marina (239-394-2502; www.rosemarina.com), 951 Bald Eagle Dr., Marco Island. Pontoon, deck, offshore, and center console boats from half- to multiple-day rentals.

Public Boat Ramps: **Caxambas Park** (239-642-0004; www.collierparks.com), 909 Collier Ct., Marco Island. Restrooms, bait, fuel, and access to Roberts Bay. Launch fee.

Cocohatchee River Park (239-513-7919; www.collierparks.com), 13531 Vanderbilt Dr., at Vanderbilt Beach, Naples. Park with three ramps onto the river (which runs to the gulf), restrooms, picnic tables, and boat rentals. Launch fee.

Collier Boulevard Boating Park (239-352-4000; www.colliergov.net). One mile before the Marco Island north bridge on CR 951. It keeps busy in season.

Delnor-Wiggins Pass State Park (239-597-6196; www.floridastateparks.org/park/Delnor-Wiggins), 11135 Gulf Shore Dr. N., Naples. The boat ramp allows access to the back bays, the Cocohatchee River, and the Gulf of Mexico, providing visitors with excellent fishing opportunities. Admission.

Naples Landing (239-213-7120; www.naplesgov.com), 1101 Ninth St. S., Naples. One ramp with playground and metered parking.

Sailboat Charters: **Serenidad Sailing Charters** (239-272-0939; www.svserenidad.com), Rose Marco River Marina, 951 Bald Eagle Dr., Marco Island. Daytime three-hour sightseeing and sunset sails aboard a forty-one-foot Beneteau yacht.

Sweet Liberty (239-793-3525; www.sweetliberty.com), 880 12th Ave. S., at the City Dock, Naples. Daily shelling/beach, sight-seeing and dolphin-spotting, and sunset sailing trips aboard a fifty-three-foot, forty-four-passenger catamaran.

Sight-Seeing & Entertainment Cruises: Look under "Wildlife Tours & Charters" for nature excursions.

Black Pearl Pirate Excursions (239-404-5422; www.piratesofmarco.com), 951 Bald Eagle Dr., at Rose Marina, Marco Island. Great for the family, the ninety-minute sunset cruise has them talking, singing, and dancing like a pirate. Includes face painting and dress up before departure, plus games and DJ entertainment along the way.

Speedy's Airboat Tours (239-695-4448 or 800-998-4448; speedysairboattours.com), 621 Begonia St., Everglades City. You'll find any number of airboat tour operators in and around Everglades City. Many, contrary to good environmental practice, feed wildlife to attract it to the boat. This one is better than others for its accessibility to grasslands and its elevated seats.

Waterskiing: **Waterski & Wakeboard Charters** (239-825-7015; www.waterskimarcoisland.com), 951 Bald Eagle Dr., Marco Island. Pulls and equipment rentals for waterskiing, wakeboarding, tubing, and barefooting. Instruction available.

FISHING Many visiting sports folk arrive at the South Coast eager to fight the big fish and brave the deep waters of the Gulf of Mexico. They come equipped with their fifty-pound test line, heavy tackle, and tall fish tales. Yet closer to home, in the back bays and shallow waters of Ten Thousand Islands, experienced fishermen find what's best about the region. Sea trout, snook, redfish, sheepshead, mangrove snapper, and pompano abound in the brackish creeks, grass flats, and channels.

Nonresidents age sixteen and older must obtain a license unless fishing from a vessel or pier covered by its own license. You can buy inexpensive, temporary, nonresident licenses at county tax collectors' offices and most Kmarts and bait shops. Check local regulations for season, size, and catch restrictions.

Fishing Charters/Outfitters: Check the large marinas for fishing guides. Experienced guides can take the intimidation and guesswork out of open-water fishing.

Pure Naples (239-263-4949; www.cruisenaplesflorida.com), 1200 Fifth Ave. S., at Tin City, Naples. Fishing boats available for deep-sea, backwater, sunset, party boat, and family fishing excursions plus private charters.

SNOOK: A PRIZED CATCH ON THE NAPLES PIER

Chokoloskee Island Outfitters (239-695-2286 or 239-695-0141; www.cyberangler.com/guides/prickett), P.O. Box 460, Chokoloskee Island, 34138. Captain Dave Prickett takes up to three passengers out into the Everglades for half- and full days.

Hickory Bay Charters (239-947-3851), 26107 Hickory Blvd., at Big Hickory Fishing Nook Marina, Bonita Springs. Board the *Ramble On III*, a thirty-foot pontoon, for four-hour fishing trips into the backcountry for up to six people. Can combine fishing excursions with sight-seeing, birding, and shelling.

Mangrove Outfitters (239-793-3370 or 888-319-9848; www.mangroveoutfitters.com), 4111 E. Tamiami Trail, Naples. Guide charters and classes on fly-tying.

Peg-Leg Charters (239-642-4333 or 239-250-0625; www.peglegcharters.com), 229 Harbor Pl. N. at Stan's Idle Hour Restaurant, Goodland. Captain Ron Kennedy takes anglers offshore for half- and full-day trips.

Sunshine Tours (239-642-5415; www.sunshinetoursmarcoisland.com), 951 Bald Eagle Dr., at Rose Marco River Marina, Marco Island. Takes small parties aboard a thirty-two-foot boat with head for offshore excursions, half- to full day. Also does backcountry fishing or shelling trips.

Fishing Piers: ✪ **Naples Pier** (239-213-7120; www.naplesgov.com), 25 12th Ave. S., Naples. The historic structure, first built in 1888, extends one thousand feet into the gulf and has a bait shop, snack bar, restrooms, and showers. It has been rebuilt three times due to hurricane damage and was newly renovated in 2016.

GOLF Naples earns its title as Golf Capital with more golf holes per capita than any other statistically tracked metropolitan area.

Public Golf Courses: ⛳ **Bonita Fairways Country Club** (239-947-9100; www.bonitafairways.com), 9751 W. Terry St., Bonita Springs. Play eighteen holes at a reasonable price. Restaurant.

Lely Resort Flamingo Island Club (239-793-2223 or 866-392-2100; www.lelyresort golfandcountryclub.com), 8004 Lely Resort Blvd., off CR 951 east of Naples. Two public courses designed by Robert Trent Jones Sr. and Lee Trevino. Offers thirty-six holes, par seventy-two.

The Links of Naples (239-417-1313; www.linksofnaples.com), 16161 E. Tamiami Trail, Naples. Lit 18-hole course with driving range, PGA lessons, rentals.

Naples Beach Hotel Golf Club (239-435-2475; www.naplesbeachhotel.com), 851 Gulf Shore Blvd. N., Naples. Naples's oldest, the eighteen-hole, par-seventy-one resort course hosts pro and amateur tournaments. The course was redesigned in 2016 in collaboration with Jack Nicklaus, who played the course as a child. Restaurant and lounge.

Tiburón Golf Club (239-593-2200; www.tiburongcnaples.com), 2620 Tiburón Dr., at the Ritz-Carlton Golf Resort, Naples. One of Naples's most exclusive golfing venues; semiprivate with two eighteen-hole courses—the Black and the Gold—and a golf academy.

Golf Instruction: **David Leadbetter Golf Academy** (239-592-1444 or 888-633-5323 [Orlando Headquarters]; davidleadbetter.com/academy/naples/), at LaPlaya Beach & Golf Resort, 333 Palm River Blvd., Naples. Offers golf school at LaPlaya Golf Course. Lessons, classes, and golf retreats can last anywhere from one hour to three days.

HEALTH & FITNESS CLUBS The following offer daily or weekly rates for visitors.

Golden Gate Fitness Center (239-252-6128; www.collierparks.com), at Golden Gate Community Park, 3300 Santa Barbara Blvd., Naples. Full range of Cybex and Keiser equipment, cardio machines, and free weights. Personal training and assessment available.

✔ **Greater Marco YMCA** (239-394-3144; www.marcoislandymca.org), 101 Sandhill St., Marco Island. Full-service gym with personal training and fitness assessment programs, swimming lessons, massage, tennis, and a wide variety of aerobic classes.

Marco Fitness Club (239-394-3705; www.marcofitnessclub.com), 871 E. Elkcam Circle, Marco Island. Top-of-the-line cardiovascular and weight machines, free weights, personal trainers, classes, and a massage therapist in a clean setting. Day passes available.

New Image Fitness (239-498-3339; www.nifitness.com), 9110 Bonita Beach Rd., Bonita Springs. CrossFit and other personal training, full cardio and weights, tanning, smoothie café.

HIKING ✪ **Big Cypress National Preserve** (239-695-2000; www.nps.gov/bicy), HCR 61, Ochopee. East of FL 29, short hiking trails lead off Route 839; longer trails begin about fifteen miles away at the Oasis Visitor Center and join up with the Florida Trail (www.floridatrail.org), a national scenic trail that traverses the state's length. A boardwalk trail at the Oasis lets visitors look down at dozens of big alligators. Another good boardwalk for gator-gazing is at H. P. Williams Roadside Park, west of the Oasis.

✪ **Collier-Seminole State Park** (239-394-3397; www.floridastateparks.org/park/ Collier-Seminole), 20200 E. Tamiami Trail, Naples. A seven-mile trail, part of the Florida Trail, winds through pine flatwoods and cypress swamp with a primitive campsite. A self-guided walk along a boardwalk leads into a salt marsh.

✪ **Fakahatchee Strand Preserve State Park** (239-695-4593; www.floridastateparks .org/park/Fakahatchee-Strand), W. J. Janes Memorial Scenic Dr., 137 Coastline Dr., Copeland. Several trails—actually, old logging tramways—traverse the strand off twelve-mile (one-way) Janes Drive from the gates on either side of the road. They range in length from one to two miles. Summer flooding can make your hike a slosh.

Park volunteers lead swamp walks November through April, when you can spot many different varieties of wild orchids.

Picayune Strand State Forest (239-348-7557; www.freshfromflorida.com), at the end of Janes Dr., Copeland. Introduces access to 3.2-mile Sabal Palm Hiking Trail, which winds through cypress forest, habitat for a variety of birds.

Ten Thousand Islands National Wildlife Refuge (239-353-8442; www.fws.gov/refuges), thirteen miles west of FL 29. Formerly accessible only by boat, the refuge recently debuted its mile-long Marsh Trail. The first quarter mile is paved and leads to a ramped observation tower overlooking the salt marshes and their hefty bird and alligator populations.

HUNTING The Everglades provides some of Florida's best shots at hunting. You must obtain a state license and a Wildlife Management Area stamp. Permits are required for early-season and special types of hunting. For information on seasons and bag limits, request a copy of the *Florida Hunting Regulations* when you buy your license. (You can also download the publications at www.myfwc.com/hunting.) Skeet and clay shooting is available at **Gulf Coast Clays** (239-642-8999; www.gulfcoastclays.com), 12425 Union Rd., between Naples and Everglades City.

KIDS' STUFF ✐ **Coral Cay Adventure Golf** (239-793-4999; www.coralcaygolf.com), 2205 E. Tamiami Trail, Naples. Eighteen-hole miniature golf course with a tropical island theme and cooling mist system. Admission.

✐ **The Edge Johnny Nocera Skate Park** (239-213-3020; www.naplesgov.com), 1600 Fleischmann Blvd., Naples. Newly renovated, it welcomes skaters and BMX bikers.

✐ **Golden Gate Community Center** (239-252-6128; www.collierparks.com), Golden Gate Community Park, 3300 Santa Barbara Blvd., Naples. Swimming fun for all ages, with water slides, wading pool and fountain, and competition pool with low and high

A NEW OBSERVATION TOWER OVERLOOKS EVERGLADES HABITAT ON THE MARSH TRAIL, THE ONLY LAND ACCESS TO TEN THOUSAND ISLANDS NATIONAL WILDLIFE REFUGE

dives. Also a BMX track and skate park (239-252-4180) at 4701 Golden Gate Pkwy. Admission.

✒ **Golf Safari** (239-947-1377; www.golfsafariminigolf.com), 3775 Bonita Beach Rd., Bonita Springs. Jungle-themed miniature golf. Go online for coupons.

♨ ✒ **River Park Aquatic Center** (239-213-3333; www.naplesgov.com), 451 11th St. N., Naples. Free swimming pool with lap lanes, a forty-seven-foot slide, interactive water fountains, and a beach entry pool.

✪ ✒ **Sun-n-Fun Lagoon** (239-252-4021; www.napleswaterpark.com), 15000 Livingston Rd., at North Collier Regional Park, Naples. Next to the Golisano Children's Museum of Naples (C'MON), it has slides, a lazy river, interactive fountain, sandy beaches, diving boards, and various pools. A concession operation sells food, ice cream, sunscreen, swim diapers, and more. Admission.

✒ **Velocity Skate Park** (239-417-0415; www.collierparks.com), 3500 Thomasson Dr., Naples. It contains a full array of pipes, drops, ramps, and rails for skaters and BMX bikers. Admission.

RACQUET SPORTS **Arthur L. Allen Tennis Center at Cambier Park** (239-213-3060; allentenniscenter.net), 735 Eighth St., Naples. Twelve lit HydroGrid tennis courts. Fee.

Tommie Barfield Elementary, 101 Kirkwood St., Goodland, Marco Island. Two lit courts.

City of Marco Island Racquet Center (239-394-5454; www.cityofmarcoisland.com), 1275 San Marco Rd., Marco Island. County facility with six clay and two regular courts, two indoor racquetball courts, a practice wall, pickleball courts, pro shop, and lessons.

Everglades City Park, Broadway at Storter Rd. Two lit courts.

TUBULAR FUN AT NAPLES'S SUN-N-FUN LAGOON

Fleischmann Park (239-213-3020; www.naplesgov.com), 1600 Fleischmann Blvd., Naples. Four lit racquetball courts.

Golden Gate Community Park (239-252-6128; www.collierparks.com), 3300 Santa Barbara Blvd., Naples. Four lit tennis and racquetball courts.

Greater Marco YMCA (239-394-3144; www.marcoislandymca.org), 101 Sandhill St., Marco Island. Eight lit clay courts with ball machine rental and round robins. Fee.

Naples Park Elementary, 685 111th Ave. N., Naples. Two lit courts.

Pelican Bay Community Park (239-598-3025; www.collliergov.net), 764 Vanderbilt Rd., Naples. Eight lit tennis and four lit racquetball courts.

Mary C. Watkins Tennis Center (239-435-4351; www.naplesbeachhotel.com), at the Naples Beach Hotel & Golf Club, 851 Gulf Shore Blvd. N., Naples. Its six HydroGrid courts are open to the public for a fee; lessons and clinics available.

SHELLING It is illegal to collect live shells in state and national parks. Collier County also discourages the collection of live shells.

Hot Shelling Spots: **Coconut Island**, north of Marco Island. A destination for most Marco Island shelling expeditions.

✪ **Key Island**, south of Naples, accessible only by boat. A partly private, partly state-owned unbridged island, Key Island (often referred to as Keewaydin) holds a great many shell prizes that are not as picked over as on beaches that are accessible by car. It is the only leashed dog-friendly beach in the Naples area. The Keewaydin Express 239-207-0403) provides shuttle service to the island.

Ten Thousand Islands, Shell Island, Kingston Key, and Mormon Key provide lots of empty shells to collect.

Shelling Charters: **Marco Island Water Sports** (239-642-2359; www.marco islandwatersports.com), 400 S. Collier Blvd., at JW Marriott Marco Island Beach Resort and other nearby resorts, Marco Island. Shelling and other boat tours aboard *Calusa Spirit*, a forty-five-foot power catamaran with canopy shade.

SPAS **Naples Beach Hotel & Golf Club** (239-261-2222 or 800-237-7600; www .naplesbeachhotel.com/spa), 851 Gulf Shore Blvd. N., Naples. This vital component to a landmark Naples hotel brings full-service spa facilities, from extensive massage services (including aromatherapy, Reiki, shiatsu, hot stone massages) to body treatments (wraps, soaks, and scrubs) and facials. A hair salon and fitness center enhance the wellness experience here.

Rick's Island Salon & Day Spa (239-642-6696; ricksislandsalon.com), 800 N. Collier Blvd., Marco Island. Luxurious setting for hair and nail care, facials, microdermabrasion, and massage.

The Ritz-Carlton Spa (239-514-6100; www.ritzcarlton.com/naples), 280 Vanderbilt Beach Rd., Naples. A divine respite from the world, it offers a full menu of massages and body treatments, hydrotherapies, and wellness evaluations and training. Signature treatments include sleep therapy and a Sea Holistic Poultice Massage. The =H2O+ café sells organic and flavorful healthy drinks, snacks, and meals.

Salt Cave (239-403-9170; www.saltcavenaples.com), 4962 Tamiami Trail N., Naples. New-age healing through salt therapy, electrotherapy, halotherapy, honey detox, and more.

Spa 41 (239-263-1664; www.spa41.net), 4910 Tamiami Trail N., Suite 200, at Tanglewood Marketplace, Naples. Offers therapeutic massage, facials, wraps, and other spa treatments. No hair or nails care.

Spa on Fifth (239-280-2777; www.innonfifth.com), at Inn on Fifth, 699 Fifth Ave. S., Naples. Full line of facials, massages, and body scrubs and wraps.

SPECTATOR SPORTS *Greyhound Racing:* **Naples-Fort Myers Greyhound Track** (239-992-2411; www.naplesfortmyersdogs.com), 10601 Bonita Beach Rd. SE, Bonita Springs. Matinees, afternoon and night races seasonally, horse race simulcasting, poker room (239-949-3511), and trackside dining. Admission.

WATER SPORTS *Extreme Water Sports:* **Marco Island Water Sports** (239-642-2359; www.marcoislandwatersports.com), 400 S. Collier Blvd., at the JW Marriott Marco Island Beach Resort and other nearby resorts, Marco Island. Parasailing and Wave-Runner and other water-bound tours.

Regency Watersports (239-389-7620;), 480 S. Collier Blvd., next to Marco Beach Ocean Resort, Marco Island. Twelve- to fifteen-minute parasail rides of 600 or 1,200 feet high.

Snorkeling & Scuba: Murky waters here send most divers to Florida's east coast and the Keys, although some charters take you out into deep local waters.

SCUBAdventures (239-434-7477; www.scubadventureslc.com), 971 Creech Rd., Naples. Supplies, instruction, and diving arrangements.

WILDERNESS CAMPING ✪ **Big Cypress National Preserve** (239-695-2000; www.nps.gov/bicy), HCR 61, Ochopee. Four primitive campgrounds and two others with limited facilities (cold showers) lie along the Tamiami Trail and Loop Road, about eighteen miles east of FL 29 in Big Cypress National Preserve, a 729 thousand-acre sanctuary adjacent to Everglades National Park. Two campgrounds close seasonally; some require an off-road vehicle permit.

✪ 🐾 **Collier-Seminole State Park** (239-394-3397; www.floridastateparks.org/park/Collier-Seminole), 20200 E. Tamiami Trail, seventeen miles south of Naples. This 7,271-acre park straddles Big Cypress Swamp and Ten Thousand Islands National Wildlife Refuge, and provides the least primitive camping in Everglades Country. There are RV hookups and tent sites; the first loop is more conducive to tenters, while the second has sites close together, a laundry, a dump station, and recreational facilities for RVers. Some sites are close to Highway 41 traffic noise. The park is full of possibilities for exploring nature and history, but no swimming is allowed.

✪ **Everglades National Park** (239-695-3311; www.nps.gov/ever) Backcountry camping along the Everglades canoe trails requires a permit, available from the Everglades City Ranger Station. Most sites provide platforms (some with shelters) on pilings with chemical toilets. Take mosquito repellent—gallons in summer.

Trail Lakes Campground (239-695-2275 or 800-504-6554; www.evergladescamping.net), 40904 US 41 E., five miles east of FL 29, Ochopee. Tent or RV camping. Also the site of Skunk Ape Research Headquarters and a live animal park. Look for the super-size statue of a Florida panther, and you know you've reached funky Old Florida.

WILDLIFE SPOTTING The Florida Everglades, Big Cypress National Preserve, and Ten Thousand Islands and Florida Panther National Wildlife Refuges are home to the reclusive golden Florida panther, along with bobcats, deer, manatees, wood storks, brown pelicans, black skimmers, roseate spoonbills, bald eagles, mangrove cuckoos, and ibises. Some creatures, such as the panther and bobcat, are rarely seen out of captivity. Others, especially the brown pelican, live side by side with residents. I've driven along FL 29 between the interstate and Tamiami Trail and spotted flocks of ibises and clumps of white-tailed deer. Deep in the 'Glades, birds flock like a blizzard. So do mosquitoes in summer. Optimum wildlife viewing is December through March, when birds migrate and dry weather concentrates them in diminished ponds and other waterways; and insects are not quite so ferocious.

EXCURSIONS: Everglades Road Trip

Head east on **Tamiami Trail (US 41)** to discover the parks, preserves, and wildlife refuges that make up the unique habitat known as the Florida Everglades. On your first stop at the **Collier-Seminole State Park** (239-394-3397; www.floridastateparks.org/park/Collier-Seminole; 20200 E. Tamiami Trail), you will get your first lesson on the monumental task of building Tamiami Trail at the Walking Dredge exhibit. Next stop, the **Marsh Trail** gives you a glimpse into **Ten Thousand Islands National Wildlife Refuge** (239-353-8442; www.fws.gov/refuges), which is otherwise accessible only by water. The refuge is part of the **Florida Panther National Wildlife Refuge** complex (www.fws.gov/refuge/Florida_Panther, intersection of SR 29 and I-75), which you can access via SR 29 if you take a left off of US 41. Along this road you first come to **W.J. Janes Memorial Scenic Drive** through **Fakahatchee Strand Preserve State Park** (239-695-4593; www.floridastateparks.org/park/Fakahatchee-Strand; 137 Coastline Dr., Copeland.) To the north lies the trailhead for Florida Panther. Return south on CR 29 and cross US 41 to reach **Everglades City** and the western access to and visitors center for **Everglades National Park** (239-695-3311; www.nps.gov/ever; 815 Oyster Bar Ln., Everglades City). The small frontier-like town offers a number of options for lunch. For another lesson on Tamiami Trail history, stop at the **Museum of the Everglades** (239-695-0008; www.colliermuseums.com, 105 W. Broadway, Everglades City). Then head back to US 41 to drive through **Big Cypress National Preserve** (239-695-2000; www.nps.gov/bicy). Visit the **Big Cypress Swamp Welcome Center** (239-695-4758; 33000 Tamiami Trail, Ochopee); stop at **Skunk Ape Headquarters** (239-695-2275; www.skunkape.info; 40904 Tamiami Trail, Ochopee) for a funky roadside attraction experience, and **H.P. Williams Roadside Park** (12580 Turner River Rd.), where you can usually watch, from the boardwalk, lots of alligators swimming. Then turn right on **Loop Road**. Most of it is unpaved, so if it's wet you may want to forego the loop. It returns you to US 41. Turn left (west) to return to the Naples area, after a stop at the **Oasis Visitor Center** (239-695-1201; 33100 Tamiami Trail, Ochopee).

Alligators: The Everglades is the New York City of Florida's alligator population. They thrive in the freshwater ponds and brackish creeks of the River of Grass. When the sun is shining along Alligator Alley (I-75) and the Tamiami Trail, you can see hundreds of these prehistoric reptiles on the banks sunning themselves. Crocodiles also live in the 'Glades, but they are rare on this side.

Birds: The South Coast is a bird-watcher's haven—especially in winter, when migrating species add to the vast variety of the coast's residential avifauna. Rare visitors and locals include roseate spoonbills, black skimmers, yellow-crowned night herons, wood storks, white pelicans, limpkins, reddish egrets, and bald eagles. More commonly seen are frigates, ospreys, little blue herons, great blue herons, ibises, snowy egrets, brown pelicans, anhingas, cormorants, terns, seagulls, plovers, pileated woodpeckers, belted kingfishers, purple gallinules, owls, and hawks.

For the best birdwatching, try ✪ **Everglades National Park**; Naples's ✪ **Corkscrew Swamp Sanctuary**, home to the largest nesting colony of wood storks in the US. ✪ **Rookery Bay National Estuarine Reserve** near Marco Island; and Ten Thousand Islands National Wildlife Refuge, a haven for waterbirds. Marco Island is a proclaimed sanctuary for bald eagles. Barfield Bay in Goodland is one of their favorite locales. At the beach, the threatened piping plover gets support and protection from local environmentalists.

The **South Florida Birding & Wildlife Trail**, the last leg of the Great Florida Birding Trail, maps the region's best spotting venues. Corkscrew Swamp Sanctuary

MUST SEE

✪ Big Cypress National Preserve (239-695-2000; www.nps.gov/bicy), HCR 61, adjacent to Everglades National Park, Ochopee. New welcome center less than five miles east of FL 29 at 33000 Tamiami Trail E., Ochopee; Oasis Visitors Center (239-695-1201; 33100 Tamiami Trail, Ochopee) about twenty-three miles east of FL 29. Welcome center and visitors center open daily 9–4:30. This 729,000-acre preserve abuts Everglades National Park to the north and Fakahatchee Strand Preserve State Park to the east. A state-of-the-art welcome center (239-695-4758; 33000 Tamiami Trail, Ochopee) features interpretive exhibits devoted to wetlands and their creatures; its boardwalk is a good vantage point for spotting manatees. From the Oasis Visitor Center you can depart on wilderness hikes to sample its Everglades environment; its small museum contains Indian artifacts and wildlife exhibits. From its boardwalk, you can usually see plenty of gators. In summer the trails—which connect to the Florida Trail—can be very wet. You'll see the grasslands and bald cypress stands for which Big Cypress is known, as well as profuse birds and an alligator nursery. The preserve boasts the state's major population of the reclusive, endangered Florida panther. Rangers lead swamp walks, bike and canoe trips, and campfire programs from both centers in season. A twenty-six-mile scenic loop road is open to vehicles when road conditions allow. Closer to Everglades City, Birdon Road (CR 841) takes a seventeen-mile trip through sawgrass prairie habitat. It connects to CR 837 and then CR 839, which leads to two 2.5-mile hiking trails, one to the north and the other to the south of the intersection.

serves as the trail's regional gateway. For a map and more information, visit www.floridabirdingtrail.com.

Nature Preserves & Eco-Attractions: ✪ ✎ 🐾 **Collier-Seminole State Park** (239-394-3397; www.floridastateparks.org/park/Collier-Seminole), 20200 E. Tamiami Trail, Naples. Open daily, 8–sundown; visitors center open 8–5. $5 per car, up to eight passengers; $4 per single-occupant vehicle; $2 per bicyclist, pedestrian, or extra passenger. Here, Naples meets the Everglades. One of the region's prettiest state parks, its 7,271 acres encompass manicured lawns to contrast with its jungle wilderness. Besides its historic attractions—a garden memorial to developer Barron Collier, the only remaining dredge used to build the Tamiami Trail across the Everglades, and a replicated Seminole War blockhouse and Seminole chikees—it harbors a wealth of birds, otters, cats, manatees, and other critters that seek shelter in the outlying Everglades. Learn about them at the little visitors center in the blockhouse, then take to the nature, bike, and paddling trails. Ranger activities provide biological background. Other features include camping and picnicking, with a children's playground.

✪ ✎ **Conservancy of Southwest Florida Nature Center** (239-262-0304; www.conservancy.org), 1495 Smith Preserve Way, one block east of Goodlette Rd., Naples. Recently remastered to bring its exhibits up to date and allow visitors opportunity to "visit" rehab patients, this tucked-away nature complex on the Gordon River was built by the Conservancy of Southwest Florida to educate the public about the environment. Within its twenty-one acres, the Nature Center encompasses a nature store; trail walks; electric boat tours of the river; a wildlife hospital nursery for public viewing; a discovery center with hands-on habitat exhibits and a juvenile loggerhead sea turtle on display in an aquarium; a theater; and a preserve. The new Little Explorer Play Zone lets kids pretend they are crawling through a gopher tortoise burrow and climbing into a bald eagle nest. The conservancy also hosts interpretive nature field trips; seasonal, guided paddle trips around the Isles of Capri; and seasonal pontoon cruises. Kayak rentals are available for use on the Gordon River.

✪ ✎ **Corkscrew Swamp Sanctuary** (239-348-9151; corkscrew.audubon.org), 375 Sanctuary Rd. W., off Naples-Immokalee Rd., twenty-one miles east of N. Tamiami

Trail, Naples. Open daily 7–5:30 (no admission less than one hour before closing). Admission: $14 adults, $6 college students with ID, $4 children ages six to eighteen. This thirteen-thousand-acre sanctuary, operated by the National Audubon Society, protects one of the largest stands of mature bald cypress trees in the country. Some of the towering specimens date back nearly five hundred years; signs point out twelve of Corkscrew's "landmark trees." The threatened wood stork once came to nest here in great numbers. Diminished populations still do, at which time the nesting area is roped off to protect them. About two hundred other species come and go or reside permanently at this keystone stop along the Great Florida Birding & Wildlife Trail. A 2.25-mile-long boardwalk takes you over swampland inhabited by rich plant and marine life. You can usually spot an alligator or two. The state-of-the-art Blair Audubon Center occupies a "stealth" building that blends with the pristine environment. Its Swamp Theater dramatically re-creates seasons and times of day on the boardwalk, plus there are hands-on opportunities for kids.

THE BOARDWALK THROUGH CORKSCREW SWAMP SANCTUARY EXPLORES A VARIETY OF ECOSYSTEMS

✎ **Delnor-Wiggins Pass State Park** (239-597-6196; www.floridastateparks.org/park/Delnor-Wiggins), 11135 Gulf Shore Dr. N., at Vanderbilt Beach, Naples. Open sunrise–sunset. $6 per car, up to eight passengers; $4 per single-occupant vehicle; $2 per bicyclist, pedestrian, or extra passenger. Prehistoric loggerhead turtles lumber ashore to lay and bury their eggs every summer, away from the lights and crowds of other area beaches. Fifty-six days later, the baby turtles emerge and scurry to the sea—hopefully before birds can snatch them up. Beach turtle talks are available during the loggerhead season. Year-round, fishing, beaching, and climbing the observation tower are popular activities.

✪ **Everglades National Park/Gulf Coast Visitor Center** (239-695-3311; www.nps.gov/ever), 815 Oyster Bar Ln., Everglades City. Tamiami Trail south of Naples; ranger station and visitors center on FL 29, before the Chokoloskee Causeway in Everglades City. Visitors center open November through May, daily 8–4:30; May through November, daily 9–4:30; concessions open daily 8:30–5. This massive wetland—home to the endangered Florida panther and other rare animals—covers 2,200 square miles and shelters more than 600 types of fish and 347 bird species. It stretches from here to the Florida Keys on the east coast. Along with Ten Thousand Islands, it also contains the largest mangrove forest in the nation. Its Marjorie Stoneman Douglas Wilderness Area is the largest wilderness area east of the Mississippi River, with 1.3 million acres. So what's the best way to see this seemingly overwhelming expanse of wildlife? Take your pick. From this end, you really can't drive into it, but you can from the eastern access, two hours away. US 41 skirts the edge of the park and Big Cypress

National Preserve, which is part of the same ecosystem. The closest access to Naples is FL 29 and Everglades City. Paddling trips from eight to ninety-nine miles long put you in closer range of birds, manatees, dolphins, alligators, and crocodiles,. There's also a variety of other options. The park offers boat tours, and private sight-seeing cruises exist. During the winter, ranger walks and canoe tours from the Gulf Coast Visitor Center teach about the unique environment. You can rent a pontoon boat or hire a charter captain in Everglades City for sight-seeing and fishing. Get advice at the visitors center, or see "Wildlife Tours & Charters." The visitors' center holds hands-on Calusa, bird, sea turtle, manatee, and other exhibits. Outdoors, tables and a chikee hut accommodate picnickers.

Fakahatchee Strand Preserve State Park (239-695-4593; www.floridastateparks .org/park/Fakahatchee-Strand), W. J. Janes Memorial Scenic Dr., 137 Coastline Dr., Copeland. Preserve administration office open weekdays 9–4. $3 per vehicle of up to eight occupants, $2 per extra person, hiker, or cyclist. Knowledgeable volunteers lead swamp walks, where you'll see wild orchids in addition to other flora and fauna, on the first, second, and third Saturday and last Tuesday of the month, November through April. You can also hike drier paths on your own. Park at the gates on either side of the road and follow the short pathways into the strand. In summer the trails are often muddy and submerged. You can also access the strand (a linear swamp forest that snakes along ancient slough valleys) via the six-mile Big Cypress Bend boardwalk trail, west of Everglades City on US 41. The ecosystem is known for its wild orchids, including forty-seven varieties of threatened and endangered species, fourteen native varieties of bromeliads, and stately stands of native royal palm. (Fakahatchee ranks as the world's largest cypress and royal palm forest.) Florida panthers, black bears, mangrove fox squirrels, and Everglades minks have all been documented along the twenty-mile-long strand. You're more likely to spot alligators, white-tailed deer, ospreys, ibises, egrets, and snakes (keep an eye out for the deadly cottonmouth). Next to the boardwalk you'll find an Indian village with a gift shop. A ranger office on W. J. Janes Memorial Scenic Drive, past the old fire tower, has displays and information on the preserve.

The Naples Preserve (239-261-4290; www.naplesgov.com), 1690 Tamiami Trail N., Naples. Open daily, dawn–dusk; eco-center open Monday to Saturday 10–4. This 9.5-acre patch of ancient ecology along the inner-city highway was recently cleaned up and fitted with a 0.4-mile boardwalk that crosses scrub oak, grassy meadow, and pine-flatwoods communities. Gopher tortoises, deer, bobcats, and birds occupy the habitat. An eco-center houses a diorama plus rotating exhibits depicting the preserve's fauna and flora and interactive programs.

✪ ✐ **Rookery Bay Environmental Learning Center** (239-530-5940; www.rookerybay .org), 300 Tower Rd., off FL 951 (Collier Blvd.) toward Marco Island. Open Monday to Saturday 9–4; closed Sunday year-round and Saturday in summer. $5 for adults, $3 for children ages six to twelve. The Gulf Coast's largest and most pristine wildlife sanctuary west of the Everglades, Rookery Bay National Estuarine Research Reserve occupies more than 110 thousand acres at the gateway to Ten Thousand Islands. It's "Ding" Darling without the crowds (or ease of accessibility), and a favorite for fishermen and bird-watchers. Rare creatures such as the American crocodile, manatee, Atlantic Green and Ridley sea turtles, bald eagle, and roseate spoonbill inhabit its backwaters and shores. For an introduction to this vast, largely inaccessible land, stop at this Department of Environmental Protection laboratory and education facility. The mangrove estuary is the star of high-tech, interactive exhibits. The centerpiece, a two-thousand-gallon aquarium, has a fifteen-foot-tall mangrove "growing" out of it and spaces into which kids can crawl and get to know the crucial habitat. Forming a backdrop to the aquarium, a curved wall holds various habitat dioramas, 3-D tactile displays of local creatures, local wildlife-artist murals, a touch tank,

Mosquito Landing, and other fun and original learning tools. The unusual polka dot batfish is the center's mascot and has been replicated in supersize proportion. Kids can climb aboard a replicated research boat to do the sea turtle dance, hear bird sounds, and watch a glass-bottom boat video. The second floor holds exhibits exploring the area's and reserve's timeline, a replica of an Old Florida homestead, and recorded stories from the different eras. A bridge leads from the second floor to a 1.5-mile nature trail on the other side of Henderson Creek. Guided tours, kayak excursions, and other educational programs are available.

   Skunk Ape Headquarters (239-695-2275; www.skunkape.info) 40904 Tamiami Trail, Ochopee. More of a funky, Old-Florida roadside attraction than a nature spot, it does harbor wild native and exotic snakes, ostriches, birds, and other creatures on its grounds and in its natural history museum. But the main thrust here revolves around the Seminole Indian legend of the smelly skunk ape, Florida's answer to Big Foot. Owner David Shealy claims to have seen it a few times and has appeared on national TV to say so. Believe it or don't. It's still fun for kids. Admission for indoor exhibits only.

   Wildlife Tours & Charters: **Conservancy of Southwest Florida Nature Center** (239-262-0304; www.conservancy.org), 1495 Smith Preserve Way, one block east of Goodlette Rd., Naples. Electric boat tours of the mangrove waterways to the Gordon River are included in admission. It also hosts wildlife cruises of Rookery Bay National Estuarine Research Reserve aboard the pontoon boat *Good Fortune*.

   Dolphin Explorer (239-642-6899; www.dolphin-explorer.com), 951 Bald Eagle Dr., at Rose Marco River Marina, Marco Island. $59 each. Lead by dolphin researchers, this excursion takes passengers on a participatory excursion with Ten Thousand Islands Dolphin Project, a scientific research study to identify and track the movement of resident dolphins in the Marco Island and Naples areas. Two three-hour survey trips depart daily, one in the morning at 9, another at 1. Advance reservations highly recommended.

   Pure Naples (239-263-4949; www.cruisenaplesflorida.com), 1200 Fifth Ave. S., at Tin City on US 41, Naples. Departs up to five times daily for a 1.5-hour narrated sight-seeing, dolphin-sighting, cruise-and-dine, family, and sunset cruises.

   Everglades National Park Boat Tours (239-695-2591; www.evergladesnationalparkboattoursgulfcoast.com), Gulf Coast Visitor Center, 815 Oyster Bar Ln., Everglades City. Naturalist-narrated tours wind through the maze of Ten Thousand Islands and its teeming bird and water life; other tours take you up the mangrove-lined Turner River.

   Florida Backcountry Adventures (239-595-7495; www.floridabackcountryadventures.com), P.O. Box 1473, Marco Island 34146. Specializes in bird and other wildlife-spotting small boat tours and eco-shelling into Ten Thousand Islands and the Everglades. Also kayak tours.

   Jet Boat Naples (239-263-4949; www.jetboatnaples.com), 1200 Fifth Ave. S., Naples, at Tin City. Eco-adventure tours of the Ten Thousand Islands.

   Manatee Sightseeing Eco-Adventure (239-642-8818; www.see-manatees.com), 525 Newport Dr., at Port of the Islands Resort and Marina, Naples. Captains Barry and Carol Berger take up to six passengers on a ninety-minute sight-seeing charter into a manatee sanctuary by appointment. If you don't see a manatee, you don't pay.

   Power Boat Eco-Excursions (239-695-3633 or 800-860-1472; evergladesareatours.com/power_boat_tours.htm), Calusa Island Marina, Goodland. An experienced naturalist leads this journey into Ten Thousand Islands and Rookery Bay to point out birds and other wildlife. Two-hour tours depart four times daily, including a sunset excursion.

   Smallwood Store Boat Tour (239-695-0016; www.smallwoodstoreboattour.com) 360 Mamie St., Chokoloskee Island 34138. The ninety-minute eco-tour explores Ten Thousand Islands. Other excursions include a two-hour historic tour or sunset cruise.

✳ Lodging

The South Coast was once a place for roughing it and low-key vacationing. The old wooden Naples Hotel, built in the 1880s by town developers, was as posh as it got. In 1946 Naples became a forerunner in the golf resort game when the Naples Hotel was bought and converted. In 1985, the Ritz-Carlton came to town and set a new tone. Naples changed forever. Naples Grande Beach Resort & Spa (formerly the Waldorf Astoria Naples) and other smaller luxury hotels followed the Ritz, including the Ritz-Carlton Golf Resort. Downtown, new properties continue to rise and tend toward intimacy and European style, giving Naples a well-rounded menu of options, from cottages and inns to golf meccas and grandes dames. A new Hyatt House extended-stay hotel opened downtown in 2016, the first new Naples accommodations in eight years. In spring 2017, the Bay House Restaurant is expected to open a twelve-suite hotel and cooking school operation. Bonita Springs, to the north, is growing into its own as a destination with fine lodging, including a Hyatt Regency. Marco Island lines up high-rise after high-rise resort and condo community along its coveted beaches. In 2017, its longtime Marriott resort completed an upgrade to the JW Marriott brand.

Privately owned second homes and condominiums provide another source of upscale accommodations along the South Coast. (Vacation brokers who match visitors with such properties are listed under "Home & Condo Rentals" at the end of this section.) Away from the metropolitan airs of Naples and Marco Island, lodging options reflect the simple, primitive nature of the Florida Everglades.

The highlights of South Coast hospitality listed here include the best and freshest in the local industry. Toll-free 800, 877, 866, or 888 reservation numbers, where available, are listed after local numbers.

Prices are normally per unit/double occupancy. The range spans low- and high-season rates and standard to deluxe accommodations. Many resorts offer packages at special rates. Prices do not include the 6 percent Florida sales tax, and some large resorts add service gratuities or maid charges. Collier County imposes a 4 percent tourist bed tax as well; proceeds from the latter go toward beach and environmental maintenance.

Rate Categories

Inexpensive   Up to $100
Moderate $100 to $200
Expensive $200 to $300
Very Expensive $300 and up

An asterisk (*) after the pricing designation indicates that at least a continental breakfast is included in the lodging rate.

Note that under the Americans with Disabilities Act (ADA), accommodations built after January 26, 1993, and containing more than five rooms must be useable by people with disabilities. I have indicated only those small places that do not make such allowances.

ACCOMMODATIONS

BONITA SPRINGS

✪ ♂ ♂ ((•)) **Hyatt Regency Coconut Point Resort & Spa** (239-444-1234 or 800-55-HYATT; www.coconutpoint.hyatt.com), 5001 Coconut Rd., 34134. This tower of luxury makes a glamour statement on the shores of pristine estuary. Despite its high-rise contrast to the surrounding low-key landscape, the resort strives to blend with its Florida setting wherever possible. The elegant Italian marble and mahogany lobby is localized with Florida-look terrazzo, and the colors of the public spaces and 454 rooms and suites reflect the sea, sand, and verdure. All rooms and suites are outfitted with mini fridges, robes, safes, and coffeemakers.

The Tarpon Bay restaurant resembles old fish-shack architecture and serves local seafood. To make up for the lack of readily available beach (guests must take a boat shuttle to a private island for sand), Hyatt's signature water features fill in with a waterslide kiddie pool, a lazy river, a toddler's pool, adult pools, stunning fountains, and a reflecting pool. In 2017, a lazy river is slated to open. Many guests are more interested in golfing, anyway, and the Hyatt pleases them with eighteen top-notch holes. A kids' camp, a spa with one of Florida's few Watsu (water + shiatsu) pools, tennis, and a medley of bars and casual eateries make this a full destination resort for those who don't mind being a short ride away from the beach, shopping, and nightlife that gets the Bonita-Naples area noticed. Moderate to Very Expensive.

✪ ⦚ **Trianon Bonita Bay** (239-948-4400 or 800-859-3939; www.trianon .com), 3401 Bay Commons Dr., 34134. The name implies "a special place" in the spirit of the Grand Trianon and Petit Trianon on the grounds of Versailles near Paris. Heavy on European influence, the hotel's lobby displays both elegance and intimacy, with polished marble and high-arched ceilings. The dramatic entryway segues into a cozy lounge/breakfast nook, where there is a fireplace and a patio with a view of green lawn and a small lake. Attention to detail is a hallmark of Trianon, which is a spin-off of a downtown Naples prototype. In its hundred spacious guest rooms and suites you'll find the same refinement previewed in the lobby: dark-wood armoires, sliding French doors to a balcony, gourmet European coffee service, roomy all-white baths, and space enough to dance. A small pool lies in the backyard of the four-story, chateaulike structure, and the Lake House Bar & Grill overlooks the pool and a pond. Shoppers will like Trianon's walking-distance proximity to The Promenade (see "Shopping"). Moderate to Expensive.

EVERGLADES CITY

🦐 ⦚ **The Ivey House** (239-695-3299 or 877-567-0679; www.iveyhouse.com), 107 Camellia St., 34139. The family-run Ivey House is tailor-made for outdoor enthusiasts. The original Ivey House Lodge, a born-again boardinghouse from the 1920s, offers eleven simple B&B rooms. The newer, seventeen-room Ivey House Inn is more modern, plus there's the Ivey House Cottage which has two small bedrooms and a three-bedroom home (Moderate to Expensive). In the original B&B, men's and women's bathrooms are separate, dorm style, from the simple, wood-paneled rooms. The newer inn's rooms, which encircle the courtyard swimming pool, have private baths and offer added style and comforts, including TVs, phones, and free WiFi. Breakfast (hot buffet in winter, cold buffet in summer) is included in all room rates. Ivey's main attraction is its proximity to Everglades waterways and its partnership with EvergladesAdventures.com (see "Paddlesports"). In fact, you could call this a B&B: bed, breakfast, and backcountry. EvergladesAdventures.com leads tours into the Ten Thousand Islands by canoe, kayak, or boat; rents equipment; and provides shuttle service to launching and landing sites. Packages are available. Inexpensive to Moderate.*

🦐 **Rod & Gun Club** (239-695-2101), 200 Riverside, 34139. Steeped in both history and outdoorsmanship, this circa-1864 lodge crowns a modest town that serves as the South Coast's gateway to the Everglades. The club's main building was built as luxury pioneer-era housing; the Old South–style mansion came under the ownership of the county's developer and namesake, Barron Collier, who turned it into a fishermen's and hunters' haven during the 1920s. A sportsman's lodge in the finest sense, it has cypress walls that are still decorated with mounted fish, animal heads, a gator hide, and tools of the fishing trade. Seventeen rooms in tin-roofed cottages scatter around the white-clapboard lodge, which has a wraparound veranda and yellow-striped awnings. The rooms are furnished for function rather than pampering—TV, paddle fan, fridge, and air-conditioning are the extent of luxury. The club's restaurant, which has a screened porch facing the river, specializes in local delicacies and will cook your catch for a nominal fee. Banana trees, lattice, and rock waterfalls decorate the swimming pool deck off the dining room. Inexpensive to Moderate. No credit cards. No handicapped access.

MARCO ISLAND

🦐 🏨 (((•))) **The Boat House Motel** (239-642-2400; www.theboathousemotel .com), 1180 Edington Place, 34145. Marco Island's north end, known as Olde Marco, reflects more strikingly the island's nautically nice personality. If you're seeking something less upscale and expensive than Marco's trademark resort scene, drive past the new Olde Marco Island Inn and turn the corner to this waterfront secret. Twenty rooms, studios, condos, and the two-bedroom gazebo house (Moderate to Expensive) run perpendicular to the boat docks and a small pool in a two-story strip. The rooms are nicely appointed, outfitted with kitchen appliances, and designed for easy, breezy waterfront living. The two end rooms have the best view and largest porch/balcony. Wireless Internet access is available throughout the resort, which is within walking distance from several restaurants. Inexpensive to Moderate.

✪ ♂ (((•))) **Marco Beach Ocean Resort** (239-393-1400 or 800-715-8517; www .marcoresort.com), 480 S. Collier Blvd., 34145. If you want the same wide beach but wish something more intimate than the JW Marriott, try this exclusive enclave just a couple of doors south. Compared to the JW Marriott, it is more compact, smaller (though still twelve stories with sheltered parking and 83 one- and 15 two-bedroom suites), and more boutique. The sumptuous rooms, redecorated in sand tones, all face the gulf, with fully equipped kitchens. The swimming pool and its pool bar are elevated to a fifth-floor rooftop. The resort's greatest asset may be Sale e Pepe, its Tuscan-style restaurant overlooking the beach. Guests have club privileges at a nearby golf and tennis facility. Moderate to Very Expensive.

🦐 (((•))) **Marco Island Lakeside Inn** (239-394-1161 or 800-729-0216; www .marcoislandlakeside.com), 155 First Ave., 34145. Escape from the madhouse traffic and high rises along the beach to this Superior Small Lodging gem on Marco Lake. Its nineteen suites offer either lakeside views from screened porches (or, on the second floor, balconies) or poolside ground-level accommodations with a shared patio. The lakeview rooms have full kitchens and one or two bedrooms (Expensive for the two-bedroom accommodations), while those around the pool have kitchenettes and no separate sleeping quarters. In all, deluxe amenities, such as pillow-top mattresses, French doors, screened balconies, and white spic-and-span tiled bathrooms, lend a boutique feel. A small sand beach with a chikee structure that edges the lake and nicely maintained landscaping have elevated the once motel-like structure into something soothing and special. Moderate.

✪ ♂ 🐚 (((•))) **JW Marriott Marco Island Beach Resort** (239-394-2511 or 800-438-4373; www.marcoislandmarriott .com), 400 S. Collier Blvd., 34145. Following nearly two years of renovations and upgrades, the forty-four-year-old Marco Island Marriott Resort transitioned into a JW Marriott-branded resort—the first beachfront JW in the continental US. Changes and improvements include a new adults-only tower, fine rooftop restaurant, entertainment center, updated and remastered existing restaurants, and other enhanced and refreshed elements with Balinese flair. One restaurant has transitioned into a fine steakhouse, the other is committed to farm-to-table freshness. Casual Quinn's on the Beach and sexy Korals Sushi and Cocktail Lobby Bar remain. The long-stretching beachfront property holds a magnificent spa that got upgraded to SPA by JW status as well and an extra-wide, shell-cluttered beach—a fantasy playground for vacationers of all ages. Families enjoy the fun water park, water-sports rentals, pizzeria, game room with table tennis, and remarkable kids' program. Adults can retire to the quieter pool, shop in the marble-floored arcade, golf at two off-site Marriott courses, dine grandly or beach style, and act like a kid when the mood strikes. To the census of 726 guest rooms and suites, the adult Lanai Tower adds ninety-four luxury accommodations. In the spa building, a state-of-the-art fitness center extracts a fee from guests; or they can use the original fitness room for free. There's a charge for WiFi use in the room, but it is complimentary in the lobby bar area. Expensive to Very Expensive.

NAPLES

✪ ♂ (𝕒) **Bellasera Hotel** (239-649-7333 or 888-612-1115; www.bellaseranaples .com), 221 Ninth Street S., 34102. Feel the warmth of Tuscany as you splash in the tiled fountain pool and sup on Italian specialties from Zizi, the poolside restaurant. Inside the lobby, a sweeping staircase and rich Tuscan tones introduce a motif that carries through in the hotel's hundred studios and one- to three-bedroom suites. In the studios, plantation shutters in the bathroom open onto the living area so you can watch TV from the jetted tub. The spacious suites include all the comforts and modern conveniences of home, plus full kitchens and screened porches and balconies overlooking the beautifully landscaped courtyard and grounds. A small fitness center fits into a second-story room on one side of the pool with the spa on the other. Location-wise, the hotel sits steps away

from the action and smart social scene of downtown Naples, but is tucked away enough to ensure peace and romance. A free shuttle whisks you off to the beach, minutes away. Moderate to Very Expensive.

🦐 (𝕒) **Cove Inn** (239-262-7161 or 800-255-4365; www.coveinnnaples.com), 900 Broad Ave. S., 34102. Back before the Ritz-Carlton and Naples Grande, Naples was about water, boating, and fishing. Cove Inn persists in the old tradition by focusing on the harbor that it edges at Naples's original, circa-1915 settlement of fishermen and builders of Tamiami Trail. Accommodations range from hotel rooms to efficiencies to one- and two-bedroom units (Expensive to Very Expensive for the latter) with separate living/dining areas. The eighty-five balconied units are individually owned and decorated; most have a view of the harbor, and even the hotel rooms come equipped with a refrigerator, coffee-maker, and microwave. An old-fashioned coffeehouse serves breakfast and lunch, and the marina-side chikee bar slaps down cold ones for sunbathers around the pool and happy hour drinkers. Part of the Crayton Cove and City Dock communities, Cove Inn is close to casual-to-fine waterfront restaurants, shops, and marina services. Inexpensive to Expensive.

♂ ⚓ (𝕒) **The Edgewater Beach Hotel** (239-403-2000 or 800-821-0196; www .edgewaternaples.com), 1901 Gulf Shore Blvd. N., 34102. The Edgewater, Naples' only all-suite property, hints at New Orleans style with lacy, white-iron balustrades on two of its three buildings, all of which face the gulf-lapped beach. You can't stay much closer to the sand than at this appropriately named hotel. Its 124 one- and two-bedroom suites are spacious, convenient, handsomely appointed, and newly renovated with clay tiles, designer furnishings, and down comforters. The floor plan of each includes a full kitchen with microwave, living/dining area, and private patio or balcony. Guests can dine in the chic lobby restaurant, Coast, or poolside under stylish market umbrellas. There's an on-site exercise room, and opportunities for other recreation nearby, including golf. Moderate to Very Expensive.

✪ 🐾 ⟨⟨⟩⟩ **Lemon Tree Inn** (239-262-1414 or 888-800-LEMON; www.lemontreeinn .com), 250 Ninth St. S., 34102. Despite its lemon-pulp-yellow paint job and free lemonade in the lobby, this condo-hotel property is anything but a lemon. At the edge of downtown's fashionable drag, it retains a humble charm, dressed in white tin roofs and flowering plants. The thirty-four rooms with porches (most are screened) are named Periwinkle, Plumosa, Poinciana, and such, after local flowers. Spacious, simple, and cottage style in décor, they are individually decorated and outfitted with a microwave, coffeemaker, and mini fridge. Around the pool and a gazebo in the courtyard, thick foliage, a butterfly garden, a gazebo, and stylish globe streetlamps create character. At the poolside breakfast nook, you can help yourself to continental goodies. Shopping is steps away, and the beach is a short drive. Moderate to Expensive.*

⟨⟨⟩⟩ **Naples Bay Resort** (239-530-1199 or 866-605-1199; www.naplesbayresort. com) 1500 Fifth Ave. S., Naples 34012. Swank and boating-oriented, this relatively new Naples property possesses all the posh and polish it takes to steal the hearts of visitors who rarely stray from the beach. By combining private yacht and recreation club settings with an Italian-motif boutique property, Naples Bay Resort can offer guests incredible amenities that include boat docking (also rentals) and a playtime complex. Said complex, a short walk away, contains a lush lazy river and four pools—lap, zero-entry for family, waterfall, and adults-only—plus an intimate spa, fitness center with personalized readouts on every weight machine, and friendly pool bar and grill. Harbor-side, 1500 South

is the Southern-inspired brainchild of a former Oprah chef. Plush accommodations with whirlpool tubs and harbor views range from hotel rooms to one- and two-bedroom suites to cottages. A free shuttle makes the short distance to the recreation club and also drives to nearby Fifth Avenue South shopping and the beach.

⚲ ⟨⟨⟩⟩ **Naples Beach Hotel & Golf Club** (239-261-2222 or 800-237-7600; www.naplesbeachhotel.com), 851 Gulf Shore Blvd. N., 34102. The doyenne of Naples resorts, this combines the best of the area—its beaches and its golf—into a three-generation tradition in the heart of town. It celebrated seventy years in 2016. The eighteen-hole golf course hosts the PGA's Naples Beach Club Senior Open. Its stand-alone spa-and-clubhouse complex overlooks the greens. The spacious facility also holds meeting rooms, a fitness center, and Broadwell's, an elegant dining room that serves breakfast. HydroGrid tennis courts, a heated pool, the Beach Klub 4 Kids (with complimentary morning programs), and water-sports equipment rentals vie for off-the-course recreational hours. The hotel's spacious lobby communicates Old Florida vacationing ease. HB's on the Gulf and the Sunset Beach Bar fill up with sunset gazers. Its 317 guest rooms, efficiencies, and suites—renovated in 2015—are done in Florida décor and display some lingering classic trademarks of yesteryear. Accommodations overlook the wide, palm-studded beach or the lush golf course. Golf, tennis, and other packages are available. Expensive to Very Expensive.

⟨⟨⟩⟩ **Port of the Islands** (239-394-3101 or 866-348-3509; www.poiresort.com), 25000 Tamiami Trail E. 34114. Poised at the brink of the Everglades, it has gone through a number of phases through the years, including a stint as a Ramada Inn. Its latest management team has spruced it up but kept its adventure escape by design. Red barrel tiles, stucco, and a faux bell tower create a Mediterranean look, and the atrium lobby feels luxury lodge-like. The rooms, however, serve the purpose of sleeping in modest comfort. They are especially plain and motel-like in the two-story main building, with a shared balcony and mini fridges. Those that encircle the pool in a one-story configuration have their own screened porch and a kitchenette. Thirty of the condo hotel complex's rooms are on the rental program, snatched up in season by fishermen, hunters, and explorers who take advantage of the resort's wilderness concierge and tour concession partners, who operate out of the property's marina. Adventure packages are available. Guests also have access to a fitness center, guest laundry, and picnic areas on the water. Continental breakfast is included in rates. Inexpensive to Moderate*.

☎ (ꞏ) **Park Shore Resort** (238-263-2222 or 800-548-2077; www.sunstream.com/naples/park-shore), 600 Neapolitan Way, 34103. Its 156 one- and two-bedroom condos stack up two to four stories high in buildings that encircle a fountained lake. A tropically landscaped island in the middle of the lake, accessible by several wooden footbridges, holds a swimming pool with a craggy waterfall backdrop. The pool complex includes a whirlpool, barbecue and sunning decks, and a poolside café. Paver stone paths travel around the pool complex and lead to racquetball, volleyball, tennis, and basketball courts. The beach is a short walk away. Tucked into one of Naples's exclusive neighborhoods, the resort is also convenient to shopping and dining. On property, guests enjoy free Internet access, a friendly atmosphere, and home-like accommodations, complete with fully equipped kitchens. Moderate to Very Expensive.

🏌 ☎ (ꞏ) **The Ritz-Carlton Golf Resort** (239-593-2000 or 800-542-8680; www.ritzcarlton.com/naplesgolf), 2600 Tiburón Dr., 34109. The golf resort operates amid twenty-seven holes of lush, Greg Norman–designed greens.

The Rick Smith Golf Academy, a putting course and practice area, and a clubhouse with pro shop make this a complete golf resort. Its sybaritic relationship with its elder sister out on the beach gives both properties the most complete menu of leisure activities possible. Guests at the golf resort have access via shuttle to the beach resort's spa, beach, kids' program, and fine restaurants. Its own Lemonia restaurant gives guests a reason to stay right on property for a fabulous Tuscan feast overlooking the links. A gourmet pastry shop, pool grill, room service, and lounges help fill the dining-entertainment bill. The golf resort also has an on-property fitness center, four lit tennis courses, and a pool. Kids from both resorts learn golf and golf etiquette at the newer resort. Overlooking the greens with private balconies, 295 rooms and suites have it all, from cuddly robes and oversize marble bathrooms to high-speed wireless Internet access and safes large enough to hold laptop computers. Very Expensive.

✪ 🏌 ☎ (ꞏ) **The Ritz-Carlton Naples** (239-598-3300 or 800-542-8680; www.ritzcarlton.com/naples), 280 Vanderbilt Beach Rd., 34108. The gold standard for regal accommodations, the Ritz-Carlton melds Old World elegance with Old Florida environment. The hotel's façade looms majestically classic. Inside,

PARK SHORE RESORT BOASTS ITS OWN ISLAND IN A LUXURIANT GREEN SETTING

oversize vases of fresh flowers, massive chandeliers, cabinets filled with priceless china, nineteenth-century oil paintings, vaulted ceilings, and crystal lamps detail Ritz extravagance. Each of the 450 units in the U-shaped configuration faces the gulf. Guest rooms and suites are dressed in fine furniture, plush carpeting, and marble bath areas. Accommodations include an honor bar, bathrobes, hypoallergenic pillows, telephones in the bathroom, clothes steamers, and private balconies overlooking the hotel's backyard, where wilderness and civility meet. In the courtyard, fountains and groomed gardens exude European character. Classic arches, stone balustrades, and majestic palm-lined stairways lead to a boardwalk that takes you through mangroves. At the end of the boardwalk lie golden sands, where Gumbo Limbo restaurant serves daytime fare and water-sports rentals are available. Nature's Sanctuary, a new interactive aquarium and touch-tank element; and the vue (Virtual User Experience with interactive games) lounge expand family leisure activity options. Other amenities and services that earn the Ritz its AAA five diamonds include afternoon tea service, a fine steak grill, a sushi bar, a gourmet coffee shop, an elegant stand-alone spa and healthy café, a lap pool and free-form family pool, a lounge, a ballroom, tennis courts, sister-property golf facilities, a fitness center, a beauty salon, children's programs, a nature walk, bicycle rentals, shops, transportation services, and twice-daily maid service. Poolside cabanas are equipped with all relaxation necessities—from high-speed Internet and a flat-panel TV with DVD player to fresh fruit and a cabana butler. Very Expensive.

✪ ♟ ♞ ((•)) **Naples Grande Beach Resort** (239-597-3232; http://www .naplesgrande.com/), 475 Seagate Dr., 34103. Formerly Waldorf Astoria Naples, its distinctive red-capped tower, villas, and fifteen championship tennis courts dominate north Naples's pristine, mangrove-fringed estuaries. Luxurious but with beach casualness, the resort's style impresses from the moment you walk through the front door into the sleek, chic lobby with its circular waterfall, smart bar, and Aura restaurant. Outside, the family pool, one of three, has a Flintstones feel with a hundred-foot on-the-rocks waterslide. Families can engage their offspring in the fine kids' program while they hit the stand-alone spa or golf course. Tram service along the boardwalk traverses estuaries to Clam Pass Park, a three-mile stretch of plush sands with all manner of water-sports rentals and a Greek-theme café. Fifty luxury bungalows edge the tennis courts; another 395 rooms and twenty-nine suites overlook the gulf. All of these are spacious and furnished with a dry bar, walk-in shower, soaking tub, and class. Guests enjoy privileges at the private eighteen-hole Naples Grande Golf Club. Five restaurants range from poolside casual to the flagship, seafood-centric Catch of the Pelican. Covered parking and fitness room use is included in a resort fee. Very Expensive.

VANDERBILT BEACH

✪ ♟ ♞ ((•)) **LaPlaya Beach & Golf Resort** (239-597-3123 or 800-237-6883; www .laplayaresort.com), 9891 Gulf Shore Dr., 34108. LaPlaya's gracious, Southern-style lobby, Thai spa, exercise room, rocky waterfall pool, pool bar, and trendy restaurant menu (see Baleen under "Where to Eat") put it on par with Miami Beach's boutique hotels. Rooms show a meticulous attention to detail; some sport Jacuzzis with sea views, and all are luxurious with four-poster beds, quality linens, goose-down pillows, private balconies, and marble baths. Of its 189 units, 141 are beachfront with private balconies. The "golf" part of the name refers to privileges on a course fifteen minutes away. The "beach" part is obvious—a delicious slice of sands that gives way to the property's lush tropical garden and

Colonial-style public areas. Moderate to Very Expensive.

🦟 ((•)) **Vanderbilt Beach Resort** (239-597-3144 or 800-243-9076; www .vanderbiltbeachresort.com), 9225 Gulf Shore Dr. N., 34108. This longtime fixture on the barefoot-casual Vanderbilt Beach scene comes in two parts: a two-story, Old Florida beach motel with a small swimming pool in the shadow of next door's towering high rise and, across the street, a four-story bayside condo building. The efficiencies and apartments in the older beach building have an easygoing feel, while the condos sport a bit more elegance. All thirty-four units come with fully equipped kitchens (no stoves in the beach efficiencies), but plan on at least one dinner at the inimitable and highly hailed Turtle Club restaurant on-site. It serves lunch and dinner inside or outside on the patio or in the sand. Other restaurants are nearby. A private fishing dock and tennis court add to the convenience of the compact property. Moderate to Expensive.

HOME & CONDO RENTALS **Royal Shell Vacations** (239-213-3311 or 855-213-3311; www.royalshellrentals.com). Rentals from Captiva Island to Naples.

RV RESORTS **Chokoloskee Island Park** (239-695-2414; www.chokoloskee.com), 1140 Hamilton Way, Chokoloskee 34138. Rustic fishing paradise with easy access to the Everglades and the gulf. Full-service marina, tackle shop, guide service, ramps, and docks. Overnight or seasonal tent and RV sites with complete hookups; efficiency and mobile home rentals.

Outdoor Resorts of Chokoloskee Island (239-695-2881; www .outdoorresortsofchokoloskee.com), 150 Smallwood Dr., Chokoloskee 34138. Marina, boat rentals, a bait-and-tackle shop, and guide service for fishing and touring. Pull into one of 283 full-service sites or stay in the motel. Either way you can take advantage of the resort's three pools, health club, lit tennis and shuffleboard courts, and marina.

((•)) **Rock Creek RV Resort** (239-643-3100; www.rockcreekrv.com), 3100 North Rd. at Airport Rd., Naples 34104. Full hookups for more than 230 RVs, pool, laundry, WiFi hot spots, and shade trees. Limited pet area.

✳ Where to Eat

Everglades City considers itself a fishing and stone-crab capital, so you can expect some highly fresh seafood in these parts. Stone crab, in fact, was discovered as a food source in the Everglades—at least that's the way some of the old-timers tell it. Before a couple of locals began trapping stone crabs and selling them to a Miami restaurant, the delicate, meaty flavor of these crustaceans went unappreciated. Along with stone crab, alligator, frogs' legs, blue crab, and other local seafood make up the substance of Everglades cookery.

Marco Island, too, is known as a good market for buying stone crab, which gets more expensive farther from the source. With more than one hundred restaurants on the island, Marco covers every genre of cuisine. Its trademark is its Old Florida style of no-nonsense, trend-resistant seafood preparation, particularly in Goodland.

Naples's dining reputation is staked on hauteur and imagination. Even the old fish houses dress up their catches in the latest fashion, which ranges from redesigned home cooking and continental nouvelle to Floribbean, Pacific Rim, and fusion styles, and of course in a town named Naples, you're going to find a lot of Italian food. Naples is a dining-out kind of place. Downtown's Fifth Avenue South and Third Street South bring their restaurants out into the street for what has been termed Naples's "café society."

The following listings sample all the variety of South Coast feasting in these price categories.

Inexpensive	Up to $15
Moderate	$15 to $25
Expensive	$25 to $35
Very Expensive	$35 or more

Cost categories are based on the range of dinner entrée prices, or, if dinner is not served, of lunch entrées.

Note: Florida law forbids smoking inside all restaurants and bars serving food. Smoking is permitted only in restaurants with outdoor seating.

BONITA BEACH

Big Hickory Seafood Grille (239-992-0991), 26107 Hickory Blvd. A masterful blend of fish-shack chic and contemporary tropical Florida style makes this longtime marinaside favorite a sure keeper. Its all-day menu adheres to its roots, with fresh seafood prepared in both traditional and creative modes. One entrées section devotes itself to Old Florida–style deep-fried seafood baskets of oysters, grouper fingers, shrimp, and scallops. The other, along with the weekly changing special menu, goes gourmet to a Caribbean beat. The Cubana Grouper is a catch in all senses of the word—a generous supply of pan-seared, banana-crusted fish swimming in a creamy banana-liqueur sauce. Salads, tacos, and sandwiches are available all day. On our latest visit, we mixed up old and new, starting with fried oysters and Mussels and Clams Chardonnay. A friend had raved about the oysters, with good reason. Small and crunchy, they were textbook old Florida style, served with a well-balanced black bean salsa. The Pine Island clams and black mussels languished in a marvelous wine and garlic broth flecked with fresh cilantro and brightened with lemon. We ordered our entrées from the Signature Dishes section. The stuffed grouper benefited from a delightfully citric sauce and slightly spicy stuffing of liberal crabmeat. The grouper tasted a little on the fishy side; the steamed vegetables were impeccably fresh and al dente. The shrimp and lobster scampi generously heaped fettuccini, large shrimp, and bits of Florida lobster into a bath of scampi sauce that more robustly pronounced its wine component than its garlic. The butterflied shrimp were masterfully cooked to perfection; the lobster bits a tad rubbery. We finished off our experience with a creamy peach tart topped with fresh fruit and almonds—a true delight, and, like its setting, truly authentic. Inexpensive to Expensive. No reservations. Closed Monday in summer and for two weeks in September.

Doc's Beach House (239-992-6444; www.docsbeachhouse.com), 27908 Hickory Blvd. This is the kind of place where Gidget and Moondoggie would hang out (if there were surfable waves, that is). It's all about being on the beach—Bonita's colorful, action-packed beach. If you can't bear leaving the sands, you can just grab a quick burger or dog and get back to it. If you need a break from the sun, duck inside. Downstairs is open and barefoot casual. Upstairs is blessedly air-conditioned and has huge picture windows so you won't miss any of the beach action. Both levels have beer and wine bars and sports TVs. The menu makes no pretense of fine dining, but the food is solidly good. Grab-and-go items include Sand Dollar Burgers, Chicago-style pizza (after 4 p.m.), tacos, chili, and sandwiches of all sorts. For dinner or a heartier lunch, add a choice of grilled seafood, strip steak, and a fried seafood combo basket. Parking is by valet. Inexpensive. No reservations. No credit cards (ATM available).

BONITA SPRINGS

Chops City Grill (239-992-4677; www.chopsbonita.com), 8200 Health Center Blvd., US 41 and Coconut Rd., at Brooks Grand Plaza. Known for its fine steaks—dry-aged in-house and reasonably priced when compared to the "name" steakhouses—this spinoff from a Naples downtown restaurant stretches far beyond beef. Recently, we started off with Caesar salad and roasted oysters "Chopafeller." Like the sourdough bread with softened butter (hard butter with bread is a pet peeve of mine) doused with parsley-infused olive oil, the starters' brilliance shone through the details. Well-seasoned and generously applied classic dressing anointed the medley of lettuce leaves and Parmesan croutons in the Caesar. We hailed it heartily. Insanely rich and multidimensional, the oysters made me want to lick the shells: jalapeno-tequila cream sauce, chipotle-spiced sausage, spinach, and pepperjack cheese. Onto the next course, the prime rib came with thickened au jus and fluffy horse-radish cream. The cinnamon butter with the sweet potato was another nice touch. Next time I'll go for the signa-ture cedar plank–roasted wild salmon blackened with bourbon-brown-sugar glaze and served with cauliflower

smash, or some grilled meat or sea-food with one of the tempting sauces or embellishments purchasable. Some other items worth mentioning from the regular menu include the roasted candy cane beets appetizer, crab and lobster cakes starter, watermelon salad with chèvre and yuzu-berry dressing, and the short rib stroganoff. Seriously fashionable, with a burnished copper bar (where the martinis are nice and icy) and modern kitchen-theater dining room, Chops's ambience sets a tone of nouvelle sophistication and fine food that blends good old American steak with Asian nuances. Moderate to Expensive. Reservations accepted.

🦐 ♿ **The Fish House** (239-495-5770; www.thefishhouserestaurants.com), 4685 Bonita Beach Rd. This place is almost too darn cute to be real. Outside, a humble, canal front facade greets you and an archway invites you to Paradise. Whether you drive or boat in, upon entering Paradise, you reach the restau-rant's open-air patio and screened porch seating on the water. Inside, where sum-mer's humidity forced me, corrugated tin and painted buoys decorate the bar,

THE FISH HOUSE—A CLASSIC FLORIDA EATERY NEAR BONITA BEACH

around which a handful of Caribbean-color wood booths with hand-painted tables huddle. The menu covers are colored by children, whose artwork also decorates the walls. There's a lot of sensory input before the food even arrives, so you're happy to find familiar seafood dishes prepared from fresh ingredients on the all-day menu. I can recommend the conch chowder and shrimp jalapeño poppers for starters; grouper tacos are a specialty. Other entrées range from sandwiches and salads to fried seafood baskets and house specialties such as coconut shrimp, shrimp and scallops over fettuccine Alfredo, bacon-wrapped scallops, and combo dinners including surf and turf. The Fish House, which has restaurants on Fort Myers Beach and Sanibel Island, is also known for its 2-4-1 Rumrunner. Inexpensive to Expensive. No reservations.

Tarpon Bay Restaurant (239-444-1234; www.coconutpoint.hyatt.com), 5001 Coconut Rd., at the Hyatt Regency Coconut Point Resort & Spa. White-clapboard fish houses were once the architectural icon of this area. The Hyatt Regency designed its restaurant to pay homage to the Old Florida it replaced. Considerably more well-dressed than the real thing, the ambience nonetheless feels cottage comfortable. (Outdoor seating overlooks a pond containing a fountain and a floating golf hole, which can provide its share of entertainment during the still-light hours.) Local and imported seafood get a tropical zing. My favorite reason for dining here is the ceviche raw bar. Besides the typical shellfish, you can sample one of eight types of raw seafood "cooked" in various citric marinades. Can't make up your mind? Try a sampler of two to eight different varieties. Also for starters, there's lobster bisque topped with caviar, grit cakes with ancho and cranberry Brussels sprouts, and fried calamari with chorizo crumbles. The entrée menu comes in two parts: a listing of house specialties and a design-your-own

section where you choose from eight sustainably fished Florida and other fresh seafood, then pair it with one of eight sauces ranging from bearnaise to yuzu ginger mole. From the house specialties, the crispy whole snapper is signature and beautifully presented with ponzu dipping sauce. Others: angel hair pasta with grilled artichokes, shrimp scampi, and filet of beef with sunny-side-up egg and tarragon-scented polenta. Ice-cream lovers can go for a sampler; our flight of three included peaches 'n' mascarpone cobbler, mojito sorbet, and Creamsicle flavors, every one as good as the next. Or try the strawberry short cake with balsamic mascarpone cream. Expensive to Very Expensive. Reservations accepted.

Wylds Café (239-947-0408; www.wyldscafe.com), 4271 Bonita Beach Rd., at Lighthouse Square. If I were to describe Wylds in a word, it would be *buttery*. So leave the diet at home and prepare to be slathered. It began with the buttery, garlicky, herby spread between the crusty bread, and ended with cinnamon bread pudding crusted with pecan praline and sauced with warm caramel and crème anglaise. Wow! The menu changes seasonally, and the lush and luscious sweet potato bisque drizzled with cinnamon crème fraîche greets fall in style. The Enigma Salad is a romaine-based creation with avocado, shiitakes, shredded duck, capers, and a rich, creamy Parmesan-peppercorn dressing. The Parmesan-crusted walleye wears a shawl of impeccable tomato-basil beurre blanc. It vies with the beef tenderloin saga for top dish. "Saga" refers to the type of blue cheese, but it could just as well be comparing this multilayered dish to a long and rousing adventure tale. Wading in a pool of demi-glace, the grilled filet mignon gets piled with shards of pommes frites and the glue of melted blue cheese—a take on steak frites that one-ups the French. The entrée menu proposes nearly twenty selections that equitably cover whims from pasta to seafood to meat, with one vegetarian dish of wild mushroom quinoa, sautéed spinach, balsamic tomatoes, and other veggies. If you are determined to eat healthy, order the grilled swordfish with wild mushroom quinoa. In a simple setting of linen and russet-textured walls and with service that was right on, the Wylds experience is as soothing as it is rich. Moderate to Expensive. Reservations accepted. Closed September.

CHOKOLOSKEE

✪ 🦞 ♿ **Havana Café** (239-695-2214; myhavanacafe.com), 191 Smallwood Dr., Chokoloskee Mall, Chokoloskee. I love Everglades food—frogs' legs, 'gator tail, and all that. But when I'm looking for a refreshing change in the Everglades City area, this is my first choice. The menu looks deceptively simple, with eggs for breakfast, sandwiches and plates for lunch, but the Cuban accent gives everything an exotic twist. The egg sandwich is pressed on Cuban bread and the *café con leche* strong and sweet. The lunch menu ranges from grilled cheese sandwich and Cuban and *medianoche* sandwiches to grouper or steak plates with rice and beans and yucca. The Cuban, with pulled pork rather than sliced (the way it's more commonly prepared), was the best we've tasted—and we've tasted plenty. We also sampled one of the day's specials, *picadilla*, a flavorful ground beef ragout with kalamata olives and bell peppers served with black beans and rice. Our server recommended the cook's special chicken wing appetizer, flavored with cilantro, garlic, and other Cuban spices, but we were saving a piece of our appetite for a slice of Key lime pie. We were happy we did: It was fluffy with a nice crumb crust and the right amount of tartness. On a nice day, choose a tile-inset cement table outside or otherwise dine among brightly painted walls at the counter or one of the floral-tableclothed tables. Inexpensive. No credit cards.

No reservations. Closed for dinner May through September.

EVERGLADES CITY

✪ 🦞 **Camellia Street Grill** (239-695-2003; 208 Camillia St.; www.facebook.com/camelliastreetgrill) Despite its funky, chic junky outdoor décor, this place is serious about its food. Strewn along the waterfront, its courtyards and patios provide a comfy alternative to the more traditional screened porch, tin-roofed dining room with its counter, where customers place their orders. Its menu covers a lot of bases, from the expected in Everglades cuisine—fried seafood baskets, oyster po' boy sandwich, and seasonal stone crab—to foodie pleasers like lima bean soup with pork hocks, chili lime catfish, herb salads, and mussels in roasted red pepper tomato sofrito. To drink, there's beer, wine, and Key lime pie shakes. Inexpensive to Moderate. No reservations.

City Seafood (239-695-4700; www.cityseafood1.com), 702 Begonia St. A couple dozen or so picnic tables on the dock outside the fresh seafood market afford guests the freshest of catches and views. High-topped tables at deck's edge are one-sided for the optimal overlook of the river and its working waterfront. There's also upstairs air-conditioned seating (no handicapped access) with table service for breakfast. For other meals, you must place your order in the fish market. Stone crab is the main currency here, in season October 15–May 15. Any time of year order up a cracked conch sandwich, blue crab cake sandwich, oyster po' boy, grilled shrimp salad, grouper wrap, fried mullet, or basket of clam strips, frogs' legs, or fried 'gator. Moderate to Expensive. No reservations.

Joanie's Blue Crab Café (239-695-2682; joaniesbluecrabcafe.com), 39395 US 41, just east of the US 41–County Route 29 (CR 29) intersection, Ochopee. Now you *know* you're in the Everglades: a

TRUE EVERGLADES FLAVOR AT JOANIE'S BLUE CRAB CAFÉ, A LONGTIME HONKY-TONK FAVORITE

shack made out of corrugated aluminum painted red, coconut heads hanging from the ceiling, a porch peering over the River of Grass, catfish sandwiches, frogs' legs, hush puppies, and what Joanie claims to be the "best 'gator in town." I have to agree. The tender little nuggets are floured and seasoned with ginger and cilantro before panfrying and serving atop Indian fry bread, a flatbread that is staple for local Indian tribes. The side of salsa contained fresh chopped tomatoes, onions, summer squash, and bell pepper in a sweet-sour bath. Joanie is also known for her homemade soups, particularly the chili, and her black beans and rice, fried green tomatoes, and softshell crab sandwich. Walk on in, grab your drink from the cooler (or wait and order a fresh mango or strawberry fruit shake), find a seat at a wood table in or out, and prepare yourself for a true swamp experience, including local bands on weekends and other days in season. Inexpensive to Moderate. No reservations. Closed Monday and Tuesday year-round and also Wednesday and Thursday in summer. Closed entirely the month of August.

Oyster House Restaurant (239-695-2073; www.oysterhouserestaurant.com), 901 S. Copeland Avd., across from the Everglades National Park Station. The very essence of the Everglades, this serves the requisite alligator nuggets, stone crab claws, fried frogs' legs, and other seafood in addition to namesake dishes. Try the sautéed gator appetizer, fried oysters or the signature grouper baked with tomatoes and green peppers, and the Key lime pie. Or bring in your filleted catch for expert preparation. Taxidermy black bears, bobcats, wild turkeys, and a rattlesnake look down upon chunky wood tables. Some have a view of the bay across the street, but you'll likely be distracted with all the pictures, slogans, clippings, license plates, and mural that claim space on the wood-panel walls. To walk off lunch, take the boardwalk next door to the bay or climb the observation tower for an Everglades overview ($2 each).

GOODLAND

Little Bar Restaurant (239-394-5663; www.littlebarrestaurant.com), 205 Harbor Pl. This place is as much about the personality as the food. Let me just mention that every year in June it throws Spammy Jammy, where people dress in pajamas and make stuff out of Spam—such as sculptures and dips. That said, the rest of the year Little Bar reflects the slightly akilter personality of Goodland with unusual décor—salvaged wood from a historic boat, pieces of pipe organ, stained glass, and various remnants with a past. As for the food, as at other Goodland restaurants, it tastes of the Everglades and the sea, but climbs a bit above typical frogs' legs fare. Yes, you'll find them on the menu—Buffalo frogs' legs, no less—but also an eclectic variety of conch chowder (served with a cruet of sherry), liverwurst with bacon sandwich, marinated herring, smoked fish spread, fried seafood baskets, kielbasa and kraut, blue crab cakes with lobster cream sauce, barbecued pork ribs, softshell crab, and blackened grouper. Most days, there's a fight for the outdoor tables on the boat docks with a view of crab trap stacks and fishing boats across the canal. You get the same view from a screened porch and the dining rooms. I'd like to recommend the peach berry tart, but it was a sellout on my last visit. The Absolut Bloody Mary, however, earns my deepest respect. Inexpensive to Moderate. No reservations. Closed July through September.

ISLES OF CAPRI

🌿 **Capri Fish House** (239-389-5555; www .caprifishhouse.com), 203 Capri Blvd. Hidden Isles of Capri has but one beach, a natural patch of sand behind this circa-1968 fish house where folks gather on Sunday for family dining, kayaking, and beaching. You can opt for an indoor air-conditioned setting in a renovated, sparkling clean setting, but most want the waterfront, open-air chikee bar even when it's warm. Paddle fans and breezes off the water cool it down. Menus offer extensive choices. For lunch, there are burgers and wraps, including Maine lobster salad, plus pasta and salads. Dinner may start out with alligator nuggets or mussels marinara and work into the signature Seafood Capri (lobster, shrimp, scallops, mussels, and clams with pasta and a cream sauce), Continental choices, such as duck à l'orange or veal parmigiana, and seafood specialties with a tropical flair—coconut shrimp, Florida lobster tail, grouper baked with tomato and artichoke hearts, and seafood kabob—flesh out the menu. Live entertainment Tuesday to Sunday. Expensive. No reservations.

MARCO ISLAND (SEE ALSO GOODLAND AND ISLES OF CAPRI)

Bistro Soleil (239-389-0981; www .bistrosoleil.net), 100 Palm St., at the Olde Marco Inn. Since the 1870s and pioneer Bill Collier, this location has fed and boarded pilgrims to this part of the world. Back in Collier's day, he advertised rooms for $1 a night, bring your own meat. Through the decades, the inn's dining room has evolved into a gracious Victorian setting with a cranberry glass chandelier and Audubon prints. Bistro Soleil, with its delightful Continental interpretations, sheds new light on the local culinary tradition. For starters, the sun-dried tomato soup gratinée with Swiss and blue cheese, or Prince Edward Island mussels steamed with herbs and white wine immerse you in Chef Denis Meurgue's irresistible style. Reasonably priced follow-up courses continue to tantalize with offerings such as wild mushroom risotto with truffle oil and fresh vegetables; slow-roasted crispy Long Island duck à l'orange; rack of lamb provencal; grouper topped with crab and capers-lemon butter sauce; fresh beignets with Chantilly; and homemade warm apple tarte tatin with vanilla ice cream and balsamic vinegar reduction. Expensive. Closed Sunday and Monday in off-season and September. Reservations accepted.

✪ ♂ (((•))) **Sale e Pepe** (239-393-1600; www.sale-e-pepe.com), 480 S. Collier Blvd., at Marco Beach Ocean Resort. Whether it's your fantasy to dine under the Tuscan sun or the Florida moon, Sale e Pepe brings it to reality in a replicated, palace-proportioned, Italian-villa setting

BISTRO SOLEIL SLANTS A RAY OF CULINARY SUNSHINE UPON A 19TH-CENTURY LODGE

with an outdoor terrace. Perched on the second floor, it affords an elevated perspective of sand and sea. Inside, you can choose a formal frescoed dining setting or a more casual lounge setting. All serve the same finely crafted, award-winning, Tuscan-based creations at dinner. Everything's made fresh, from the crusty olive and rustic herb breads to the pasta, soup, sausage, and tiramisu al limoncello. The menu adapts to the seasons, always paying tribute to the main Tuscan food groups: antipasto (featuring imported cheeses and charcuterie), fish, meat, and pasta. In the pasta department, there's Buffalo caciotta cheese–stuffed marjoram ravioli and ricotta cavatelli with smoked Maine lobster and sweet garlic mascarpone thyme sauce. From the *terra*, try veal scaloppine saltimbocca; from the *mare*, grilled breaded swordfish steaks with eggplant caponata and ricotta mint mousse. The formal dining room also offers a tasting menu and, in summer, early dining specials. Lunch and breakfast on the terrace and in the lounge disappoints with its departure from Italian to humdrum, although the spinach-mushroom pizza I tasted recently was exceptional. Stop in the huge gaslit bar, a shrine to artist Toulouse-Lautrec, for an after-dinner drink. Or take the staircase down to the beach to walk off the dinner in which you've most likely overindulged. Moderate to Expensive. Reservations accepted.

✎ & **Snook Inn** (239-394-3313; www .snookinn.com), 1215 Bald Eagle Dr. Snook Inn's tiki bar packs them in despite the less-than-stellar talent of its musicians. The view of the Marco River and the feeling of Margaritaville *are* stellar, however. And the food? Dependably tasty and just enough old-fashioned to ensure its longevity. Inside, where some retreat in summer's swelter, the salad bar, with its huge barrel of dill pickle chunks, is signature. It comes with every sandwich or entrée lunch and dinner. For lunch, I recommend the beer-battered grouper sandwich. For the ultimate

decadence, order Shrimp Denny—stuffed with scallops, wrapped in bacon, deep-fried (wait, it's not over yet), and topped with hollandaise! The dinner menu does seafood and meat with equal confidence: fried or stuffed grouper, blackened catch of the day, Cuban-style barbecued ribs, and surf and turf. If you can fit it in, there's chocolate toffee mousse cake to further wreak havoc on your diet. Inexpensive to Moderate. No reservations.

NAPLES

USA TODAY's 10Best.com readers ranked Naples as having the #9 Best Small Town Food Scenes in the US. In 2014, *Conde Nast Traveler* magazine listed Naples number seventeen of its Top Cities for Foodies readers' choice awards. For a taste tour of Naples, visit www.naplesfoodtours.com.

Barbatella (239.263.1955; www .barbatellanaples.com), 1290 Third Street S., Naples. Another brainchild of the talented team of Sea Salt's Chef Fabrizio Aielli and his wife, Ingrid, this one presents a number of different Italian experiences in one sidewalk-front cluster. In the bar, long "community tables" encourage meeting new people as you share in European noshes from figs with burrata cheese to Caesar salad with artichoke hearts, and soppressata with caramelized onion and pickled cauliflower mayo paninimini (small sandwich). At its doorstep spreads al fresco tables and umbrellas for a convivial sidewalk café scene. Adjacent, a gelato shop with take-out pizza operation affords a view of a kitchen that seems miniscule for its diverse output. I like the opportunity to try the unusual, or to stick with traditional Italian pasta dishes prepared with Old World care, whether I'm in for lunch and dinner. Wood-fired pizzettes, too, range from traditional margherita to eggplant and sausage with buffalo mozzarella. There's so much more to choose from at dinner—charcuterie, full-sized pizza, fresh pasta, and fresh fish.

The saffron cavatelli pasta with Maine lobster and mascarpone sauce will give you a fair sampling of what Barbatella's is about. You can't go wrong with the lasagna, rabbit cacciatore, or Ligurian Seafood platter (lobster, shrimp, octopus, mussels, and calamari on spaghettini with a light tomato broth). Then you've gotta gelato—the Italian sundaes are especially seductive, but the Nutella and caramelized banana pizza makes its own case for crumbling willpower.

✪ **Bha! Bha!** (239-594-5557; www.bhabhapersianbistro.com), 865 Fifth Ave. S. With its air of "chic desert oasis," Bha! Bha! serves a widely embraced brand of "Persian bistro" cuisine. In an Iranian dialect the name means "Yum! Yum!" And that's where Chef Michael Mir comes in. He fuses his native background with his experience in fine American kitchens to present an intriguing menu that maintains the authenticity and boldness of Middle Eastern cuisine, while employing a few tricks of classic Continental and experimental new American styles. Prepare your palate for a magic carpet ride. *Aash*, a peasant-style herbed bean and noodle soup, starts out simple but, as you nibble into the center garnish of yogurt and onions, becomes more and more complex and extraordinary. In the appetizer of eggplant and artichoke, we could discern an orchestra of flavors: distinctive Bulgarian feta, dill, and a hint of sweetness in the mustard sauce, and the peanut oil in which the eggplant was sautéed. Yum, yum. The menu is divided between classic and innovative Persian cuisine and *khoreshes* (specialties). I recommend the spicy *kermani* beef, its dark saffron sauce enlivened by pepperoncini and cucumber yogurt; char-broiled lamb (incredibly beautiful and tasty); garlic eggplant chicken (wonderful!); and duck *fesenjune*, braised in orange saffron stock and served with pomegranate walnut sauce (a bit heavy sweet). Turkish coffee comes served in a delicate espresso service with an ornamental wooden box full of rock candy and sugar. Try the seasonal sorbet such as pomegranate-strawberry with rosewater or gooey baklava for dessert. Moderate to Expensive. Reservations accepted. Closed Monday in off-season. No lunch.

Bistro 821 (239-261-5821; www.bistro821.com), 821 Fifth Ave. S. Bistro 821, the maverick of Fifth Avenue South and trendsetter in the local bistro craze when it opened in 1994, still leads today despite a swell of competition in its wake. The menu benefits from an injection of fearless creativity. Small plates range from the familiar escargot and fried calamari to the inventive shrimp and spiced beef *chiles rellenos* and grilled prawn with crispy sushi rice cake. Most salads come in appetizer and full portions (be sure to indicate "appetizer" even if you order it as a first course). One menu section is devoted to pasta and risotto, some also as half and full options, with such tempters as tenderloin tips and gorgonzola over penne and seafood risotto. Entrées, too, wax from such traditional bistro fare as meatloaf and pot roast to house specialties: honey mustard–glazed roasted duck, seafood paella, and miso-sake roasted sea bass. The signature coconut, ginger, and lemongrass–encrusted snapper with coconut-ginger jasmine rice and Thai chile peanut sauce will dazzle any sweet tooth. A gluten-free menu, robust wine list, handsome indoor-outdoor dining space, and intriguing dessert menu round out the reasons Bistro 821 will always remain at the Fifth Avenue forefront. Moderate to Expensive. No reservations. No lunch.

The Continental (239-657-0007; damicoscontinental.com), 1205 Third St. S. To call The Continental a "steakhouse" does not do justice. Fine aged, ranch beef certainly takes center stage on the menu, and its interior space has the ornate feel of a traditional steakhouse. But from there on, the restaurant breaks all the rules, spilling out onto a flowered courtyard that sets a more casual tone with its craft-cocktail bar and live music

en papillote, shrimp Provençal, roasted duck with classic orange sauce, and New Zealand rack of lamb. For lighter fare, you may want to dabble in the intriguing starters and small plates: homemade pork terrine with wild mushrooms, Jura salade (beets, green lentils, bacon, Jura cheese, and vanilla dressing), chicken liver with caramelized onions and mushrooms, artisinal cheese plate, fondue of gruyere and Emmentaler cheeses with breads and veggies, and signature onion soup. Even the children's menu is sophisticated, designed by owner/chef Lisa Boët's daughter. The napoleon layers pastry, Chantilly cream, crème anglaise, and berries is a dessert for the books. Or dip fruit and madeleine cookies into decadent fondue *au chocolat*—56 percent cacao couverture. Expensive. Reservations accepted.

○ ❀ ✿ **The Dock at Crayton Cove** (239-263-9940; www.dockcraytoncove .com), 845 12th Ave. S. The Dock remembers what Naples is about—clear down to its roots—while keeping up with what Naples has become. The roots part is reflected in the fun, casual, waterlogged atmosphere exuded from its breeze-through setup and location along Naples's original, circa-1915 fishing harbor. Opened in 1976, the fish house–style eatery has kept abreast of Naples's sophistication with remakes and menu upgrades. Once a purveyor of typical fried seafood fare, today it takes a serious stance among the town's tough culinary standards. Seafood still reigns in traditions such as grouper and chips, Ipswich clams, and fried oysters, but island and Cajun influences have washed in to give us such offerings as Red Stripe baby back ribs with guava sauce, Key lime grouper, and pineapple-glazed sea bass. Chefs execute the creative offerings with complexity. Crafty salads, sandwiches, and specials complete the luncheon offerings, plus the all-day menu offers six fresh catches simply grilled and brushed with Key lime butter. Inexpensive to Expensive. No reservations.

into the wee hours. But back to the menu: Should you decide you're not in the mood for a $46 eight-ounce Piedmontese filet mignon from Italy or Japanese Wagyu priced by the ounce, the day's fresh seafood selections and dishes such as Kurobuta pork chop, cappellini with shrimp, and the best dang burger around provide options. Don't-miss starters and sides include the yellow tail carpaccio, onion soup with bone marrow and pork belly, Brussels sprouts gratin, and potatoes gratin with serrano ham. The dessert menu changes daily. If you see Key lime blackberry pie, grab it. Or end the meal with one of the bar's original and cleverly named cocktails like the Nada Colada. Expensive to Very Expensive. Reservations accepted.

Chez Boët (239-643-6177; www .chezboetnaples.com), 755 12th Ave. S., Naples. It bills its fare as "French home cooking," and much of the product the kitchen uses is local and organic. Reminiscent of the French owners' favorite Parisian haunts, whimsical faces wallpaper brightens the cozy dining space. I'm a big fan of the lamb tagine, a Moroccan form of exotic comfort food with prunes, curry, and couscous; it also comes in seafood and chicken varieties. The *moules frites*—mussels in white wine with hand-cut French fries—ranks a close second. There's also yellowtail snapper

Escargot 41 (239-793-5000; www
.escargot41.com), 4339 N. Tamiami Trail,
at Park Shore Shopping Center. Who
would have thought: near-perfect French
cuisine with only a dozen tables in the
corner of a shopping center next to Party
City? The wine list, nearly as big in size
as the restaurant itself, came as the first
surprise. Our white Bordeaux, Château
Peyruchet, started out light but opened
up marvelously to meet the rich creaminess of our appetizers, which followed a
charming amuse-bouche of puréed eggplant and goat cheese. We felt we must
try escargot, and so opted for the night's
special appetizer in cognac cream. They
were as divine as our mussels appetizer
in their soup of wine, tomatoes, basil, and
a touch of cream. You can also choose
smoked salmon, foie gras, onion soup,
lobster bisque, and Caesar salad to kick
off the meal. As far as entrées go, the
fruits de mer aux morilles delightfully
surprised us next by sheer nonstingy
volume of the morel strips tucked among
shrimp, scallops, and mushrooms—all
luxuriously napped in a champagne
cream sauce with a subtle thyme under-
tone. The yellowtail snapper is fresh,
lightly pan-fried, and served in a Merlot
brown sauce with bacon, baby shrimp,
and mushrooms. Other entrées wander
into meat categories: tournedos sautéed with anchovy butter, duck in plum
port wine sauce, and veal scaloppine in
Calvados cream sauce. For dessert, the
vanilla crème brûlée came heavily caramel crusted in a heart-shaped dish. The
velvety smooth underlie was a creamy
counterpoint, and we toasted it with a
small glass of port and bubbly kir royale.
It was the perfect wrap to a perfect dining experience. Moderate to Expensive.
Reservations required. No lunch,.

Osteria Tulia (239-213-2073; www
.tulianaples.com), 466 Fifth Ave. S. It's
not easy opening an Italian restaurant
in a town fat with them. You need a new
hook, and owner-chef Vicenzo Betulia
came up with "rustic Italian." The theme
applies from the barn-wood paneling

in the cozy restaurant with sidewalk
seating to a menu that employs fine
ingredients, Old World recipes, and
homemade cooking. From the antipasti
selections, we sampled Brussels sprouts
caramelized with house-made fennel
sausage and a warm, creamy herbed
ricotta studded with walnuts and served
with bruschetta. Both marvelous. The
Sicilian meatballs pack the added serendipity of pine nuts, currants, and chili
flakes. The sauce demanded sopping
up with the slices of artisanal bread
provided with crockery cruets of fine
Italian olive oil. Pizzas on the lunch and
dinner menus are cute: Mary Had a Little
Lamb features lamb sausage and ricotta,
for instance. The kitchen also produces
its own pasta, and we sampled it in the
garganelli—penne tossed with a wonderful braised lamb Bolognese-type sauce
and sheep cheese. Wood-roasted Faroe
Island salmon with Marcona almonds
and yogurt, and wood-grilled pork ribeye
with blistered avocado-cilantro-lime give
you an inkling of how the entrees delight
the senses. The lunch menu carries many
of the same dishes plus panini. Craft
cocktails from the bar cap off the experience. Betulia also operates Bar Tulia next
door, an Italian gastropub with its own
kitchen, if you're looking for tapas-style
fare. Reservations accepted at the osteria
only.

Sam-Bucco Bistro (239-592-6050;
www.sambuccobistro.com), 14700 Tamiami Trail N. #5, Naples. The menu here
flexes beyond traditional Italian with
other Mediterranean influences. The
inviting atmosphere of earth tones, linens, low lights, and heavy drapes feels
as warm as the Mediterranean sun. Chef
Sam Tadros, who roams freely to regale
guests like old friends (many are!), made
his recommendations from a menu that
defies decision-making. He was right
about the mushroom soup: Who knew
that old pantry staple could taste so silky
marvelous. I mopped up the very last drop
with the coarse bread that had arrived
earlier along with a flavorful sun-dried

tomato and olive oil dip. Simplicity and quality ingredients made the bruschetta appetizer a pleasure; the Caesar salad, too, weighed in as an unassailable classic. There's also eggplant rollatini, Turkish grilled calamari, and baby greens topped with pine nuts and Roquefort cheese to get this party started. We also took Chef's advice on the fettuccine bolognese, fresh and meaty with a kiss of nutmeg; and the grilled scallops and shrimps with chorizo, braised pear, and asparagus. A tangy pomegranate and sun-dried tomato sauce pulled together the salty and sweet components with delightful dexterity. Italian cuisine figures importantly into the scheme of Chef Sam's vast repertoire, including whole wheat penne with spinach, mushrooms, tomatoes, Gorgonzola, and tomato sauce; porcini risotto; veal piccata or marsala; and the light-as-a-dream tiramisu. Moderate. Reservations recommended.

✪ ☙ **Sea Salt** (239-434-7258; www .seasaltnaples.com), 1186 Third St. S. With 130 or more different types of sea salt in-house on any given day, salt-tasting becomes central to this award-winning dining experience. Then there's also Chef Fabrizio Aielli's Venetian birthright and obvious penchant for global flavors, a whole organic and hormone-free commitment, wines from everywhere, and Norman Love Chocolates. On my recent dining experience, first came a flight of salt with lovely bread and olive oil. The tray contained *kala namak* from India, sel gris from France, and a smoky red clay salt from Hawaii. Flights of six are available upon request, bearing flavored salts such as chipotle or truffle. From the fresh seafood showcase I ordered the whole Mediterranean branzino, which I could then taste with the salts for a different flavor at each bite. Other seafood specialties on the ever-changing menu may include ora king salmon with lentil ragu and crispy hogfish with ricotta gnocchi. In the pasta department, chef's Italian shines through with creative interpretations such as braised veal house-made ravioli with creamy black truffle sauce. Meat comes from local farms when possible: boneless wagyu short ribs, grass-fed Delmonico, and free-range chicken, for instance. For starters, Sea Salt imports the finest charcuterie, cheese, olives, and other tapas and also offers a well-rounded selection of American oysters. The charred octopus is also a popular appetizer. Lunch and bar menus allow you to sample the goodness in lighter, earlier-in-the-day portions, sandwiches, and small plates. Desserts come bite size. In addition to Love truffles, gelato and other confections vie for attention. Moderate to Very Expensive. Reservations recommended.

VANDERBILT BEACH

✪ ♂ **Baleen** (239-598-5707; www .laplayaresort.com), 9891 Gulf Shore Dr., at LaPlaya Beach & Golf Resort, Naples. The best place to sit at Baleen is outdoors on the porch or lamp-lit beach at heavy teak tables and chairs with a front-row seat of the sunset and percussion of the surf. Inside feels dark and formal in comparison. The dinner menu allows you to order your seafood and meat simple—roasted, grilled, or sautéed—or dressed in all the trappings of creative New World cuisine. The signature dish, to illustrate the latter, glazes

SEA SALT SERVES AND SELLS MORE THAN 130 VARIETIES OF NATURAL AND INFUSED SALTS

local snapper with miso and serves with a fire-roasted, head-on prawn. Parsnip puree and butternut squash jam accompany the seared diver scallops. Duck fat-roasted marble potatoes side meat dishes such as herb-roasted chicken and grilled strip steak. For lunch, try the lobster Cobb salad or guava-glazed pork BBQ sandwich. Baleen also serves such breakfast and Sunday entrées as roasted eggs with andouille, lobster, and chipotle crème; and coconut brioche French toast. Expensive to Very Expensive. Reservations accepted.

BAKERIES Bakeries here are often combined with delis, grocery stores, and even wine shops.

Café Chic (239-643-0004; the-cafechic.com), 4360 Gulf Shore Blvd. N., #506 at the Village on Venetian Bay, Naples. A French bakery selling scrumptious pastries, breads, croissant sandwiches, and crepes, plus hot and iced coffees and teas.

Tony's Off Third (239-262-7999; www .tonysoffthird.com), 1300 Third Ave. S., Naples. Dessert bakery featuring legendary cakes, pastries, muffins, and tarts and a well-respected selection of wine and coffee, plus deli and take-out items and sandwiches.

Mon "Key" Bread Factory (239-793-5203; www.monkeybreadfactory.com), 1200 Fifth Ave. S. at Tin City, Naples. Breads, rolls, buns, and other confections with the flavors of the tropics—Key lime, banana, cinnamon, pecan, and coconut.

BREAKFAST ❂ **Breakfast Plus** (239-642-6900), 1035 N. Collier Blvd. #302, at Marco Town Center, Marco Island. The best and most unusual selection of breakfast items around: apple dumplings, peach-stuffed French toast, scrambled eggs and chicken livers, berry crepes, latkes, and more. The New Orleans–style Benedict, egg Hussarde, is phenomenal. Serves breakfast until 2:30 (1:30 in summer), lunch starting at 11. Cash only.

Hoot's (239-394-4644; hootsbreakfast andlunch.com), 563 E. Elkcam Circle, Marco Island; and (239-304-4644), 12676 Tamiami Trail E., Shops at Eagle Creek, Naples. Breakfast served all day (until 2); known for its bread baked fresh daily. Also lunch.

Joe's Diner (239-254-7929; www .joesdiners.com), 9331 Tamiami Trail N., Naples. In an old-fashioned diner setting with outdoor seating, pick from a wide selection of hardy breakfasts all day. Muffins, egg sandwiches, benedicts (love the pot roast benny!), scrambles, cakes: Joe's has it all. Also serves lunch and dinner.

❂ **Old 41 Restaurant** (239-948-4123; www.old41.com), 25091 Bernwood Dr., at Old 41, Bonita Springs. It serves both breakfast and lunch 7–3. The kitchen grinds its own Colombian coffee and makes everything from scratch, with a Philly nod: Taylor pork roll, scrapple, corned beef hash homemade from Boar's Head meat, killer Texas-style French toast with homemade caramel sauce and pecans, Carbon's malted Belgian waffles, omelets, Benedicts, and more.

❂ **Stage Deli Fine Foods** (239-597-2800; www.stage62deli.com), 9105 Strada Pl. at Mercato, Naples. A true Jewish deli, it's all-day breakfast appeals to anyone looking for imagination in their morning repast. The Bloody Mary garnished with a "new pickle," is a good way to start. Pick from one of four hashes with poached eggs, huevos rancheros, omelets, benedicts, and blintzes, and don't skip the bagels.

BREWERIES, WINERIES, DISTILLERIES **Momentum Brewhouse** (239-949-9945; www .momentumbrewhouse.com), 9786 Bonita Beach Rd. SE #1, Bonita Springs. An unusually bright, spacious taproom whose beer is, well, gaining momentum in the local craft beers scene.

Naples Beach Brewing (239-304-8795; www.naplesbeachbrewery.com), 4120 Enterprise Ave. #116, Naples. Sip a Liquid

Sunshine weissbier or Paddle Board pale ale at this, the region's first craft brewery.

Riptide Brewing Company (239-228-6533; riptidebrewingcompany.com), 987 Third Ave. N., Naples. One of the region's newest, its taproom is set in the midst of the brewing operations. Order-in and food truck dining available.

CANDY & ICE CREAM ✎ **The Chocolate Strawberry** (239-394-5999), 937 N. Collier Blvd., Marco Island. The specialty is strawberries hand-dipped in various types of chocolate; also sells truffles, Italian gelato, smoothies, coffee, and chocolates in the shape of turtles, shells, dolphins, and other local critters.

Divino Gelato (239-949-3770, www .divinogelatocafe.com). 26841 S. Bay Dr. #154, Bonita Springs at Promenade at Bonita Bay. Authentic gelato in twenty-four flavors, plus dairy-free sorbetto, gelato javas—milkshakes with a shot of espresso—and bubble tea.

Olde Naples Chocolate (239-262-3975; www.oldenapleschocolate.com), 945 Fifth Ave. N., Naples. An old-fashioned chocolate shop offering choco-late-making classes.

(((•))) **Regina's Ice Cream** (239-434-8181), 824 Fifth Ave. S., Naples. An old-fashioned soda fountain with modern frozen yogurts, sorbets, and sugar-free and name-brand ice cream.

(((•))) ✪ **Sweet Annie's Ice Cream & Candy** (239-642-7180;), 692 Bald Eagle Dr., Marco Island. Old-fashioned-style parlor with black-and-white tiled floor, counter, and chrome-legged stools. It serves more than thirty flavors of ice cream, including sugar-free, frozen yogurt, gelato, and frozen custard.

Sweet Mayberry's Café and Gifts (239-695-0092; www.facebook.com/ sweetmayberryscafe) 207 Broadway W., Everglades City. Near the city park and historical museum, it sells gelato, coffee, and desserts in a cheerful setting.

COFFEE ✪ (((•))) **5th Avenue Coffee Company** (239-261-5757;

www.5thavncoffeeco.com), 599 Fifth Ave. S., Naples. Hot and iced coffee and tea, cappuccino, caffè latte, macchata, bakery goods. Seating indoors and out with high-speed wireless Internet connections.

Peace Love & Little Donuts (239-213-0188; www.peaceloveandlittledonuts .com), 3106 Tamiami Tr. N., Naples. Besides mini-doughnuts in such fla-vors as maple-bacon, spicy Mexican chocolate, lemon ginger, Boston cream pie, chocolate pretzel with sea salt, and strawberry cheesecake, this place pours a great cup of fresh-roasted hot and iced coffee.

Sweet Mayberry's Café and Gifts (239-695-0092; www.facebook.com/ sweetmayberryscafe) 207 Broadway W., Everglades City. Espresso, latte, and other coffee drinks plus gelato and pastries.

(((•))) **Café Chic** (239-643-0004; the cafechic.com), 4360 Gulf Shore Blvd. N., #506 at the Village on Venetian Bay, Naples. Billed as a French café and bak-ery it serves pastries, and sandwiches along with fine hot and iced coffee, cap-puccino, , chai latte, iced coffee and tea.

DELI & SPECIALTY FOODS ✪ **DeRo-mo's Gourmet Market** (239-325-3583; www.deromos.com), 26811 S. Bay Dr. at The Promenade, Bonita Springs. A food-ie's haven of everything fine from fresh produce and deli goods to coffee, pas-tries, and prepared foods.

The Italian Deli & Market (239-394-9493; www.marcoislanditaliandeli.com) 247 Collier Blvd., Marco Island. Highly rated New York-style pizza to go plus cold and hot heroes, foot-long ciabattas, salads, and soups.

Jimmy P's Butcher Shop & Deli (239-643-6328 or 866-998-8927; www .jimmypsbutchershop.com), 1833 Tami-ami Trail N., Naples. This longtime North Naples fixture sells the finest cuts of meat, including Wagyu beef and Kuro-buta pork, plus frozen exotic meats and seafood and deli sandwiches. In 2015, the restaurant Jimmy P's Charred opened next door.

Pepper's Fine Food (239-643-2008; www.peppersnaples.com), 4165 Corporate Square, Naples. Butcher shop with every kind of sausage, plus cheeses, fresh sauerkraut, potato salad, hot lunches, and other German foods.

Ródes Seafood Restaurant & Marketplace (239-992-4040 or 800-786-0450;), 3756 Bonita Beach Rd., Bonita Beach. Fresh produce and local seafood market. Also sells fresh breads and gourmet groceries.

Tony's Off Third (239-262-7999; www.tonysoffthird.com), 1300 Third St. S., Naples. Breakfast and lunch sandwiches, prepackaged deli salads, and yummy muffins and pastries.

Wynn's (239-261-7157; www.wynnsonline.com), 141 Ninth St. N., Naples. Since 1948 the Wynn family has operated this landmark, most famous for its fine selection of wine, seafood, fresh bakery goodies, desserts, and hot-and-cold prepared deli foods.

FRUIT & VEGETABLE STANDS **Bonita Springs Lions Farmers' Market** (239-992-4011), Old 41 Rd. and Pennsylvania, Riverside Park, Bonita Springs. Fresh fruits and vegetables and baked goods every Wednesday 8–1.

Marco Island Farmers' Market (239-642-0575; www.cityofmarcoisland.com), Veteran's Community Park, 901 Park Ave., Marco Island. Fresh local produce, flowers, sauces, honey, seafood, and artisan works. Every Wednesday 7:30-1 through mid-April.

Third Street South Farmers' Market (239-434-6533; www.thirdstreetsouth.com/farmersmarket.html), parking lot at Third St. S. and 13th Ave., Old Naples. Every Saturday 7:30–11:30 a.m. year-round.

✪ **Oakes Farms Market** (239-732-0144; www.oakesfarms.com), 2205 Davis Blvd., Naples. A supermarket of super fresh food picks: organic and other produce, fine meats, bakery goods, gourmet items, fresh-ground nut butters, and deli and prepared food options.

NATURAL FOODS **Food & Thought Organic Market & Restaurant** (239-213-2222; www.foodandthought.com), 2132 Tamiami Trail N., at Gateway Plaza, Naples. Smoothies and juice bar; fresh, prepared, and preserved organic food; indoor and outdoor seating.

For Goodness Sake (239-992-5838; fgsorganicmarkets.com), 9118 Bonita Beach Rd. E., at Sunshine Plaza, Bonita Springs; and (239-353-7778), 7211 Radio Rd., Naples. Full line of health groceries, including local honey, fresh produce, frozen products, and a menu of salads, sandwiches, and fruit or protein smoothies.

Summer Day Market and Café (239-394-8361; www.summerdaymarket.com), 1069 N. Collier Blvd. #215, in Marco Town Center, Marco Island. Inviting market with full line of fresh, frozen, bulk, and processed organic, gluten-free, and low-carb products, including baby food. Sandwich and smoothie-juice and salad bars with outdoor tables.

PIZZA & TAKE-OUT **Aurelio's** (239-403-8882; www.aureliospizza.com), 2048 N. Tamiami Trail at Coastland Center, Naples. Since 1959, this Chicago-born chain has served pizza, pasta, and other Italian specialties to eat in or to go. Mama Aurelio's Calabrese, stuffed with spinach and cheese, is especially tasty.

✪ **Oakes Farms Market** (239-732-0144; www.oakesfarms.com), 2205 Davis Blvd., Naples. Deli and hot sandwiches, homemade soup, burgers, salads, pizza, and hot entrées in a market setting with some seating.

Three60 Market (239-732-7331; three60market.com), 2891 Bayview Dr. Fresh-made breads and other bakery treats, THE BEST tomato pie, plus salads, sandwiches, pasta dishes, and other tasty entrée stations for take-out and eat-in (outside on the waterside deck) breakfast and lunch. Also affordable wine.

SEAFOOD **Captain & Krewe Seafood Market & Raw Bar** (239-263-1976; http: www.cknaples.com), 629 Eighth St. S., Naples. Formerly Capt. Kirk's, new owners have created a bright, cheerful space for buying fresh seafood or eating in, just off Fifth Avenue South.

City Seafood (239-695-4700 www .cityseafood1.com), 702 Begonia St., Everglades City. Find all that's fresh and special about Everglades cuisine: stone crab in season, alligator tail, frogs' legs, lobster, grouper, and Key lime pie. Serves breakfast, lunch, and early dinner dockside.

Kirk Fish Co. (239-394-8616; kirkfish .com) 417 Papaya St., Goodland. Friendly little fish market right on Goodland's working waterfront, surrounded by crab traps. All varieties of local shell and fin fish.

Lee Be Fish Company (239-389-0580; www.leebefish.com), 350 Royal Palm Dr., Old Marco Shops, Marco Island. Everything local and beyond—from shrimp, stone crab claws, and grouper to oysters, clams, and Maine lobster. Also prepared take-out such as fried fish baskets and seafood tacos.

Ródes Seafood Restaurant & Marketplace (239-992-4040 or 800-786-0450), 3756 Bonita Beach Rd., Bonita Springs. Fresh produce and local seafood market inside a restaurant.

✳ Selective Shopping

Custom-designed jewelry, exclusive top-designer fashion lines, original masterpiece art, and the world's first street concierge make the experience of browsing, buying, and window-yearning in Naples entirely unique. Naples ranks with Palm Beach's Worth Avenue and Sarasota's St. Armands Circle among Florida's most chic arenas for spending. Downtown concentrates the shopping frenzy in the Old Naples districts of Fifth Avenue South and Third Street South, but a number of other fashionable shopping centers are found throughout town. Downtown shops are known for their individually owned and one-of-a-kind galleries and designer outlets.

SHOPPING CENTERS & MALLS **10th Street Design District** (10th St. and Central Ave., Naples) Around this intersection, shoppers find a collection of flooring, interiors, lighting, and architectural stores, plus antique and secondhand shops.

Coastland Center (239-262-2323; www.coastlandcenter.com), 1900 Tamiami Trail N. at Golden Gate Pkwy., Naples. Naples's largest and only enclosed, climate-controlled shopping center has 150 stores and eateries, including a full array of shopping options, from major department stores to small specialty shops. Chain names include, Sears, Old Navy, Victoria's Secret, Bath & Body Works, and Starbucks.

Marco Town Center Mall, Collier Blvd. and Bald Eagle Dr., Marco Island. A popular cluster of more than ten distinctive eateries and forty shops. There's live entertainment January to April on Wednesday evenings at 6–8.

Mercato (239-254-1080; www .mercatoshops.com), 9132 Strada Pl. #11103, Tamiami Trail at Vanderbilt Rd., Naples. Its stores, boutiques, restaurants, and bars are mostly of the high-end franchise variety, such as Whole Foods, Sur La Table, Books-A-Million, Coldwater Creek, Jos. A. Bank, and Capital Grille, plus the luxury Silverspot movie experience. Mercato hosts outdoor movies and live music throughout the year.

Promenade at Bonita Bay (239-949-1573; www.promenadeshops.com) 26795-26851 S. Bay Dr., Bonita Springs. This once-fashionable al fresco shopping center has risen again after a recessional downfall. Anchored by the new DeRomo's Gourmet Market & Restaurant, it comprises a number of fine jewelry and clothing stores.

MUST SEE

⊙ **Fifth Avenue South** (239-692-8436; www.fifthavenuesouth. com), Naples. Once upon an eon, members of the Seminole tribe sold their crafts from a stand on Fifth Avenue. Today it's one of Naples's most fashionable addresses. In 1996, a movement started to update the historic district, which had begun to look run-down. Famed Florida planner Andrés Duany was hired to breathe new life into the district. Besides making cosmetic improvements, he brought a new bustle to the street. Tony hotels, shops, and twenty-plus restaurants and sidewalk cafés attract Naples's "café society." Live entertainment and special events are regularly scheduled.

Shops of Marco, San Marco Rd. and Barfield Dr., Marco Island. One-of-a-kind clothing and gift shops.

Third Street South (239-434-6533; www.thirdstreetsouth.com), Naples. Visit this upscale shopping quarter in Old Naples, the heart of the arts scene. The Plaza shopping scene in recent years has declined, but new, vaunted restaurants and bars keep the district lively. Saturdays in season, a farmers' market convenes in the main parking lot. There's music and other entertainment every Thursday evening in season (November–May) 6–9; the third Thursday in the off-season.

🐚 **Tin City** (239-262-4200; www.tin -city.com), 1200 Fifth Ave. S., US 41 at Goodlette Rd., Naples. I love the structure of this mall, which resurrected old tin-roofed docks. Its thirty shops in two buildings tend to be touristy, selling mainly nautical gifts and resort wear. But it also offers enjoyable waterfront restaurants, plus it's a good place to catch a fishing or sight-seeing tour.

⊙ **The Village on Venetian Bay** (239-261-6100; www.venetianvillage.com), 4200 Gulf Shore Blvd., at Park Shore Dr., Naples. An upscale, Mediterranean-style domain of fashion, jewelry, and art located on the waterfront. The complex holds more than forty-five restaurants

SHOP UNTIL YOU DINE: MERCATO, NAPLES' NEWEST SHOPPING VENUE, IS EQUALLY KNOWN FOR ITS RESTAURANTS AND CLUBS

THE ARCHITECTURE OF THE VILLAGE ON VENETIAN BAY SHOPPING DISTRICT CONTRIBUTES TO THE ITALIAN FLAVOR OF AMERICA'S NAPLES

and stores plus an interactive water fountain.

Waterside Shops at Pelican Bay (239-598-1605; www.watersideshops.com), 5415 Tamiami Trail, Naples. This shopping enclave features Saks Fifth Avenue, Nordstrom, Williams-Sonoma, Ann Taylor, other high-end chains, and some fun dining options—all located in a setting of contemporary stainless steel, cascading waters, and lush foliage. Covered parking available.

WELCOME TO TIN CITY—NAUTICAL KITSCH AT ITS BEST

ANTIQUES & COLLECTIBLES **Ashley Adams Arts & Antiques** (239-435-7273), 795 Fifth Ave. S., Naples. Literally packed with large European, Oriental, and American bronze, silver, and porcelain sculptures, plus clocks, furniture, and more, both new and old.

The Englishman (239-649-8088; www.theenglishmanusa.com), 1190 Third St. S. Naples. For top-shelf European furniture, oil paintings, and sculpture from the nineteenth and twentieth centuries, browse the fine treasures here.

BOOKS **Sunshine Booksellers** (239-393-0353; www.sunshinebooksellers.com), 677 S. Collier Blvd., Marco Island; and (239-394-5343), 1000 N. Collier Blvd., Marco Island. Large, modern stores with a complete line of books, plus greeting cards, gifts, puzzles, games, and toys.

CLOTHING **All About April** (239-430-0444; www.allaboutapril), 4350 Gulf Shore Blvd. N. at Village on Venetian Bay, Naples. Simply adorable, but pricey fashions for doted-upon kids and grandkids.

Children's Couture (239-405-7401), 26811 S. Bay Dr., Bonita Springs at Promenade at Bonita Bay. It carries a delightful line of clothes, gifts, toys and books for the wee ones.

Butterfly Beach 9239-394-0837; www.butterflybeachclothing.com), 760 N. Collier, at the Esplanade, Marco Island. Colorful and casual tropical fashions, shoes, and other affordable accessories.

Fia's Island Woman (239-642-6116; www.fiasislandwoman.com), 217 Harbor Pl., Goodland. Goodland's answer to a department store: hand-painted silk fashions, gemstone jewelry, T-shirts, sarongs, tropical art, crafts, wild wigs, and other crazy stuff.

John Craig Clothiers (239-301-2080; johncraigclothier.com), 26832 S. Bay Dr. #106, Bonita Springs at Promenade at Bonita Bay. Men's fine dress wear.

Kay's on the Beach (239-394-1033), 1089 Bald Eagle Dr., Marco Island. A distinctive blend of suits and gorgeous formal wear for mature women. Also locations at Promenade at Bonita Bay in Bonita Springs and on Fifth Avenue South in Naples.

Marco Island Clothing Co. (239-642-7277;), 117 S. Barfield Dr., at Shops of Marco, Marco Island. Stylish name-brand women's swimsuits, shoes, tropical resort fashions, and accessories.

Marissa Collections (239-263-4333 or 800-581-6641; www.marissacollections.com), 1167 Third St. S., Naples. Carries prestige designer labels such as Givenchy, Michael Kors, Marchesa, Bruno Cucinelli, and Oscar de la Renta.

Mondo Uomo (239-434-9484; mondouomo.com), 4232 Gulf Shore Blvd., at the Village on Venetian Bay, Naples. Fine, tasteful fashion and European styles for men: tropical wool, German cotton, sweaters, and distinctive casual and dress wear for Gulf Coast climes. The Promenade store is called Mondo Uomo & Donna, and also carries stylish name-brand women's wear.

Obsession (239-393-6332; obsessionmarco.boutiquewindow.com), 124 Barfield Dr., at Shops of Marco, Marco Island. This boutique appeals to thirty-something women with casual clothing and jewelry that spells individual style.

Old Naples Surf Shop (239-262-1877; www.oldnaplessurfshop.com), 1311 Third St. S., Naples. Every Florida town must have one, whether or not surfing conditions exist there. This one carries the usual selection of brand-name surf apparel and accessories, plus surf, skim, and stand-up paddle boards.

OMG That's Chic (239-970-2101; www.omgthatschic.com), 1089 N. Collier Blvd., at Marco Town Center, Marco Island. You'll find lace-trimmed jeans, animal prints, cowboy styles and even Mexican-style muumuus for women, plus shoes, jewelry, and other accessories.

Signatures (239-676-7290; www.signaturesnaples.com), 26795 S. Bay Dr. #164, Bonita Springs at Promenade at Bonita Bay. Stylish fashions for the mature woman.

Simply Natural (239-643-5571; www.venetianvillage.com/simply-natural), 4330 Gulf Shore Blvd. N., Suite 302, at the Village on Venetian Bay, Naples. High-end youthful women's fashions in lace, denim, and other contemporary fabrics and styles. Also stores on Fifth Ave. S. and in Mercato.

Wildflower (239-643-6776; wildflower boutique.biz), 4222 Gulf Shore Blvd. N., at the Village on Venetian Bay, Naples. Distinctive fun and formal women's wear with Florida flair and style.

CONSIGNMENT Naples is a second-hand shopper's paradise. In many of the clothing consignment shops you can find designer fashions with the price tags still attached. Oh, the joys of hunting down the castoffs of the well-to-do!

Encore Retail Shop (239-775-0032; www.davidlawrencecenter.org/encore. php), 3105 Davis Blvd., Naples. Designer furniture, paintings, decorative items, and collectibles.

New to You Consignment (239-263-8400), 933 Creech Rd., Naples. Women's designer clothing and high-end furniture and decorative items.

FACTORY OUTLET CENTERS **Naples Outlet Center** (239-775-8083 or 888-545-7196; www.primeoutlets.com), 6060 Collier Blvd. #121, Naples. Though the location is looking a bit deserted these days, you can still find Izod, Coach, Samsonite, Bass, Ann Taylor, and a smattering of other stores open.

FLEA MARKETS & BAZAARS **Flamingo Island Flea Market** (239-948-7799; www .flamingoisland.com), 11902 Bonita Beach Rd., Bonita Springs. Open Friday to Sunday 8–4, with up to six hundred retail, services, and food vendors.

GALLERIES Naples has earned a reputation as a mecca for fine art. Gallery Row, along Broad Avenue South at Third Street South, is a good place to begin your art quest. Galleries line the street and sell a wide spectrum of art. Several more lie in the immediate vicinity. Fifth Avenue South is another area, although the galleries there are more spread out.

Casanova Art Gallery (239-571-1610; www.casanovaart.com), 4320 Gulf Shore Blvd. N., at Village on Venetian Bay, Naples. Casanova occupies two

ART AND GREENERY MAKE WINDOW-SHOPPING ALONG NAPLES'S THIRD STREET SOUTH A MULTIDIMENSIONAL EXPERIENCE

store-fronts at this shopping complex, but the Venetian glass gallery impresses most with its two floors of exquisite Murano vessels, chandeliers, masks, sculptures, and clowns. At the other, you will find fine oils and sculptures.

Local Color Art Gallery (239-394-2787, www.malendatrick.com/localcolor), 258 Royal Palm Drive at the Shops of Olde Marco, Marco Island. Ten local artists display and sell their wares on the second floor of the shopping center. Media ranges from watercolors to photography, sculpture, and jewelry.

Nora Butler Designs (239-403-8287; www.norabutler.com), 800 12th Ave. S., Naples, at Crayton Cove. The namesake artist has licensed her trademark colored-pencil tropical designs to national note card and gift companies. Here she sells prints and Giclées on canvas of her whimsical pelicans, mermaids, seashells, and more.

The Darvish Collection (239-261-7581; www.artnet.com/darvish.html), 1199 Third St. S. #2, Naples. Features the work of North American and European masters within its seven wood-lined, clublike galleries. Most works in the four- to six-figure range.

East West Fine Art (239-220-7503; eastwestfineart.com), 9115 Strada Pl. #5130 at Mercato, Naples; and 2425 Tamiami Trail N. #102 at Bigham Galleries, Naples. Formerly the Gallery on Fifth at Mercato, it has expanded and changed names to reflect its global range. Modern, striking paintings and mixed media pieces with Russian and other international influence.

Gallery One (239-263-0835; www.galleryonenaples.com), 770 Fifth Ave. S., Naples. My favorite Naples gallery, it exhibits mostly 3-D art, including a preponderance of glass.

Guess-Fisher Gallery (239-403-8393 or 239-659-2787; www.philfisherfineart.com), 810 12th Ave. S., Naples, at Crayton Cove. The husband-and-wife team of Phil Fisher and Natalie Guess sells mostly their own work here near the water. He specializes in bright impressionistic paintings of local themes, she in batik.

HW Gallery (239-263-6640; www.hwgallery.com), 1305 Third St. S., Naples. Look here for the work of celebrated artists, such as Britto, Warhol, Peter Max, and Rauschenberg.

Native Visions Gallery (239-643-3785; www.callofafrica.com), 737 Fifth Ave. S., Naples. Remarkable works themed around Africa, the sea, and the environment.

Riverside Park (239-949-6262), Old US 41 Rd. and Pennsylvania, downtown Bonita Springs. City officials saved a row of historic circa-1954 fish shacks from demolition by renovating them and turning them into a string of six art galleries/shops. You'll find the most activity the second Friday of each month, when "Evening in the Park" takes place during season, and Thursdays 10–4 when visitors can meet the artists.

Silver Eagle (239-403-3033; www.silvereaglegallery.com), 850 Fifth Ave. S., Naples. Decorative Native American drums, blankets, and headdresses; paintings and beautiful silver and turquoise jewelry.

Sweet Art (239-597-2110; www.thesweetartgallery.com), 2054 Trade Center Way, Naples. Affordable tropical decorative art and home accessories.

GIFTS Some of Naples's best souvenirs are found in the gift shops at the town's visitor attractions.

The Blue Mangrove Gallery (239-393-2405; www.bluemangrovegallery.com), 1089 N. Collier Blvd. #417, at Marco Town Center, Marco Island. Baby and children's gifts, jewelry, furniture and accessories, photography, and art, all with a local slant.

Pucci & Catana (239-263-9663; www.pucciandcatana.com), 647 Fifth Ave. S., Naples. Over-the-top designer doggy outfits and accessories, plus fun gifts for pet-lovers.

Regatta (239-262-3929), 760 Fifth Ave. S., Naples. Regatta's subtitle describes it best: "fun things for fun people." Clothes, toys, and things for the home, all in a fine and whimsical tone.

Ship's Store (23-394-2502; www.rosemarina.com/ships-store.htm), 951 Bald Eagle Dr., at Rose Marco River Marina, Marco Island. Something of a nautical department store, with everything from select women's, children's, and men's outdoor fashions to beachy home accessorites, bait, and fishing/boating gear.

JEWELRY **Antica Murrina** (239-362-1789), 26821 S. Bay Dr. #119, Bonita Springs at Promenade at Bonita Bay. Florida's only outlet for this brand of fine artisan Murano glass jewelry from Venice, Italy.

Cleopatra's Barge (239-261-7952 or 800-678-7934; www.cleopatrasbarge .com), 1197 Third St. S., Naples. Home of "Naples Medallion" jewelry and other fine handcrafted and traditional pieces. Certified jewelers and diamond setters.

DuFrane Jewelers (239-495-9005 or 888-DUFRANE; www.dufranejewelers .com), 8200 Health Center Blvd. #103, Bonita Springs. Besides gorgeous diamond jewelry and watches, this large outlet sells fine china and crystal and other elegant table- and barware.

Exquisite Timepieces (239-262-4545; www.exquisitetimepieces.com), 4380 Gulf Shore Blvd. #800 at Village on Venetian Bay, Naples. New and preowned brand-name men's and ladies' watches from Aquadiva to Zannetti.

Golden Gate Jewelers of Marco (239-259-8937; ggjmarco.com) 133 Barfield Dr., in Shops of Marco, Marco Island. It sells sea- and island-themed pieces, including customizable Marco charms.

Pearl (239-643-9779; www .bluediamondjewelers.com), 4320 Gulfshore Blvd. N. #209, Naples, at the Village on Venetian Bay. Specializing in pearls from around the world.

✪ **Port Royal Jewelers** (239-263-3071; www.portroyaljewelers.com), 623 Fifth Ave. S., Naples. This place is like a museum: It includes eighteenth-century royal jewels and antique pieces in art deco, Edwardian, Georgian, and Victorian styles, as well as custom-designed and estate jewelry. It's so exclusive you have to ring a doorbell to get in, and there's a special vault containing the real treasures.

Thalheimers Fine Jewelers (239-261-8422; thalheimers.com), 3200 Tamiami Trail N. #100, Naples. This well-respected name in jewelers carries quality watches, diamond jewelry, gems, crystal, and porcelain. Watchmaker, designer, and appraiser on premises.

✪ **Wm. Phelps, Custom Jeweler** (239-434-2233 or 888-757-2233; www .phelpsjewelers.com), 4380 Gulf Shore Blvd. N. #812, at the Village on Venetian Bay, Naples. Fine-crafted pendants, rings, earrings, and pins on display, including its signature nature collection of gorgeous birds and shells, plus colored stones and diamonds for customizing.

Yamron Jewelers (239-592-7707 or 800-492-6766; www.yamron.com), 5415 Tamiami Trail N., at Waterside Shops, Naples. A select stock of exquisite diamond and other precious stone jewelry and Swiss watches.

KITCHENWARE & HOME DÉCOR **Fabec-Young & Co.** (239-649-5501; www.venetianvillage.com/fabec -young-co), 4360 Gulf Shore Blvd. N., #604, at the Village on Venetian Bay, Naples. Unusual table settings, including napkins, candles, glassware, silver, and ceramics.

Gattle's (239-262-4791 or 800-344-4552; www.gattles.com), 1250 Third St. S., Naples. Fine linens for bed, bath, and table; home accessories and art.

The Good Life (239-514-4663; good-lifenaples.com), 2355 Vanderbilt Beach Rd. #176. This longtime Naples fixture (originally located in the Third Street South Plaza) has stocked cooks with the finest variety of cookware and entertaining accessories for decades. It hosts cooking classes throughout the year.

A Horse of a Different Color (239-261-1252), 4226 Gulf Shore Blvd. N., at the Village on Venetian Bay, Naples. Pricey, one-of-a-kind, highly contemporary and casual gifts, tableware, and home accents.

SHELL SHOPS **The Blue Mussel** (239-262-4814; www.bluemussel.com), 757 Fifth Ave. S., Naples. Specimen shells and shell-themed jewelry and gifts.

Kelly's Shell Shack (239-774-0494; kellysfishhousediningroom.com/shell -shack.html), 1302 Fifth Ave. S., Naples. Shells, sponges, sharks teeth, fossils, jewelry and nautical gifts. All guests go home with a free seashell. Shop for craft supplies, books, windsocks, and stuffed toys.

Marco Craft & Shell Company (239-394-7020; www
.marcocraftandshellcompany.com), 1089
N. Collier Blvd. #424, at Marco Town
Center Mall, Marco Island. Craft and
specimen shells, locally handcrafted
gifts, other craft supplies.

Sea Shell Co. (239-390-1815), 4461
Bonita Beach Rd., Bonita Springs. Pristine as an art gallery, it displays fine
specimen shells along with shell craft
supplies, jewelry, and other gifts.

✳ Special Events

January: **Bonita Springs National
Art Festival** (239-495-8989; www
.artcenterbonita.org/artfest), Riverside
Park, 10450 Reynolds St., Bonita Springs.
A top-rated, two-day show midmonth featuring fine artists from around the world.
Also in February and March. **Downtown
Naples New Year's Eve Art Fair** (239-
262-6517www.naplesart.org), Fifth Ave.
S., Naples. Fine artisans fill the street the
weekend after New Year's.

**Marco National Fine Arts & Fine
Crafts Festival** (239-394-4221; www
.marcoislandart.com), 1010 Winterberry
Dr., at the Art League of Marco Island
grounds, Marco Island. Two days midmonth for an outdoor art fling. **Mullet
Festival** (239-394-3041 or 877-387-2582;
www.stansidlehour.com), Stan's Idle
Hour restaurant, Goodland. Celebrating
Goodland's fishing heritage with an
extravaganza of music and tomfoolery,
including the Buzzard Queen contest.
Three days the weekend before Super
Bowl. **Naples Winter Wine Festival**
(239-514-2239 or 888-837-4919; www
.napleswinefestival.com), 4305 Exchange
Ave., Naples. Held throughout Naples, it
benefits local children with a high-yielding live auction and pricey vintner dinners in private homes. **Southwest Florida
Nature Festival** (239-530-5940; www
.rookerybay.org), Rookery Bay National
Estuarine Research Reserve, Naples.
Weekend midmonth; live animals, family

activities, guided field trips, children's
programs. **Swamp Buggy Races**
(239-774-2701 or 800-897-2701; www
.swampbuggy.com), Florida Sports Park,
CR 951, East Naples. Nationally televised
event; the Everglades equivalent of tractor pulls or monster truck racing.

February: **Jammin' in the Hammock
Annual Bluegrass Festival** (239-394-
3397; www.floridastateparks.org/
park/Collier-Seminole), Collier-
Seminole State Park. Second weekend
of the month. Admission. ✪ **Everglades
Seafood Festival** (239-695-2277; www
.evergladesseafoodfestival.org), Everglades City. Three days of music, arts
and crafts, carnival rides, and fresh seafood. Early in the month. **Greek
Festival** (239-591-3430; stkatherine.net),
St. Katherine's Greek Orthodox
Church, 7100 Airport Rd., Naples.
Greek food specialties, music, costumed
dancers, and exhibits. Five days at the
end of the month. **Marjory Stoneman
Douglas Festival** (239-695-0008; www
.colliermuseums.com/events), Museum
of the Everglades, Everglades City. Pays
tribute to author Douglas's groundbreaking work in preserving the Everglades
with talks, boat tours, guided walks, and
canoe trips. Late month. **Naples National
Art Festival** (239-262-6517; www
.naplesart.org), Cambier Park, downtown
Naples. This prime art festival event
takes place over two days midmonth.
Donation suggested.

March: ✿ **Collier County Fair** (239-
455-1444; www.colliercountyfair.com),
Collier County Fairgrounds, 751 39th
Ave. NE, Naples. A good old-fashioned
fair with rides and exhibits. Midmonth
for eleven days. Also in January. **Marco
Island Seafood Festival** (239-394-7549;
www.marcoislandseafoodfestival.com),
Veterans Park, 403 Elkam Circle, Marco
Island. Seafood, music, and good times.
One weekend late in the month. **Naples
St. Patrick's Day Parade** (naplesparade.
com). Celebrate in true Irish spirit as this
parade makes its way through Fifth Avenue South and Third Street South one

day mid-March. ✍ **Old Florida Festival** (239-252-8476; www.colliermuseums .com), Collier County Museum, Naples. Living history from the Stone Age to World War II, with food, crafts, games, demonstrations, and reenactments. One weekend early in the month.

April: **Swamp Buggy Races** (239-774-2701 or 800-897-2701; www.swampbuggy .com), Florida Sports Park, CR 951, East Naples. See January. The Conservancy of Southwest Florida (239-262-0304; www.conservancy.org) hosts ✍ **Earth Day Festival** each year on the Saturday closest to April 22.

May: **Stay in May** (239-390-2788; stayinmay.com) Two weeks of music, dance, film, theater, and culinary arts in Naples early in the month. **A Taste of Collier** (239-331-7371; www.tasteofcollier. com), Fifth Ave. S., Naples. Naples's renowned restaurants serve samples of their culinary specialties. Live music. One Sunday early in the month. **Great Dock Canoe Race** (239-404-6718; www. greatdockcanoerace.com), the Dock at Crayton Cove restaurant, 12th Ave. S., Naples. More than two hundred teams, many in festive costumes, paddle across Naples Bay in good-spirited competition that kicks off with a parade. One Saturday midmonth.

June: **Spammy Jammy** (239-394-5663; www.littlebarrestaurant.com), The Little Bar, Goodland. A wacky one-night celebration befitting Goodland, featuring Spam creations, nighttime apparel, and a good bit of drinking. End of month. **SummerJazz** (239-261-2222; www.naplesbeachhotel.com), Naples Beach Hotel & Golf Club, Naples. A series of sunset concerts under the stars one Saturday every month, June through September.

October: ✍ **Boo at the Zoo** (239-262-5409; www.napleszoo.org), Naples Zoo, 1590 Goodlette-Frank Rd., Naples. One afternoon of trick-or-treating close to Halloween. Shortly after the opening of stone crab season on October 15, Naples celebrates with a weekend-long **Stone Crab Festival** (www.stonecrabfestival. org) at Tin City. **Swamp Buggy Races**. See January. The October races kick off the season with a parade. Late month.

November: **Festival of Lights** (239-434-6533; www.thirdstreetsouth.com), Third St. S., Naples. Holiday street- and tree-lighting festivities, open houses at shops, and music. Five days around Thanksgiving. **Naples International Film Festival** (239-877-2819; www .naplesfilmfest.com), Silverspot at Mercato, US 41 and Vanderbilt Beach Rd. Five days early in the month. Also a summer series. ✍ **Old Florida Festival** (239-252-8476; www.colliermuseums.com), Collier County Museum, Naples. Living history from the Stone Age to World War II, with food, crafts, games, demonstrations, and reenactments. One weekend late in the month.

HIGHLIGHTS

If Time Is Short

Not enough time to do it all on this trip to southwest Florida? Here are some highlights I suggest to weekenders and short-term vacationers who wonder how they can best spend their precious time. Beach time, of course, is a high priority for those with only a few days to spend in the sun. I list must-see beaches as well as other attractions, adventures, restaurants, and lodgings you should not miss.

BRADENTON & MID-COAST

The beaches of Anna Maria Island are a clear highlight of any visit to Manatee County. For a splurge dine-out adventure, dine on the gulf at **Beach Bistro** (941-778-6444; www.beachbistro.com; 6600 Gulf Dr., Holmes Beach).

✪ **Longboat Key** provides a drive on the coast's wealthy side. Dine in the spirit of maritime fun at ✪ **Mar Vista Dockside Restaurant & Pub** (941-383-2391; www.groupersandwich.com; 760 Broadway St., Longboat Key).

Downtown Bradenton and its **Riverwalk** deserve an afternoon's stroll. Across the river, **Palmetto** offers a historic park and **Emerson Point Preserve** (941-721-6885; www.mymanatee.org; 5801 17th St. W., Palmetto) for biking, hiking, and exploring an ancient Indian mound. Spend the night at historic **Palmetto Riverside Bed & Breakfast** (941-981-5331; www.palmettoriverside.com; 1102 Riverside Dr., Palmetto). For a trip to old Florida, visit the museums, fish houses, and working waterfront in **Cortez**.

SARASOTA BAY COAST

✪ **Siesta Beach** (941-861-5000; 948 Beach Way Dr., Siesta Key), despite its weekend and high-season crowds, is the area's ultimate beach. Its sands are white and fluffy beyond belief. Have dinner at **Ophelia's on the Bay** (941-349-2212; opheliasonthe-bay.net; 9105 Midnight Pass Rd., Siesta Key), ingenious fare with a calming view.

✪ **Downtown Sarasota** is a happening place. Take in a play and circle the galleries of the Theatre and Arts District. Don't miss the shops of **Palm Avenue** (www.palmavenue.org) and the galleries of ✪ **Towles Court Artist Colony** (www.towlescourt.com; 1938 Adams Ln., Sarasota).

PUNTA GORDA'S HISTORIC CITY HALL

HEED THIS WARNING SIGN AT PINE ISLAND'S "WORLD'S FISHINGEST BRIDGE."

✪ **The Ringling Museum of Art**, , and the complex's various circus and Gilded Age attractions (941-355-5101; www .ringling.org; 5401 Bay Shore Rd., Sarasota) crown in glory Sarasota's famed cultural scene.

CHARLOTTE HARBOR COAST

The best of Charlotte Harbor lies in its hidden-from-the-spotlight barrier islands. **Manasota Key** and **Englewood Beach** boast sunny beaches flecked with shark teeth. For a unique and nature-intensive lodging experience, book at ✪ **Manasota Beach Club** (941-474-2614; www .manasotabeachclub.com; 7660 Manasota Key Rd., Englewood), a long-standing beach resort with accommodations from rustic to lavish.

On Gasparilla Island, **Boca Grande** supplies a full day of beaching, shopping, and dining. Have lunch or dinner at ✪ **PJ's Seagrille** (239-964-0806; www.pjseagrille.com; 312 Park Ave., Boca Grande) and savor something from the sea, inventive and well crafted. For a different flavor of island life, take a room at the old, gracious **Gasparilla Inn** (239-964-4500 or 800-996-1913; www.gasparillainn.com; 500 Palm Ave., Boca Grande), as the Vanderbilts and Du Ponts did starting back in the 1910s.

For an island wilderness adventure that returns you to the days of Florida cow-hunting, ride the bouncy swamp buggy through a modern-day cattle ranch at ✪ **Babcock Ranch Preserve Eco-Tour** (941-637-0551 or 800-500-5583; www.myfwc.com/viewing/ recreation/wmas/cooperative/babcock-ranch-preserve; 800 FL 31, Punta Gorda).

ISLAND COAST

Fort Myers's finest attraction, the ✪ **Edison & Ford Winter Estates** (239-334-7419; www .edisonfordwinterestates.org; 2350 McGregor Blvd., Fort Myers), peeks into the times and genius of America's greatest inventors, who lived side by side in winter months long past. Dine Victorian in the two historic homes that make up ✪ **The Veranda** (239-332-2065; www.verandarestaurant.com; 2122 Second St., Fort Myers), which specializes in Southern charm and fine cuisine.

Much of what's special about the Island Coast has to do with what's wild. More than half of Sanibel Island is devoted to the ✪ **J. N. "Ding" Darling National Wildlife Refuge** (239-472-1100; www.fws.gov/refuge/jn_ding_darling/; 1 Wildlife Dr., off Sanibel-Captiva Rd., Sanibel Island), home to alligators, roseate spoonbills, manatees, river otters, and bobcats. The best way to see it is by tram or paddling tour from **Tarpon Bay Explorers** (239-472-8900; www.tarponbayexplorers.com; 900 Tarpon Bay Rd., Sanibel Island).

Sanibel's beaches are renowned for their bountiful shells and minimal impact on nature's birthright beauty. Most natural and secluded is ✪ **Bowman's Beach** (Bowman's Beach Rd. off Sanibel-Captiva Rd.). To find the utmost in remote beaches, rent a boat or hop a charter to unbridged **Cayo Costa Island** and **North Captiva Island** (www .floridastateparks.org), where state parks preserve slices of Old Florida.

For lively beaching, follow CR 865 through Estero Island's **Fort Myers Beach** and down along lovely, undeveloped Lovers Key en route to ✪ **Bonita Beach**. On the way you'll pass bustling resort scenes and quiet island vistas.

SOUTH COAST

To explore the highbrow face of Naples and its environs, stop for afternoon tea at the ✪ **Ritz-Carlton Naples** (239-598-3300 or 800-241-3333; www.ritzcarlton.com/naples; 280 Vanderbilt Beach Rd., Naples) and take in a concert and art stroll at the **Artis–Naples** (239-597-1900 or 800-597-1900; artisnaples.org; 5833 Pelican Bay Blvd., Naples) and ✪ **The Baker Museum** next door (239-597-1900; artisnaples.org; 5833 Pelican Bay Blvd., Naples). Downtown's ✪ **Fifth Avenue South** has evolved into a fashionable shopping and sidewalk-dining district. Try **Osteria Tulia** (239-213-2073; www.tulianaples.com, 466 Fifth Ave. S.) for an example of the finest in Naples's cutting-edge Italian cuisine.

To really have experienced Naples, you must do sunset at the ✪ **Naples Pier** (12th Ave. S.). It's a nightly ritual for fishermen, strollers, lovers, and pelicans. By day the pier is the center of activity along a beach that stretches for miles.

My favorite part of Marco Island is ✪ **Goodland**. A little fishing village "on pause," it serves fresh seafood and country fun in its restaurants and introduces the unruly flavor of Ten Thousand Islands and the Florida Everglades.

✪ **Everglades City** is headquarters for tours that explore this labyrinthine land down under. ✪ **Everglades National Park** (239-695-3311 or 239-695-2591 for boat tours; www.nps.gov/ever; Everglades Ranger Station, Everglades City) has a base here, conducts boat tours, and rents kayaks for launching into the 99-mile **Wilderness Trail**.

Chelle's High Fives

Here, I give a "high five" to my top picks in a number of offbeat categories. These are the crème de la crème of Southwest Florida, whether you're looking for the best martini or the swankiest jewelry. Within the chapters, look for starred entries to indicate the High Fivers.

BEACHY KEEN RESORTS
1. Palm Island Resort, Cape Haze
2. Manasota Beach Club, Manasota Key
3. Longboat Key Club & Resort, Longboat Key
4. JW Marriott Marco Island Beach Resort, Marco Island
5. LaPlaya Beach & Golf Resort, Vanderbilt Beach

FAMILY-LOVING RESORTS
1. Sundial Beach Resort, Sanibel Island
2. Ritz-Carlton Naples
3. Hyatt Regency Coconut Point Resort & Spa, Bonita Springs
4. Palm Island Resort, Cape Haze
5. South Seas Island Resort, Captiva Island

CITY-SMART HOTELS
1. The Ritz-Carlton Sarasota
2. Bellasera Hotel, Naples
3. Trianon Bonita Bay, Bonita Springs
4. Hotel Indigo, Sarasota
5. Courtyard by Marriott Bradenton Sarasota Riverfront

INNS & B&BS
1. Harrington House B&B, Sarasota
2. Collier Inn & Cottages, Useppa Island
3. Gasparilla Inn, Boca Grande
4. Palmetto Riverside Bed & Breakfast
5. Island Inn, Sanibel Island

COTTAGE BY THE SEA
1. Rolling Waves Cottages, Longboat Key
2. Cabbage Key Inn, Cabbage Key
3. Jensen's Twin Palm Cottages & Marina, Captiva Island
4. Gulf Breeze Cottages and Motel, Sanibel Island
5. Manasota Beach Club, Manasota Key

SPLURGE ACCOMMODATIONS
1. The Ritz-Carlton Naples
2. Sanibel Harbour Resort & Spa, Fort Myers
3. Naples Grande Beach Resort
4. Marco Beach Ocean Resort, Marco Island
5. Hyatt Regency Coconut Point Resort & Spa, Bonita Springs

MARTINI MECCAS
1. Blu Sushi, Fort Myers
2. 7th Avenue Social, Naples
3. The Continental, Naples
4. Chops City Grill, Bonita Springs
5. Blue Water Bistro, Estero

TABLES WITH A WATER VIEW
1. Sale e Pepe, Marco Island
2. Old Salty Dog, Lido Key
3. Baleen, Naples
4. The Crow's Nest, Venice
5. The Dock at Crayton Cove, Naples

SEAFOOD NOSHING
1. PJ's Seagrille, Boca Grande
2. Lucky Pelican Bistro, Sarasota
3. Star Fish Company, Cortez
4. Captain Eddie's Seafood Restaurant, Nokomis
5. Casey Key Fish House, Casey Key

KEY LIME PIE-IN-THE-SKY
1. Ophelia's on the Bay, Siesta Key
2. Gramma Dot's, Sanibel Island
3. Havana Café, Chokoloskee Island
4. Bayfront Bistro, Fort Myers Beach
5. Casey Key Fish House, Osprey

ROMANTIC RESTAURANTS
1. Beach Bistro, Holmes Beach
2. Sale e Pepe, Marco Island
3. The Veranda, Fort Myers
4. Café L'Europe, Sarasota
5. Gulf View Grill, Englewood Beach

CREATIVE CUISINE
1. Sea Salt, Naples
2. The Perfect Caper, Punta Gorda
3. Libby's Café + Bar, Sarasota
4. Cork Soakers Deck & Wine Bar, Cape Coral
5. Beach Bistro, Holmes Beach

ETHNIC EATS
1. Bha! Bha!, Naples
2. Selva Grill, Sarasota
3. Blu Sushi, Fort Myers
4. Alvarez Mexican Food, Palmetto
5. Havana Café, Chokoloskee Island

OLD FLORIDA FUNK
1. Cabbage Key Inn, Cabbage Key
2. Little Bar Restaurant, Goodland
3. New Pass Baithouse & Grill, Lido Key
4. Capri Fish House, Isles of Capri
5. Owen's Fish Camp, Sarasota

BREAKFAST
1. CRaVE, Fort Myers
2. Breakfast Plus, Marco Island
3. Old 41 Restaurant, Bonita Springs
4. Stage Deli Fine Foods, Naples
5. Station 400, Sarasota

DELI/FOOD MARKETS
1. Morton's Market, Sarasota
2. Wynn's, Naples
3. DeRomo's Gourmet Market, Bonita Springs
4. Oakes Farms Market, Naples
5. Mario's Italian Meat Market & Deli, Fort Myers

ARCHITECTURAL GEMS
1. Cà d'Zan, Ringling Estates, Sarasota
2. Gamble Plantation Mansion, Bradenton
3. Sarasota Opera House
4. Gasparilla Inn, Boca Grande
5. Van Wezel Performing Arts Hall, Sarasota

HISTORY ALIVE
1. Historic Spanish Point, Osprey
2. Edison & Ford Winter Estates, Fort Myers
3. De Soto National Memorial, Bradenton
4. Koreshan State Historic Site, Estero
5. Sanibel Historical Museum & Village

KID COOL
1. Golisano Children's Museum of Naples (CMON)
2. Imaginarium, Fort Myers
3. Sun-n-Fun Lagoon, Naples
4. Sarasota Jungle Gardens
5. Sun Splash Family Waterpark, Cape Coral

QUIRKY MUSEUMS
1. Gasparilla Island Maritime Museum, Boca Grande
2. Ringling Circus Museum & Tibbals Learning Center, Sarasota
3. Sarasota Classic Car Museum, Sarasota
4. Anna Maria Island Historical Museum
5. Bailey-Matthews National Shell Museum, Sanibel Island

ON STAGE
1. Van Wezel Performing Arts Hall, Sarasota
2. Asolo Center for the Performing Arts, Sarasota
3. Artis-Naples
4. Barbara B. Mann Performing Arts Hall, Fort Myers
5. Circus Arts Conservatory, Sarasota

NIGHT PROWLING
1. Beach Club, Siesta Key
2. The Gator Club, Sarasota
3. Crow's Nest Beach Bar & Grille, 'Tween Waters Inn, Captiva Island
4. 7th Avenue Social, Naples
5. Dixie Roadhouse, Cape Coral

BOATING ADVENTURES
1. Florida Sailing & Cruising School, North Fort Myers
2. Offshore Sailing School, Captiva Island
3. Pure Naples
4. Captiva Cruises, Captiva Island
5. King Fisher Cruise Lines, Punta Gorda

JAMES NEWTON'S AUTOBIOGRAPHY, UNCOMMON FRIENDS, INSPIRED THIS DOWNTOWN FORT MYERS SCULPTURE, WHICH PORTRAYS CAMPING TRIPS THAT HENRY FORD, HARVEY FIRESTONE, AND THOMAS EDISON SHARED DURING THEIR VISITS TO THE AREA

NATURE PRESERVED
1. Everglades National Park
2. J. N. "Ding" Darling National Wildlife Refuge, Sanibel Island
3. Rookery Bay National Estuarine Research Reserve, Naples
4. Corkscrew Swamp Sanctuary, Naples
5. Collier-Seminole State Park, Naples

ECO-ATTRACTIONS
1. Mote Marine Aquarium, Sarasota
2. Babcock Ranch Preserve Eco-Tour, Punta Gorda
3. Rookery Bay Environmental Learning Center, Naples
4. Manatee Park, Fort Myers
5. Conservancy of Southwest Florida Nature Center, Naples

BIKEWAYS
1. W. J. Janes Memorial Scenic Drive, Fakahatchee Strand Preserve State Park, Naples
2. Sanibel Island
3. Longboat Key
4. Cape Haze Pioneer Trail, Cape Haze
5. Punta Gorda Riverwalk

PADDLE HAPPY
1. Wilderness Waterway, Everglades National Park
2. Great Calusa Blueway, Greater Fort Myers
3. Paradise Coast Blueway, Greater Naples
4. Tarpon Bay/J. N. "Ding" Darling National Wildlife Refuge, Sanibel Island
5. Matlacha Aquatic Preserve, Pine Island

TAKE A HIKE
1. Fakahatchee Strand Preserve State Park, Naples
2. Big Cypress National Preserve, Everglades City
3. Collier-Seminole State Park, Naples
4. Oscar Scherer State Park, Osprey
5. J. N. "Ding" Darling National Wildlife Refuge, Sanibel Island

SHELL-SHOCKED BEACHES
1. Bowman's Beach, Sanibel Island
2. Cayo Costa State Park/Johnson Shoals
3. Bonita Beach
4. Key Island, Naples
5. Venice Beach

SECLUDED BEACHES
1. Cayo Costa State Park, Boca Grande
2. Key Island, Naples
3. Stump Pass Beach State Park, Englewood Beach
4. Don Pedro Island State Park, Boca Grande
5. Palmer Point Beach, Siesta Key

PLAYFUL BEACHES
1. Siesta Beach, Siesta Key
2. Lynn Hall Memorial Park, Fort Myers Beach
3. Manatee County Park, Holmes Beach
4. Coquina Beach, Bradenton Beach
5. Lowdermilk Park, Naples

REEL FISHY
1. Boca Grande Pass, Boca Grande
2. Nokomis Beach's North Jetty, Casey Key
3. Venice Fishing Pier
4. Naples Pier
5. Fort Myers Beach Pier

SHOPPING ARENAS
1. St. Armands Circle, Sarasota
2. Fifth Avenue South, Naples
3. Downtown Sarasota
4. The Village on Venetian Bay, Naples
5. Downtown Venice

ART APPRECIATION
1. The Ringling Museum of Art, Sarasota
2. The Baker Museum, Naples
3. Towles Court Artist Colony, Sarasota
4. Village of the Arts, Bradenton
5. The von Liebig Art Center, Naples

BLING!
1. Port Royal Jewelers, Naples
2. Sarasota Estate & Jewelry
3. June Simmons Designs, Sarasota
4. Congress Jewelers, Sanibel Island
5. Wm. Phelps, Custom Jeweler, Naples

FESTIVALS
1. Edison Festival of Light, February, Fort Myers
2. De Soto Heritage Festival, April, Bradenton
3. Everglades Seafood Festival, February, Everglades City
4. MangoMania Tropical Fruit Fair, July, Pine Island/Cape Coral
5. Shark's Tooth & Seafood Festival, April, Venice

HOMEY HOMETOWNS
1. Goodland
2. Punta Gorda
3. Englewood
4. Everglades City
5. Matlacha

INDEX